CONVEYANCING

Volume 1

CONVEYANCING

Volume 1

Editors
Gabriel Brennan
Nuala Casey

OXFORD
UNIVERSITY PRESS

OXFORD

UNIVERSITY PRESS

Great Clarendon Street, Oxford ox2 6DP

Oxford University Press is a department of the University of Oxford.
It furthers the University's objective of excellence in research, scholarship,
and education by publishing worldwide in

Oxford New York

Auckland Bangkok Buenos Aires Cape Town Chennai
Dar es Salaam Delhi Hong Kong Istanbul Karachi Kolkata
Kuala Lumpur Madrid Melbourne Mexico City Mumbai Nairobi
São Paulo Shanghai Taipei Tokyo Toronto

Oxford is a registered trade mark of Oxford University Press
in the UK and in certain other countries

Published in the United States
by Oxford University Press Inc., New York

First published Blackstone Press 2000

A catalogue record for this title is available from the British Library

Library of Congress Cataloging in Publication Data
(Data available)
ISBN 0 19 925553 9

10 9 8 7 6 5 4 3

Typeset by Newgen Imaging Systems (P) Ltd., Chennai, India
Printed in Great Britain
on acid-free paper by
Antony Rowe Limited, Chippenham

AUTHORS OF THIS VOLUME

Owen Binchy is a partner in James Binchy & Son, Solicitors, Charleville. He is a member of the Registration of Title Rules Committee, is a former Chairman of the Law Society's Conveyancing Committee and has been a regular contributor to the Law Society's Continuing Legal Education programme.

Gabriel Brennan is a solicitor with the Law Society. She is responsible for the presentation of the conveyancing and landlord and tenant law modules on the Law School's courses. She has lectured on the Law Society's Continuing Legal Education courses on landlord and tenant law and has been a member of the Law Society's Conveyancing Committee since 1998. Gabriel was formerly in practice with Abercorn, Solicitors.

Nuala Casey is a lecturer and tutor on the Law Society's conveyancing and probate modules on both Professional Practice Courses. She is a registered trust and estate practitioner and acts as a consultant solicitor, advising in all aspects of conveyancing, probate and estate management. She formerly practised in her family firm in County Clare and, latterly, was in private practice in Dublin.

Deirdre Fox is a lecturer on the Law Society's conveyancing module on the Professional Practice Courses and has lectured extensively on conveyancing practice. A member of the Conveyancing Committee since 1996, she has recently been involved in a revision of the Conveyancing Handbook. Deirdre Fox has been head of the Conveyancing Department of the legal office of eircom plc since 1997.

Lorcan Gogan is a lecturer on the Law Society's conveyancing module on the Professional Practice Courses and has also lectured on the Law Society's Continuing Legal Education courses on registered land conveyancing. He qualified as a solicitor in 1992 and entered private practice in 1993, after working in the Land Registry for twenty years.

Brian Magee has been a lecturer and tutor on the Law Society's conveyancing module on the Professional Practice Courses for twenty years. He is a practising solicitor with unbroken service with the Dublin firm of Maurice E Veale & Company since August 1954; he has been a partner since 1970. His practice concentrates on conveyancing, probate, capital taxes on death and landlord and tenant.

Anne McKenna qualified as a solicitor in 1977 and was a sole practitioner in Dublin until recently when she joined the practice of Daly Lynch Crowe & Morris as consultant. She also practises in Northern Ireland having been admitted to the Law Society of Ireland in 1988. Anne is a lecturer and tutor in the Law Society's conveyancing and probate modules. She also participates in the Institute of Professional Legal Studies in Belfast.

Pat O'Brien has been a lecturer on the Law Society's conveyancing module on the Professional Practice Courses since 1981. He was a practising solicitor from 1959 to 1963 when he joined the Land Registry as a legal assistant. He later became senior legal assistant, examiner of titles, and chief examiner of titles, retiring in 1999.

Anne Stephenson, formerly a partner with Peter Morrissey & Company in Dublin, is a founding partner of Fallon & Stephenson, a specialist practice providing advisory services for solicitors and financial institutions in the areas of wills, trust and administration and tax planning. Anne tutors and lectures on the Law Society's Professional Practice Courses and has lectured on the Law Society's Continuing Legal Education courses in the areas of wills, trusts and probate, tax planning and conveyancing.

PREFACE

Our aim in writing this book is to provide students with a comprehensive text dealing with all the fundamental aspects of conveyancing practice and procedure. The primary focus of the text is to prepare trainee solicitors for practice. Where necessary academic law is referred to; it is assumed, however, that readers have a basic knowledge of land law and contract law, upon which the practice of conveyancing rests.

This text is designed for the guidance of trainee solicitors attending the Law Society's Law School. It is anticipated that the text will provide a foundation for their learning and also assist them once their apprenticeship period is concluded and they have entered the profession. Indeed, it is hoped that the text will provide assistance to all practitioners in the conveyancing field. If utilised in practice, the sample forms and precedents included in the text should be adapted as appropriate to the transaction in question.

It is recognised that conveyancing practice and procedures throughout Ireland vary and, while acknowledging these variations, the text reflects Law Society recommended practice.

While the authors are jointly and severally responsible for this book, primary responsibility is as follows: chapters 1, 2, 3 and 16—Brian Magee; chapters 4, 5 and 15—Owen Binchy; chapters 6, 7 and 12—Deirdre Fox; chapter 8—Anne McKenna; chapters 9 and 10—Gabriel Brennan; chapter 11—Anne Stephenson; chapters 13 and 17—Nuala Casey; chapter 14—Pat O'Brien and Lorcan Gogan.

The practice of conveyancing, like all aspects of law, is constantly evolving. The authors have taken every care to ensure that conveyancing law, practice and procedure are correctly stated as at 1 October 2002 in accordance with Law Society recommended practice.

While every effort has been made to ensure that the text is accurate, the authors would be grateful to learn of any errors or omissions. Any comments or queries on the content of this manual should be sent to the general editors at the Law School.

Thanks to all in the Law School who offered their assistance and, finally, special thanks to our husbands Bill and Edwin for their unfailing encouragement and support.

Gabriel Brennan
Nuala Casey
October 2002

ACKNOWLEDGEMENTS

While the individual authors are, of course, solely responsible for the contents of the manual, we would like to express our gratitude to the many colleagues who so ably assisted us in this project.

In particular, our collective thanks to Brendan McDonnell, Solicitor, Dublin, one of the longest serving members of the Law Society's Conveyancing Committee, who expended a great amount of time in reading and commenting on the entire draft manuscript. His invaluable contribution to the project is very much appreciated.

Grateful acknowledgements are due to the many members of the profession who helped bring this manual about by reading individual chapters at various stages, offering invaluable advice and judicious improvements. The project would have been impossible without the contributions of: Paul Kerrigan, David Larney, Margaret Hegarty, Rory O'Donnell, Patrick Sweetman, Michelle Linnane, David Soden, Niall Casey, Rory Casey, Sean Casey, Brian Gallagher, William Devine, Rosemarie McLoughlin, Jeanne Cullen, Liam Young, Michael Staines, Ernest Farrell, Dr Eamonn Hall, the Register of Titles, Catherine Treacy and her staff at the Land Registry, Moling Ryan, Marie Whelan-Flanagan, Seamus Carey, Padraic Courtney, Mary Upton, Keyna McEvoy, Trina Murphy, Niamh O'Keeffe and Emer Murray. Thanks also to Mr Seamus Carey and Mr Kim Unger of the Office of the Revenue Commissioners for their assistance.

DISCLAIMER

OUTLINE CONTENTS

CONTENTS

CONTENTS

CONTENTS

TABLE OF STATUTES

TABLE OF STATUTES

TABLE OF STATUTES

TABLE OF RULES AND REGULATIONS

TABLE OF RULES AND REGULATIONS

LIST OF CASES

CHAPTER 1

INTRODUCTION

1.1   Introduction

Conveyancing is the sum of the procedures used in the disposal and acquisition of immovable property. It is the procedural side of the coin of which the law of property is the substantive side.

Conveyancers are the qualified professionals retained by the parties to a transaction to ensure the proper disposal and acquisition of the title to the property involved and to secure the mortgage or charge of any lending institution involved. In Ireland conveyancing for reward can only be carried out by qualified solicitors.

Conveyancing is the generic term used to describe property transactions whether they be in respect of a commercial property, a residential property, an agricultural property or a mix of all or any of them. The basic rules and principles of conveyancing apply with equal force irrespective of the nature of the property. However, the practice may vary somewhat in respect of the different types of properties, eg if the property in question was a commercial property such as licensed premises there are certain essential pre-contract enquiries and requisitions that will be raised which would not be relevant to the acquisition of a title to a residential property.

Likewise, there are certain pre-contract enquiries and requisitions that might be raised if the property being acquired was an agricultural holding.

The general objective of this manual is to:

(a)   explain a conveyancer's role and function in acquiring and disposing of an interest in immovable property (property meaning both buildings and lands) and how this is achieved;

(b)   establish the basic principles involved in passing good title;

(c)   identify and explain the two systems of registration in operation in Ireland, viz the Registry of Deeds and the Land Registry, and how they work;

(d)   establish the documentation and evidence required for a good marketable title and, in particular, identify what is a good root and what is not a good root of title;

(e)   clarify the length of title required;

(f)   advise on and outline current practice in conveyancing;

(g)   identify standard documentation currently in use;

(h)   identify current legislation, ie within the past thirty years or so, which has had a substantial impact on conveyancing practice;

(i)   identify and explain the terminology used by conveyancers; and

(j)   deal with any other matter generally arising.

1

1.1.1 WORDS AND PHRASES COMMONLY USED

As in all professions, there are words and phrases used which are meaningless to a lay person, particularly when an abbreviation is used. The following is a list of the most commonly used terms in conveyancing and its associated field of Landlord and Tenant:

ASSENT: Describes the document under the terms of which an executor vests title to a property in a beneficiary under the will or on the intestacy of a deceased.

ASSIGN: The act of transferring leasehold title.

ASSIGNMENT: Describes the deed transferring leasehold title.

ASSURANCE: A generic term for any document transferring title.

CAT CERT: A clearance certificate from the capital taxes branch of the Revenue Commissioners certifying that all capital acquisitions tax on a property has been discharged where there is a death or a gift on title. Such a certificate may be qualified or absolute.

CERTIFICATE OF COMPLIANCE: Used to describe a certificate endorsed on a lease by the lessor to confirm that a particular covenant in a lease has been complied with, usually a covenant to build. Also used to describe a certificate from an architect or an engineer confirming that a property or a development to a property has been built in accordance with the relevant planning permission and the building regulations or that the development is exempt. This is now usually done by way of an opinion rather than a certificate.

CERTIFICATE OF TITLE: Certificate given by a purchaser's solicitor to a lending institution that the title on which they are taking a charge or mortgage is a good marketable title. There is a standard form used, the terms of which have been agreed between the Law Society, the building societies and the banks and which are used only in respect of residential properties.

CGT CERT: Exemption certificate issued by the Revenue Commissioners under the capital gains tax legislation as amended exempting a purchaser from making any deduction from the purchase monies on closing when the consideration exceeds the relevant current threshold set by the legislation, which is usually updated on an annual basis. NB This certificate is required for all sales which exceed the relevant threshold, irrespective of whether there is capital gains tax payable on the disposal or not, and if not available on closing, the purchaser must deduct 15 per cent of the purchase price in a relevant case from the full purchase price on closing and forthwith remit it to the Revenue Commissioners.

CONVEY: The act of transferring a freehold title.

CONVEYANCE: Describes the deed transferring a freehold title.

DEED: A document executed under seal.

DEMISE: Used as a noun to describe a lease and as a verb to describe the act of leasing.

EQUITY NOTE: A note entered on pre-1967 Land Registry folios to protect any interest prior to the registered owners, which are not shown on the face of the folio (if any). In post-1967 folios, such titles are shown as possessory.

FAMILY HOME/LAW DECLARATIONS: Statutory declaration by a vendor (and spouse if married) to establish whether the property being sold is or is not a family home as defined in the Family Home Protection Act, 1976 as amended. Such declarations also deal with the provisions of the Family Law Act, 1981, the Judicial Separation and Family Law Reform Act, 1989, the Family Law Act, 1995 and the Family Law (Divorce) Act, 1996 and any matters arising thereunder.

HEREDITAMENT: A parcel of freehold land.

PARCEL: A separately identified plot of land either by reason of its boundaries or it having a separate or distinct title.

PER REPS (PERSONAL REPRESENTATIVES): A generic term used to describe executors and administrators of an estate.

POSSESSORY TITLE: A term used to describe a title in the Land Registry post 1967 (see Equity Note above).

REVERSIONARY LEASE: A lease granted during the currency of an existing lease for a term of years, which commences on the expiration of the current lease.

SECTION 72 DECLARATION: Statutory declaration by the registered owner of a title registered in the Land Registry to confirm that none of the burdens which can affect registered land without registration as set out in s 72 of the Registration of Title Act, 1964 as amended affect the subject property and that there are no deaths or voluntary dispositions on title in the last twelve years.

SECTION 12 CONSENT: Consent to the subdivision or subletting of an agricultural holding under s 12 of the Land Act, 1965.

SECTION 45 CONSENT: Consent under the Land Act, 1965 to the purchase of land by a non-qualified person.

TRANSFER: Used as a term to describe the deed used for both freehold and leasehold titles in Land Registry titles.

VESTING CERT: Document issued by the Registrar of Titles in the Land Registry vesting the freehold and all superior leasehold title in a lessee under the provisions of the Landlord and Tenant (Ground Rents) (No 2) Act, 1978.

For further definitions relevant to landlord and tenant matters, the Law Society's manual on Landlord and Tenant chapter 1.2, paras 2, 3 and 4 should be consulted.

1.2   Role of Conveyancers

A conveyancer's role generally falls under one of three headings, viz:

(a)   representing a vendor on the sale or transfer of an interest in property;

(b)   representing a purchaser on the purchase or acquisition of an interest in property; or

(c)   representing a lending institution which is advancing money by way of a loan on the security of a property.

Occasionally a solicitor will also be asked to give independent legal advice to a party who is asked to execute a document relating to a conveyancing transaction, eg to advise a spouse on the legal significance of executing a consent under the provisions of the Family Home Protection Act, 1976 as amended, or advising a life tenant or a person with a right of residence in a property who is asked to sign a document postponing that interest in favour of a lending institution so as to give that lending institution a first charge on the property involved.

1.2.1   THE STATUTE OF FRAUDS

Section 2 of the Statute of Frauds (Ireland) Act, 1695 provides that, in order to be enforceable, the contract for sale of land must be in writing or there must be a note or memorandum of the agreement.

Section 2 states:

And be it further enacted by the authority aforesaid that from and after the said feast day of the nativity of St John the Baptist, which shall be in the said year of our Lord one thousand six hundred and ninety six, no action shall be brought whereby to charge any executor or admin-istrator upon any special promise, to answer damages out of his own estate, or whereby to charge the defendant upon any special promise, to answer for the debt, default, or miscarriage of another person, or to charge any person upon any agreement made upon consideration of marriage, or upon any contract for sale of lands, tenements or hereditaments, or any interest in or concerning them, or upon any agreement that is not to be performed within the space of one year from the making thereof, unless the agreement upon which such action shall be brought, or some mem-orandum or note thereof, shall be in writing, and signed by the party to be charged therewith, or some other person thereunto by him lawfully authorised.

Under Deasy's Act, 1860, s 4 oral tenancies from year to year or lesser periods are enforce-able without a memorandum or note in writing. This is the only amendment to s 2 of the Statue of Frauds (Ireland) Act, 1695.

If s 2 is not complied with, the agreement is unenforceable.

The memorandum or note must contain the following details:

(a) parties (and their capacities);

(b) price;

(c) property;

(d) particulars, ie statement of material terms.

1.3 Certificates of Title

In a conveyancing transaction involving the purchase of a residential property it is now standard practice for lending institutions to allow the purchaser's solicitor exclusively to investigate the title and, on completion of the purchase, to allow the purchaser's solicitor to take responsibility for having the mortgage duly executed by the borrowers, stamping and registering the borrower's title and furnishing a certificate of title to the lending institution. This practice was adopted some years ago as a result of public pressure on lending institu-tions, in particular building societies, as purchasers at that time were obliged not only to pay their own solicitor on the purchase of the property but also to pay the building society's solicitor who independently investigated the title. The object of the exercise in introducing the certificate of title procedure was to save the purchaser the expense of having to pay fees to two solicitors for performing what, in the view of the public, was the same work.

This certification of title procedure is confined exclusively to residential property purchases. Since it was first introduced the system has been refined by the Conveyancing Committee of the Law Society in conjunction with the representatives of the lending insti-tutions. The current format of the certificate and guidance notes relating to it are those issued by the Conveyancing Committee in March 1999. It is the view of the Conveyancing Committee that this current form of certification should not be departed from by any solicitor acting for a purchaser of residential property under any circumstances. In com-mercial conveyancing transactions, ie transactions relating to a commercial property or the acquisition of an agricultural holding, this certification procedure is not used and was never intended to be used.

In some residential purchases where the lending institution considers the purchase to be a commercial purchase, ie one intended as an investment by the purchaser, the lend-ing institution may retain its own solicitor.

1.4 Conflicts of Interest

A solicitor should give careful consideration to the difficulties and possible conflict of interest that may arise if both parties to a transaction require that solicitor to act for both parties. Prior to the certificate of title procedure above referred to, and which is dealt with in detail in chapter 9: Mortgages, a practice had emerged of certain lending institutions requiring the purchaser's solicitor to act for the lending institution as well as the purchaser in connection with his or her mortgage and security on the property being purchased. In so doing it became clear that a conflict of interest could arise and, accordingly, the current certification procedure makes it clear that a purchaser's solicitor does not act for a lending institution as well as a purchaser but should merely represent the purchaser and certify the title on the basis of the normal conveyancing practice and procedure adopted on behalf of a purchaser.

A situation may also arise in a transaction where a conflict of interest will occur, eg if a spouse's prior consent is required to the sale or a mortgage of a property governed by the provisions of the Family Home Protection Act, 1976 as amended. It is imperative that the spouse who is asked to sign such a prior consent fully understands the nature and implication of what is being signed. Recently the Supreme Court ruled in *Bank of Ireland v Smyth* [1996] ILRM 401 that what is required in such cases is a fully informed consent. If there is any doubt in the matter such a spouse should be separately advised by another independent solicitor.

1.5   Registry of Deeds

1.5.1   GENERALLY

To fully understand the practice of conveyancing one must first of all become familiar with the two systems of registration currently in operation in Ireland. The first one introduced in Ireland was the Registry of Deeds established under the Registration of Deeds (Ireland) Act, 1707 (the 1707 Act), which was established for the purpose of giving priority to registered deeds and the prevention of fraud in dealing with the transfer of ownership of land. It is the registration system which is most frequently encountered in dealing with titles in urban areas. Most of the titles outside urban areas are dealt with in the Land Registry. There are a number of points to be noted in respect of the Registry of Deeds system:

(a)   It deals with the registration of documents, not the registration of the title dealt with by the documents.

(b)   Registration in the Registry of Deeds is not compulsory under the 1707 Act. It is, however, obligatory upon a solicitor to ensure the registration of a purchase deed or a mortgage deed for the purpose of obtaining the priority afforded by the legislation.

(c)   Registration is not necessary to transfer the title as title passes when the deed is delivered and the purchase money is paid.

(d)   While the Act is called the Registration of Deeds (Ireland) Act, 1707, the Registry will accept the registration of other documents which are not deeds, eg a contract for sale, an option to buy land. In fact any type of document in writing relating to a transaction in respect of land duly executed and witnessed and with the appropriate memorial duly completed will be accepted by the Registry and registered.

(e)   The registration of a deed or other document in the Registry of Deeds is not notice under the doctrine of notice. The effectiveness of the registration is governed by the statutory provisions which grant priority to a registered deed.

(f)   The Registry of Deeds has no responsibility for the effectiveness of the deed or other document being presented to it for registration. This remains the sole responsibility of the parties preparing the document.

(g) The 1707 Act grants priority because of registration, ie the first registered of two registered deeds gets priority under s 4 according to the time of its registration, irrespective of its date, and a registered deed gains priority over an unregistered deed under s 5 because of its registration. The Act has no application as between two unregistered deeds or between a registered deed and an unregisterable transaction, eg a registered deed as against documents of title lodged by way of an equitable deposit with a lending institution as, in the latter case, there is no document executed capable of registration.

(h) It should be noted that in respect of the statutory protection afforded by the actual registered deed against an unregistered deed the courts of equity have intervened to make it clear that they will not allow the statute to be used as an instrument of fraud. A party cannot claim the protection of the Act on foot of a registered deed when that party has *actual notice* of an unregistered deed. What is required is actual notice not actual knowledge. Constructive notice is not sufficient. A recent modern case of *O'Connor v McCarthy* [1982] IR 161 demonstrates this principle and the continuing effectiveness of the Act notwithstanding its age. There is a very detailed and well-written judgment of Costello J in that case which deals not only with the priority granted under the Act but also looks very fully at the whole question of notice. That case incidentally also turns on the registration of a contract for sale which was not a deed.

(i) Section 17 of the Act provides that a lease for a term not exceeding twenty-one years where actual possession goes with it is not registerable. In such a case possession is considered notice to a purchaser to make enquiries. It is interesting to note that a similar provision to the same effect is contained in the Registration of Title Act, 1964, s 69 in respect of similar leases in Land Registry cases.

1.5.2 METHOD OF REGISTRATION

The registration of a deed or other document in the Registry of Deeds is achieved by the completion of a memorial. A memorial is an extract (now typed rather than handwritten) from the deed or other document containing the date of the deed, the names and addresses of the parties to the deed, the nature of the deed, the effect of the deed and a full description of the property affected by it. Details of the due execution of the deed or other document by the parties is noted with the full names and addresses of the witnesses also noted on the memorial. The memorial should then be executed by the party disposing of the interest in the land, eg in the case of a sale of property by the vendor, in the case of a mortgage by the mortgagor, or in the case of a lease by the lessor. A memorial executed in this fashion will be accepted in due course as evidence against the parties to the deed of the contents thereof. It has, however, become commonplace for the memorial to be executed by any of the parties to the deed and this is accepted for registration purposes.

The execution of the memorial must have two witnesses who must sign their names, and one of these witnesses must also be a common witness to the deed itself. There is an affidavit at the foot of the memorial which must be sworn by this common witness attesting to the fact that the witness saw the deed and memorial duly executed by the named party and that his or her signature to the deed and memorial is in the witness's name and handwriting. This memorial must be sworn before a commissioner for oaths or a practising solicitor.

This memorial when duly stamped, and when the deed has also been duly executed and stamped, is taken to the Registry of Deeds which for titles in the Republic of Ireland is in Henrietta Street in Dublin. There is a separate office in Belfast for Northern Ireland titles. The officials in Henrietta Street compare the memorial with the deed and, if it is a proper extract and is executed in accordance with the Act, the deed and the memorial are taken to the Registrar who registers the deed, keeps the memorial and gives back the original deed with the registration particulars duly endorsed thereon. The registration particulars contain the precise time and date when the deed is registered and each individual deed is given a separate and distinct registration number.

One of the advantages of the Registry of Deeds system is that if a deed or other document which is registered has been lost or mislaid, a certified copy of the memorial may be obtained which will prove the existence of the deeds, the execution of the deed by the parties to it, the property affected and the parties to the deed and, possibly, a description of the title and the effect of the deed. This is of considerable help in reconstituting a title if an original deed is lost or destroyed. Such certified copy memorials are secondary evidence of the existence of the deed and, where a deed has been lost, are generally accepted as sufficient evidence of the existence and execution of the original deed, coupled with a properly completed statutory declaration dealing with the loss of the original. The practice has developed in recent years of putting in the memorial the minimum amount of data from the deed sufficient to enable the Registry to accept it for registration purposes. This is not necessarily the best practice and practitioners in the future, who are endeavouring to reconstitute a title from memorials where deeds have been lost or destroyed, may be more appreciative of those practitioners who flesh out their memorials with a little bit more detail from the relevant deeds.

1.5.3   INDEX OF NAMES AND LANDS

The Registry of Deeds today functions on an Index of Names only. Up to 1947 the Registry of Deeds also kept an Index of Lands but that Index has not been kept up to date and lapsed in 1947. It is, however, still available if endeavouring to trace registered documentation prior to 1947 in respect of a particular piece of land where precise information as to the parties involved in any particular deed is not available.

The Index of Names is maintained under the name of the person or party disposing of or granting an interest under the registered document, eg a lease will be registered under the name of the lessor, a conveyance or assignment under the name of the vendor and a mortgage under the name of the mortgagor. The only variation in that practice is that since the introduction of vesting certificates, ie a document issued by the Land Registry under the Landlord and Tenant (Ground Rents) (No 2) Act, 1978 vesting the freehold in a lessee, the Registry of Deeds index maintains such vesting certificates in the name of the person acquiring the freehold title rather than in the name of the person disposing of it.

Care must be taken when searching against names on the Index of Names as the Names Index is kept very precisely on the basis of the spelling contained in a particular deed. This name may have many variations in practice, eg the common practice with Irish surnames spelt with or without 'Mc' or a surname with or without an 'O', eg McGee or Magee or Connor or O'Connor. It is accordingly important when making the search to check the deeds to ascertain the spelling of the name used and also to check the signature to see if the individual signed his or her name differently from the spelling on the deed itself. Any alternative spelling should always be included to ensure that the search made is accurate.

1.5.4   SEARCHES

1.5.4.1   Formal searches

The key to the operation of the Registry of Deeds is the system of searching on the Index of Names. The Registry of Deeds itself provides two official searches, one a negative search and the other a common search. A negative search is one carried out by two searchers the results of which are fully guaranteed by the Registry, whereas a common search is carried out by one searcher only. A common search is slightly cheaper to obtain than a negative search but it is recommended for conveyancing purposes that a negative search must always be obtained as the comparative cost in today's terms is minimal.

The search is obtained by completing and signing a formal requisition which is lodged in the Registry of Deeds indicating the parties against whom the search is to be made, a full description of the property and the relevant dates to be covered by the search. When perusing a title to determine what searches are to be made, first of all check to see what searches are already made on the title, as searches should have been made when each transaction on the title was taking place and the results of such searches should be with the title deeds. It is common practice now not to go back more than twenty years with searches but there may be circumstances where a longer search may be necessary, eg if a property is owned by the one person for a substantial number of years then obviously the search will have to start from the date that person acquired the property.

The searches are made in the Registry of Deeds against a party from the time that party acquired the property until such time as the deed under which they parted with their interest in the property is registered in the Registry of Deeds. An example of this would be if John Brown acquired the property by a deed dated 1 January 1980. He sold the property by a deed dated 10 July 1985 and that deed was then registered in the Registry of Deeds on 3 September 1985. In that situation, if subsequently acquiring an interest in that property, then the period of the searches should cover John Brown from 1 January 1980 up to 3 September 1985 and not to 10 July 1985. The reason for this is that on the registration of the purchase deed from John Brown that registration gives priority to the deed over any other unregistered deed or a later registered deed and consequently there is no need to search any later than the date of registration of the deed under which John Brown parted with his interest.

1.5.4.2 Hand searches

The above are the only formal searches issued by the Registry of Deeds. However, in addition, it is necessary to have further searches carried out up to the time a transaction is being completed, as in most cases either the search requisition lodged with the Registry of Deeds will not have produced the necessary result prior to the completion, or, if it has, there will be a gap between the date up to which that search is made and the date of closing. These additional searches are called hand searches and are carried out by professional searchers, of whom there are a number of firms operating, and any firm used should be checked regularly to ensure that it has proper insurance cover against any claims. All of the firms concerned provide a very speedy and reliable service and are an essential part of the conveyancing procedure.

In addition to covering gaps in Registry of Deeds searches, these professional searchers also deal with additional searches required on the closing day of the sale in the Land Registry, the Companies Registration Office, the Bankruptcy Office, the Judgments Office and the Sheriff's Office, but more information on this aspect of conveyancing is furnished in chapter 10: Searches.

1.6 Land Registry

1.6.1 GENERALLY

1.6.1.1 Registry of deeds distinguised

The second system of registration in Ireland is the Land Registry and this system is the alternative registration system to the Registry of Deeds. The crucial and essential difference between the two systems is that in the Registry of Deeds system all that is registered is the document, whereas in the Land Registry it is the title itself that is registered. Thus conveyancers, when they talk about the Registry of Deeds, talk about an 'unregistered title', whereas in Land Registry cases they talk about a 'registered title'. This terminology is strictly speaking correct but should not be confused with the phrase 'unregistered' in the Registry of Deeds system as registration of deeds is still required.

1.6.1.2   Establishment

The Land Registry was formally established in Ireland under the Local Registration of Title Act, 1891 (the 1891 Act). Prior to that there was the Record of Title Act, 1865. This earlier Act, however, provided only for a voluntary registration system and no more than 700 to 800 titles were registered under it. For the first time under the 1891 Act registration in the Land Registry was compulsory in certain cases. It was introduced originally to deal with the vast volume of titles that were being transferred under the major land reforms at the end of the nineteenth century when substantial government funds were provided to purchase agricultural land. It was felt that a proper registration system was needed for these titles to protect the State's investment and hence the Land Registry was established. Land acquired by the Land Commission had to be registered under the compulsory registration system introduced under the 1891 Act. The legislation was eventually extended to cover labourers' cottages and dwellings purchased under the Small Dwellings Act, 1899 and the Labourers Act, 1906 by local authorities. It also allowed for voluntary registration of a title.

The 1891 Act was replaced by a modern statute which is the Registration of Title Act, 1964 (the 1964 Act) which came into effect on 1 January 1967. Its operation coincided with the coming into operation of the Succession Act, 1965 and both pieces of legislation were brought into operation contemporaneously.

1.6.1.3   Registration of Title Act, 1964

Under the 1964 Act compulsory registration was extended under ss 23 and 24. Section 23 provided for compulsory registration in the following cases:

(a)   where the land has been or is deemed to have been at any time sold and conveyed to or vested in any person under any of the provisions of the Land Purchase Acts or the Labourers Acts, 1883 to 1962;

(b)   where the land is acquired after the commencement of the 1964 Act (ie 1 January 1967) by a statutory authority (this includes a local or public authority); and

(c)   in any case to which s 24(2) applies.

Section 23 further provides that the registration of the ownership of a leasehold interest is compulsory in the following cases:

(a)   where the interest is acquired after the commencement of the Act by a statutory authority, or

(b)   in any case to which s 24(2) applies.

Section 24 was intended to be the key section in the Act under the terms of which compulsory registration would be extended to all land in the State, both urban and rural. It was intended that this would be achieved by designating areas in the State as being liable to compulsory purchase under s 24(2). So far only three areas in the State have been designated, namely the counties of Meath, Carlow and Laois with effect from 1 January 1970. In those areas, the registration of ownership if not already compulsory became compulsory in the following circumstances:

(a)   in the case of freehold land upon conveyance on sale, and

(b)   in the case of a leasehold interest on the grant or assignment on sale of such an interest.

'On sale' means for money or money's worth and accordingly would not apply to a voluntary transfer of title by way of gift or a title transferred on death.

Section 25 of the 1964 Act provides that where registration becomes compulsory it must be carried out within six months after the relevant document becomes operative, otherwise no title passes to the transferee. The Registrar has power to extend this period of six months. The section does not clarify where ownership of the title goes after the six-month period has expired without an application being made for registration. The Registrar of Titles will generally extend the six-month period for registration but if for any reason he should refuse then the court has power to do so.

A much more detailed examination of the Land Registry system is dealt with in **chapter 14** but the following is a brief explanation of how the system works in practice.

1.6.2 DOCUMENTS

1.6.2.1 The map

The entire system is based on the boundaries of the particular property in respect of which the title is registered being shown on an Ordnance Survey map. This OS map is not part of the register and is accordingly not automatically issued with a copy of the folio or the land certificate and must be specifically requisitioned. However, as the map or the file plan is a key part to identifying the land covered by the title registered it should always be obtained as part of the documentary evidence of the title and should bear a date contemporaneous with the copy folio.

However, it is one of the drawbacks of the Land Registry system that the official map or file plan is not conclusive of the extent of the land or the boundaries shown and this is provided for in the 1964 Act, s 85.

This provision is said to be consistent with an unregistered title where the description of the land is often described as 'more or less' or 'thereabouts'. Accordingly it is important that the client is shown any such map and asked to confirm or check that the boundaries shown are correct. It is possible under the 1964 Act, s 86 and rules 148 to 151 of the Land Registration Rules, 1972 for adjoining owners to agree on the precise location of their boundaries and to have this agreement recorded on their respective folios. A recent case, *Tomkins Estates Ltd v O'Callaghan*, 16 March 1995, McCracken J (29 May 1995 ITLR) highlighted the problem that this lack of conclusiveness in the boundaries of Registry maps can cause. The case involved a dispute relating to a laneway at the rear of No 1 Merrion Square, Dublin, the ownership of which was claimed by the owner of No 3 Merrion Square, Dublin on whose Land Registry map the laneway was clearly shown as part of the land in respect of which his title was registered. However, the owner of No 1 had an unregistered title which also showed ownership of the laneway. McCracken J held that as the 1964 Act, s 85 made it clear that the Registry map was not conclusive of the boundaries shown, the registered owner of the land could not rely on it and accepted the evidence of the title deeds of the owner of No 1 as having a freehold title to the laneway in question.

1.6.2.2 The folio

The folio is the actual register of the title and is set out in three parts. The heading on the folio shows the folio number and the county to which it relates and which register the title is on, viz freehold, leasehold or subsidiary. Part 1 gives details of the property and specifies the map reference on the Registry map. It also sometimes specifies the area of the land. If it does specify the area, it usually includes one-half of any adjoining roadway. One should be careful of this in rural areas particularly, as a large farm might have extensive road frontage which could account for several acres of the area shown on the folio thus reducing the actual area of the farm land. Part 2 shows the class of title and ownership and Part 3 shows the burdens and notices of burdens. Some of the counties are computerised now and the folios will be produced on a typical computer printout in a somewhat different layout but still containing all the relevant information and data required. The 1964 Act prescribes the registers that are kept in the Land Registry. These are dealt with later.

Each registered title has a separate folio number under the relevant county in which it is situate. If it is a freehold title it merely bears a reference number but in modern folios has the letter F after the relevant number. If the title is a leasehold folio then the letter L is appended to the folio number.

There are various categories of title which would be registered either in the freehold register or the leasehold register. There is a third register, known as a Register of Subsidiary Interests, and if there is a folio issued under that category the letter S is appended to the folio number. These are, however, rare. They would cover such matters as the ownership of a rent payable out of a freehold title, eg a fee farm rent which would rarely be registered. They would also include interests such as an inchoate interest, eg an interest vested in a Minister for State to supervise from the bank of a river fisheries under the control of the State.

1.6.2.3 The land certificate

The Land Registry will on request issue a land certificate in respect of a folio. The issue of a land certificate is not an essential document to establish title and a copy of the folio issued by the Land Registry and certified by it as a true copy of the folio is sufficient evidence of the title to that particular land on the date the folio was issued. However, if a land certificate is issued it will be noted on the front of the folio that it has issued and it then becomes an important document of title. It must always be produced in respect of any transaction under which title is being transferred. It should be noted that a land certificate is not evidence of the current state of the title, as it only speaks from the date that it is issued which may be some considerable time prior to the date that the title is being considered.

1.6.2.4 Certificates of charge

The Land Registry also issues certificates of charge under rule 156 or 157, these being the relevant rules under the 1972 Land Registration Rules, which are the basic rules under which the Land Registry currently functions with some small subsequent amendments. A rule 156 charge is an endorsement on the deed of charge itself and is not a separate document. A rule 157 charge, however, is a certificate of the ownership of the charge and is the equivalent of a land certificate and must always be produced when the charge is being cleared off or being otherwise dealt with.

1.6.2.5 Transfers

In Land Registry titles ownership is dealt with under the forms provided for in the 1972 Rules. There is one form only used for the transfer of title inter vivos, namely a deed of transfer and this is used both for freehold and leasehold titles. It is important to note that title in a Land Registry case only passes when the title has been registered (see Registration of Title Act, 1964, s 51). The 1972 Rules provide a substantial variety of forms to be used in virtually all cases that will be experienced in dealing with registered land and if the rules are followed and the documentation properly completed, then the transaction will be registered without any query. Transactions which may take several weeks to complete will gain priority from the time they are lodged in the Land Registry and registration will relate back to the date of lodgement assuming that no query has been raised or that the dealing is not subsequently rejected by the Land Registry. If the dealing is rejected and sent back then priority will only arise again from the date of relodgement of the dealing with the queries discharged.

1.6.3 EFFECT OF REGISTRATION IN THE LAND REGISTRY

The effect of registration of a title in the Land Registry is that such title falls out of the Registry of Deeds system. The two systems are mutually exclusive. The title in the Land Registry carries with it a State guarantee that it is valid. It is, however, crucial to remember that they are mutually exclusive only in respect of the same title and not in respect of the same property. It is commonplace to find property with several titles affecting it, eg a freehold title, a leasehold title and possibly a sub-leasehold title. The freehold title may be registered in the Land Registry, while the documents relating to the leasehold and the sub-leasehold title may be registered in the Registry of Deeds. The crucial difference here is that they are different titles affecting the same property and each title coexists quite happily with the other in a different registration system. If those titles should merge at any stage, eg if the sub-leasehold interest enlarged its interest under the Landlord and Tenant (Ground Rents) (No 2) Act, 1978 into a full freehold by acquiring the superior leasehold and the registered freehold, then it would be advisable to take the entire leasehold and sub-leasehold title into the Land Registry and convert the entire title into a registered freehold, at which stage the leasehold and the sub-leasehold would cease to exist and thereafter, the entire title would be dealt with in the Land Registry system.

1.7 Standard Documentation

1.7.1 CONTRACTS

For a long number of years there were a substantial variety of contracts in use for the purchase and sale of land and, likewise, building contracts in respect of the construction of new houses. Practically every auctioneer had his or her own conditions of sale and every law stationer also had its own conditions of sale. This was a most unsatisfactory situation which persuaded the Law Society to produce its first edition of a standard Contract for Sale in 1976. This Contract for Sale was introduced to give a fair balance of rights between a vendor and a purchaser and proved extremely successful. It has been revised from time to time and the current edition is the 2001 edition. This form of contract for sale has now become the standard contract for sale used by the legal profession in all types of sales and purchases. It incorporates terms and conditions which are appropriate to both a sale by auction, as well as for a sale by private treaty.

Likewise, in the private house building sector, a standard building agreement was developed and its current edition issued in 2001 is now recommended for use in the purchase and sale of new houses.

In the standard certification of title for private dwellings referred to above, the certificate provides that the standard contract for sale issued by the Law Society has been used or if the property is a new house, the standard building agreement has been used.

As in all of these cases it should never be overlooked that these contracts are standard contracts for use in general conveyancing practice and regard must always be had to variations which may be required from time to time in respect of any particular transaction.

1.7.2 REQUISITIONS ON TITLE

Requisitions on title are the queries raised in all conveyancing transactions in respect of the vendor's title and many ancillary matters relevant to the property in question. The requisitions cover a multitude of matters, not all of which may be relevant to the particular transaction being dealt with. The form of requisitions on title has again been standardised by the Law Society and the current edition of them, viz the 2001, is now in general use in all conveyancing transactions. The requisitions have also been transferred onto computer (the CORT system) and these are sometimes issued with standard replies which may be adequate for standard residential house sales. However, it is vitally important to check that if replies are being given that the replies are accurate.

Because of the multiplicity of additional factors which all conveyancers now have to take into account, a substantial number of requisitions have been added to the standard ones. These are incorporated in the printed forms issued by the Law Society but are to be excluded in cases to which they do not apply, eg there are separate requisitions on title covering matters like licensing, second-hand apartments, multi-storey buildings, restaurant certificates, etc.

1.7.3 FAMILY LAW DECLARATIONS

Because of the development since 1976 of legislation dealing with family law, it has become essential for conveyancers to have regard to a number of legislative provisions which may affect property transactions, ie Family Home Protection Act, 1976, Family Law Act, 1981, Judicial Separation and Family Law Reform Act, 1989, Family Law Act, 1995 and Family Law (Divorce) Act, 1996.

In order to deal with this developing branch of conveyancing, standard declarations recommended for use by the solicitors' profession have been prepared and issued by the Law Society. These have been updated and amended from time to time and the declarations are recommended for standard use as being adequate to deal with the various matters raised in the legislation. It is important to emphasise, however, that they should not be used without giving proper consideration to the contents thereof to ensure that, where necessary, relevant amendments are made to cover any particular situation that may arise. This is still a developing area of law and these standard declarations may require amendment from time to time.

The reader is referred to **chapter 6**, which deals with this topic for further details of the particular elements of the legislation to which conveyancers must have regard.

1.8 Ethics

The New Oxford Dictionary of English defines ethics as 'moral principles that govern a person's behaviour or the conducting of an activity' or in the singular as 'the branch of knowledge that deals with moral principles'. It then goes on to say:

> 'Schools of ethics in Western philosophy can be divided, very roughly, into three sorts. The first, drawing on the works of Aristotle, holds that the virtues (such as justice, charity and generosity) are dispositions to act in ways that benefit both the person possessing them and that person's society. The second, defended particularly by Kant, makes the concept of duty central to morality: humans are bound, from a knowledge of their duty as rational beings, to obey the categorical imperative to respect other rational beings. Thirdly, utilitarianism asserts that the guiding principle of conduct should be the greatest happiness or benefit of the greatest number.'

The three key words in this statement are Virtues, Duty and Conduct.

In conveyancing, there are professional codes of practice that fall directly under the heading of ethics and that must be followed as a matter of course by all solicitors and their staff in dealing with their colleagues and other parties and institutions engaged in the conveyancing area, eg banks, building societies, lending institutions and local authorities. Any behaviour considered to be a breach of ethical conduct may lead to disciplinary proceedings by the Law Society. The following is a short list of some of the more obvious matters:

(a) fair dealing and courtesy with your colleagues, avoiding any sharp practices or dishonesty;

(b) all dealings for or with your client to be honest and above board;

(c) full observance and performance of any undertakings. Failure to do so may lead to civil litigation against you as well as disciplinary proceedings by the Law Society;

(d) proper files and books of account to be kept, the latter to conform fully with the Solicitor Accounts regulations;

(e) all correspondence and enquiries from the Law Society relating to the conduct of a client's affairs to be dealt with immediately; and

(f) to ensure that all actions taken by you are in the client's best interest and are in accordance with the client's instructions.

1.9 Chart of Basic Steps in a Residential Conveyancing Transaction

BASIC STEPS IN A RESIDENTIAL CONVEYANCING TRANSACTION

Vendor's Solicitor   Purchaser's Solicitor

Take full instructions and furnish section 68 letter

Vendor's Solicitor side:

Obtain title deeds from client or lending institution. Client's authority required to take deeds up on accountable trust receipt.

Investigate title.

Draft contract in duplicate.

Send contract and copy title listed in documents schedule to purchaser's solicitor. Mark letter 'subject to contract/contract denied'.

Agree/Disagree with proposed amendments to draft contract.

If amendments are required have these approved by the vendor's solicitor.

Send executed contract in duplicate and deposit cheque to vendor's solicitor to be held as stakeholder pending completion.

Check that contract is unchanged or contains only the agreed amendments.
Have contract executed in duplicate by vendor once the terms have been explained by you. If property is a family home not in joint names the spouse's prior consent must be endorsed on the contract prior to its execution by the vendor. Hold deposit as stakeholder pending completion.

Return one contract to purchaser's solicitor.

Send balance of title to purchaser's solicitor within seven working days of date of sale.

Send objections (if any) and requisitions on title to vendor's solicitor within fourteen working days after delivery of the balance of the title. Any made outside this time and not going to the root of the title are deemed to have been waived.

On the basis of vendor's instructions reply to objections (if any) and requisitions on title. Have vendor sign a file copy of the replies by way of confirmation of your instructions.

Return objections (if any) and requisitions with replies to the purchaser's solicitor.

Purchaser's Solicitor side:

Carry out any required pre-contract enquiries, eg planning, user, finance, identity.

Advise client in writing to carry out an independent survey.

Check the terms of the contract and peruse the title documents.

Once terms of the contract are agreed explain them to the purchaser along with any matters arising in relation to the title. Ensure purchaser has loan approval. Furnish undertaking to lending institution and agree any qualifications on title in writing. If purchaser is happy to proceed have contract executed in duplicate by purchaser.
Obtain cheque for deposit (less booking deposit).

Binding contract now exists.
At this stage the purchaser should have insurance cover on the property.

Peruse full title and raise objections (if any) and requisitions on title.

15

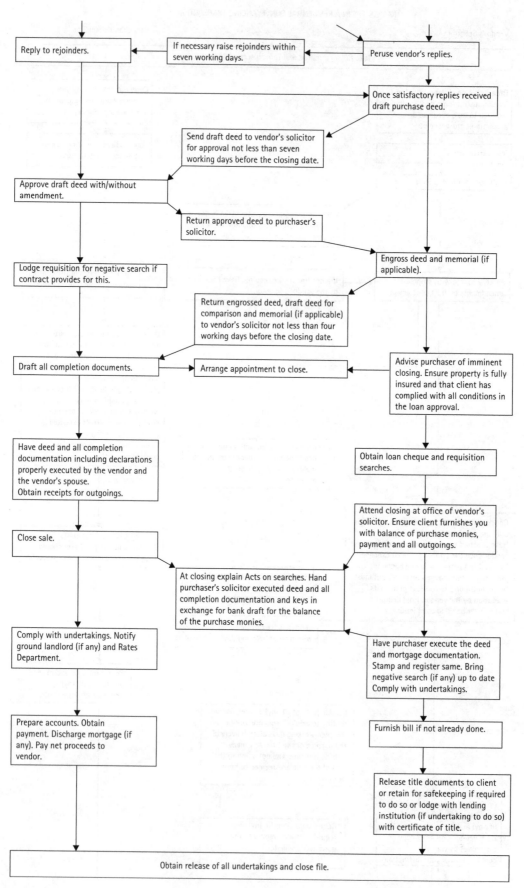

Reply to rejoinders.

If necessary raise rejoinders within seven working days.

Peruse vendor's replies.

Once satisfactory replies received draft purchase deed.

Send draft deed to vendor's solicitor for approval not less than seven working days before the closing date.

Approve draft deed with/without amendment.

Return approved deed to purchaser's solicitor.

Lodge requisition for negative search if contract provides for this.

Engross deed and memorial (if applicable).

Return engrossed deed, draft deed for comparison and memorial (if applicable) to vendor's solicitor not less than four working days before the closing date.

Draft all completion documents.

Arrange appointment to close.

Advise purchaser of imminent closing. Ensure property is fully insured and that client has complied with all conditions in the loan approval.

Have deed and all completion documentation including declarations properly executed by the vendor and the vendor's spouse.
Obtain receipts for outgoings.

Obtain loan cheque and requisition searches.

Close sale.

Attend closing at office of vendor's solicitor. Ensure client furnishes you with balance of purchase monies, payment and all outgoings.

At closing explain Acts on searches. Hand purchaser's solicitor executed deed and all completion documentation and keys in exchange for bank draft for the balance of the purchase monies.

Comply with undertakings. Notify ground landlord (if any) and Rates Department.

Have purchaser execute the deed and mortgage documentation. Stamp and register same. Bring negative search (if any) up to date Comply with undertakings.

Prepare accounts. Obtain payment. Discharge mortgage (if any). Pay net proceeds to vendor.

Furnish bill if not already done.

Release title documents to client or retain for safekeeping if required to do so or lodge with lending institution (if undertaking to do so) with certificate of title.

Obtain release of all undertakings and close file.

CHAPTER 2

TITLE

2.1 Good Title

A person who is either disposing of or acquiring a property generally describes his disposal or acquisition as the purchase of a house, a factory, a farm etc. In legal terms what that person is doing is disposing of or acquiring a particular title to the property in question. The nature of the title being disposed of or acquired may vary from a simple weekly tenancy to a full unencumbered fee simple. In between those two extremes of title may be a variety of different types, eg short leaseholds, long leaseholds, fee farm grant interests, life estates, leases for lives renewable forever, etc. Some of the titles concerned may impose severe restrictions on the use of the property or may impose substantial conditions on the person holding the current interest in the property, eg there may be a very severe repairing clause imposed upon a lessee in a leasehold title. However, irrespective of the nature of the title to the property, a conveyancer is obliged to ensure that what is being disposed of and what is being acquired is a good marketable title.

2.2 Marketable Title

2.2.1 GENERALLY

A good marketable title is a term adopted over many years and is understood by conveyancers to mean the standard of title which is given and accepted by conveyancers following what is regarded as good conveyancing rules and practice. There is no statutory definition of a good marketable title and hence conveyancers have determined their own code of practice supported by the views of the courts as to what constitutes a good marketable title.

The introduction by the Law Society of a standard contract for sale, standard requisitions on title, practice recommendations on issues that arise in practice from time to time and the preparation of standard documentation dealing with the provisions of the Family Home Protection Act, 1976 as amended, have been decisive matters in establishing an acceptable balancing of the conflicting rights that arise between vendors and purchasers. These documents, when used in conjunction with such statutory provisions as there are, dealing with the length of title to be furnished, have established a clearly understood concept of what is a good marketable title in modern conveyancing. It has to be emphasised that such procedures and rules as there are in conveyancing (apart from such statutory provisions as there are in the Vendor and Purchaser Act, 1874, the Conveyancing Act, 1881 and the Registration of Title Act, 1964) are matters that have developed from the practice of conveyancing. There will always be occasions when, for one reason or another, the standard procedures and rules of practice may not be applicable. For example, in the purchase of a private dwellinghouse where it is intended to continue the residential use, a vendor's solicitor may offer, and a purchaser's solicitor may be satisfied to accept in accordance with standard recommended practice, a title which commenced with a good root of title twenty-five years old. A title of similar length may not be acceptable to a purchaser's solicitor if he or she is purchasing a substantial property where, for example, the purchaser intends to carry out substantial development works. In such a case it may be necessary and advisable for a purchaser's solicitor to carry out a much more in-depth investigation of the title and he or she may wish to extend his or her investigation for a period substantially in excess of the twenty-five-year period above referred to. It must also be borne in mind, having regard to the nature of some titles, that the root of title may of necessity have to be older than the recommended period of time because there is no suitable document which would be acceptable as a good root of title within the shorter period referred to or it may have to satisfy the first registration requirements of the Land Registry where a minimum of thirty years' title is required.

2.2.2 COURTS OF EQUITY

The ultimate test as to what is a good marketable title is that a court of equity will not enforce a contract against a purchaser unless the vendor makes out and shows a good marketable title in accordance with the contract. The courts of equity will not force a purchaser to take a bad title. It is a well-settled principle that, in so far as the enforcement of a contract for a sale of property is concerned, a purchaser is entitled to a good title and that, accordingly, a vendor must give one and that, in addition, a vendor must make out or show his or her title. This broad principle has been stated by judges over the years in different cases of which the following are two examples:

(a) In the case of *Clarke v Taylor* [1899] IR 449, Walker LJ stated the 'law of the land applicable to vendors and purchasers always has been that where a man proposes to sell land he must make out his title'. In the same case Lord Ashbourne stated that this stems from the ordinary right of a purchaser to see that he is getting what he desires to buy.

(b) In *Re Flynn and Newman's Contract* [1948] IR 104, Kingsmill Moore J stated:

'in the absence of any express provision to the contrary the vendor undertakes and is bound in law to show a good title to the property to be sold and to convey land corresponding substantially in all respects with the description contained in the contract'.

Whether this right arises as an implied term of the contract or exists as a rule of law was at one stage considered to be of some consequence but the distinction now seems to be purely academic.

2.2.3 CLOSED AND OPEN CONTRACTS

The duty to provide, and the entitlement to receive, a good marketable title is said to have two aspects:

(a) to *show* good title in the sense of stating all matters essential to the title contracted to be sold, and

(b) to *make* good title in the sense of proving by proper evidence those matters.

The full force of this duty arises only in open contracts, ie a contract which contains no restrictions on the purchaser's right to investigate the title of the vendor. An open contract of this nature is one which rarely exists in practice and, if it does exist, would normally arise where a note or memorandum enforceable under the Statute of Frauds, 1695 has been entered into by a vendor and a purchaser without the assistance of any legal advice. In everyday conveyancing matters a vendor's solicitor will restrict the purchaser's enquiry into the title being offered and, in some very limited circumstances, may in fact exclude the purchaser's normal right by appropriate conditions in the contract for sale. This is a practice which should create no difficulty provided that the vendor's solicitor inserts conditions on the purchaser's solicitor's right to investigate the title in terms which are considered to be fair and reasonable and which are not fraudulent or ambiguous. If in fact conditions are inserted which are considered by the courts to be unduly onerous, then the contract will be construed against the vendor and specific performance will be refused.

The leading case in this matter is *White and Hague's Contract* [1921] 1 IR 138. In that case the vendor's solicitor seriously overstepped the mark in drawing special conditions in the contract which were so unreasonable and restrictive that no purchaser could be asked to complete on foot of them. In his judgment in that case O'Connor MR stated:

'and there is also authority for a further proposition that a contract by a purchaser to take such title as the vendor has does not relieve the vendor from the necessity of showing a bona fide title and producing the best title he can from the material in his power, a proposition which has special application to a case in which no explanation can be offered for refusal to make title except dishonesty or perversity'.

In *Re Flynn and Newman's Contract* Kingsmill Moore J stated:

'the vendor may of course limit his obligations to good title by suitable special conditions but if he does so he must fairly indicate what is the defect in his title to which the purchaser must submit and must also take care that he is not guilty of misrepresentation'.

2.2.4 DEFECTIVE TITLES

It should also be remembered that a condition in the contract restricting investigation of a particular part of a vendor's title does not relieve the vendor from disclosing latent defects in title of which the vendor is, or ought to have been, aware. Furthermore, the Law of Property Amendment Acts, 1859 and 1860 make it both a criminal offence and a civil wrong actionable in damages by the purchaser or persons deriving title under him or her for the vendor or his or her solicitor or other agent to conceal *with intent to defraud* from the purchaser any instrument or incumbrance material to the title or to falsify any pedigree upon which the title may depend in order to induce the purchaser to accept the title offered or produced.

It must be remembered that there will always be titles which fall short both in their nature and documentation of what would normally be sought and given. One of the prime examples of this type of title is what is known as a 'squatters' title, ie a title acquired under the Statute of Limitations, 1957 where somebody has entered into possession of a property adverse to the owner's title and occupied it for more than twelve years without acknowledging the true owner's title. In such a case, if the vendor is proposing to dispose of the interest that he or she has established in the property, he or she will have no documentary evidence whatsoever other than providing a statutory declaration made by himself or herself and any other party who may have knowledge of the length and nature of his or her occupation. In very many cases he or she may not even be able to establish the nature of the title that he or she is barring. In such a case, if a vendor fairly discloses all the facts surrounding the nature of the title he or she is offering for sale, and if a purchaser, having been given all of the relevant information, contracts to purchase such an interest, then the courts will enforce the contract.

Likewise, while good conveyancing practice insists upon a title starting with a good root of title (a concept which is dealt with later), it is always open to a purchaser to accept what is considered to be a bad root of title. In considering this proposition it is important to distinguish between a valid deed and a defective deed. A bad root of title may of itself be a perfectly valid deed but for other reasons which are explained later is not acceptable as a good root. In a leading case on this point, *Marsh v Earl of Granville* (1882) 24 Ch D 11, it was stated in the contract that the title to a certain freehold property would commence with a deed of conveyance less than forty years old. After the contracts had been exchanged and title furnished it transpired that the deed referred to was a voluntary deed, ie one in which there was no valuable consideration paid for the transfer of ownership, but this was not stated in the contract. It was held in that case that the purchaser was justified in refusing to complete and was entitled to assume, as nothing had been stated to the contrary in the contract, that the deed was a conveyance for value which would have been accepted as a good root of title. Accordingly, if intending to furnish a contract starting with a document which would be classified as a bad root of title then the nature of that document should be clearly specified in the special conditions of the contract so that the proposed purchaser is put on full notice of the nature and content of it.

2.2.5 CERTIFICATES OF TITLE

In residential conveyancing matters the approved form of certificate of title (being the 1999 edition approved by the Law Society) states that a good marketable title within that system means a title of a quality commensurate with prudent standards of current conveyancing practice in Ireland. These standards require, inter alia, that the purchase was effected on foot of the current Law Society Contract for Sale and/or Building Agreement. They also require that the investigation of title to the property was made in accordance with the current Law Society Requisitions on Title together with any additional requisitions appropriate to the property and that satisfactory replies have been received. Where the property is already owned by the borrower, title shall be so investigated that if the said requisitions had been raised satisfactory replies would have been obtained.

The certificate goes on to provide that any dispute with regard to the quality of any title (within the foregoing definitions) may be referred for a ruling to the Conveyancing Committee of the Law Society but without prejudice to the right of either party to seek a determination by the court on the issue. Thus, within conveyancing of residential property using the certificate of title system, there is a facility whereby any dispute may be dealt with if agreed between the parties without going to court. The alternative in residential conveyancing and in any other type of conveyancing is to go to court on foot of a vendor and purchaser summons. This is a summons issued under the provisions of the Vendor and Purchaser Act, 1874 which enables parties to go to court for a ruling where a dispute has arisen under the terms of the contract in respect of the title and is a relatively quick and cheap way of resolving any disputes.

2.3 Roots of Title

2.3.1 INTRODUCTION

The concept of a good title essentially hangs on the quality of the root of title offered and its age. A good root of title is the document from which the vendor proposes to show that his or her title starts, and the rest of his or her title from that time onwards is literally rooted in that document. It is accordingly an essential prerequisite to a good marketable title that what has become accepted as a good root of title is used by a vendor to commence his or her title.

2.3.2 DEFINITION

There is no statutory definition of a good root of title but many years of conveyancing practice and court decisions have laid down the guidelines which must be followed in identifying a good root. One of the classic textbooks, *Williams on Title* (23rd edn), pp 651–652 gives a good definition of what is required in a good root of title which covers all the essential ingredients as follows:

> 'An instrument of disposition dealing with or proving on the face of it without the aid of extrinsic evidence the ownership of the whole legal and equitable estate in the property sold containing a description by which the property can be identified and showing nothing to cast a doubt on the title of the disposing parties.'

In addition to all of the characteristics specified in this definition, the age of the root as has been stated is also a key factor.

2.3.3 GOOD ROOTS

The following documents are examples of, and have become accepted as being, good roots of title:

(a) where land is vested by the Crown (pre-1922) or by an Act of the Oireachtas;

(b) a conveyance or a lease for value;

(c) a Land Registry folio with title absolute;

(d) a landed estates court conveyance;

(e) a settlement in consideration of marriage;

(f) an ante-nuptial settlement, the consideration being marriage;

(g) a legal mortgage in fee simple;

(h) a fee farm grant (distinguished from a fee farm conversion grant);

(i) a fee farm conversion grant converted under the Renewable Leasehold Conversion Act, 1849 converting a lease for lives into a freehold title. Note that this form of grant was previously considered to be a bad root as it relied for its validity upon the converted lease but, in modern conveyancing practice, it is now generally accepted as a good root, particularly if the original lease for lives is available. However, in a substantial number of cases these leases for lives are not available, but because of their antiquity and if the property concerned has been used for the same purpose for a substantial number of years without any notices from the grantor, they are generally accepted; and

(j) a specific devise in a will of a person who died prior to 1 June 1959. Note that this form of root is not acceptable for any person who died on or after 1 June 1959 as the Administration of Estates Act, 1959 provided that, on or after 1 June 1959 a written assent to a beneficiary in a will was required. Thus after 1 June 1959 what would be required is not one, but two, documents, namely a specific devise in a will coupled with the subsequent assent from the personal representative in favour of the beneficiary.

2.3.4 DEVOLUTION OF TITLE FROM THE ROOT

In cases involving a leasehold title, or a fee farm grant (a hybrid freehold containing many of the characteristics of a leasehold), the root will always be the lease, or the fee farm grant, no matter how old it is, as the terms and conditions and covenants contained therein will always continue to affect the subject property.

The vendor will then be entitled to skip to a later deed at least twenty years old which conforms to the definition of a good root, eg an assignment for valuable consideration. In that context, the provisions of the Vendor and Purchaser Act, 1874, s 2 are helpful and the relevant part of that section reads as follows:

> *Recitals, statements and descriptions of facts, matters and parties contained in deeds, instruments, acts of parliament or statutory declarations twenty years old at the date of the contract shall unless and except so far as they shall be proven to be inaccurate be taken to be sufficient evidence of the truth of such facts, matters and descriptions.*

If the title is based on a fee farm grant, which will contain covenants and conditions similar to those in a lease, the title should always start with the grant in question and skip to a document which conforms to the definition of a good root at least twenty years old. If the title is based on a lease for lives renewable forever that has been converted to a fee farm grant under the Renewable Leasehold Conversion Act, 1849, then the lease for lives is where the title must start and not the fee farm grant, as the covenants and conditions in the lease are grafted onto the grant and are preserved. This means that the covenants and conditions are carried forward and in effect incorporated into the fee farm grant.

If the lease for lives is dated earlier than 1 August 1849 and has not been converted under the 1849 Act, it is automatically converted to a freehold title under the Landlord and Tenant (Amendment) Act 1980, s 74 and that freehold title is deemed to be a graft on the previous interest and is subject to any rights or equities arising from its being such a graft. In such a title, the lease for lives will be the starting point for the title. It appears that the estate created under this section is not a fee farm grant but may be a new form of statutory fee simple. For a detailed comment on this aspect of the section, see Wylie, *Irish Landlord and Tenant Law* (3rd edn) p 1181, note 718.

2.3.5 BAD ROOTS

The following are examples of bad roots of title:

(a) general devise in a will;

(b) voluntary conveyance;

(c) deed of appointment of trustees;

(d) conveyance under a power of sale;

(e) post-nuptial settlement;

(f) post-1959 will on its own;

(g) possessory title in the Land Registry;

(h) legal mortgage by demise;

(i) disentailing deed; and

(j) deed of assignment.

2.3.6 LEASES

In a leasehold title always start with the original lease irrespective of how old the lease is as the purchaser will be bound by the covenants and conditions in the lease and will always want to know what they are even if the lease should be 500 years old. If it is necessary to go back for a substantial period of time to find a good root, the vendor would then be entitled to skip to an assignment or, if freehold, a conveyance for value in the recent past more than twenty years old in accordance with the rules discussed later and there should be no need to investigate the title during the intervening period.

2.3.7 BASIC PRINCIPLE

The basic principle involved in selecting the type of deeds referred to above as good roots is that in all of those cases an investigation of the title would have been carried out by the solicitor acting on behalf of the recipient of the property or, alternatively, title would have passed on foot of the statutory authority contained in some Act of Parliament or of the Oireachtas. In relation to those documents specified as being bad roots, they would be instruments in which either no prior investigation of title would have taken place as there was no valuable consideration passing, eg the voluntary conveyance or the documents relied for their validity upon the contents and existence of an earlier document such as a conveyance under a power of sale.

2.3.8 AGE OF ROOTS OF TITLE

The next important matter to be considered in connection with roots is their age. Here the modern conveyancer is in something of a quandary as there are no modern statutory rules that may be relied upon to establish how old a root of title must be. Instead it is necessary to fall back on what is considered in modern times to be a reasonable length of time for the age of the root as recommended by the Law Society coupled with the length of time required by the Land Registry under the Registration of Title Act, 1964 and the Land Registry Rules in respect of first registration applications and the conversion of possessory titles to absolute titles.

2.3.9 STATUTORY PROVISIONS

2.3.9.1 Generally

The old common law rule prior to the introduction of the provisions of the Vendor and Purchaser Act, 1874 and the Conveyancing Act, 1881 was that a good root of title must be at least sixty years old. This meant that it was necessary to go back at least sixty years and if necessary beyond the sixty years until a good root of title with which to start was found. This common law rule was first amended by statutory provisions in the Vendor and Purchaser Act, 1874 and then by the Conveyancing Act, 1881. These Acts reduced the period of time to forty years for freeholds and introduced special rules for leaseholds. However, these statutory provisions apply with their full rigour only to open contracts, ie contracts where the title to be furnished is not restricted by the special conditions. As stated at **2.2.3**, in practice an open contract is rarely encountered and is likely only to arise in an exchange of documents between a vendor and a purchaser without legal advice, which satisfy the conditions as to enforceability under the provisions of the Statute of Frauds (Ireland), 1695, and which bind the parties. The decision of the Supreme Court in *Boyle v Lee* [1992] 1 IR 555 delivered on 12 December 1991, in which the court fully reviewed the manner in which the Statute of Frauds, 1695 should be applied, makes it even less likely that an open contract will be encountered in practice.

Notwithstanding the foregoing, however, it is important that conveyancers should be familiar with these statutory provisions as there are consequences for a purchaser if he or she accepts less than the statutory minimum title provided for in these Acts even in a closed contract situation, ie a contract which restricts the extent of the title to be provided by the vendor. The relevant provisions are contained in the Vendor and Purchaser Act, 1874 (the 1874 Act), ss 1 and 2 and the Conveyancing Act, 1881 (the 1881 Act), ss 3(1) and 13(1). On the question of the creation and enforceability of a legally binding contract for the sale of land, the reader is referred to the detailed consideration of this respect of conveyancing at **16.2.1.14**.

2.3.9.2 Vendor and Purchaser Act, 1874

Under the 1874 Act, s 1 title must be deduced for a period of at least forty years and this means going back further than this if necessary to find a good root. This applies to both freehold and leasehold except to the extent that the provisions are restricted by other statutory provisions. Section 2 of the 1874 Act states:

under a contract to grant or assign a term of years derived or to be derived out of a freehold or a leasehold estate the intended lessee or assignee shall not be entitled to call for the title to the freehold.

2.3.9.3 Conveyancing Act, 1881

Section 3(1) of the 1881 Act states:

under a contract to sell and assign a term of years derived out of a leasehold interest in land, the intended assignee shall not have the right to call for the leasehold reversion.

Section 13(1) of the 1881 Act states:

on a contract to grant a lease for a term of years to be derived out of a leasehold interest with a leasehold reversion, the intended lessee shall not have the right to call for the title to that reversion.

2.3.9.4 Effect of leasehold titles

It may be seen from these provisions that a person dealing with the acquisition of a leasehold interest may be very restricted in the length of title that he or she is entitled to get. The combined effect of these provisions may be summarised as follows:

(a) in the case of a lease the lessee cannot call for the freehold;

(b) the sublessee may get the original lease, however old, and see the title for the last forty years if the lease is that old;

(c) the sublessee may not call for the freehold;

(d) in the case of a sub-sublessee, the sub-sublessee may get the sublease, however old, and see the title to the last forty years if the sublease is that old;

(e) but the sub-sublessee may not call for the leasehold reversion or the freehold reversion; and

(f) on the assignment of a lease or a sublease or a sub-sublease the respective assignees are entitled to see the lease or sublease or the sub-sublease, however old, and all dealings therewith for the last forty years if the lease, sublease or sub-sublease is that old.

While these provisions may appear at first sight to be satisfactory, in practice they may not be as in a case where the lease might be only, say, six years old. For some more detailed consideration of the operation of these sections consult Wylie, *Irish Conveyancing Law* (2nd edn, 1996) pp 484–487 where he gives some detailed examples of how these provisions might work in a number of situations.

2.3.10 RULE IN *PATMAN v HARLAND*

Prior to the enactment of these statutory provisions, the common law rule appeared to be that a purchaser of leasehold property was entitled to call for his lessor's title but this could be restricted by an express contractual provision. After the passing of the legislation, the question arose as to what the purchaser's position was under an open contract which precluded an investigation of the freehold or leasehold reversion. It was soon decided in 1881, under what has become known as the rule in *Patman v Harland* (1881) 17 Ch D 353, a case decided in relation to the Vendor and Purchaser Act 1874, s 2 that a purchaser is fixed with constructive notice not only of matters that he or she would have discovered by investigating that title he or she is allowed to see under the statutory provisions, but also all matters he or she would have discovered by investigating the superior title which the statutory provisions precluded him or her from investigating on an open contract. In other words, the purchaser runs the risk of being affected by hidden defects or encumbrances in the superior title both if he or she contracts for less than the legislation allows him or her and if he or she fails to contract for more than the legislation allows him or her. Accordingly, the only safe option for a purchaser is to contract for more than the legislation allows him or her and not to leave the contract open, as the above provisions apply only to the extent that the contract does not otherwise provide (Vendor and Purchaser Act, 1874, s 2 and Conveyancing Act, 1881, ss 3(9) and 13(2)).

2.3.11   EFFECT OF RULE

The object of the rule in *Patman v Harland* is to protect the interest of superior owners in relation to a transaction in which they are not parties and may not even know is taking place. In England the rule has been altered by the Law of Property Act, 1925 and many critics of the change argue that the cure is worse than the disease. However, it is still in operation in Ireland. The extent to which conveyancers should be concerned with its operation will, to a large extent, depend on the nature of the title being offered, the length of that title and the use to which the property is to be put either in the short term or the long term. Each case will have to be considered on its own merits and it would be dangerous to generalise. It will be appreciated that conveyancing practice has been considerably refined since the passing of the 1874 and 1881 Acts and the failure to pass amended legislation to update these Acts and bring them in line with modern conveyancing practice has led the solicitors' profession into adopting its own code of practice on what length of title it is reasonable to offer and to look for on a purchase and sale of a property. It should be noted that in England the statutory period for a freehold title was reduced in 1925 to thirty years and was further reduced in 1969 to fifteen years.

2.3.12   LAW SOCIETY GUIDELINES

However, as has been pointed out, these statutory periods are applicable only where there are no contractual provisions closing down the title and it is very rare to come across an open contract with no restrictions on the title to be furnished. In current conveyancing practice it is recommended by the Law Society Conveyancing Committee that, in general, a minimum period of twenty years' title shall be provided and sought in closed contracts but that anything less than that minimum period is not acceptable. This means that a root of title should be at least twenty years old and comply with the definition of a good root of title detailed earlier in this chapter. In many cases it will be necessary because of the nature of the title being dealt with to start with a root that is much older than twenty years. A root that is less than twenty years should never be accepted.

2.3.13   CURRENT PRACTICE

The basic reason for adopting this twenty-year rule is the frequency with which property now changes hands compared to the situation in 1874 and 1881 when the above Acts were passed. The earlier periods of sixty and forty years are essentially arbitrary periods even though the latter is fixed by statute. With the huge increase of the development of urban land which took place in Ireland in the 1950s and 1960s and which continues to this day, it became commonplace for large tracts of land for housing and for commercial use to be developed. Each such tract of land would have a single title from which the title for each individual property was carved. Such titles were read and accepted by a substantial number of different solicitors acting for each individual purchaser as well as the solicitors acting for each lending institution who advanced money on the security of each title. Thus, each of such titles was scrutinised many times and if any defects were found, such defects were corrected at that time. As the properties and the titles aged it was felt that adherence to the strict forty-year period was unnecessary.

Accordingly, in order to simplify conveyancing practice and to reduce the volume of paper work each time a property changed hands, the period of time to be shown for the root gradually shortened to the now generally accepted minimum of twenty years. It must again be emphasised that this is a recommended period only and has no force of law although it does have the support of the Law Society's Conveyancing Committee as good practice in modern conveyancing.

There will be undoubtedly many cases where a practitioner might not be prepared to accept such a short period of title, eg where the title is a one-off title not forming part of a larger development, or the property is being bought for development purposes, or the purchaser may require more than twenty years to enable the title to be registered in the Land Registry. It is not possible to lay down hard and fast rules on this matter other than to indicate the general recommendations of the Law Society Conveyancing Committee. As a conveyancer gains experience he or she will be better able to assess those titles where it is advisable to go beyond the recommended twenty-year minimum period.

The issue of the length of title was considered by the Law Reform Commission recently and in 1989 it issued a recommendation that the statutory period of forty years in the Vendor and Purchaser Act, 1874 be reduced to twenty years and this recommendation is contained in the Law Reform Commission Report 30, 1989, chapter 2. This recommendation has not yet been enacted in legislation but it does give strong support to the view of the Law Society Conveyancing Committee.

2.3.14 REGISTERED TITLES

2.3.14.1 Generally

The foregoing observations in respect of roots and lengths of title apply mainly in respect of unregistered titles, ie titles which are in the Registry of Deeds system and are not in the Land Registry system. The classes of title that are registered in the Land Registry are covered in **chapter 14**. In respect of two of these classes, namely absolute freehold and absolute leasehold, the above observations in respect of roots of title and lengths of title have no application. The effect of the registration of these two classes of title is as later stated and a conveyancer is spared any further investigation beyond what is stated on the register *irrespective of the date of registration of the registered owner*. Neither the forty-year nor the twenty-year rule has any relevance and one is entitled to rely on the register without looking behind it and the State guarantee that the register is correct.

2.3.14.2 Investigation of prior title

There is one class of title, however, where the title prior to the registration must be investigated and that is where the title is registered subject to equities or, in modern folios, registered with a possessory title in both freehold and leasehold titles. In such cases evidence must be obtained to enable the purchaser to apply and have the equity note discharged or the possessory note converted to absolute or good leasehold. The Registration of Title Act, 1964 (the 1964 Act), s 50 and the Land Registration Rules, 1972 (as amended) deal with the documentation required for this purpose.

There is one other class of title in the Land Registry where additional title beyond that shown on the register may be required, ie good leasehold title. Section 45 of the 1964 Act states that registration with a good leasehold title shall not affect or prejudice the enforcement of any right adverse to or in derogation of the title of the lessor to grant the lease. This in effect means that in registering the title the Registrar did not investigate the title of the lessor to grant the lease but only investigated the title of the lessee. Accordingly, in such cases one must apply the twenty-year rule to the lease. If the lease is less then twenty years old then one should look for the title of the lessor to grant the lease and if satisfied with that title it is not necessary to have the leasehold title converted to absolute. If the lease is more than twenty years old then if it is acceptable as a good root it is not necessary to enquire beyond the register and the twenty-year rule may be applied. Always remember, even in Land Registry cases, that the original lease must be obtained.

2.3.14.3 First registration

Part 2 (rules 14–51) of the Land Registration Rules, 1972 as amended deals with first registration, conversion of possessory and qualified titles and other registrations involving examinations of title. The Land Registry requirements are set out in these rules. On a first registration application rule 19 allows the title to commence with a disposition of the property made not less than thirty years prior to the date of the application that would be a good root of title under a contract limiting only the length of title to be shown. Where the market value of the property is shown to the satisfaction of the Registrar not to exceed €317,435 (this is the current figure and is subject to change), the length of title to be shown may be reduced to twenty or twelve years on the terms set out in the Rules. If the application is by a statutory authority the Registrar may dispense with any examination of title and rely on a certificate of title to be provided by the solicitor for the authority in the form set out in the Rules.

It will be seen from the foregoing that the State registering authority for Land Registry titles does not seek to impose the forty-year rule and may even in specified cases accept less than the minimum twenty years recommended as general practice by the Law Society. In the light of these factors and the absence of modern legislative provisions it is acceptable practice to adopt the twenty-year rule as set out above and to recommend that rule as good modern conveyancing practice.

2.3.14.4 The registers

The 1964 Act prescribes the registers that shall be kept in the Land Registry. Section 8(a) provides that there shall be a register of ownership of freehold land and of leasehold land. Section 8(b) provides for what is called the subsidiary register, eg incorporeal hereditaments held in gross and such other rights as may be prescribed. Section 83 of the Act and rules 223 and 227 of the 1972 Rules prescribe the contents and procedures under s 8(b). This subsidiary register deals with such matters as rent charges, fee farm rents and fishing rights. This subsidiary register is rarely encountered in practice and is not considered here in any detail but the same principles apply to it as to the other registers.

These other registers are self-explanatory, dealing with freehold and leasehold title. There are four classes of ownership, namely full owner and limited owner for freeholds and full owner and limited owner for leaseholds. Section 27 of the 1964 Act provides for the registration of these classes as follows:

(a)   as full owner of freehold land, that is to say, as tenant in fee simple;

(b)   in the case of freehold land as limited owner thereof, that is to say, as tenant for life or a person having the power of a tenant for life under the Settled Land Acts;

(c)   as full owner of a leasehold interest, that is to say, as the person in whom the leasehold interest is vested in possession; or

(d)   in the case of leasehold land as limited owner thereof, that is to say, as tenant for life or a person having the power of a tenant for life under the Settled Land Acts.

A sale by a limited owner will require evidence of the nature of his power of sale and may require the consent or joinder of some third party as rights of third parties under the settlement on foot of which the limited owner was registered may be protected by an inhibition registered on the folio. Students are referred to Fitzgerald, *Land Registry Practice* (2nd edn, 1989) p 101 for a more detailed discussion on this class of ownership.

2.3.14.5 Classes of title

Sections 33 and 40 of the 1964 Act deal with the classes of title for freehold and leasehold respectively. These classifications identify the quality of the title registered. Both sections provide for title to be registered as absolute, possessory or qualified. In the case of a leasehold title, there is an additional category known as good leasehold. In both freehold and leasehold, the Registrar will always prefer to give an absolute title but may be obliged to give a qualified title. A qualified title is the same as an absolute title (s 39) but it will be qualified by excepting from the effect of registration any right

    (a)   arising before a specified date; or

    (b)   arising under a specified instrument; or

    (c)   otherwise particularly described in the register (see s 33(5)).

If such a registration is given, a purchaser should carefully examine the nature of the qualification and should always seek whatever documents or evidence are required to convert to absolute title in accordance with the provisions of the Act, s 50. In respect of a person registered as full owner of freehold land with absolute title, s 37(1) provides that there shall vest in the person so registered an estate in fee simple in the land, together with all implied or express rights, privileges and appurtenances belonging or appurtenant thereto.

In respect of a limited owner of freehold land, s 37(2) provides that, on registration of a person as limited owner of freehold land with an absolute title, an estate in fee simple in the land, together with all implied or express rights, privileges and appurtenances belonging or appurtenant thereto, shall vest in the person so registered and the other persons entitled to the several estates and interests comprised in the subject of the settlement collectively, according to such estates and interests respectively. In both cases, the estate of the registered owner shall be subject to all registered burdens and all s 72 burdens but shall be free from all other rights, including rights of the State. With regard to possessory title, s 38 provides that the registration of a person as first registered full or limited owner of freehold land with a possessory title shall not effect or prejudice the enforcement of any right adverse to or in derogation of the title of that person and subsisting or capable of arising at the time of registration, but, save as aforesaid, shall have the same effect as registration with an absolute title. Possessory title is the modern equivalent of titles formerly registered 'subject to equities'. With regard to leaseholds, s 40(4) provides that a person shall be registered as owner with an absolute title where the title both to the leasehold interest and to the freehold estate, and to any intermediate leasehold interest that may exist, is approved by the Registrar.

Section 40(5) provides that a person shall be registered as owner with a good leasehold title where the title to the leasehold interest is approved by the Registrar. Section 40(6) deals with the registration of a leasehold title as a qualified title and contains much the same provisions as s 39 for freehold title. Sections 44 and 46 deal with the effect of registration as a full or limited owner of a freehold estate with absolute or possessory title in much the same way as ss 37 and 38 deal with freehold title. With regard to the separate category of good leasehold, s 45 provides that the registration of a person as first registered full or limited owner of a leasehold interest with a good leasehold title shall not affect or prejudice the enforcement of any right adverse to or in derogation of the title of the lessor to grant the lease, but, save as aforesaid, shall have the same effect as registration with an absolute title.

The quality of the various titles in the Land Registry and the way they fit into the practice of conveyancing are considered later in these notes when we come to consider the whole question of roots of title and the quality of what is required for a 'good root', a good root being the document on which a good or marketable title is based. In so far as the transfer of ownership of a registered title is concerned, the 1972 Rules lay down the forms to be used, whether the transfer is between living persons or following a death. A simple form of transfer between living persons is used for both freehold and leasehold and avoids the sometimes complex but often necessary recitals in the transfer of unregistered title.

Such a transfer will not, however, form part of the title documents in a registered title as it is retained in the Land Registry once the change of ownership has been registered. Apart from the transfer, there are a substantial number of other forms used in Land Registry dealings which are dealt with in more detail in **chapter 14**.

CHAPTER 3

INVESTIGATION OF TITLE

3.1 Why Investigate Title?

This chapter considers matters relevant to the actual investigation of a title. It deals with the type of documentation that will be encountered in various types of titles and the main points to have regard to when reading a title. It is worth stating at this stage that reading a title is just as important for a vendor's solicitor as for a purchaser's solicitor as it is the duty of the vendor's solicitor to prepare the contract for sale, and to enable him or her to do that properly on behalf of the vendor he or she must first read the title to determine the manner in which the contract is to be drawn and, indeed, to identify precisely the nature of the vendor's title that the vendor is contracting to sell. Having said that, however, the main onus thereafter is on the purchaser's solicitor to read the title and satisfy himself or herself that he or she can acquire a good marketable title on behalf of the purchaser, that the title being provided is that contracted for in the contract for sale, and that the property contracted to be sold is properly and adequately identified in the title deeds.

3.2 Bona Fide Purchaser for Value Without Notice

It is a well-settled principle of law that a bona fide purchaser for value without notice acquires a good title to property unaffected by matters of which he had no notice. The question of notice may arise either by some matter arising from the documentation either contained in the title deeds themselves or given in response to replies to requisitions on title or that may be apparent from an inspection of the premises. Those apparent from an inspection of the premises are generally described as patent defects and those not apparent from an inspection of the premises are generally described as latent defects.

3.2.1 PATENT DEFECTS

In *Re Flanagan and McGarvey and Thompson's Contract* [1945] NI 32 Black J stated:

> 'It is well settled that the purchaser of the property must take it subject to any defects which are patent on an inspection and are not inconsistent with the description contained in the contract for sale. In order that a defect may be a patent defect within the meaning of this rule it is not enough that there exists on the land an object of sense that might put a careful purchaser on enquiry. To be a patent defect the defect must either be visible to the eye or arisen by necessary implication from something visible to the eye.'

In that case the question being considered was a right of way claimed by another landowner and Black J concluded as follows:

'I think that the existence and the nature of the path leading nowhere but to the back door of the house showed that it served no purpose other than as a way from the road to this back door to which there was no other means of access and necessarily indicated as a practical certainty to anyone who saw it that the occupier of the house would have a right of way over it to the back door of the house.'

3.2.2 LATENT DEFECTS

3.2.2.1 *Somers v Weir*

The broad basis upon which the principle works in relation to latent defects was well stated by Henchy J in the case of *Somers v Weir* [1979] IR 94. This case was the first major case dealing with the notice provisions contained in the Family Home Protection Act, 1976 (the 1976 Act) and in that case Henchy J stated that the nub of the case was whether the purchaser was 'an assignee who in good faith acquires an estate or interest in property?' Henchy J stated the law as follows:

'The question whether a purchaser has acted in good faith necessarily depends on the extent of his knowledge of the relevant circumstances. In earlier times the tendency was to judge a purchaser solely by the facts that had actually come to his knowledge. In the course of time it came to be held in the Court of Chancery that it would be unconscionable for the purchaser to take a stand on the facts that had come to his notice to the exclusion of those which ordinary prudence or circumspection or skill should have called to his attention. When the facts at his command beckoned him to look and enquire further and he refrained from doing so, Equity fixed him with constructive notice of what he would have ascertained if he had pursued the further investigation which a person of reasonable care and skill would have felt proper to make in the circumstances. He would not be allowed to say "I acted in good faith in ignorance of those facts of which I learned only after I took the conveyance", if those facts were such as a reasonable man in the circumstances would have brought within his knowledge.

'When the Supreme Court of Judicature Act (Ireland), 1877 brought the rules of Equity into play in all courts the equitable doctrine of notice was given supremacy. Further it was given statutory expression in s 3 of the Conveyancing Act, 1882. For the purposes of this case the relevant parts of that section are contained in subsection 1 which states:

(1) A purchaser shall not be prejudicially affected by notice of any instrument, fact or thing unless

(i)   It is within his own knowledge or would have come to his knowledge if such enquiries and inspections had been made as ought reasonably to have been made by him or

(ii) In the same transaction with respect to which a question of notice to the purchaser arises it has come to the knowledge of his counsel as such or of his solicitor or other agent as such if such enquiries and inspections had been made as ought reasonably to have been made by the solicitor or other agent.'

Henchy J then went on to point out:

'that Section 3 of the Family Home Protection Act, 1976 was to be operated within this doctrine of notice was emphasised by the fact that subsection 7 of that section amends section 3 of the 1882 Act by deleting from it the words "as such" (which appeared after the word counsel and after the word solicitor or other agent) thus extending the reach of constructive notice'.

Accordingly, in this case it was held unanimously by the Supreme Court that the purchaser did not acquire a good title as the purchaser failed to satisfy the court that he had acted in good faith within the meaning of the 1976 Act, s 3 in the purchase of the property.

3.2.2.2 *O'Connor v McCarthy*

There is another recent Irish case of *O'Connor v McCarthy* [1982] IR 161 in which the entire question of notice was considered in detail by Costello J. That case turned upon the registration of a contract for sale in the Registry of Deeds which was the second contract signed in respect of the sale of the same premises. As the first contract (though valid and enforceable) was not registered the purchaser under the second contract claimed that his contract had priority under the Registration of Deeds (Ireland) Act, 1707 (the 1707 Act) as it was registered, whereas the first contract, although dated earlier, was not registered. It was sought to upset this claim by establishing that the purchaser under the second contract had notice of the existence of the first contract. Costello J deals fully with the question of constructive notice, actual notice and whether the 'flying rumours' in respect of the first sale which it was claimed circulated in the district where the property was situate were sufficient to defeat the second purchaser's claim. In that case on the facts determined by Costello J he held in favour of the purchaser under the second contract and declared that as the second purchaser did not have actual notice of the first contract, he was entitled to purchase the property by virtue of the priority which the registration of the contract gave him under the 1707 Act.

3.2.2.3 Family law matters

This concept of a purchaser for valuable consideration in good faith without notice has been further extended in family law matters and incorporated into the Judicial Separation and Family Law Reform Act, 1989, s 29, the Family Law Act, 1995, s 35 and the Family Law (Divorce) Act, 1996, s 37 in the context of a reviewable disposition under those three pieces of legislation.

3.2.2.4 Notice

There is an ongoing debate among conveyancers on the question of notice arising from a practice which is becoming more common among solicitors of furnishing all the vendor's title documents to the purchaser's solicitor with the draft contract before a binding contract between the parties comes into existence. This is regarded as a bad practice and further comments are made upon this matter in **chapter 16**.

3.3 Types of Title

The types of title that a solicitor will be dealing with are basically either a freehold or a leasehold title and this applies to registered and unregistered titles.

3.3.1 LEASEHOLD UNREGISTERED TITLES

In cases involving a leasehold title, the root of title (see **chapter 2**) will always be the lease, no matter how old it is, as the terms and conditions and covenants contained therein will always continue to affect the subject property. It is important to recognise that while the lease under which the vendor holds the property will always be the root, provided the rules relating to good roots of title are observed it may be necessary to seek copies of any head leases as the terms, covenants and conditions contained in any of the head leases may in fact continue to affect the property. While most of these terms, covenants and conditions will usually be reflected, if not actually repeated, in the vendor's lease, it is important for a purchaser to at least be aware of the nature of the superior covenants and as to whether or not any of such covenants may impose restrictions which he or she might otherwise not be aware of. Having commenced with a good root the vendor would then be entitled to skip to a later deed at least twenty years old which contains all the characteristics of a good root of title, eg an assignment for valuable consideration. Accordingly, the title intervening between the root and the subsequent assignment for value is not investigated, nor are any of those deeds furnished to the purchaser's solicitor during the course of the transaction. They are, however, usually handed over on closing without prejudice to the terms of the contract. The object of doing so is to cut down as much as possible on the necessity to investigate unnecessarily all of the documentation that came into being between the date of the root and the assignment for valuable consideration more than twenty years old on the understanding and belief that on the assignment for valuable consideration the purchaser's solicitor at that time would have investigated the intervening title (also called intermediate title). In that context also the provisions of the Vendor and Purchaser Act, 1874, s 2 are helpful and the relevant part of that section reads as follows:

> *Recitals, statements and descriptions of facts, matters and parties contained in deeds, instruments, acts of parliament or statutory declarations twenty years old at the date of the contract shall unless and except so far as they shall be proven to be inaccurate be taken to be sufficient evidence of the truth of such facts, matters and descriptions.*

Thereafter the vendor must trace by subsequent documentary evidence (referred to as the chain of title) each change of ownership down to the present vendor's acquisition of the property.

3.3.2 FEE FARM GRANTS UNDER THE RENEWABLE LEASEHOLD CONVERSION ACT, 1849

Fee farm grants have already been discussed in **chapter 2**. If the title is based on a lease for lives renewable forever that has been converted to a fee farm grant under the Renewable Leasehold Conversion Act, 1849 (the 1849 Act) then the lease for lives is where the title should start and not the fee farm grant as the covenants and conditions in the lease are grafted on to the grant and are preserved.

If the lease for lives is dated earlier than 1 August 1849 and has not been converted under the 1849 Act it is automatically converted to a freehold title under the Landlord and Tenant (Amendment) Act, 1980, s 74. That freehold is deemed to be a graft on the previous interest and is subject to any rights or equities arising from its being such a graft. In such a title the lease for lives will be the starting point for the title. It appears that the estate created under this section may not be a fee farm grant but may be a new form of statutory fee simple. This possibility has been raised in Wylie, *Irish Landlord and Tenant Law* (3rd edn) p 1181, note 718 and the reader is referred to that book for a further discussion on this point.

In practice the lease for lives may not be available and is not available in many titles. Consequently the fee farm grant may be the only document upon which the title can be based. In such cases it has become accepted practice to treat the fee farm grant as a good root even though technically it does not conform to the definition of a good root set out in **chapter 2**. In many cases this will not create any problems for a purchaser if the property has been continuously used for the same purpose for a substantial number of years without any notices having been served or any other action taken by the superior owner of the rent for a breach of any of the terms, covenants and conditions contained in the lease for lives which have been grafted onto the fee farm grant. However, if the purchaser intends to materially change the established use or carry out a major development of the property then the terms of the lease for lives would have to be established or alternatively the interest of the superior owner may have to be bought out.

The devolution of this type of title will follow the same format as that for leases.

3.3.3 FREEHOLD UNREGISTERED TITLES

In freehold titles the normal root of title is a conveyance for value but may also be one of the documents specified in **chapter 2** as a good root of title. In unregistered titles the devolution of the title will follow the same format as for leases and for fee farm grants, namely that the vendor would be entitled to skip down to a document for valuable consideration more than twenty years old and deduce title from that document down to the present vendor. In such a case the benefit of the Vendor and Purchaser Act, 1874, s 2 referred to above would apply.

3.3.4 REGISTERED TITLES

In a registered title that is registered with title absolute the only document of title required is an official copy of the Land Registry folio on which the title is registered, coupled with the land certificate, if it has issued, together with a copy of the map or file plan issued in respect of the lands registered. If it is a leasehold title then again, if the title is absolute, the original lease and an up-to-date copy of the folio and map or file plan, together with a land certificate, if issued, consist of the title. In such cases there is no need to have any other documentation produced as one of the primary aims of the Land Registry is to take out of the conveyancing system all documents of title other than the Land Registry folio.

However, as previously discussed, if the title is either registered subject to equities or is a possessory title then the vendor should produce documentary evidence to enable such titles to be converted to absolute or to have the equity note discharged. If registered as good leasehold then evidence of the lessor's title to grant the lease should be obtained if the lease is less than twenty years old.

3.4 Documents Produced with the Contract

In terms of the documentation that should be produced at the initial stage of the transaction, ie when contracts are being prepared and issued, the recommended practice of the Conveyancing Committee of the Law Society is that the only documents at that stage that should be produced are the root of title, any document from which title is being deduced, any document referred to in the special conditions and planning documentation (see Law Society Gazette, May 2000). If there are no documents referred to in the special conditions which are required to be produced, then the only documents that should be listed and produced at the contract stage are the root of title, the document from which title is being deduced and the planning documentation. In the case of a registered title a copy of the folio with the map or file plan is the relevant document. It is only after contracts have been signed and exchanged and become binding that the balance of the title is furnished. The Law Society's Conveyancing Committee had to issue, on three occasions in recent years (see Law Society Gazette Practice Note, January/February 1991, March 1995 and May 2000), a practice note emphasising the importance of following this recommended practice as a contrary practice had become commonplace of vendors' solicitors issuing at the contract stage copies of the entire title to the property for sale. This raised difficult questions of practice because by doing so the vendor is putting the purchaser on notice of the contents of all of the documents and may oblige the purchaser to raise requisitions on title before any binding contract comes into existence. This is a practice which is commonplace in England, but is not the practice here and it is a practice which the

Conveyancing Committee strongly discourages. Indeed, it is an open question as to whether such pre-contract queries may be raised as requisitions and whether any replies given bind the vendor as there is no legal relationship between the parties until they are contractually bound to each other.

3.5   Pre-contract Enquiries

3.5.1   GENERALLY

As a result of the increasing complexity in respect of all matters relating to property transactions in recent years it has become necessary for conveyancers to consider the extent and nature of what pre-contract enquiries should be made by a purchaser's solicitor before allowing a purchaser to sign a contract. In England the practice is that all enquiries in relation to title matters are dealt with before binding contracts come into existence and the sale is completed more or less contemporaneously with the exchange of signed contracts. This is not the practice in Ireland, but there are a number of areas where a strong view has developed for pre-contract enquiries to be made, eg apartments. The Conveyancing Committee took this factor into account some years ago and in the current requisitions on title there are several areas where separate pages are printed as part of the requisitions which may be extracted and furnished as pre-contract enquiries rather than left to be dealt with after binding contracts have been exchanged. If any such pre-contract enquiries are made and answered by the vendor's solicitor they should be repeated as formal requisitions on title after the exchange of binding contracts so as to legally bind the vendor to the replies given. Set out below are most of the areas which would be covered by these pre-contract enquiries.

Since the decision of the Supreme Court in the case of *Frascati Estates Ltd v Walker* [1975] IR 177, decisions affecting premises under the Planning Acts and the various amendments and regulations are now matters of title. Many practitioners consider the warranties under condition 36 of the General Conditions of Sale in the Law Society contract to be too wide-ranging. It has now become commonplace for the vendor's solicitor in the special conditions of the contract to restrict, or in some cases delete completely, the provisions of general condition 36 by providing specifically for the documentation that will be furnished by a vendor in respect of any developments that have taken place on the property since 1 October 1964 when the first Planning Acts came into operation. Planning law is an entire branch of law which has developed its own expertise and **chapter 11** deals with the matters under planning law that should concern a purchaser's solicitors. Planning permissions may sometimes be very complex and lengthy documents, particularly where the property being purchased is a large and perhaps multi-user property, eg a combined shopping centre cum office cum residential, and particular attention should be paid to this aspect of a property before contracts are signed. This view has been endorsed by the Law Society in a recent practice note (Law Society Gazette, May 2000).

There is accordingly a developing view that this is an area that should be dealt with and terms agreed between the parties prior to the exchange of binding contracts.

3.5.2   SPECIFIC EXAMPLES

The following types of properties will also, in the majority of cases, require pre-contract enquiries to be raised and satisfied:

(a)   licensed premises be they public house, restaurant, hotel or off-licence;

(b)   a commercial property where there may be many enquiries to be made in respect of planning, building control regulations and fire regulations and user;

    (c)   investment properties, eg an office block containing multi-user tenants all with separate leases perhaps for different lengths of time and subject to rent reviews;

    (d)   new or second-hand apartments or flats;

    (e)   agricultural properties where there may be a milk quota or where there may be problems arising under environmental legislation; and

    (f)   premises being sold with the benefit of a special tax incentive of which there are at present a substantial number of different ones. However, it is again emphasised that a purchaser's solicitor should not rely exclusively on replies to such pre-contract enquiries and should repeat the enquiries as requisitions on title after the parties are contractually bound.

Each of the foregoing requires a particular expertise because of the type and nature of the property. The title itself may in fact be quite simple and very often a conveyancer has to spend far more time dealing with planning matters, registration matters, fire safety requirements etc than with the actual title to the property itself. It is important for conveyancers to recognise areas of special difficulty and they should not hesitate to seek the assistance of specialists in any particular area to ensure that the purchaser is adequately protected.

3.6   Important Statutory Provisions

The provisions referred to here are those which have been implemented for the purpose of assisting in the conveyancing procedure and are as follows:

    (a)   Vendor and Purchaser Act, 1874, s 2 which enables conveyancers to accept recitals and documents twenty years old as sufficient evidence unless proven to be inaccurate.

    (b)   Conveyancing Act, 1881, s 3(4) which provides that the production of the last receipt for rent payable under a lease is acceptable as conclusive evidence of compliance with the terms of the lease unless the contrary is proven.

    (c)   Conveyancing Act, 1881, s 56 which provides that a receipt clause in a deed of assurance, apart from giving a discharge to the person paying the consideration, entitles a solicitor acting for a vendor to collect the consideration in exchange for the deed and to give a valid receipt for it.

    (d)   Conveyancing Act, 1881, s 63 (known as the 'all estates clause') provides that a conveyance shall be effectual to pass all the estate, right, title and interest vested in the conveying party to a purchaser unless a contrary intention is expressed in the conveyance. This section was intended to catch any interest inferior to the freehold which was vested in the vendor without the necessity of having to have full recitals in the deed.

    (e)   Statutory acknowledgements and undertakings in respect of original documents which are retained by the vendor impose obligations upon the vendor to produce the documents for inspection, to produce them in court on a hearing to establish title and to furnish copies on request and also oblige the vendor to keep the documents safe and whole unless destroyed by fire. This is provided in the Conveyancing Act, 1881, s 9.

3.7   The Chain of Title

The chain of title is the term used to describe all of the connected events on a title from the root of title down to the document or event that vested the ownership of the property in the current vendor or owner. This chain of title may consist of a variety of documents or events, eg conveyances, assignments, wills, grants of probate, assents, court orders, transfers, deaths, bankruptcies, liquidations etc. The conveyancer's task is to ensure that from the root of title down to the document or event that vested title in the current vendor or owner there is an unbroken series of documents or events not only marking the change of ownership but also ensuring that the document or event properly transfers title from one owner to another.

It is important where technical words are required that they are used and used properly. Such technical words apply with full force where the title being transferred is a freehold unregistered title. There are no words of limitation required in a deed of transfer in the Land Registry. The words of limitation in a conveyance of an unregistered title are as follows:

(a) 'Unto and to the use of the purchaser and his heirs'; or, alternatively

(b) 'Unto and to the use of the purchaser in fee simple.'

The above alternative phrases will convey a full freehold to an individual. When the conveyance is to a corporation sole or a company or a corporation the words used are as follows:

(c) 'Unto the purchaser, its successors and assigns.'

The first phrase at head (a) above was that used prior to the Conveyancing Act, 1881. The Conveyancing Act, 1881, s 51 introduced the term 'in fee simple' as equal to the use of the words 'and his heirs' to convey the entire of the freehold interest. The failure to use these technical words will result in the conveyance of an interest which is less than a full freehold, eg it may only confer a life interest or a base fee.

3.8   Events on Title

There are some events on the title which a conveyancer will commonly come across. These are set out at **3.8.1** to **3.8.5** below.

3.8.1   DEATHS ON TITLE

Prior to 1 June 1959 a devise of freehold property vested directly in the beneficiary and not in the executor or administrator. Pure personalty, ie a leasehold interest, vested in the personal representative, but on completion of the administration the beneficiary assumed occupation and ownership without any further formal documentation. In respect of all deaths on or after 1 June 1959, under the Administration of Estates Act, 1959, all titles vested in the personal representative and thereafter no interest passed to a beneficiary without a written assent from the personal representative.

Thus, if a beneficiary wished to pass title in respect of an interest acquired under a death which occurred on or after 1 June 1959, the paper documentation required to establish the title was the grant of probate incorporating the original will, or a grant of administration with the will annexed incorporating the original will, or a grant of letters of administration intestate coupled with the assent or assignment or conveyance from the personal representative formally vesting title to the property in the beneficiary.

Alternatively the property could be sold by the personal representative and this power of sale is now contained in the Succession Act, 1965. In such cases the purchaser from a personal representative is relieved of the responsibility of having any beneficiary join in the sale.

Where the property is held jointly, the title automatically devolves on the surviving joint owner on the death of one or more of the other joint owners and the only evidence required in respect of the passing of the title is a copy of the deceased joint owner's death certificate exhibited in a statutory declaration identifying the deceased joint owner as the person named in the death certificate with a confirmatory declaration by the surviving joint owner that the joint tenancy was never severed.

Where the property is held in common ownership, as tenants in common then each owner has a separate interest in the property which does not devolve upon the survivors when one tenant in common dies. In such a case the title will have to be traced through his or her will or on intestacy.

3.8.2   VOLUNTARY CONVEYANCES

Voluntary conveyances are normally conveyances between related parties where one owner transfers a property to another for 'natural love and affection'. There is no formal consideration in money terms paid. These deeds are perfectly valid but they are liable to be set aside. If, for example, the donor is made a bankrupt within two years of the deed, then the deed is void. If within five years and after two years the donor is made bankrupt, the deed is void unless the donor can establish that he or she was solvent at the time without relying on the property (Bankruptcy Act, 1988, s 59). A deed of this nature will accordingly require a statutory declaration by the donor (referred to in practice as a Declaration of Solvency) confirming that the transfer to the donee was effected for natural love and affection without any intent to defraud his or her creditors and for the purpose of conferring a benefit upon the donee and that in doing so the donor was solvent and able to meet his or her other creditors without the benefit of the property transferred. In addition a bankruptcy search will be required. If, in fact, a transfer from the donee to another party has taken place within two years then an indemnity bond for the value of the property from an insurance company may be required to protect the purchaser from such a donee. As in the case of deaths on title a deed of this nature is taxable as a gift and consequently appropriate capital acquisitions tax clearance certificates have to be obtained on a death in respect of any inheritance tax payable and on a voluntary deed in respect of any gift tax payable. A practice note in the April 1998 Law Society Gazette advises that a bond should not now be required once a declaration of solvency is produced by the doner.

3.8.3   LOST DEEDS

It is not uncommon to come across cases where either an entire set of documents of title or some of the documents in the chain of title have been lost. This situation will occasionally apply in Land Registry cases where the original land certificate is lost. If a land certificate is lost a duplicate must be issued before a transaction can be completed as the Land Registry will not deal with any application for registration of a subsequent owner without the original land certificate.

In Registry of Deeds cases, what is required to perfect the chain of title are certified copies of the missing deeds or official copies of the memorials of any deeds registered in the Registry of Deeds. The copy memorials are readily procurable from the Registry of Deeds once the names of the parties and the approximate dates of the deeds are known. Apart from production of copies of the relevant documents a full detailed statutory declaration should be obtained from the vendor, and if necessary, confirmed by any other party who may have knowledge, fully setting out the circumstances in which the deeds were lost and, most importantly, confirming that the deeds were not pledged or lodged in any way as security for a loan or otherwise. Appropriate searches must also be conducted for the entire of the period covered by the title to ensure that there are no outstanding charges registered which have not been cleared off.

In some cases it may be necessary to obtain an insurance company indemnity bond for the value of the premises to protect the purchaser against any claim that might be made if the deeds should turn up in the hands of some person who has a sustainable claim against the property but such bonds are quite expensive. If a satisfactory explanation is forthcoming, supported by sworn declarations, and copies of the relevant deeds are made available, then a bond should not be necessary but this is a matter which can only be judged in each individual case.

3.8.4   CERTIFIED COPY DEEDS

It is commonplace in urban areas for the root of title, eg a lease, to cover a number of properties. As these properties are sold off individually, some of the property owners will get only certified copies of the original deeds and the original owner will normally retain possession of the originals. This is a perfectly acceptable practice provided that contained in each deed where a part of the property is sold off there is a statutory acknowledgement by the vendor of the time who retains possession of the original deeds acknowledging the right of the purchaser to the production of the original deeds and undertaking for their safe custody. Such documents would normally be listed in the deed and the benefit of this would pass to all subsequent owners.

3.8.5   DEEDS OF RECTIFICATION

Deeds of rectification may turn up on the title occasionally where there has been some error in an earlier deed which has been identified and the relevant parties would join in for the purpose of correcting the error, eg incorrect words of limitation may have been used which prevented the full title passing and it may be necessary to get an appropriate deed of rectification from the previous owner rectifying the defect in the deed.

3.9   Capacity of Vendors

It is important to appreciate that the mere fact that a person or body makes a contractual commitment to sell a particular property does not automatically mean that such a person or body has any legal title to do so. An ordinary individual, if he or she buys a property, would have legal entitlement to subsequently sell it. However, there are a number of categories of persons in respect of whom further enquiries must be made and documentation obtained to establish that they do have a legal title and the following is a list of those to which special attention must be paid.

3.9.1   TRUSTEE

If a trust is disclosed on the title then a trustee as such has no power to sell unless the trust document gives the trustee power to sell. The power of sale can arise under a power of sale contained in a trust document or a trust for sale and may be under a settlement inter vivos or under a will. If the trust is a charitable trust then it may be necessary to obtain the consent of the Commissioners for Charitable Donations and Bequests to the sale under the provisions of the Charities Acts, 1961–73. If a trust is not shown on the title furnished the solicitor should not raise any specific requisitions enquiring if such trust exists as he or she may be creating difficulties by putting himself or herself on notice of the trust where the title furnished does not so disclose.

3.9.2   A COMMITTEE OF A WARD OF COURT

A committee of a ward of court is a person appointed by the court to look after the person and property of a person taken into wardship. A committee has no authority to sell the property belonging to a ward of court without a court order. The requisite documents that are necessary are a copy of the order appointing the committee and a copy of the order authorising the committee to sell the ward's property. Probably the production of the second order would be adequate as the court undoubtedly would not make any such order unless the committee was properly appointed. The order permitting the committee to sell will also contain detailed provisions as to how the property is to be sold and the various steps to be taken in respect of lodgement of the deposit, purchase money etc.

3.9.3   A COMPANY

In the case of a company the first matter to be checked is that the company was properly registered and this is done by the production of a certified copy of the certificate of incorporation. It is also very important in modern day conveyancing, having regard to the powers now vested in the Registrar of Companies, to ensure that the company is still on the register of companies. If it is not, then it would either have to be restored to the register before the sale may proceed or, alternatively, it is necessary to investigate the operation of the statutes under the terms of which the assets of all companies struck off the register are vested in the Minister for Finance. In such cases, if a restoration to the register of companies is not possible, then the only party who may have any title to transfer may be the Minister for Finance. In addition, the memorandum of the company, ie the objects for which it was founded, should include an entitlement, first to acquire property, and secondly to sell property. Finally, the articles of association should always be checked to see in what way the company is authorised to affix the seal to the purchase deed. If the company was incorporated under the Companies Act, 1908 then the sealing requirements under that Act were for the seal to be countersigned by two directors and the secretary, whereas in most modern companies it is one director and the secretary, or two directors, or one director and a nominated person.

If the company is one not registered in this jurisdiction then be particularly careful in determining the company's authority to sell and, in particular, the manner in which the company is authorised to execute documents as some foreign companies do not have a seal.

3.9.4   STATUTORY BODY

In the case of statutory bodies it is necessary to check the relevant statute under which the body was founded to establish the statutory authority of the body to sell and also whether there are any prior consents required, eg from the Minister for Finance, before a valid conveyance may be executed. With a sale by local authority, evidence must be produced of compliance with the Local Government Act, 1946, s 46.

3.9.5   LIFE TENANT

Under the provisions of the Settled Land Acts 1882–1890 a life tenant has an in-built power of sale. However, such a life tenant does not have any entitlement to receive the proceeds of sale which must be paid to two trustees of the settlement. If a valid receipt is not obtained in the deed witnessed by two trustees the deed is void. It is essential that there are two trustees unless the trust authorises the payment to one trustee as sufficient discharge. In cases where an infant in his or her own right is seised of or entitled in possession to land, the land is deemed settled land and the infant a tenant for life. In such a case the trustees of the settlement, or if there are no such persons, whoever the court orders, may exercise the statutory power of sale of the tenant for life on behalf of the infant, this being one of the rare cases in which the trustees do have a power of sale although not specifically conferred upon them by the instrument setting up the trust (see Trustee Act, 1882, ss 59 and 60). Further provisions are contained in the Succession Act, 1965, ss 57 and 58 giving powers of sale to trustees of an infant's property.

3.9.6 PERSONAL REPRESENTATIVE

A personal representative is authorised to sell the property of a deceased under the provisions of the Succession Act, 1965, s 50. There is a protection contained in the Act for bona fide purchasers for value who do not have to enquire as to whether the personal representatives have followed all the statutory provisions contained in the Act in respect of consulting with the beneficiaries. It is not necessary in a sale by a personal representative to join any of the beneficiaries in the deed.

3.9.7 A BENEFICIARY UNDER A WILL

As previously stated at **3.8.1** if the vendor is a beneficiary under a will in respect of a death which occurred on or after 1 June 1959 then, in addition to the grant of probate which contains a copy of the will, a formal assent from the executor is required and this must be in writing. Any such vendor is selling as full beneficial owner. Similarly, a beneficiary under an intestacy will require to furnish a copy of the grant of administration intestate and the assignment, conveyance or assent vesting title to the property in him or her.

3.9.8 ATTORNEY

Originally powers of attorney were dealt with under the provisions of the Conveyancing Act, 1881 and a properly drawn power of attorney was declared to be irrevocable for a period of twelve months. Accordingly, a purchaser from an attorney under such a power did not have to make any enquiries if the power was no more than twelve months old. If the power, however, was older than twelve months then a purchaser was put on notice to make enquiries as to the fact that the donor of the power was still alive and that such donor was capable. The death of a donor or his or her incapacity rendered such a power of attorney invalid.

There are now two new forms of power of attorney under the Enduring Power of Attorneys Act, 1996. The first type, namely the enduring power of attorney only comes into operation under this Act when the donor of the power becomes incapable from mental incapacity of conducting his or her own affairs and not otherwise. Such a power of attorney must then be registered in the Wards of Court Office and the persons specified in the power formally notified that it has come into operation before it becomes effective.

In addition, this Act introduces in s 16 a very short form of power of attorney which gives extremely wide powers to the donee of the power. Under any other form of power of attorney it is crucial to check and ensure that the power gives the grantee of the power the right to sell. The original power is normally retained by the vendor and a certified copy only is produced. If the original is registered in the Central Office then an attested copy from the Central Office is normally furnished.

3.9.9 SURVIVING JOINT TENANT

The first matter to check in the case of a surviving joint tenant is that the original deed did in fact create a joint tenancy and not a tenancy in common. If the surviving joint tenant is selling, then evidence is required as stated at **3.8.1** that the other joint tenant is deceased by exhibiting a death certificate in a statutory declaration and confirming that the joint tenancy was not severed prior to the death.

3.9.10 MORTGAGEE IN POSSESSION

Mortgage documents are highly technical and there are a number of steps which mortgagees must follow before they are entitled to exercise their powers of sale. However, a purchaser from a mortgagee in possession is relieved from the responsibility of ensuring that all of the necessary technical steps have been taken and accordingly a purchaser from a mortgagee in possession need only satisfy himself or herself on the following points:

(a) obtain a copy of the mortgage deed to ensure that the mortgagee did have a right of re-entry and sale;

(b) evidence that the amount due on foot of the mortgage became due and payable;

(c) evidence that the mortgagee properly obtained possession of the property either by way of a surrender to it by the mortgagor or on foot of a court order;

(d) if on foot of a court order a copy of the ejectment decree showing it having been executed by the sheriff should be obtained; and

(e) if the property is a residential property then it is necessary to ensure that the mortgage was properly executed in full compliance with the provisions of the Family Home Protection Act, 1976.

3.9.11 COURT ORDER

There are circumstances in which the court will order a sale of a particular property and a purchaser is entitled to rely exclusively upon the terms of the court order as sufficient evidence that the person designated in the order as the person entitled to sell the property has a proper title to do so. An attested copy of the court order and compliance with any of the terms and conditions set out in the court order is all that is required.

3.9.12 CHARITABLE ORGANISATION

In the case of a charitable organisation, if there is no power of sale contained in the document establishing the trust, then the consent of the Commissioners for Charitable Donations and Bequests is required.

3.9.13 THE COUNTY REGISTRAR

There are provisions in the Landlord and Tenant (Ground Rents) Act, 1967 that where a superior owner cannot be identified or located, the county registrar has power to appoint a person (or on an appeal from the county registrar the court may so order) to sign the deed in respect of the transfer or conveyance of the freehold on behalf of the unknown person and all that is required as evidence in this case is a certified copy of the relevant court order of the order of the county registrar.

3.9.14 UNINCORPORATED BODY

The category of unincorporated bodies would include, for example, a club. In such a case it is necessary to look to the club rules to see what provision is made by them for the sale.

The procedures laid down must be carefully followed and documented by the club secretary and the actual parties entitled to convey (usually the club trustees) identified and the necessary resolutions by the club members (a common enough requirement) authorising the sale must be passed and authenticated by the club secretary.

3.10 Analysis of Deeds of Conveyance and Assignment (Notes on Title)

There are quite a number of headings of matters that are contained in deeds of conveyance and assignment which a conveyancer needs to check.

3.10.1 REVENUE STAMP

On the front page of each deed will be impressed the Revenue Stamp showing the stamp duty paid in respect of that particular deed. It is important to check that the correct amount of stamp duty relevant at the date of the deed is properly impressed. A Particulars Delivered Stamp is also impressed on the deed, namely a statutory form to be filed with each deed when it is being stamped giving particulars of the vendor and purchaser, the premises and the purchase price. When stamped each document is given a unique document identification number (see Revenue Leaflet SD8 and Law Society Gazette, November 1999).

3.10.2 DATE AND TIME OF REGISTRATION

On the front page of each deed in an unregistered title will be imprinted the details of the date and time of registration of the deed in the Registry of Deeds and it is important to check that the deed has been registered and that the deed has been registered in its correct priority.

The actual deed itself will be headed with the date of the deed and again it is important to check that this date is in the correct date order with the remainder of the documents of title.

3.10.3 THE PARTIES

The next part of the deed contains the names and addresses of the parties and, again, these should be carefully checked and compared with deeds prior and subsequent to it so as to ensure that the parties are correctly identified and are the correct parties who are either transferring or receiving the title, or who are required to join in the deed for the purpose of ensuring that a full title passes to the purchaser.

3.10.4 RECITALS

The next part of the deed normally contains recitals, eg this part normally recites the root of title be it a conveyance for value or a lease with which the title starts. It also very often gives a detailed description of the property for sale as contained in the earlier deed or a description of the property from which it is carved. It may also be necessary here to trace the title in some detail from the root if its devolution is not straightforward. This part of the deed can be of considerable importance to later conveyancers who may be entitled to rely upon the recitals contained if they are more than twenty years old in accordance with the previously recited provisions contained in the Vendor and Purchaser Act, 1874.

3.10.5 CONTRACT FOR SALE

The contract for sale is then recited between the parties to the deed and the purchase price specified. It is also important at this stage that if there are any other parties to the deed, apart from the vendor and the purchaser, that the reason for their joining in the deed should be set out here, and their function, and the particular interest that they may be joining in the deed to convey or assign.

3.10.6 CONVEYANCE OR ASSIGNMENT OF PROPERTY

The deed then recites the conveyance or assignment of the property for the specified consideration and at this point must contain a receipt clause by the vendor acknowledging receipt of the agreed purchase money. The vendor should convey as beneficial owner which implies all the relevant covenants under the provisions of the Conveyancing Act, 1881, s 7 (these being the implied covenants that the vendor has the right to convey, covenant for quiet enjoyment, covenant that the property is free from encumbrances and a covenant for further assurance). If the vendor is not selling as beneficial owner then the capacity in which the vendor is selling should be specified. Such alternative capacity may imply covenants less extensive than those of a beneficial owner.

3.10.7 DESCRIPTION OF PROPERTY

A full description of the property being conveyed or leased or assigned should next be inserted and this will very often be taken first from earlier documents, eg from the original lease if it is a leasehold title, and then go on to describe the property by reference to its modern description. It may be necessary in some cases to properly identify it by reference to a map attached to the deed. It is important to remember that the basic principle is that the words of the deed will be relied upon for the description of the property in preference to the map attached and it is only if such description of the deed is ambiguous that the map may be relied upon.

It is important here that the necessary words of limitation as to how the purchaser is thenceforward to hold the property are inserted and the correct words of limitation as previously specified must be used.

3.10.8 EXCEPTIONS AND RESERVATIONS

In a leasehold assignment the deed will contain covenants by the purchaser to observe and perform all the covenants and conditions in the lease and to pay any rent reserved and to indemnify the vendor against any claims in respect of any breach, non-performance or non-observance of the covenants or the non-payment of the rent. Such covenants obviously will not appear in a conveyance of a freehold. However, at this stage there may be further provisions incorporated such as exceptions and reservations in favour of the vendor, eg a reservation of a right of way or right of access to and the use of sewers or water pipes or something of that nature and this is the place in which it would be contained.

If the original deeds are not being handed over then the acknowledgement and undertaking in respect of safe custody of the original deeds should be inserted here.

3.10.9 FINANCE CERTIFICATES

In modern-day conveyancing one or more of a number of alternative finance certificates must be inserted here in order to comply with the relevant provisions of the legislation dealing with stamp duty on the purchase deed. There has now developed a multiplicity of these types of certificates depending upon the nature of the property, what it is being acquired for and what its use is going to be, and regard must be had to current certificates at all times.

3.10.10 CERTIFICATES OF CITIZENSHIP

It may also be necessary here to insert certificates of citizenship or other qualification to acquire the property under the Land Act, 1965, s 45 depending upon where the property is located and who the purchaser is.

3.10.11 EXECUTION OF THE DEED

Finally the deed will then be executed by the parties and should be signed, sealed and delivered by the vendor and purchaser or executed by a company or statutory body under its corporate or common seal.

   If the property is a family home where the spouse's prior consent is required this consent appears at the end of the deed. It must be remembered that it is of crucial importance that such prior consent must be signed by the spouse prior to the deed being executed by the vendor; otherwise the consent is totally ineffective under the provisions of the Family Home Protection Act, 1976.

   It is of course of crucial importance that the execution by any of the parties to the deed should be properly witnessed and the name, address and occupation of the witness inserted in the appropriate place beside the execution of the parties. It is useful to remember that any signatures which are difficult to decipher should be printed so as to assist any future parties who may require to identify the witness in event of any dispute arising over the contents or execution of the deed.

CHAPTER 4

PRE-CONTRACT ENQUIRIES

4.1 Introduction

When acting for a purchaser, a solicitor has to be aware of the terms and conditions of the Contract for Sale. He has to decide what matters need to be dealt with before the contract is signed and what matters may be left outstanding until after the signing of the contract. These vary from case to case and may also depend on the actual purchaser.

Take the example of a land-locked field. If an adjoining landowner buys, he or she will provide his or her own access and will bring the other services which he or she needs to the property through his or her existing holding. If the purchaser of the field is not an adjoining owner, then the question of access, water supply, electricity etc become major issues which need to be clarified before a contract is signed.

This leads to the division between the pre-contract enquiries which must be made (ie before the purchaser has signed the contract) and the requisitions on title which must be raised after the contract has been signed by all necessary parties. (Requisitions on title are dealt with in **chapter 15**.)

The purchaser's pre-contract enquiries may be broken into two categories:

(a) those relating to the physical condition and location of the property, and

(b) enquiries arising out of the documents including the contract furnished.

While enquiries in relation to the contract and title documents are, in the main, directed to the vendor's solicitor, the other enquiries are not.

To assist the purchaser, the Contract for Sale (the 2001 edition) includes a non-title information sheet for completion by the vendor covering many of the matters which a purchaser may require to have clarified before signing the contract. This checklist which forms part of the standard contract is reproduced in **Appendix 5.1**. General condition 33(b) outlines penalties to be imposed on the vendor in respect of omissions or misstatements etc, contained in this non-title information sheet. This information sheet is inserted after the special conditions.

4.2 Enquiries in Relation to Physical Condition and Location of Property

The basic legal rule which applies is caveat emptor, ie buyer beware (see general condition 16 of the Contract for Sale).

46

4.2.1 PHYSICAL STATE OF THE PROPERTY

The purchaser buys the property as it stands. The vendor is not under a duty to disclose any physical defects in the property. A purchaser must be advised of this and must be advised that in order to protect himself or herself he or she should have the property fully surveyed before the contract is signed. The vast majority of buyers will have the property surveyed without question and will, in all probability, furnish a copy of the survey to their solicitor. Once the solicitor has the copy of the survey it is evidence in his or her file that he or she has given the buyer the necessary advice. However, if a client decides not to have the property surveyed then his or her solicitor needs to be extremely careful to ensure that the file is in order and that he or she is not leaving himself or herself open to a subsequent action for negligence. To protect himself or herself, the purchaser's solicitor should ensure that he or she has on file a letter to the purchaser setting out the legal position and that he or she has an acknowledgement from the purchaser that he or she has received this letter.

A purchaser's solicitor should never put the following or similar terms in to the contract: 'The sale is subject to the purchaser obtaining a satisfactory survey of the property.' Only a court could determine what the words 'satisfactory survey' mean. If the timber in one of the windows has rotted does this entitle the buyer to throw up the purchase?

Where the purchaser is buying a house in the course of construction the position is different. At the stage of the contract being signed no building work may have commenced and therefore it would not be possible to have the property surveyed. In such cases the purchaser's rights are governed by the terms and conditions of the building contract and the warranties given in the building contract.

Occasionally, a vendor's solicitor will issue a contract for sale in respect of a house in the course of construction without including a building contract for the work which remains to be completed. A purchaser's solicitor should never accept this arrangement and should always insist on having a building contract as well.

4.2.2 GENERAL LOCATION OF THE PROPERTY

A vendor gives no warranty as to the use or occupation of property adjoining the property he is selling. Accordingly, the purchaser should be advised to check out certain matters before he or she signs the contract.

4.2.2.1 Other planning permissions

Depending on the property in question, it may well be that planning permission has already been granted for development on the adjoining property which would affect the property in sale. For example, a purchaser might not be too happy to discover that a substantial factory could be looking into his or her back garden at a future date.

4.2.2.2 Road widening

With the current economic boom and the infrastructural developments which are taking place, it is very important that a purchaser checks to ensure that the building of a new road or the widening of an existing road will not have a negative impact on the property being bought.

The necessity for advising the client in relation to these matters depends on the location of the property. If a purchaser is buying a house within a cluster of 200 new houses in a housing estate, it is unlikely the local authority is going to consider building a new road through the existing development.

4.2.3 ACCESS TO THE PROPERTY

As indicated at **4.1,** it depends on the circumstances of the transaction whether or not the purchaser requires access to the property being bought. The legal right to gain access to the property must be evidenced prior to the signing of the contract. It is too late to discover the problem when replies to the requisitions on title are returned to the purchaser's solicitor's desk.

In many cases it is clear from the inspection of the property that it is abutting the public road. In the new development situation it is necessary to ensure that there is a grant of right of way contained in the deed of conveyance or deed of transfer. This grant of right of way must be from the property in sale to a roadway already taken in charge.

Access to the property in sale may be one of the following:

(a)   by abutting the public highway;

(b)   by an appurtenant right of way granted by deed;

(c)   by an appurtenant right of way created by long usage; or

(d)   by adjoining a public right of way not taken in charge by the local authority.

Most agricultural rights of way are not registered. When the Land Commission purchased the estates from the landlords and vested them in the existing tenants no references were made to rights of way. In the later years of the Land Commission, when it acquired land for redistribution, it did create registered rights of way.

A purchaser's solicitor will refer, in the first instance to the replies given by the vendor to query 1.ii of the non-title information sheet attached to the contract.

4.2.4   WATER SUPPLY

A contract for sale does not warrant that the property has a water supply. While this does not normally create a difficulty in the urban situation this is not necessarily so in rural areas. The property owner may have been allowed to take water from a well on an adjoining property on a temporary basis or may have been given permission, on a temporary basis, to place a waterline on an adjoining property. Accordingly, a purchaser must be satisfied that the necessary easements and wayleaves are in place to ensure a water supply to the property.

A purchaser's solicitor will refer, in the first instance, to the replies given by the vendor to query 1.i of the non-title information sheet attached to the contract.

4.2.5   OTHER SERVICES

A purchaser's solicitor needs to be satisfied that the septic tank and its soakage area are within the site being purchased. If the property is served by the local authority sewer, do the pipes go directly from the property in sale to the local authority system? If they pass through intervening properties have legal wayleaves been created?

A purchaser's solicitor will refer, in the first instance, to the replies given by the vendor to query 1.iii of the non-title information sheet attached to the contract.

4.2.6   OTHER PRE-CONTRACT MATTERS

The purchaser will be concerned with the outgoings in respect of the property. Information regarding this will be given on the non-title information sheet in reply to query 3.ii. He or she may want to know about rents, rates, service charges and the like.

While totally unconnected with title investigation, a purchaser's solicitor should advise the purchaser of the necessity of having finance arranged to enable the transaction to be completed.

4.3 Enquiries Arising out of Documents Including the Contract

4.3.1 THE WORDING OF THE CONTRACT

If the title to be produced is limited under the contract then a purchaser's solicitor may need to do pre-contract enquiries in relation to the title furnished before allowing the purchaser to sign the contract. If the title furnished was not limited then the same enquiries would be raised with the requisitions on title.

For example, if a licensed premises are being sold with 'the ordinary seven-day publican's licence attached thereto', then it is a matter for requisitions on title for proof of the type of licence, whereas if the contract says the property 'together with the intoxicating liquor licence attached thereto' then, before the purchaser signs a contract, the purchaser's solicitor must ensure what type of licence is attached because the vendor has not warranted that it is a seven-day ordinary licence with that wording.

4.3.2 PURCHASER ON NOTICE OF CERTAIN DOCUMENTS

General condition 6 of the Contract for Sale states:

'The documents specified in the Document's Schedule or copies thereof have been available for inspection by the Purchaser or his Solicitor prior to the Date of Sale. If all or any of the Subject Property is stated in the Particulars or in the Special Conditions to be held under a lease or to be subject to any covenants, conditions, rights, liabilities or restrictions, and the lease or other document containing the same is specified in the Documents Schedule, the Purchaser, whether availing of such opportunity of inspection or not, shall be deemed to have purchased with full knowledge of the contents thereof, notwithstanding any partial statement of such contents in the Particulars or in the Conditions.'

A purchaser's solicitor must satisfy himself or herself that he or she has all the documents as listed in the documents schedule. He or she must read through these documents and satisfy himself or herself that there is no matter contained therein which gives rise for concern. Because the purchaser is deemed to be on notice of the contents it is too late to raise queries in relation to the contents of the documents produced, after the contract has been signed.

Good conveyancing practice in preparing a contract is to provide the purchaser with:

(a) the root of title;

(b) any document to which title is stated to pass under the special conditions;

(c) any document which is specifically referred to in the special conditions (see Law Society Gazette, January/February 1990 and March 1995); and

(d) planning documentation (see Law Society Gazette, May 2000).

If this is done the purchaser is not on notice of the contents of any of the intervening documents and is entitled to raise requisitions to deduce title from the root of title to the last assurance.

4.3.3 PRIOR LEASEHOLD TITLE

Both under general conditions 10(a) and 16 of the Contract for Sale and by statute there is a restriction on the right of a purchaser to obtain evidence of the landlord's title. Where a property is held under lease if a purchaser's solicitor feels that, in the particular circumstances of the case, he or she should have evidence of the landlord's title then this must be done pre-contract or by amendment to the contract to provide for production of the landlord's title.

4.3.4 RESTRICTION OF PURCHASER'S RIGHT TO INVESTIGATE CERTAIN MATTERS IN RELATION TO LEASEHOLD TITLE

General condition 10 of the Contract for Sale restricts the purchaser's right to raise any objection or requisition in relation to:

10(b)(i)   lack of consent of a superior owner to the apportionment of rent between sublessees, and

10(b)(ii) by reason of any discrepancy between the covenants, conditions and provisions contained in any sublease and those in any superior lease (unless they were such as would give rise to forfeiture or a right of re-entry).

General condition 10(b)(iii) provides that the production of the receipt for the last gale of rent reserved shall be accepted as conclusive evidence that all rent accrued and due has been paid and that all the covenants and conditions in the lease have been performed and observed.

General condition 10(b)(iv) provides that the vendor shall not be required to institute legal proceedings to obtain the landlord's consent to alienate where a landlord's consent is required but withheld. However, if this consent is not obtained 'either party may rescind the sale by seven days' prior notice to the other'.

4.3.5 INVESTIGATING OF PRIOR AND INTERMEDIATE TITLE

Condition 11 of the Contract for Sale provides that the purchaser is not entitled to investigate or object to the title prior to the date of the instrument specified in the special conditions as the commencement of title.

Condition 12 prohibits the investigation of the intermediate title (ie where the title commences with a particular instrument and then passes to a second instrument or to a specified event).

A vendor's solicitor has a duty to his or her client to ensure that in preparing the contract he or she does not unnecessarily limit the title being furnished to a purchaser. Accordingly, in normal circumstances this condition will not create problems for a buyer's solicitor. However, in the occasional case where a vendor's solicitor has unduly limited the title furnished, a purchaser's solicitor needs to be aware that it is too late to raise queries at the requisitions stage.

4.3.6 IDENTITY OF PROPERTY IN SALE

Condition 14 limits the purchaser's right to evidence of identity of the property in sale. Once the contract has been signed the purchaser is entitled to the evidence of identity as may be gathered from the documents furnished together with a 'statutory declaration to be made by a competent person, at the purchaser's expense, that the subject property has been held and enjoyed for at least twelve years in accordance with the title shown'. There is no obligation to identify boundaries, party or party walls or to identify parts of the property in sale held under different titles.

4.3.7 DISCLOSURE OF MATTERS AFFECTING THE PROPERTY IN SALE

General condition 15 requires the vendor to disclose before the sale all easements, rights, privileges, taxes and other liabilities, which are known by the vendor to affect the property or to be likely to affect it following the completion of the sale. Subject to this, condition 16 then states that the purchaser is deemed to buy with full notice of the actual state and condition of the property and subject to all leases mentioned in the particulars and special conditions and to all easements, rights, reservations, exceptions, privileges, covenants, restrictions, rents, taxes, liabilities, outgoings and incidents of tenure.

Condition 35 provides that the purchaser may rescind the sale if he or she has not been furnished with notices given or otherwise known to the vendor at the date of sale which affect the property.

4.4 Summary

What has been dealt with are the pre-contract enquiries which are made in ordinary residential transactions. In many of the specialist transactions it is necessary to raise the requisitions on title, in relation to that type of transaction, pre-contract. Properties to which this applies include:

    (a)   licensed premises;

    (b)   other commercial premises;

    (c)   new apartments;

    (d)   second-hand apartments; and

    (e)   agricultural land with milk quota attached.

A solicitor should not undertake the conveyancing of any of the above without being fully familiar with all the legal implications of the transaction. For example, environmental law might play a major part in the purchase of a factory.

The following prepared by the Law School are set out hereunder:

Instruction sheet for basic conveyancing transaction from the point of view of the vendor (**4.5**).

Instruction sheet for basic conveyancing transaction from the point of view of the purchaser (**4.6**).

Particulars of vendor: checklist (**4.7**).
(Pre-contract questionnaire for property sale)

Particulars of purchaser: checklist (**4.8**).
(Pre-contract questionnaire for property sale)

Conveyancing—Instruction Sheet (**4.9**).

4.5 Checklist for the Vendor

SALE OF PREMISES: PRE-CONTRACT INFORMATION

1.   Boundaries

        (i)   which are shared and which are in common
        (ii)   any special agreements
        (iii) all maps and identity to be checked

PRE-CONTRACT ENQUIRIES

2. Services

    (i)   drainage
    (ii) water
    (iii) electricity
    (iv) telephone
    (v)   gas
    (vi) alarm system—number/code

3. Services

    (i)   in charge
    (ii) private—details/indemnity

4. Easements

    (i)   right of way/light
    (ii) services
    (iii) others

5. Forestry/fishing/sporting

6. Tenancies/vacant possession

7. PLV

8. Outgoings

    (i)   ground rent
    (ii) rates
    (iii) water rates/water charges
    (iv) service charge
    (v)   insurance contribution
    (vi) receipts and vouchers

9. Notices

    (i)   served
    (ii) given
    (iii) CPO

10. Encumbrances/proceedings

    (i)   mortgage of vendor
    (ii) litigation/disputes
    (iii) grants—are they repayable

11. Voluntary dispositions

12. Taxation

    (i)   capital acquisitions tax—certificate of discharge
    (ii) probate tax—certificate of discharge
    (iii) capital gains tax—clearance certificate
    (iv) VAT
    (v)   residential property tax—clearance certificate/certificate of discharge
    (vi) details of PPS number and details of inspector of taxes (name and address and district no), details of PPS number of purchasers for the Contract for Sale residential property tax form and PD form. From 19 June 2000 RSI numbers

were replaced by PPS numbers which will be traced or allocated through the Department of Social, Community and Family Affairs

13. Body corporate/trustee

   (i)   memo and articles
   (ii) Companies Office search
   (iii) rules
   (iv) trust instrument

14. Family law

   (i)   all relevant State certificates
   (ii) is the property anybody else's family home?
   (iii) other information

15. Planning/building bye-law approval/building regulations/fire certificate/Fire Services Act/environment

16. Food hygiene regulations

17. Landlord and tenant/lease

   (i)   consent to assign
   (ii) consent to change of use

18. Fee simple—acquired?

19. Multi-storey building, apartment/second-hand apartment

Use copy of relevant requisitions to take detailed instructions

20. Licensing/restaurant/hotel/special restaurant dancing/music/singing/Fire Services Act

Use copy of relevant requisitions to take detailed instructions

21. Inventory

22. Insurance

Increase to full replacement value if necessary and advise in writing pre-contract

4.6 Checklist for the Purchaser

1. DETAILS VENDOR

   (i)   name
   (ii) address
   (iii) price
   (iv) deposit
   (v) loan clause
   (vi) solicitors for vendor

2. FINANCE

   (i)   deposit/equity from sale of house
   (ii) loan—amount €
      (a) name of lending institution

    (b) branch/address
    (c) position of loan application
    (d) survey/fire cover/life cover
  (iii) bridging accommodation
  (iv) undertaking and irrevocable authority
  (v) prepare and furnish financial memo

3. ITEMS INCLUDED IN SALE

  (i) inventory
  (ii) value

4. PURCHASE OF PART

  (i) map
  (ii) easements including:
    (a) right of way/light
    (b) services
    (c) maintenance

5. STRUCTURE/SURVEY

  (i) inspection by expert independent of lending institution
  (ii) check re survey/valuer's report for lending institution (advise in writing)

6. PLANNING

  (i) planning search (pre-contract)
  (ii) any change in planning unit/division
  (iii) any change in use/intensification
  (iv) fire certificate/building regulations

7. INSURANCE

  (i) cover from date of contract/roofing if new building
  (ii) life cover/mortgage protection

4.7 Particulars of Vendor: Checklist

DATE

GENERAL

1. CLIENT

  (i) name
  (ii) address and occupation
  (iii) status/age—married/single/separated/divorced
  (iv) Irish citizen
  (v) telephone/fax
  (vi) PPS/tax number

2. SPOUSE

  (i) name
  (ii) Irish citizen
  (iii) other details
  (iv) PPS/tax number

3. BANK

    (i)   name
    (ii)   address
    (iii) contact (name)
    (iv) undertaking
    (v)   financial arrangements

4. CLOSING DATE

    (i)   desired closing date
    (ii) alternative

5. DETAILS OF PURCHASERS

    (i)   names
    (ii)   address
    (iii) price
    (iv) deposit
    (v)   loan clause
    (vi) PPS/tax number of purchasers
    (vii) solicitors for purchaser

6. MORTGAGOR OF VENDORS

    (i)   name of lending institution
    (ii)   branch/address
    (iii) amount due
    (iv) authority re deeds
    (v)   any other encumbrances
    (vi) undertaking—retainer and irrevocable authority

7. ITEMS INCLUDED IN SALE

    (i)   inventory
    (ii) value

8. SALE OF PART

    (i)   map
    (ii) easements including
        (a) right of way/light
        (b) services
        (c) maintenance

9. INSURANCE

    (i)   any general conditions re risk remaining
    (ii) is property insured to full replacement value?

10. INFORMATION—REPLIES TO REQUISITIONS

4.8   Particulars of Purchaser: Checklist

DATE: ....

PURCHASER'S NAME: ....

....

ADDRESS: ....

....

OCCUPATION: ....

HOME TELEPHONE NUMBER: ....   OFFICE: ....

FAX NO: ....

MARRIED/SINGLE/DIVORCED/SEPARATED/ENGAGED: ....

IF MARRIED NAME OF SPOUSE AND DATE AND PLACE OF MARRIAGE:

....

....

AGE: ....

IF JOINT PURCHASE—IS PROPERTY TO BE TAKEN AS JOINT TENANTS OR TENANTS IN COMMON:

....

VENDOR'S NAME: ....

ADDRESS: ....

....

VENDOR'S SOLICITOR: ....

....

ADDRESS OF PROPERTY TO BE PURCHASED: ....

IS PURCHASER AN IRISH CITIZEN OR NOT: ....

....

BORROWING ARRANGEMENT: ....

NAME AND ADDRESS OF BANK/BUILDING SOCIETY: ....

....

CHECK IF BRIDGING FINANCE WILL BE NECESSARY: . . . .

. . . .

GET IRREVOCABLE AUTHORITY FROM THE PURCHASER AND HIS WIFE, IF APPLIC-
ABLE, TO COMPLETE PURCHASE AND TO GIVE RELEVANT UNDERTAKING TO THE
BANK:

. . . .

ITEMS AGREED WITH VENDOR TO BE INCLUDED IN THE PURCHASE: . . . .

. . . .

. . . .

DESIRED CLOSING DATE: . . . .

ADVISE CLIENT TO HAVE HOUSE CHECKED BY ARCHITECT: . . . .

ADVISE CLIENT TO HAVE HOUSE INSURED: . . . .

ESTIMATED COST OF TRANSACTION: . . . .

Stamp duty on assurance	€
Land Registry/Registry of Deeds etc	€
Marriage certificate	€
Searches	€
Surveyor's fees	€
Stamp duty on mortgage	€
Land Registry/Registry of Deeds fees on mortgage	€
Sundries	€
Own professional fee	€
VAT	€

4.9   Conveyancing—Instruction Sheet

DATE:

GENERAL:

1.   CLIENT

> (i)   name
> (ii)   address and occupation
> (iii) status/age
>   married/single/separated/divorced
> (iv)   Irish citizen
> (v)   telephone/fax
> (vi)   PPS/tax number

2.   SPOUSE

> (i)   name
> (ii)   Irish citizen

      (iii)   other details
      (iv)   PPS/tax number

3.   BANK

      (i)   name
      (ii)   address
      (iii)   contact (name)
      (iv)   undertaking
      (v)   financial arrangements

4.   CLOSING DATE

      (i)   desired closing date
      (ii)   alternative

SALE

1.   DETAILS OF PURCHASERS

      (i)   names
      (ii)   address
      (iii)   price
      (iv)   deposit
      (v)   loan clause
      (vi)   PPS/tax number of purchasers
      (vii) solicitors for purchaser

2.   MORTGAGOR OF VENDORS

      (i)   name lending institution
      (ii)   branch/address
      (iii)   amount due
      (iv)   authority re deeds
      (v)   any other encumbrances
      (vi)   undertaking—retainer and irrevocable authority

3.   ITEMS INCLUDED IN SALE

      (i)   inventory
      (ii)   value

4.   SALE OF PART

      (i)   map
      (ii)   easements including
          (a)   right of way/light
          (b)   services
          (c)   maintenance

5.   INSURANCE

      (i)   any general conditions re risk remaining
      (ii)   is property insured to full replacement value?

6.   INFORMATION—REPLIES TO REQUISITIONS

PURCHASE

1. DETAILS VENDOR

   (i) name
   (ii) address
   (iii) price
   (iv) deposit
   (v) loan clause
   (vi) solicitors for vendor

2. FINANCE

   (i) deposit/equity from sale of house
   (ii) loan—amount €
       (a) name of lending institution
       (b) branch/address
       (c) position of loan application
       (d) survey/fire cover/life cover
   (iii) bridging accommodation
   (iv) undertaking and irrevocable authority
   (v) prepare and furnish financial memo

3. ITEMS INCLUDED IN SALE

   (i) inventory
   (ii) value

4. PURCHASE OF PART

   (i) map
   (ii) easements including
       (a) right of way/light
       (b) services
       (c) maintenance

5. STRUCTURE/SURVEY

   (i) inspection by expert independent of lending institution
   (ii) check re survey/valuer's report for lending institution

6. PLANNING

   (i) planning search (pre-contract)
   (ii) any change in planning unit/division
   (iii) any change in use/intensification
   (iv) fire certificate/building regulations

7. INSURANCE

   (i) cover from date of contract/roofing if new building
   (ii) life cover/mortgage protection

CHAPTER 5

CONTRACT FOR SALE

5.1 Introduction

Nowadays, we take the existence of the Standard Law Society Contract for Sale for granted. Before the introduction of the Standard Contract for Sale by the Law Society, every solicitor had his or her own contract. At public auction, the full contract including all the general conditions was read by the vendor's solicitor. The result of this was that most solicitors could recite by heart their own contracts for sale. The downside was that a purchaser's solicitor had no idea what was likely to be in the contract for sale prepared by the vendor's solicitor.

Nowadays it is unheard of to have the general conditions of the Standard Law Society Contract read out. A solicitor would merely refer to them as being the Standard and Current Conditions of Sale of the Law Society. Because the conditions are no longer read out, people have become far less familiar with them. However, it is vital that conveyancing solicitors familiarise themselves with each and every one of the general conditions. For example, general condition 36, which deals with planning, is relevant to almost every single transaction. The vendor is giving a warranty that all development which has taken place on the property since 1 October 1964 is in compliance with the planning legislation. If this warranty is to be altered in any way in the special conditions, the vendor's solicitor must satisfy himself or herself as to the position in relation to development prior to the preparation of the contract.

When the 1995 edition of the Contract for Sale was being launched the Conveyancing Committee of the Law Society issued an explanatory memorandum setting out the changes in the contract and also made a number of general points. Among the general points made by the committee were:

(a) Where a purchaser's solicitor makes any amendment or alteration to any of the first four pages of the contract for sale or to any map this alteration or amendment should be highlighted in the covering letter returning the contracts for sale. Otherwise, a vendor's solicitor is entitled to assume that 'the contract' which he or she sent out is 'the contract' which was returned to him or her.

(b) It is bad practice to use a limited form of contract referring to the general conditions without setting them out. The committee has recommended that all contracts should contain physically a full set of the standard general conditions.

The current Contract for Sale (the 2001 edition) is a twenty-six page document containing fifty-one general conditions, three special conditions, a memorandum page, a particulars and tenure, a documents schedule, a searches schedule and space to include any additional special conditions which the parties wish to insert in the contract together with a two-page query sheet for non-title information.

An explanatory memorandum has been issued by the Conveyancing Committee high-lighting the changes which have been made in the current contract.

Unlike the requisitions on title, which relate to the various statutory provisions covering conveyancing, the contract is a stand-alone document. Therefore, it is very important that conveyancers are familiar with it in its entirety. It is recommended that before going any further, readers should familiarise themselves with the contract and each condition in it. The Contract for Sale is set out at **Appendix 5.1.**

Because the contract speaks for itself, it is not proposed to go through it condition by condition. Rather, it is dealt with under the following headings:

(a)   portions of the contract which need to be filled in by a vendor, and

(b)   general conditions of the Contract for Sale.

5.2   Portions of the Contract to be Filled in by Vendor

5.2.1   INTRODUCTION

The portions of the contract to be completed by the vendor are:

(a)   cover page;

(b)   memorandum of agreement including the vendor's PPS number;

(c)   particulars and tenure;

(d)   the documents schedule;

(e)   the searches; and

(f)   any additional special conditions other than the three already contained in the contract.

5.2.2   COVER PAGE

From a contractual point of view, it is of no importance whether the cover page is filled in or left blank.

5.2.3   MEMORANDUM OF AGREEMENT

5.2.3.1   Generally

The memorandum of agreement is p 1 of the contract document. It sets out the name and address of the vendor and of the purchaser, their PPS numbers, the purchase price, the deposit (usually 10 per cent of the purchase price), the closing date, and the interest rate payable in the event of late closing. (If no interest rate is specified, the 'Stipulated Interest Rate' as set out in the definitions shall apply.) It has spaces for the vendor and the purchaser to sign and have their signatures witnessed and also provides for payment of the deposit as stakeholder. This page also has provision for the spouse of the vendor to give his or her consent under the Family Home Protection Act, 1976 where a family home is being sold.

The memorandum of agreement will be dated when it is signed by the last necessary party. The last necessary party will normally be the vendor.

5.2.3.2 Closing date

General condition 2 of the contract defines closing date as:

> 'the date specified as such in the Memorandum, or, if no date is specified, the first Working Day after the expiration of five weeks computed from the Date of Sale'.

In relation to the interest rate, it is defined in general condition 2 as:

> 'the interest rate specified in the Memorandum, or, if no rate is so specified, such rate as shall equate to 4 per centum per annum above the Court Rate obtaining pursuant to Section 22, Courts Act, 1981 and ruling at the date from which interest is to run'.

These two definitions, which are relatively new to the contract, are very important protections for the vendor. While the interest rate is a matter for the vendor, insertion of a figure may often be overlooked in the rush to issue contracts. Assuming that the sale goes through as agreed, the interest rate is of no consequence. Normally when a contract is being signed, the parties are not expecting any hitch and therefore the interest rate payable by a defaulting purchaser will not be to the forefront of the party's mind.

The closing date is something which may not have been agreed when the other terms and conditions of the contract were finalised between the parties. Contracts are issued frequently with no closing date inserted, on the basis that the purchaser will insert the closing date when signing the contract. The purchaser's solicitor may return the contract without having inserted the closing date. Before the alternative closing date was provided by the definition section, the vendor's solicitor would have had to revert to the purchaser's solicitor and agree the closing date before allowing his or her client to sign. By virtue of the current definition, he or she can allow his or her client to sign on the basis of a five-week closing date.

5.2.3.3 Receipt of deposit

Page 1 also includes a space for the solicitor to sign the receipt of the deposit which the vendor's solicitor will hold as stakeholder pending the completion of the sale.

In private treaty sales the vendor's solicitor may receive the deposit prior to the date of sale. General condition 5(c) provides that such a deposit will be held by the vendor's solicitor as trustee for the purchaser until the date of sale. (There is an argument as to the effectiveness of clause 5(c). 'Date of sale' is defined in the definition section as being the date upon which the contract for the sale shall have become binding on the vendor and the purchaser. If the contract is not binding before then, how can condition 5(c) bind the parties?)

5.2.3.4 Summary

In order to complete the memorandum of agreement the vendor or his or her auctioneer will need to give the vendor's solicitor the name and address of the purchaser, the purchase price and the agreed closing date. The vendor's solicitor will also need to have clarified the position in relation to the Family Home Protection Act, 1976. Is the property in sale a family home or is it not? If it is a family home the spouse's consent must be available.

5.2.4 PARTICULARS AND TENURE

Under the particulars and tenure section, the vendor's solicitor fills in particulars of the property being sold as found in the documents relating to the property (as distinct from the postal address).

An example of what might be found under this heading would be something along the lines of the following:

> ALL THAT AND THOSE the dwellinghouse and premises known as No 196 Brownwood Avenue, Rathmines situate in the Parish of St George formerly in the County but now in the City of Dublin HELD under an Indenture of Lease dated the 1st day of January 1900 and made BETWEEN Joseph Black of the One Part and Mary White of the Other Part for a term of Nine Hundred and Ninety Nine Years from 1st day of January 1900 subject to the annual rent of Ten Pounds Ten Shillings and Sixpence thereby reserved and to the covenants on the part of the lessee and conditions therein contained. Rateable Valuation: £14

5.2.4.1 Summary

In order to prepare the particulars and tenure the vendor's solicitor will need to have the title documents in his or her possession or to have copies of them. The information for this section will be derived mainly from the vendor's title documents.

5.2.5 THE DOCUMENTS SCHEDULE

The documents schedule identifies the documents which are being produced by the vendor with the contract for sale. The Conveyancing Committee has issued practice notes (Law Society Gazette, March 1995 and May 2000) setting out what should be included and what should not be included in the documents schedule. The 1995 practice note referred to the practice of including all the documents of title in the documents schedule and states:

> 'the Conveyancing Committee disapproves of the foregoing practice and recommends that in accordance with established Conveyancing practice, the documents listed in the Documents Schedule should be limited to:

> (a) The root of title being shown.

> (b) Any document to which title is stated to have passed under the Special Conditions.

> (c) Any document which is specifically referred to in a Special Condition'.

The May 2000 practice note adds planning documentation to this list.

5.2.6 THE SEARCHES SCHEDULE

General condition 19 provides that the purchaser shall be furnished with the searches (if any) specified in the searches schedule and any searches already in the vendor's possession which are relevant to the title or titles on offer.

In Land Registry transactions, the folio will be furnished and it will be a matter for the purchaser to make any other searches which he or she wishes.

In rural areas, it is not the practice for the vendor to lodge a negative search in the Registry of Deeds; instead, the purchaser will rely on a hand search. However, because of the computerisation of the Registry of Deeds, negative searches are now available in short periods and they should be made available to a purchaser.

Searches are covered in detail in **chapter 10**.

5.2.7 THE SPECIAL CONDITIONS

The printed standard contract contains three special conditions. The first special condition provides that the definitions and provisions of the general conditions shall apply to the special conditions in the contract. Special condition 2 provides that if there is an amendment to the general conditions, this amendment is effective only if there is a special condition included amending the general conditions. If this special condition was not in the contract, then a party could delete one of the general conditions without the other party being aware of it.

When a vendor's solicitor issues a contract for sale, he or she is entitled to assume that the document being returned to him or her has not been altered. If the solicitor for the purchaser makes any alteration to the document (eg the price, closing date etc) the alteration should be referred to in the covering letter returning the contract. This need to alert the vendor is even more important where there has been a change to the special conditions. While a vendor's solicitor will have p 1 open in front of him when he is getting his or her client to sign (and is therefore likely to notice any change), he or she will have no reason to look at p 4.

It was stated in the Law Society Gazette, October 1993:

'The view of the Professional Purposes Committee is that when a solicitor furnishes a contract to a purchaser's solicitor, he must expect that no amendments will have been made to the contract, or to any map attached to the contract, unless this fact is clearly stated in the purchaser's solicitor's covering letter returning the contract. Accordingly, it is the recommendation of the Professional Purposes Committee that a vendor's solicitor must be clearly alerted by the covering letter that a contract or map has been amended. Failure to so alert, will be regarded by the Committee as a breach of the professional etiquette which exists between colleagues.'

It depends on the circumstances what other special conditions the vendor's solicitor will put in. Fixtures may be excluded from sale, fittings may be included, the warranty in condition 36 may be altered, the title may be limited to certain documents or to commence with a certain document, it may be subject to the purchaser obtaining loan sanction or obtaining planning permission for a particular development etc.

The contract document (p 7) provides that where a vendor is altering or deleting a general condition in the contract that the reason for this change should be given to the purchaser, unless the reason is self evident.

Below, at **5.2.8**, are some Law School specimen special conditions.

5.2.8   SPECIMEN SPECIAL CONDITIONS

1.   The title shall commence with Indenture of Lease dated the 1st day of January 1930 and made between John Smith of the One Part and Anthony Jones of the Other Part and shall then pass to an Indenture of Assignment made the 4th day of July 1972 and made between Tony Ryan of the One Part and James O'Reilly of the Other Part and shall be deducted therefrom. No objection, requisition or enquiry shall be raised in relation to the intermediate title but without prejudice the vendor will furnish all documents of intermediate title in his possession on closing.

The Purchaser shall conclusively assume that the said Indenture of Lease was validly granted and is a valid and subsisting lease and shall raise no objection, requisition or enquiry in relation to title prior thereto.

2.   The title shall commence with Indenture of Conveyance dated the 2nd day of March 1977 and made between Martin O'Neill of the One Part and Maureen Hara of the Other Part and shall be deduced therefrom.

3.   The title shall consist of official certified copy folio and file plan (map) of Folio 1705 of the Register of Freeholders County Dublin.

4.   The title to the property shall commence with Indenture of Lease dated the 17th day of October 1938 and made between Joseph Flynn and Others of the One Part and Brigid Flynn of the Other Part and shall then pass without objection requisition or

enquiry in relation to the intermediate title to Indenture of Assignment dated the 31st day of December 1969 and made between Gail Ward of the One Part and Francis Bouchier of the Part and shall be deduced therefrom.

5. This contract shall be subject to the purchaser obtaining approval for a loan of €150,000 from First Active Building Society on the security of the premises PROVIDED ALWAYS that if this loan has not been approved in writing within 4 weeks from the date hereof either party shall be entitled to rescind this contract and in such event the purchaser shall be refunded his deposit without interest costs or compensation thereon.

If the loan approval is conditional on a survey satisfactory to the lending institution or a mortgage protection or life assurance policy being taken out or some other condition compliance with which is not within the control of the purchaser the loan shall not be deemed to be approved until the purchaser is in a position to accept the loan on terms which are within his reasonable power or procurement.

The sale shall be completed 14 days after the issue of the loan approval.

6. Included in the contract price are the fitted carpets, curtains and light fittings presently in the premises.

7. This contract is conditional upon the vendor obtaining within 10 days from the date hereof subdivision consent under Section 12 of the Land Act, 1965 in respect of the lands being sold hereunder. If such consent is not forthcoming within 10 days from the date hereof (unless the time shall be extended by agreement between the parties) the purchaser shall be refunded his deposit but without interest, costs or compensation thereon and thereupon this contract shall be null and void.

8. This contract is subject to and conditional upon the present Lessors, Irish Life Limited, consenting within four weeks from the date hereof to the assignment of the premises to the purchasers and to the premises being used as a retail shoe shop. The purchaser hereby agrees that he shall furnish without delay such references and reasonable information as may be required by the Landlord.

9. The sale is conditional upon the purchaser obtaining planning permission for the erection on the land described in the Particulars and Tenure of 72 houses in accordance with plans and specifications whereof details will be submitted to the Planning Authority for the purposes of obtaining such permission. If at the expiration of six months from the date hereof planning permission as aforesaid shall not have been granted or shall have been granted subject to conditions which are unacceptable to the purchaser and that fact shall have been notified to the vendor within seven days after the expiration of the said period then either party may be notified in writing in that behalf served upon the other rescind this agreement whereupon the vendor shall return the deposit to the purchaser but without interest costs or compensation and the purchaser shall return the copy title deeds and any other papers furnished to him and neither party shall be entitled to any sum in respect of costs, compensation or otherwise.

10. This contract is conditional upon the vendor obtaining within 3 months from the date hereof planning permission for the retention of the kitchen recently built by the vendor. If the said planning permission is not obtained within the said period of 3 months the purchaser shall be refunded his deposit without interest costs or compensation and this contract shall be null and void. The purchaser shall accept the vendor's Architect's Certificate that the extension complies with all conditions (if any) in the retention permission and in his view would have complied with Building Bye Laws if they had been applied for at the time of the erection of the extension. General Condition 36 is hereby varied accordingly.

11. The property being sold under this contract is at present subject to a mortgage in favour of EBS Building Society. Prior to completion the vendor shall inform the purchaser of the sum required to repay the mortgage and the balance purchase money shall be paid at the purchaser's expense to the vendor's solicitor in the following manner:

    (a) a bank draft in favour of EBS Building Society for the balance outstanding to the said Building Society; and

    (b) a bank draft for the remaining balance of the purchase price in favour of the vendor's solicitor.

    The purchaser shall on closing accept the vendor's solicitor's undertaking to immediately forward the bank draft for the redemption monies to the Building Society and to furnish a vacate of the said mortgage duly registered in the Registry of Deeds as soon as possible thereafter.

12. This contract is signed subject to the purchaser obtaining consent from the Land Commission under Section 45 of the Land Act, 1965 to the vesting in himself of the property being sold under this contract.
    If such consent has not been received within 6 weeks from the date of this contract the purchaser's deposit shall be refunded to him but without interest costs or compensation and thereupon this agreement shall be at an end.

13. The purchaser shall raise no objection, requisition or enquiry regarding the fact that the Deed of Conveyance dated the 4th day of March, 1946 did not contain an express Declaration of Merger. The purchaser shall conclusively assume that the leasehold interest merged in the freehold reversion expectant upon the determination thereof by virtue of the said Deed of Conveyance of the 4th day of March 1946.

14. The vendor is selling in her capacity as personal representative of the estate of Bridget Maher deceased. On closing the purchaser will accept the vendor's solicitor's undertaking to hold sufficient monies out of the sale proceeds to discharge Capital Acquisitions Tax due in respect of the death of the said Bridget Maher deceased and to discharge same and furnish an unconditional Certificate of Discharge when same becomes available from the Revenue Commissioners.

15. The vendor will assign to the purchaser the benefit of the consent of the freehold owner to the acquisition of the fee simple under the provisions of the Landlord and Tenant (Ground Rents) (No. 2) Act, 1978.

16. This sale is subject to the consent of Clare County Council being first had and obtained. The vendor will immediately apply for such consent and the purchaser will furnish the vendor with any information and comply with conditions required by Clare County Council in respect of such application. If such consent is not forthcoming within six weeks from the date hereof this agreement shall be rescinded and the purchaser's deposit shall be returned without interest costs or compensation. If such consent is forthcoming the sealing of the Deed of Assurance shall be the responsibility of the purchaser.

17. The vendor is selling in her capacity as Tenant for Life for the purposes of the Settled Land Acts and Mary Lynch and Tom Humble will join in the Deed as Trustees of the Settlement for the purpose of giving a receipt. (Check this is a Settled Land Act Trust otherwise Trustees may not have power of sale.)

18. The purchaser is furnished with a letter dated the 16th December, 1986 from Dun Laoghaire Corporation confirming that the roads, footpaths and services abutting the premises are in charge of the Local Authority and will not raise any objection, requisition or enquiry in relation thereto.

19. The purchaser is referred to Voluntary Deed of Assignment dated the 4th November 1982 and made between Francis J Bouchier of the One Part and his wife Katherine Deirdre Bouchier of the Other Part affected under the provisions of Section 14 of the Family Home Protection Act, 1976. A Statutory Declaration re the Family Home Protection Act, 1976 and the Family Law Act, 1981 was not obtained at the date of this deed. The vendor relies on the provision of Section 54 of the Family Law Act, 1995 and no objection, requisition or enquiry may be raised as to the non-availability of this Statutory Declaration.

20. The Deed of Assent referred to at document number 3 of the Documents Schedule hereto was not registered in the Registry of Deeds. The purchaser will not raise any objection, requisition or enquiry regarding this and will not look for the registration of same. The purchaser is referred to Section 53(1)(c) of the Succession Act, 1965. (Registration of an Assent is not compulsory but if not registered the beneficiary runs the risk of losing his priority.)

21. The vendor has applied for a Grant of Probate in the estate of the deceased owner. The closing date hereof shall be seven days after the purchaser's solicitor has been notified by the vendor's solicitor that the said Grant of Probate has issued.

22. On the closing of the sale the purchaser shall accept the vendor's solicitor's undertaking to hold sufficient monies out of the sale proceeds to discharge Capital Acquisitions Tax and Probate Tax due in respect of the death of the said Kathleen McLoughlin deceased and to discharge same and to furnish an unconditional Certificate of Discharge when same becomes available from the Revenue Commissioners.

23. The vendors will forthwith apply to purchaser the freehold interest in the premises from Pembroke Estates Holdings Limited, the party entitled to the said freehold interest. If the said freehold interest shall have been acquired at the time of completion of the sale herein then the vendors shall convey the freehold interest at the time of completion. If the freehold interest shall not have been acquired before completion of the sale then the vendors will convey the freehold interest to the purchaser as soon as possible thereafter. The vendors shall be responsible for the purchase price of the fee simple interest and also for any legal costs involved in the acquisition thereof.

5.2.9   OTHER SPECIAL CONDITIONS

Other special conditions which may be inserted by a vendor's solicitor are set out below.

The following is an example of a special condition inserted in a contract where a title document that forms part of the 'chain of title' is missing. The vendor's solicitor is aware of this at the time of drafting the contract and has made a search in the Registry of Deeds, has located the memorial and has obtained an attested copy. All due enquiries as to the whereabouts of the missing deed have been made and a draft statutory declaration has been prepared for completion by the vendor as well as a statutory declaration by the firm who acted at the time the vendor purchased.

> Deed dated   day of   and made between A of the one part and B of the other part has been mislaid. On closing the vendor will furnish an attested copy Memorial of the said deed together with Statutory Declaration of the vendor's solicitor regarding same in the form of the drafts referred to in the Documents Schedule herein. The purchaser shall accept said documentation and no further objection or requisition or enquiry shall be raised in relation to same.

The attested copy memorial and the draft statutory declarations should be exhibited in the documents schedule of the contract.

Where the entire title documents are missing it may be possible to reconstruct the chain of title by means of attested copy memorials, possibly supported by copies of some of the deeds and an insurance company bond (see Law Society Gazette Practice Note, July 1997 in relation to bonds).

An example would be in the case of a leasehold interest where the original lease and subsequent assignments are missing or destroyed. Enquiries may be made to ascertain the party entitled to the lessor's interest and an approach made to them to obtain a certified copy of the counterpart lease which they would hold. Searches may then be made in the Registry of Deeds to try to trace the chain down. It is also possible, by checking the solicitors' files and papers at the time the vendor purchased, that copy documents may have been retained on the file which, backed up by attested copy memorials, would help. Again, the loss of the documents would be supported by statutory declarations from the last party who would have had them and from the solicitors acting for any lending institution who had held them as security pending the discharge of a mortgage.

5.2.10 NON-TITLE INFORMATION SHEET

This sheet appears at pp 5 and 6 of the contract document. It is a new departure by the Conveyancing Committee and should be beneficial to both the vendor's solicitor and the purchaser's solicitor. If the vendor goes through it, it will enable him or her to identify any problems which exist, before he or she issues the contract. For the purchaser's solicitor, it will mean that the information will be available to him or her without having to make enquiries in relation to the particular matters contained therein.

General condition 33(a) caters for the situation where the information contained in the non-title information sheet is inaccurate.

5.3 General Conditions

5.3.1 DEFINITIONS AND INTERPRETATION

Definitions and interpretation are covered by conditions 1 to 3. The closing date and the interest rate have already been covered at **5.2.3** dealing with the memorandum of agreement. The other definition requiring comment is that of the 'purchase price'. The definition provides that where goodwill, crops or purchased chattels are included, then the purchase price extends to the money payable for these. Because the contract provides for the payment of the balance of the purchase money on closing (general condition 24(a)) by virtue of this definition, a purchaser cannot avoid paying for goodwill crops or purchased chattels on the closing date.

In the 2001 edition of the contract, general condition 3 has been expanded to cover the situation where the contract includes a special condition which is void, illegal or invalid. This condition now provides that provided the condition does not go to the root of the contract, such a special condition shall be deemed to have been severed and omitted from the conditions.

5.3.2 SALE BY AUCTION AND PRIVATE TREATY

Conditions 4 and 5 are alternative conditions. Condition 4 applies where the sale is by public auction and condition 5 deals with the situation where the property is sold by private treaty. Where the sale is by public auction the deposit is payable to the vendor's solicitor as stakeholder. Wylie, *Irish Conveyancing Law* (2nd edn) para 10.26 states:

'if the deposit is paid to a stakeholder, it is settled that he is personally responsible for its safekeeping and must not hand it over to the vendor without the purchaser's permission. In this respect, he is agent for both parties, obliged to hold onto the deposit until the vendor becomes entitled to it, e.g. on forfeiture due to default by the purchaser or on completion of the transaction, or the purchaser becomes entitled to its return, e.g. on rescission of the contract due to the vendor's default'.

Where the sale is by private treaty the deposit is paid to the vendor's solicitor as trustee for the purchaser until the date of sale and thereafter as stakeholder.

5.3.3 NUTS AND BOLTS OF THE TROUBLE-FREE TRANSACTION

5.3.3.1 Delivery of title

Condition 7 provides that within seven working days from the date of sale, the vendor shall deliver or send by post to the purchaser or his solicitor copies of the documents necessary to vouch the title to be shown in accordance with the conditions.

It is on receipt of these documents that the purchaser will raise requisitions on title.

5.3.3.2 Requisitions on title

Under condition 17, the purchaser shall, within fourteen working days after the later of the date of sale or the delivery of copy documents of title in accordance with condition 7, send to the vendor's solicitors his objections and requisitions on title. The vendor's replies to any objections or requisitions shall be answered by the purchaser in writing within seven working days after the delivery thereof. The purchaser has a right to raise rejoinders to the requisitions on title and likewise the seven-day time limit applies.

5.3.3.3 The assurance

Condition 20 provides that the purchaser shall submit a draft deed of assurance, ie the conveyance, transfer or assignment, not less than seven working days, and the engrossment not less than four working days, before the closing date.

At common law, the production of a draft deed portrays the presumption of the acceptance of the title furnished. For convenience solicitors deliver the draft deed at any early stage. Frequently, it is delivered with the requisitions on title. So as to negative this presumption of acceptance of title, condition 20 states: 'the delivery of the said draft or engrossment shall not prejudice any outstanding Objection or Requisition validly made'. General condition 20(b) provides that a completed PD form shall be handed over to the purchaser on or before handing over the assurance.

5.3.3.4 Completion and interest

Conditions 24 to 26 deal with the completion of the sale and the payment of interest. As already mentioned at **5.3.1** the purchase price as defined by the definition section must be paid on or before the closing date.

Condition 24(b) provides for the sale to be completed at the office of the vendor's solicitor. This is a very important condition. Purchasers' solicitors frequently overlook this. However, the vendor's solicitor is entitled always to insist that closing takes place in his or her office. It is not an economic proposition in rural areas to close sales personally at the vendor's solicitor's office. Provided all the parties agree, then a postal closing is acceptable. The Conveyancing Committee devised a system for postal closing, setting out the procedures to be adopted when sales are being closed through the post (see Law Society Gazette, January/February 1996, July 1987 and December 1996).

When the sale is closed pursuant to condition 24(b) the vendor is entitled to release the purchase money forthwith. Similarly, on a postal closing, the vendor's solicitor should be in a similar position. It is not acceptable practice for a purchaser's solicitor to forward the balance of the purchase money to a vendor's solicitor 'on trust pending receipt of all documents of title as per my Requisitions on Title' or on similar terms. If money is sent on this basis, a vendor's solicitor should retain same in his or her client account and insist on a formal closing in accordance with condition 24(b) or, alternatively, offer to close the sale on the basis of the Law Society Code of Practice for postal closings. The contract now provides at general condition 25(c) that the vendor is not allowed to delay completion solely with regard to liability for interest.

5.3.3.5 Documents of title relating to other property

Condition 34 deals with the situation where the documents of title relate to other property as well as the property in sale. It provides that the vendor will give certified copies of the relevant documents, together with a statutory acknowledgement of the right of production, and also an undertaking for safe custody of all documents retained by him. It also provides that the purchaser shall furnish a counterpart deed to the vendor after it has been stamped and registered. The purpose of giving the counterpart deed to the vendor is so as to enable him or her to use it for the purpose of explaining and discharging searches which will arise on subsequent transactions in respect of the balance of the property. General condition 34 does not deal with registered land. In the case of registered land the Land Registry will open a new folio for the portion being transferred.

5.3.3.6 Risk

General condition 43 deals with the passing of the risk in respect of the property to the purchaser. The current position is that the risk passes to the purchaser when the sale is closed. If the sale is closed at the office of the vendor's solicitor or is closed through the post on the basis of the Law Society Code of Practice, then it is quite clear when the risk has passed to the purchaser. The vendor must be advised to maintain insurance cover until the sale has been completed. In practice most lending institutions require the premises to be insured before issuing the loan cheque. Therefore, in most transactions the premises will be doubly insured for a certain period prior to the closing.

5.3.3.7 Inspection

Condition 47 gives the purchaser a right to inspect the property on a reasonable number of occasions and at reasonable times prior to the closing of the sale. Thus, if the purchaser wishes to inspect the property on the day of the closing, he has a right to do so under this condition.

5.3.3.8 Non-merger

Condition 48 is headed 'Non-Merger'. At common law the contract is deemed to merge with the conveyance. This means that once the sale is closed, the vendor's obligations under the contract cease and it is only those obligations, if any, contained in the conveyance which survive.

However, general condition 48 provides that notwithstanding delivery of the deed to the purchaser

'all obligations and provisions designed to survive completion of the Sale and all warranties in the Conditions contained, which shall not have been implemented by the said Assurance, and which shall be capable of continuing or taking effect after such completion, shall enure and remain in full force and effect'.

Examples of this would be the planning warranty given under condition 36 and the warranty given in relation to chattel property under condition 46. Another area where it arises is where fencing is involved. In particular, if a purchaser has bought a site from a farmer, the contract will include a provision such as

'prior to the commencement of any work on the site the Purchaser shall erect a stock proof fence at least 4.5 feet high between the property sold and the property being retained by the Vendor'.

If there was merger, the deed of conveyance would have had to include a covenant about fencing.

5.3.4 CONTRACTUAL RESTRICTIONS PLACED ON PURCHASER

As already mentioned at **4.3.2** in the context of pre-contract enquiry, the purchaser is deemed to be on notice of the contents of the documents specified in the documents schedule of the contract.

5.3.4.1 Title

General condition 8(a) limits the title to be shown to the property in sale to such as is set forth in the special conditions. The special conditions will normally contain a clause stating 'the title shall commence with Assurance dated . . .'. Again, as mentioned in the context of pre-contract enquiries, condition 10(a) provides in relation to a lease that 'the Purchaser shall not call for or investigate the title of the grantor or lessor to make the same, but shall conclusively assume that it was well and validly made and is a valid and subsisting lease'.

Again, general condition 10, which relates to leasehold title, places various limitations on the purchaser:

(a) no objection or requisition shall be raised in respect of apportionment of rent on the ground of any superior owner not having concurred in the apportionment or to the exclusive charge of the rent to a particular portion of the demised property, or

(b) no objection or requisition shall be made by reason of any discrepancy between the covenants, conditions and provisions contained in any sublease and those in any superior lease, unless such give rise to forfeiture or a right of re-entry, or

(c) the purchaser shall accept the production of the receipt for the last gale of rent as conclusive evidence of various matters arising between the landlord and the lessee.

5.3.4.2 Prior title and intermediate title

General conditions 11 and 12 respectively limit the purchaser's right to investigate the title prior to the date of the instrument specified in the special conditions as a commencement of title and limit the purchaser's right to investigate the title where the special conditions provide that the title shall commence with a particular document and then pass to a second instrument or to a specified event.

5.3.4.3 Registered land

General condition 13 deals with registered land. This condition provides that where registration is subject to equities, the vendor will not be obliged to have the equities discharged but merely to furnish sufficient evidence to enable the purchaser to procure their discharge.

Where the title is registered as possessory, again the vendor is not obliged to convert the title to absolute but only to furnish sufficient documentation to the purchaser to enable the purchaser to be registered with an absolute title. It is acknowledged in general condition 13(h) that the vendor and not the vendor's solicitor shall deal with Land Registry mapping queries.

5.3.4.4 Identity

General condition 14 deals with the identity of the property in sale. Again this matter has been dealt with in the context of pre-contract enquiries. The vendor:

'shall not be required to define exact boundaries, fences, ditches, hedges or walls or to specify which (if any) of the same are of a party nature, nor shall the Vendor be required to identify parts of the Subject Property held under different titles'.

After the contract has been signed, all that the vendor is entitled to (and only if the circumstances require) is a statutory declaration to be made by a competent person at the purchaser's expense, setting out that the subject property has been held and enjoyed for at least twelve years in accordance with the title shown.

5.3.4.5 Caveat emptor: condition of subject property

General condition 16 provides that the purchaser shall be deemed to buy:

'(a) with full notice of the actual state and condition of the Subject Property; and

(b) subject to (i) all leases (if any) mentioned in the Particulars or in the Special Conditions and (ii) all easements, rights, reservations, privileges, covenants, restrictions, rents, taxes, liabilities, outgoings and all incidents of tenure affecting the Subject Property.'

5.3.4.6 Rights: liabilities of subject property

General condition 15 places certain obligations on the vendor and these are dealt with in the context of the obligations placed on the vendor by the contract. However, the vendor's obligation of disclosure does not extend to matters already known to the purchaser or which are apparent from inspection.

As a matter of prudence, when drafting a contract for sale, a vendor's solicitor should give details of all the rights and liabilities affecting the property even if they are known to the purchaser or apparent from inspection. By doing so, he or she will avoid any arguments in that regard in the future.

5.3.4.7 Land Act, 1965, s 45 consent

General condition 28 deals with consent under the Land Act, 1965, s 45. Section 45 prohibited non-Irish citizens (now non-EU and EEAA citizens) from purchasing agricultural land in Ireland without Land Commission consent. Unless there is a special provision to the contrary, such purchasers are warranting that they will get the necessary Land Commission consents and, as the condition provides that 'the Sale is not conditional upon such consent being obtained', the purchaser will lose his deposit if the consent is not forthcoming.

5.3.4.8 Compulsory acquisition

General condition 29(b) provides that where the transaction gives rise to compulsory registration in the Land Registry, such registration shall be a matter for the purchaser.

5.3.4.9 Differences: errors

General condition 33(d) limits the purchaser's right (and also the vendor's) to annul the sale in the event of any error.

5.3.4.10 Risk

General condition 44 limits the liability imposed on the vendor by condition 43 of the contract in respect of the risk to the property between the signing of the contract for sale and the closing of the sale.

The vendor has no liability in respect of:

(a) inconsequential damage or insubstantial deterioration from reasonable wear and tear in the course of normal occupation and use and not materially affecting value; or

(b) damage occasioned by operations reasonably undertaken by the vendor in his or her removal from, and vacation of, the subject property, provided that the same are so undertaken with reasonable care; or

(c) where any such loss or damage has resulted from a requirement restriction or obligation imposed by a competent authority after the date of sale.

5.3.5 OBLIGATIONS PLACED ON VENDOR BY FORMAL WARRANTY IN CONTRACT FOR SALE

The obligations placed on the vendor by the Contract for Sale may be broken into two sections:

(a) the formal warranty given by the vendor under the contract for sale, and

(b) the other obligations placed on the vendor under the contract.

5.3.5.1 Registered land

Under general condition 13(a) and (b) in respect of possessory title and title registered subject to equities, the vendor warrants that he will furnish sufficient evidence to enable the purchaser to register his title as absolute.

Under general condition 13(d) the vendor warrants that a statutory declaration in respect of the non-existence of any burdens which, under the Registration of Title Act, 1964, affect registered land without registration (s 72: burdens), will be available on closing. Burdens specified or mentioned in the particulars or in the special conditions are excluded from this warranty.

5.3.5.2 Searches

Under general condition 19, the vendor warrants that he will be in a position to explain and discharge any acts appearing on the purchaser's searches covering the period from the date stipulated or implied from the commencement of title to the date of actual completion.

5.3.5.3 Vacant possession

Under general condition 21, the vendor warrants that the purchaser will get vacant possession of the property in sale on closing. This warranty applies unless there is a contrary provision in the particulars or in the conditions or unless it is otherwise implied by the nature of the transaction that there will not be vacant possession.

5.3.5.4 Leases

Under general condition 23, the vendor warrants that in the case where the property sold is subject to any lease

'that there has been no variation in the terms and conditions of said Lease (other than such as may be evident from an inspection of the Subject Property or apparent from the Particulars or the documents furnished to the Purchaser prior to the Sale), and that the said terms and conditions (save those pertaining to the actual state and condition of the Subject Property) have been complied with'.

5.3.5.5 Planning

Under general condition 36, the vendor gives the planning warranty. Planning is dealt with extensively in **chapter 11**.

Under condition 36 the vendor warrants there has been no development since 1 October 1964 or, alternatively, that there have been developments after that date but that all planning permissions and building bye-law approvals relevant to the property have been complied with substantially.

Under condition 36(d), the vendor warrants that in all appropriate cases, there has been substantial compliance with the Building Regulations made under the Building Control Act, 1990. This general condition now contains a proviso that the warranty will not extend to approvals under the Building Bye Laws or compliance with such Building Bye-Laws in respect of development or works carried out prior to 13 December 1989.

5.3.5.6 Chattels

Under general condition 46 the vendor warrants that all chattel property included in the sale is not 'subject to any lease, rental hire, hire-purchase or credit sale agreement or chattel mortgage'.

5.3.6 OTHER OBLIGATIONS PLACED ON THE VENDOR UNDER THE CONTRACT

5.3.6.1 Title

Under general condition 8(b), if the title is based on possession, the vendor agrees to furnish a certificate from the Revenue Commissioners pursuant to the Finance Act, 1994, s 146 as amended by Finance Act, 1996, s 128. Under that section the certificate to be issued is to the effect that the Revenue is satisfied:

(a) that the property did not become charged with gift tax or inheritance tax during the relevant period, or

(b) that any charge for gift tax or inheritance tax to which the property became subject during that period has been discharged or will to the extent that it has not been discharged within a time considered by the Revenue Commissioners to be reasonable.

Condition 8(c) was introduced in the 1995 General Conditions of Sale, and specifically states that the vendor is obliged to discharge all mortgages and charges for the payment of money affecting the property at or before the sale.

5.3.6.2 Foreign vendor

General condition 9 provides that where the vendor is a company established outside the State, this should be disclosed in the Special Conditions.

The purpose of the condition is to put the purchaser on notice so that the necessary enquiries can be made pre-contract. A practice note headed 'Foreign Lawyer's Opinion' at p 34 of the Law Society Gazette of March 2001 sets out the intricacies of acting for a purchaser where the vendor is a foreign company.

5.3.6.3 Prior title

Condition 11(b) is again a provision introduced in the 1995 edition of the General Conditions of Sale.

74

Under general condition 11(a) there is the provision that the purchaser shall not object to or investigate the title prior to the date of the instrument specified in the special conditions of the Contract for Sale as the commencement of title, ie the root of title. However, in the case of registered land this condition is too restrictive and hence paragraph (b) putting the obligation on the vendor to deal with matters arising under the following:

(a)   the Registration of Title Act, 1964, s 52;

(b)   the Registration of Title Act, 1964, s 115; and

(c)   the Succession Act, 1965, s 121 as extended by the Family Law Act, 1995, s 25(s).

This condition was designed to meet difficulties on the investigation of registered titles in the area of capital acquisitions tax and voluntary dispositions.

(a) Registration of Title Act, 1964, s 52

Section 52(1) provides that on foot of a transfer of freehold land:

there shall be vested in the registered Transferee an estate in fee simple in the land transferred together with all implied or expressed rights, privileges and appurtenances, belonging or appurtenant thereto subject to (a) the burdens, if any, registered as effecting the land, and (b) the burdens to which, though not registered, the land is subject by virtue of Section 72, but shall be free from all other rights including rights of the state.

Section 52(2) provides that where the transfer is made without valuable consideration, it shall:

so far as concerns the Transferee and persons claiming under him otherwise than from valuable consideration, be subject to all unregistered rights subject to which the Transferor held the land transferred.

(b) Registration of Title Act, 1964, s 115

Section 115 states:

Every stipulation in a Contract for the Sale or Charge of registered land or for the Transfer of a registered charge whereby the Purchaser or intending Chargeant or the intending Transferee (as the case may be), is precluded from making Requisitions in relation to burdens generally or any particular burden which, by virtue of Section 72, may affect the land shall be void.

(c) Succession Act, 1965, s 121

Section 121(1) states:

this Section applies to a disposition of property (other than a testamentary disposition or a disposition to a Purchaser) under which the beneficial ownership of the property vests in possession in the Donee within three years before the death of the person who made it or on his death or later.

Section 121(2) provides that if a court is satisfied that the disposition was made for the purpose of defeating or substantially diminishing the share of the disponer's spouse, whether as a legal right or on intestacy, or the intestate share of any of his children or of leaving any of his children insufficiently provided for, then the court is entitled to, among other remedies, set aside the disposition.

5.3.6.4   Prior title

By virtue of general condition 11(b) the vendor is obliged to deal with requisitions on title covered by the statutory provisions at **5.3.6.3**.

5.3.6.5   Registered land

Under general condition 13(g) the vendor is obliged to redeem any land purchase annuity affecting the property in sale.

Under general condition 13(h) the vendor, where the property in sale is part only of a folio, agrees to satisfy any Land Registry mapping queries arising on the registration of the purchaser's title and to pay and discharge any additional Land Registry fees which might arise where fees are attributable to default on the part of the vendor.

5.3.6.6 Rights: liabilities

Under general condition 15, the vendor is obliged to disclose to the purchaser 'all easements, rights, reservations, exceptions, privileges, covenants, restrictions, rents, taxes and other liabilities (not already known to the Purchaser or apparent from inspection) which are known by the Vendor to affect the Subject Property and are likely to affect it', following completion of the sale.

This condition places an onerous obligation of disclosure on the vendor. Once disclosure has been made the vendor is protected by general condition 16.

5.3.6.7 Leases

General condition 22 relates to property which is sold subject to lease. This condition obliges the vendor to furnish a copy of the lease together with copies of any notices in the vendor's possession served by or on the lessee.

5.3.6.8 Completion and interest

General condition 25(b) requires a defaulting vendor to give his purchaser five working days' notice of his ultimate ability to complete. This condition was included in the contract so as to avoid a situation where, after the vendor's delay, the purchaser is asked to close immediately. The purchaser will need time to reorganise his or her finances and put himself or herself in a position where he or she is ready to close. General condition 25(c) provides that the vendor is not allowed to delay completion if the purchaser refuses to pay interest.

5.3.6.9 Compulsory registration

General condition 29(a) obliges the vendor to procure registration of his title prior to the completion of the sale in any case where the property was subject to compulsory registration prior to the date of sale.

This is an important clause in the context of the church temporalities cases. Since the Registration of Title Act, 1964, it has become compulsory to register title in the Land Registry, where the land has been or is deemed to have been at any time sold and conveyed to or vested in any person under the provisions of the Land Purchase Acts.

Land held by the Commissioners of Church Temporalities in Ireland is deemed to have been purchased under the Land Purchase Acts. The obligation to register such titles is frequently overlooked. In any of the cases where it has been overlooked, the purchaser is entitled to insist that the vendor registers his or her title prior to the closing of the sale.

Under Compulsory Registration of Ownership (Carlow, Laoighis and Meath) Order, 1969 (SI 1987/69), compulsory registration in the Land Registry was introduced for the counties of Meath, Carlow and Laois. Where there is a transaction in respect of an unregistered title in these counties, it must be registered. Again, under condition 29(a) the vendor will be obliged to register prior to closing.

Provided the difficulty is adverted to prior to the preparation of the contract, a vendor's solicitor will normally include a clause obliging the purchaser to do the first registration.

5.3.6.10 Differences: errors

General condition 33(b) obliges the vendor to compensate the purchaser for

'any loss suffered by the Purchaser in his bargain relative to the Sale as a result of an error made by or on behalf of the Vendor provided however that no compensation shall be payable for loss of trifling materiality unless attributable to recklessness or fraud on behalf of the Vendor nor in respect of any matter of which the Purchaser shall be deemed to have had notice under Condition 16(a) nor in relation to any error in a location or similar plan furnished for identification only'.

Further, under general condition 33(c) it states:

'Nothing in the Memorandum, the Particulars or the Conditions shall:

(i)   entitle the Vendor to require the Purchaser to accept property which differs substantially from the property agreed to be sold whether in quantity, quality, tenure or otherwise, if the Purchaser would be prejudiced materially by reason of any such difference or

(ii)   affect the right of the Purchaser to rescind or repudiate the Sale where compensation for a claim attributable to a material error made by or on behalf of the Vendor cannot be reasonably assessed.'

Under condition 33(d) neither the vendor nor the purchaser is entitled to annul the sale or be discharged therefrom except in accordance with this condition.

5.3.6.11   Disclosure of notices

General condition 35 deals with the disclosure of notices by the vendor. The vendor is obliged to disclose, prior to the sale, any closing, demolition or clearance order or any notice for compulsory acquisition or any other notice made or issued by or at the behest of a competent authority in respect of the subject property and affecting same at the date of sale. The vendor is not obliged to disclose the contents of the development plan in respect of the area 'other than an actual or proposed designation of all or any part of the subject property for compulsory acquisition'. The vendor is not obliged to disclose any notice, details of which are required to be entered in the Planning Register. (See Planning and Development Act, 2000, s 7 for the proposed changes to the Planning Register.)

Subject to the limitations set out in the condition, the purchaser may give notice to the vendor to rescind the sale where there is non-disclosure by the vendor of such notices.

5.3.7   CONDITIONS RELATING TO PROBLEM TRANSACTIONS

It is proposed to outline hereunder the conditions in the Contract for Sale which deal with transactions where problems arise.

5.3.7.1   Title

General condition 10(b)(iv) deals with the situation where a landlord's consent to alienation is required but is not forthcoming. The condition provides that if the consent is refused or is issued subject to a condition which the purchaser, on reasonable grounds, refuses to accept, either party may rescind the sale by seven days' prior notice to the other.

5.3.7.2   Requisitions on title

General condition 17 deals with the time limit set for raising and replying to requisitions and objections on title. The contract provides that time is of the essence in respect of these time limits. The condition states 'any Objection or Requisition not made within the time aforesaid and not going to the root of the title shall be deemed to have been waived'. Therefore, the vendor is not obliged to reply to any requisition on title raised outside the time limit set in the condition unless the matter raised goes to the root of the title.

General condition 18 entitles the vendor to rescind the sale by giving not less than five working days' notice to the purchaser where the purchaser insists on any objection or requisition as to the title 'which the Vendor shall, on the grounds of unreasonable delay or expense or other reasonable ground be unable or unwilling to remove or comply with'. The purchaser is entitled to withdraw the objection or requisition before the expiration of the five working days. Then, the sale is not rescinded.

The implications of general condition 18 are discussed at length in Wylie, *Irish Conveyancing Law*, paras 15.27 to 15.35. At para 15.30 Wylie states:

'this right of rescission constitutes a considerable restriction on the purchaser's rights and so it is not surprising that the courts have been alert to see that it is not abused. In fact the courts have laid down a number of qualifications to the vendor's right of rescission. First, it is settled that the vendor must exercise it in a reasonable manner or, as it is more usually put, he must not invoke it without reasonable cause. He must not act capriciously or arbitrarily and if necessary will have to convince the court that the objection or requisition which has caused him to invoke his right of rescission is one which will cause him substantial expense or involve him in litigation if he is to comply with or remove it. Thus, he cannot use the right as a convenient method of getting out of his Contract with the Purchaser eg in order to be able to accept a higher offer for the property from a Third Party'.

5.3.7.3 Completion and interest

General condition 25 of the contract deals with the situation where there is default either by the purchaser or by the vendor.

General condition 25(a) provides that where there is default on the part of the purchaser in not closing the sale at the closing date, the purchaser shall pay interest at the contract rate and the vendor shall be entitled to the rents and profits of the property up to the actual date of closing.

Under general condition 25(b), if the vendor is in default and has not been ready, willing and able to complete on the closing date, he is obliged to give the purchaser at least five working days' notice of any proposed new closing date.

General condition 25(c) provides that the vendor shall not be entitled to delay the closing of the sale solely because there is a dispute as to whether interest is payable or there is a dispute as to the amount of interest payable. However, the condition provides that the sale shall be closed without prejudice to the vendor's right to pursue his claim for interest.

5.3.7.4 Signing: 'in trust' or 'as agent'

General condition 30 deals with the situation where the contract has been signed 'in Trust' or 'as Agent' without identifying the true purchaser. The condition provides that the person who signs the memorandum is personally liable to complete the sale 'unless and until he shall have disclosed to the Vendor the name of his principal or other such party'.

5.3.7.5 Failure to pay deposit

General conditions 31 and 32 deal with the situation where there is a failure to pay in full the deposit or where the deposit cheque has not been honoured. If either of these events occur then the vendor may elect either:

'(a) to treat the Contract evidenced by the Memorandum, the Particulars and Conditions as having been discharged by breach thereof on the Purchaser's part or

(b) to enforce payment of the deposit as a deposit by suing on the cheque or otherwise'.

5.3.7.6 Differences: errors

General condition 33 deals with differences and errors. This has already been dealt with at **5.3.6.10** in the context of the vendor's obligations under the contract.

5.3.7.7 Rescission

General conditions 37, 38 and 39 relate to the situation where the sale is rescinded in accordance with any of the provisions of the Contract for Sale. The conditions provide that, where there is rescission, the purchaser is entitled to a refund of his deposit without interest and the purchaser must submit to the vendor all documents in his possession belonging to the vendor and procure the calculation of any entry relating to the sale in any register.

If the vendor does not return the deposit to the purchaser within five working days from the date upon which the sale has been rescinded, the purchaser is entitled to interest (at the rate specified at the definition section) from the expiration of a period of five days until actual payment.

5.3.7.8 Completion notices

General condition 40 deals with the issue of completion notices where one of the parties fails to complete the sale on the closing date.

Condition 40 deals with all contracts of sale where time is not of the essence in respect of the closing date. While, from a preliminary viewpoint, it may seem sensible to make time of the essence of the contract, in practice this creates as many difficulties for the vendor as it does for the purchaser.

If, for any reason, the vendor is unable to complete on the day, he will be bound by the terms of his own contract.

The purpose of general condition 40 is to enable either party to the contract to make time of the essence, thereby creating a cut-off point.

The condition provides for the issue of twenty-eight-day notices (which are in reality a number of days longer). The period is twenty-eight days after the service of the notice but excluding the date of service. Under general condition 49 the date of service is either the date of delivery or, when posted, the expiration of three working days after the envelope has been put in the post. (General condition 50 also deals with matters in relation to working days and in particular, where the last day for doing something is a day other than a working day, it extends the time to the next following working day.)

The twenty-eight-day notice does not terminate the contract but makes time of the essence of the contract and enables the party giving the notice to exercise his rights under the contract.

The requirement of general condition 40(b) is that notice be given to the other party. While the Law School has drafted a sample notice (set out below), the non-use of this sample will not in itself make the notice defective. The service of this notice is governed by general condition 49. This condition provides for service of the notice by:

(a) delivery;

(b) post; and

(c) by facsimile transmission.

It should be noted that there is no provision for use of the Document Exchange, facsimile or e-mail.

5.3.7.9   Sample notice: general condition 40

Law Society Contract for Sale

IN THE MATTER OF: A Contract dated the   day of 20

VENDOR:
PURCHASER:
CONSIDERATION:

Purchase Price	€	
Less Deposit	€_____	
Balance	€_____	

CLOSING DATE:
INTEREST RATE: 20

                                                                                  per cent per annum

PARTICULARS AND TENURE: ALL THAT (quote exactly from the Particulars and Tenure in the Contract).

<u>NOTICE</u>

TAKE NOTICE that, the closing date in the above Contract having passed without completion having taken place, pursuant to the provisions of the above Contract and without prejudice to the generality thereof pursuant to General Condition 40, the Vendor/Purchaser hereby:

(i)   notifies the Purchaser/Vendor that the Vendor/Purchaser is ready willing and able to complete and has been so ready willing and able to complete from the closing date,

(ii)   (without prejudice to any intermediate right of rescission) gives notice to and calls upon the Purchaser/Vendor to complete the sale herein without any further delay whatever, but in any event within a period of twenty eight days after the service of this notice (excluding the day of service) and in this respect time is hereby made of the essence,

(iii) notifies the Purchaser/Vendor that if the Purchaser/Vendor does not comply with the terms of this Notice within the period referred to in paragraph (ii) hereof he shall be deemed to have failed to comply with the above Contract and the conditions therein in a material respect And in which event the Vendor/Purchaser will enforce against the Purchaser/Vendor without further notice such rights and remedies as may be available to the Vendor/Purchaser at law or in equity, or (without prejudice to such rights and remedies) may invoke and impose the provision of General Condition 41 of the above Contract,

[Additional paragraph required if default is on the part of the Purchaser.]

AND FURTHER TAKE NOTICE that as the sale herein was not completed on or before the closing date by reason of default on the part of the Purchaser and on which date the Vendor was and continues to be ready, willing and able to complete, the Vendor requires that the Purchaser shall pay interest to the Vendor on the balance of the purchase price which remains unpaid, namely € at the stipulated interest rate, namely % per annum (which interest amounts to € per annum of € per diem) for the period between the closing date and the date of actual completion of the sale.

Dated the   day of   20

SIGNED:_____

M/s

Solicitors for the Vendor/Purchaser

of

in the city of

To: Purchaser/Vendor

C/o Solicitors for the Purchaser/Vendor,

of,

in the city of

5.3.7.10   Forfeiture of deposit and resale

General condition 41(a) provides for forfeiture of the deposit by the vendor and the resale of the property. This condition provides that if the property is resold within one year after the closing date:

'the deficiency (if any) arising on such re-sale and all costs and expenses attending the same or on any attempted re-sale shall (without prejudice to such damages to which the Vendor shall otherwise be entitled) be made good to the Vendor by the Purchaser, who shall be allowed credit against same for the deposit so forfeited. Any increase in price obtained by the Vendor on any re-sale, whenever effected, shall belong to the Vendor'.

General condition 41(b) is a new condition which has been inserted in the 2001 contract by way of protection of the solicitor who has held the deposit as stakeholder. It does not limit the purchaser's right to sue the vendor where it is claimed that the deposit has been wrongly forfeited.

5.3.7.11   Damages for default

General condition 42(a) provides that a purchaser who obtains specific performance is not precluded from an award of damages at law or in equity in the event of such order not being complied with.

General condition 42(b) excludes the application of the rule in *Bain v Fothergill*. That rule provided that damages could not be awarded in an action for breach of contract against a vendor who has failed to show good title. The exclusion of this rule places an additional onus on the vendor's solicitor in respect of the preparation of the contract.

5.3.7.12   Arbitration

Condition 51 provides for arbitration between the parties. It sets out the mechanisms for the appointment of the arbitrator and lists the matters in respect of which there must be arbitration between the parties.

These are:

'(a)   whether the rent is or is not a rack rent for the purpose of Condition 10(c), or

(b)   the identification of the Apportionment Date, or the treatment or quantification of any item pursuant to the provisions for apportionment in the Conditions, or

(c)   any issue on foot of Condition 33, including the applicability of said Condition, and the amount of compensation payable thereunder, or

(d)   the materiality of any matter for the purpose of Condition 36(a), or

(e)   the materiality of damage or any other question involving any of the provisions in Conditions 43, 44 and 45 including the amount of compensation (if any) payable, or

(f)   whether any particular item or thing is or is not included in the Sale, or otherwise as to the nature or condition thereof.'

General Conditions of Sale

Law Society of Ireland

GENERAL CONDITIONS OF SALE (2001 EDITION)

PARTICULARS
and
CONDITIONS OF SALE
of

*SALE BY PRIVATE TREATY
*SALE BY AUCTION

to be held at

on   the   day of   ,200

at   o'clock

*Auctioneer:

*Address:

Vendor:

Vendor's Solicitor:

Address:

Reference:

_____

*Delete, if inappropriate

WARNING: IT IS RECOMMENDED THAT THE WITHIN SHOULD NOT BE COMPLETED WITHOUT PRIOR LEGAL ADVICE

FAMILY HOME PROTECTION ACT, 1976 SPOUSAL CONSENT

I, being the Spouse of the under-named Vendor hereby, for the purposes of Section 3, Family Home Protection Act, 1976, consent to the proposed sale of the property described in the within Particulars at the price mentioned below.

SIGNED by the said Spouse
in the presence of:

MEMORANDUM OF AGREEMENT made this   day of   200
BETWEEN

of

PPS Number(s)   ('VENDOR')

AND

of

PPS Number(s)   ('PURCHASER')

whereby it is agreed that the Vendor shall sell and the Purchaser shall purchase in accordance with the annexed Special and General Conditions of Sale the property described in the within Particulars at the Purchase Price mentioned below.

Purchase Price _____   Closing Date: _____

less deposit   _____   Interest Rate: _____ per cent per annum

Balance   _____

SIGNED   _____   SIGNED   _____

                 _____   _____
                              (Vendor)   (Purchaser)

Witness   _____   Witness   _____

Occupation   _____   Occupation   _____

Address   _____   Address   _____

                 _____   _____

                 _____   _____

(*For Sale by Auction*)   As Stakeholder   I/We   acknowledge receipt of Bank Draft/Cheque for _____ in respect of deposit.

SIGNED _____

GENERAL CONDITIONS OF SALE

PARTICULARS AND TENURE

DOCUMENTS SCHEDULE

SEARCHES SCHEDULE

1. Negative Search in the Registry of Deeds on the Index of Names only for all acts affecting the Subject Property by the Vendor from the   day of

and

SPECIAL CONDITIONS

1. Save where the context otherwise requires or implies or the text hereof expresses to the contrary, the definitions and provisions as to interpretation set forth in the within General Conditions shall be applied for the purposes of these Special Conditions.

2. The said General Conditions shall:

    (a) apply to the sale in so far as the same are not hereby altered or varied, and these Special Conditions shall prevail in case of any conflict between them and the General Conditions

    (b) be read and construed without regard to any amendment therein, unless such amendment shall be referred to specifically in these Special Conditions.

3. In addition to the Purchase Price, the Purchaser shall pay to the Vendor an amount equivalent to such Value-Added Tax as shall be exigible in relation to the sale or (as the case may be) the Assurance, same to be calculated in accordance with the provisions of the Value Added Tax Act, 1972, and to be paid on completion of the sale or forthwith upon receipt by the Purchaser of an appropriate invoice (whichever shall be the later).

(It may be appropriate to delete this Condition or, in certain assignments or surrenders of leasehold interests, to adjust its wording).

84

NON-TITLE INFORMATION

Query   Reply (Please tick and / or insert comments as appropriate)

1. SERVICES

	Yes	No	Comment

i. How is the Subject Property serviced as to:
   (a) drainage;
   (b) water supply;
   (c) electricity;
   (d) gas; and
   (g) otherwise.

ii. Have the services (including roads, lanes, footpaths, sewers and drains) abutting or servicing the Subject Property been taken over by the Local Authority.

Will a letter from the Local Authority or a solicitor's certificate to vouch the position be furnished on or before closing.

If services are not in charge, are there appropriate easements and indemnities in existence.

iii. Is the Subject Property serviced by:
   (a) septic tank; or,
   (b) private drainage scheme.

iv. Is the Subject Property serviced for television and if so is it by;
   (a) Cable T.V.;
   (b) Satellite Dish;
   (c) MMDF;
   (d) TV aerial owned by Vendor; or
   (e) TV aerial owned by another.

If (b) or (d) applies, will it be included in the Purchase Price.

v. Is there a telephone line to be supplied with the Subject Property.

vi. Is there an ISDN line to be supplied with the Subject Property.

	Yes	No	Comment

2. CONTENTS

i. Are there any contents included in the Purchase Price.

   If so, give Vendor's estimate of value.

ii. Are there any fixtures, fittings or chattels included in this Sale which are the subject of any Lease, Rent, Hire Purchase Agreement or Chattel Mortgage.

   If so, furnish now the Agreement and on closing proof of payment to date or discharge thereof.

3. OUTGOINGS

i. What is the Rateable Valuation of:
   (a) Lands;
   (b) Buildings.

ii. Give particulars of any other periodic or annual charge which affects the Subject Property or any part of it.

NOTE

These General Conditions are not to be altered or deleted other than by way of Special Condition. A Special Condition altering or deleting a General Condition should give the reason for such variation, unless manifestly evident.

Special Conditions should be utilised in instances where it is required to adopt Recommendations or Advices of the Law Society or of any Committee associated with it, where such Recommendations or Advices are at variance with provisions expressed in the General Conditions.

General Conditions of Sale

DEFINITIONS

1. In these General Conditions:

   'Conditions' means the attached Special Conditions and these General Conditions

   'Documents Schedule', *'Searches Schedule'* and *'Special Conditions'* mean respectively the attached Documents Schedule, Searches Schedule and Special Conditions.

   'Memorandum' means the Memorandum of Agreement on Page 1 hereof

   'Particulars' means the Particulars and Tenure on Page 2 hereof and any extension of the same

   'Purchaser' means the party identified as such in the Memorandum

   'Sale' means the transaction evidenced by the Memorandum, the Particulars and the Conditions

   'Subject Property' means the property or interest in property which is the subject of the Sale

   'Vendor' means the party identified as such in the Memorandum.

2. In the Conditions save where the context otherwise requires or implies:

   'Apportionment Date' means either (a) the later of (i) the Closing Date (as defined hereunder) and (ii) such subsequent date from which delay in completing the Sale shall cease to be attributable to default on the part of the Vendor or (b) in the event of the Vendor exercising the right referred to in Condition 25 (a)(ii) hereunder, the date of actual completion of the Sale or (c) such other date as may be agreed by the Vendor and the Purchaser to be the Apportionment Date for the purpose of this definition

   'Assurance' means the document or documents whereby the Sale is to be carried into effect

   'Closing Date' means the date specified as such in the Memorandum, or, if no date is specified, the first Working Day after the expiration of five weeks computed from the Date of Sale

   'Competent Authority' includes the State, any Minister thereof, Government Department, State Authority, Local Authority, Planning Authority, Sanitary Authority, Building Control Authority, Fire Authority, Statutory Undertaker or any Department, Body or person by statutory provision or order for the time being in force authorised directly or indirectly to control, regulate, modify or restrict the development, use or servicing of land or buildings, or empowered to acquire land by compulsory process

   'Date of Sale' means the date of the auction when the Sale shall have been by auction, and otherwise means the date upon which the contract for the Sale shall have become binding on the Vendor and the Purchaser

'*Development*' has the meaning ascribed to it by the Local Government (Planning and Development Act) 1963 or by the Planning and Development Act, 2000 which ever meaning shall be applicable to the circumstances

'*Lease*' includes (a) a fee farm grant and every contract (whether or not in writing or howsoever effected, derived or evidenced) whereby the relationship of Landlord and Tenant is or is intended to be created and whether for any freehold or leasehold estate or interest and (b) licences and agreements relating to the occupation and use of land, cognate words being construed accordingly

'*Non-Title Information Sheet*' means the Non-Title Information sheet attached hereto

'*Planning Legislation*' means the Local Government (Planning and Development) Acts 1963 to 1999, the Planning and Development Act, 2000, Building Bye Laws, the Building Control Act 1990, and all regulations made under those Acts

'*Purchased Chattels*' means such chattels, fittings, tenant's fixtures and other items as are included in the Sale

'*Purchase Price*' means the Purchase Price specified in the Memorandum PROVIDED HOWEVER that, if the Sale provides for additional moneys to be paid by the Purchaser for goodwill, crops or Purchased Chattels, the expression '*Purchase Price*' shall be extended to include such additional moneys

'*Requisitions*' include Requisitions on the title or titles as such of the Subject Property and with regard to rents, outgoings, rights, covenants, conditions, liabilities (actual or potential), planning and kindred matters and taxation issues material to such property

'*Stipulated Interest Rate*' means the interest rate specified in the Memorandum, or, if no rate is so specified, such rate as shall equate to 4 per centum per annum above the Court Rate obtaining pursuant to Section 22, Courts Act, 1981 and ruling at the date from which interest is to run

'*Working Day*' does not include any Saturday or Sunday or any Bank or Public Holiday or any of the seven days immediately succeeding Christmas Day.

INTERPRETATION

3.   In the Conditions save where the context otherwise requires or implies:

Words importing the masculine gender only include the feminine, neuter and common genders, and words importing the singular number only include the plural number and vice versa

The words 'Vendor' and 'Purchaser' respectively include (where appropriate) parties deriving title under them or either of them and shall apply to any one or more of several Vendors and Purchasers as the case may be and so that the stipulations in the Conditions contained shall be capable of being enforced on a joint and several basis

Any condition (or, as the case may be, any part of any condition) herein contained, not going to the root of the Contract, which shall be or become void, illegal or invalid or shall contravene any legislation for the time being in force, shall, while the same shall continue to be void, illegal, invalid, or so in contravention be deemed to have been severed and omitted from the Conditions PROVIDED HOWEVER that neither its inclusion in the first instance nor its deemed severance and omission as aforesaid shall prejudice the enforceability of the Conditions nor affect or curtail the other stipulations and provisions herein set forth

Unless the contrary appears, any reference hereunder:

(a)   to a particular Condition shall be to such of these General Conditions of Sale as is identified by said reference

(b) to a Statute or Regulation or a combination of Statutes or Regulations shall include any extension, amendment, modification or re-enactment thereof, and any Rule, Regulation, Order or Instrument made thereunder, and for the time being in force

Headings and marginal notes inserted in the Conditions shall not affect the construction thereof nor shall the same have any contractual significance.

AUCTION

4.   Where the Sale is by auction, the following provisions shall apply:

(a)   the Vendor may divide the property set forth in the Particulars into lots and sub-divide, consolidate or alter the order of sale of any lots

(b)   there shall be a reserve price for the Subject Property whether the same shall comprise the whole or any part of the property set forth in the Particulars and the Auctioneer may refuse to accept any bid. If any dispute shall arise as to any bidding the Auctioneer shall (at his option) either determine the dispute or again put up the property in question at the last undisputed bid. No person shall advance at a bidding a sum less than that fixed by the Auctioneer, and no accepted bid shall be retracted. Subject to the foregoing, the highest accepted bidder shall be the Purchaser

(c)   the Vendor may:

(i)   bid himself, or by an agent, up to the reserve price

(ii)   withdraw the whole of the property set forth in the Particulars or, where such property has been divided into lots, withdraw any one or more of such lots at any time before the same has been sold without disclosing the reserve price

(d)   the Purchaser shall forthwith pay to the Vendor's Solicitor as stakeholder a deposit of ten per centum (10%) of the Purchase Price in part payment thereof, and shall execute an agreement in the form of the Memorandum to complete the purchase of the Subject Property in accordance with the Conditions.

PRIVATE TREATY SALE

5.   Where the sale is by private treaty, the following provisions shall apply:

(a)   the Purchaser shall, on or before the Date of Sale, pay to the Vendor's Solicitor a deposit of the amount stated in the Memorandum in part payment of the Purchase Price, which deposit is, with effect on and from the Date of Sale, to be held by the said Solicitor as stakeholder

(b)   if notwithstanding Condition 5(a) a part of such deposit has been or is paid to any other person appointed or nominated by the Vendor, that other person, with effect as from the Date of Sale, shall be deemed to receive or to have received said part as stakeholder

(c)   any moneys paid by way of deposit by or on behalf of the Purchaser prior to the Date of Sale to the Vendor's Solicitor or to any such other person as aforesaid shall, up to the Date of Sale, be held by the recipient thereof as trustee for the Purchaser.

The Following Conditions Apply Whether the Sale is by Auction or by Private Treaty

PURCHASER ON NOTICE OF CERTAIN DOCUMENTS

6. The documents specified in the Documents Schedule or copies thereof have been available for inspection by the Purchaser or his Solicitor prior to the Date of Sale. If all or any of the Subject Property is stated in the Particulars or in the Special Conditions to be held under a lease or to be subject to any covenants, conditions, rights, liabilities or restrictions, and the lease or other document containing the same is specified in the Documents Schedule, the Purchaser, whether availing of such opportunity of inspection or not, shall be deemed to have purchased with full knowledge of the contents thereof, notwithstanding any partial statement of such contents in the Particulars or in the Conditions.

DELIVERY OF TITLE

7. Within seven Working Days from the Date of Sale, the Vendor shall deliver or send by post to the Purchaser or his Solicitor copies of the documents necessary to vouch the title to be shown in accordance with the Conditions.

TITLE

8. (a)   The Title to be shown to the Subject Property shall be such as is set forth in the Special Conditions

    (b)   Where the title to be shown to the whole or any part of the Subject Property is based on possession, the Vendor shall, in addition to vouching that title and dealing with such further matters as are required of him by the Conditions, furnish to the Purchaser on or before completion of the Sale a certificate from the Revenue Commissioners to the effect (i) that the Subject Property or (as the case may be) such part of the same as aforesaid is not charged with any of the taxes covered by the provisions of Section 146, Finance Act, 1994 as amended by Section 128 Finance Act, 1996 or (ii) that the Revenue Commissioners are satisfied that any such charge will be discharged within a time considered by them to be reasonable

    (c)   Save as stipulated in the Special Conditions the Vendor shall, prior to or at the completion of the Sale, discharge all mortgages and charges for the payment of money (other than items apportionable under Condition 27(b)) which affect the Subject Property.

FOREIGN VENDOR

9. Where the Vendor is a company, corporation, association or other similar entity incorporated, formed or established outside the State, the Vendor shall disclose this fact in the Special Conditions.

LEASEHOLD TITLE

10. (a)   Where any of the Subject Property is held under a lease, the Purchaser shall not call for or investigate the title of the grantor or lessor to make the same,

but shall conclusively assume that it was well and validly made, and is a valid and subsisting lease.

(b) Where any of the Subject Property is stated to be held under a lease or an agreement therefor then:

(i) no Objection or Requisition shall be made or indemnity required on account of such lease or agreement being (if such is the case) a sublease or agreement therefor, or on account of any superior lease comprising other property apart from the Subject Property or reserving a larger rent, or on the ground of any superior owner not having concurred in any apportionment or exclusive charge of rent

(ii) no Objection or Requisition shall be made by reason of any discrepancy between the covenants, conditions and provisions contained in any sublease and those in any superior lease, unless such as could give rise to forfeiture or a right of re-entry

(iii) the production of the receipt for the last gale of rent reserved by the lease or agreement therefor, under which the whole or any part of the Subject Property is held, (without proof of the title or authority of the person giving such receipt) shall (unless the contrary appears) be accepted as conclusive evidence that all rent accrued due has been paid and all covenants and conditions in such lease or agreement and in every (if any) superior lease have been duly performed and observed or any breaches thereof (past or continuing) effectively waived or sanctioned up to the actual completion of the Sale, whether or not it shall appear that the lessor or reversioner was aware of such breaches. If the said rent (not being a rack rent) shall not have been paid in circumstances where the party entitled to receive the same is not known to the Vendor, or if the Subject Property is indemnified against payment of rent, the production of a Statutory Declaration so stating shall (unless the contrary appears) be accepted as such conclusive evidence, provided that the Declaration further indicates that no notices or rent demands have been served on or received by the Vendor under the lease or agreement on foot of which the Subject Property is held; that the Vendor has complied with all the covenants (other than those in respect of payment of rent) on the part of the lessee and the conditions contained in such lease or agreement, and that he is not aware of any breaches thereof either by himself or by any of his predecessors in title

(iv) if any of the Subject Property is held under a lease or agreement for lease requiring consent to alienation, the Vendor shall apply for and endeavour to obtain such consent, and the Purchaser shall deal expeditiously and constructively with and shall satisfy all reasonable requirements of the lessor in relation to the application therefor, but the Vendor shall not be required to institute legal proceedings to enforce the issue of any such consent or otherwise as to the withholding of the same. If such consent shall have been refused or shall not have been procured and written evidence of the same furnished to the Purchaser on or before the Closing Date, or if any such consent is issued subject to a condition, which the Purchaser on reasonable grounds refuses to accept, either party may rescind the Sale by seven days prior notice to the other.

PRIOR TITLE

11. (a) The title to the Subject Property prior to the date of the instrument specified in the Special Conditions as the commencement of title, whether or not

appearing by recital, inference or otherwise, shall not be required, objected to or investigated.

(b) In the case of registered freehold or leasehold land registered under the Registration of Title Acts, 1891 to 1942 or the Registration of Title Act, 1964 the provisions of subparagraph (a) of this Condition shall apply without prejudice to Sections 52 and 115 of the last mentioned Act and shall not disentitle the Purchaser from investigating the possibility of there having been a voluntary disposition on the title within the period of twelve years immediately preceding the Date of Sale or a disposition falling within Section 121, Succession Act, 1965 as extended by Section 25 (5), Family Law Act, 1995 and the Vendor shall be required to deal with all points properly taken in or arising out of such investigation.

INTERMEDIATE TITLE

12. Where in the Special Conditions it is provided that the title is to commence with a particular instrument and then to pass to a second instrument or to a specified event, the title intervening between the first instrument and the second instrument or the specified event, whether or not appearing by recital, inference or otherwise, shall not be required, objected to or investigated.

REGISTERED LAND

13. Where all or any of the Subject Property consists of freehold or leasehold registered land registered under the Registration of Title Acts, 1891 to 1942 ('the Acts of 1891 to 1942') or the Registration of Title Act, 1964 ('the Act of 1964') then:

(a) if the registration is subject to equities under the Acts of 1891 to 1942, the Purchaser shall not require the equities to be discharged, but the Vendor shall, with the copy documents to be delivered or sent in accordance with Condition 7, furnish sufficient evidence of title prior to first registration or otherwise to enable the Purchaser to procure their discharge

(b) if the registration is with a possessory title under the Act of 1964 the Purchaser shall not require the Vendor to be registered with an absolute title, but the Vendor shall, with the copy documents to be delivered or sent in accordance with Condition 7, furnish sufficient evidence of the title prior to such registration or otherwise to enable the Purchaser to be registered with an absolute title

(c) the Vendor shall, with the copy documents to be delivered or sent in accordance with Condition 7, furnish to the Purchaser a copy of the Land Registry Folio or Folios relating to the Subject Property written up-to-date (or as nearly as practicable up-to-date), together with a copy of the relevant Land Registry map or file plan

(d) the Vendor shall furnish a Statutory Declaration, by some person competent to make it, confirming that there are not in existence any burdens which under the Act of 1964 affect registered land without registration, save such (if any) as are specifically mentioned in the Particulars or the Special Conditions

(e) if the Land Certificate has been issued to the Land Commission or if no such Certificate has been issued, the Purchaser shall not be entitled to require such Certificate to be produced, handed over on completion or issued

(f) the Purchaser shall procure himself to be registered as owner of the Subject Property at his own expense

(g) in the event of the Subject Property being subject to a Land Purchase Annuity the Vendor shall, prior to completion, redeem the same or (as the case may be) such proportion thereof as may be allocated to the Subject Property

(h) where the Subject Property is part only of the lands in a Folio, the Vendor shall (i) do everything within the reasonable power or procurement of the Vendor to satisfy within a reasonable time any Land Registry mapping queries arising on the registration of the Assurance to the Purchaser so far as it affects that land, and (ii) pay and discharge any outlay to the Land Registry which ought properly to be paid by the Vendor, including additional fees attributable to default on the part of the Vendor.

IDENTITY

14. The Purchaser shall accept such evidence of identity as may be gathered from the descriptions in the documents of title plus (if circumstances require) a statutory declaration to be made by a competent person, at the Purchaser's expense, that the Subject Property has been held and enjoyed for at least twelve years in accordance with the title shown. The Vendor shall be obliged to furnish such information as is in his possession relative to the identity and extent of the Subject Property, but shall not be required to define exact boundaries, fences, ditches, hedges or walls or to specify which (if any) of the same are of a party nature, nor shall the Vendor be required to identify parts of the Subject Property held under different titles.

RIGHTS—LIABILITIES—CONDITION OF SUBJECT PROPERTY

15. The Vendor shall disclose before the Date of Sale, in the Particulars the Special Conditions or otherwise, all easements, rights, reservations, exceptions, privileges, covenants, restrictions, rents, taxes and other liabilities (not already known to the Purchaser or apparent from inspection) which are known by the Vendor to affect the Subject Property and are likely to affect it following completion of the Sale.

16. Subject to Condition 15, the Purchaser shall be deemed to buy:

(a) with full notice of the actual state and condition of the Subject Property and

(b) subject to (i) all leases (if any) mentioned in the Particulars or in the Special Conditions and (ii) all easements, rights, reservations, exceptions, privileges, covenants, restrictions, rents, taxes, liabilities, outgoings and all incidents of tenure affecting the Subject Property.

REQUISITIONS

17. The Purchaser shall, within fourteen Working Days after the later of (i) the Date of Sale or (ii) the delivery of the copy documents of title in accordance with Condition 7, send to the Vendor's Solicitor a written statement of his Objections (if any) on the title and his Requisitions. Any Objection or Requisition not made within the time aforesaid and not going to the root of the title shall be deemed to have been waived. The Vendor's Replies to any Objections or Requisitions shall be answered by the Purchaser in writing within seven Working Days after the delivery thereof and so on toties quoties, and, if not so answered, shall be considered to have been accepted as satisfactory. In all respects time shall be deemed to be of the essence of this Condition.

GENERAL CONDITIONS OF SALE

18. If the Purchaser shall make and insist on any Objection or Requisition as to the title, the Assurance to him or any other matter relating or incidental to the Sale, which the Vendor shall, on the grounds of unreasonable delay or expense or other reasonable ground, be unable or unwilling to remove or comply with, the Vendor shall be at liberty (notwithstanding any intermediate negotiation or litigation or attempts to remove or comply with the same) by giving to the Purchaser or his Solicitor not less than five Working Days notice to rescind the Sale. In that case, unless the Objection or Requisition in question shall in the meantime have been withdrawn, the Sale shall be rescinded at the expiration of such notice.

SEARCHES

19. The Purchaser shall be furnished with the searches (if any) specified in the Searches Schedule and any searches already in the Vendor's possession, which are relevant to the title or titles on offer. Any other searches required by the Purchaser must be obtained by him at his own expense. Where the Special Conditions provide that the title shall commence with a particular instrument and then pass to a second instrument or to a specified event, the Vendor shall not be obliged to explain and discharge any act which appears on a search covering the period between such particular instrument and the date of the second instrument or specified event, unless same goes to the root of the title. Subject as aforesaid the Vendor shall explain and discharge any acts appearing on Searches covering the period from the date stipulated or implied for the commencement of the title to the date of actual completion.

ASSURANCE

20. (a) On payment of all moneys payable by him in respect of the Sale, and subject to the provisions of Section 980, Taxes Consolidation Act, 1997, and (if relevant) to those contained in Section 107, Finance Act, 1993 (in relation to Residential Property Tax), the Purchaser shall be entitled to a proper Assurance of the Subject Property from the Vendor and all other (if any) necessary parties, such Assurance to be prepared by and at the expense of the Purchaser. The draft thereof shall be submitted to the Vendor's Solicitor not less than seven Working Days, and the engrossment not less than four Working Days, before the Closing Date. The delivery of the said draft or engrossment shall not prejudice any outstanding Objection or Requisition validly made.

(b) If the Stamp Duty (Particulars to be Delivered) Regulations, 1995 apply to the Sale, the Vendor shall, on or before handing over the Assurance, furnish to the Purchaser the Form referred to in such Regulations duly completed in accordance therewith.

VACANT POSSESSION

21. Subject to any provision to the contrary in the Particulars or in the Conditions or implied by the nature of the transaction, the Purchaser shall be entitled to vacant possession of the Subject Property on completion of the Sale.

LEASES

22. Where the Subject Property is sold subject to any lease, a copy of the same (or, if the provisions thereof have not been reduced to writing, such evidence of its nature and terms as the Vendor shall be able to supply) together with copies of any notices in the Vendor's possession served by or on the lessee (and of continuing and material

94

relevance) shall, prior to the Sale, be made available for inspection by the Purchaser or his Solicitor.

23.   Unless the Special Conditions provide to the contrary, the Purchaser shall be entitled to assume that, at the Date of Sale, the lessee named in any such Lease (as is referred to in Condition 22) is still the lessee; that there has been no variation in the terms and conditions of said Lease (other than such as may be evident from an inspection of the Subject Property or apparent from the Particulars or the documents furnished to the Purchaser prior to the Sale), and that the said terms and conditions (save those pertaining to the actual state and condition of the Subject Property) have been complied with.

COMPLETION AND INTEREST

24.   (a)   The Sale shall be completed and the balance of the Purchase Price paid by the Purchaser on or before the Closing Date.

       (b)   Completion shall take place at the Office of the Vendor's Solicitor.

25.   (a)   If by reason of any default on the part of the Purchaser, the purchase shall not have been completed on or before the later of (a) the Closing Date or (b) such subsequent date whereafter delay in completing shall not be attributable to default on the part of the Vendor

              (i)   the Purchaser shall pay interest to the Vendor on the balance of the Purchase Price remaining unpaid at the Stipulated Interest Rate for the period between the Closing Date (or as the case may be such subsequent date as aforesaid) and the date of actual completion of the Sale. Such interest shall accrue from day to day and shall be payable before and after any judgment and

              (ii)   the Vendor shall in addition to being entitled to receive such interest, have the right to take the rents and profits less the outgoings of the Subject Property up to the date of the actual completion of the Sale

       (b)   If the Vendor by reason of his default shall not be able, ready and willing to complete the Sale on the Closing Date he shall thereafter give to the Purchaser at least five Working Days prior notice of a date upon which he shall be so able ready and willing and the Purchaser shall not before the expiration of that notice be deemed to be in default for the purpose of this Condition provided that no such notice shall be required if the Vendor is prevented from being able and ready to complete or to give said notice by reason of the act or default of the Purchaser

       (c)   The Vendor shall not be entitled to delay completion solely because of a dispute between the parties with regard to liability for such interest or as to the amount of interest payable PROVIDED ALWAYS that such completion and the delivery of any Assurance on foot of these Conditions shall be had strictly without prejudice to the right of the Vendor to pursue his claim for interest.

26.   The submission of an Apportionment Account made up to a particular date or other corresponding step taken in anticipation of completing the Sale shall not per se preclude the Vendor from exercising his rights under the provisions of Condition 25 and in the event of such exercise the said Apportionment Account or the said other corresponding step shall (if appropriate) be deemed not to have been furnished or taken, and the Vendor shall be entitled to furnish a further Apportionment Account.

APPORTIONMENT AND POSSESSION

27. (a) Subject to the stipulations contained in the Conditions, the Purchaser, on pay-ing the Purchase Price shall be entitled to vacant possession of the Subject Property or (as the case may be) the rents and profits thereout with effect from the Apportionment Date

(b) All rents, profits, rates, outgoings and moneys (including rent, outgoings and money payable in advance but not including impositions derived from hypo-thecation) referable to the Subject Property shall for the purpose of this Condition, be apportioned (whether apportionable by law or not) on a day to day basis as at the Apportionment Date, up to which the liability for or the entitlement to the same shall (subject to apportionment as aforesaid to accord with the position obtaining as to moneys paid or due at such date) be for the account of the Vendor and thereafter for that of the Purchaser provided that if completion shall have been delayed through the default of the Vendor the Purchaser may opt for apportionment under this Condition as at the Closing Date or at the date at which the Purchaser (if also in default) shall have ceased to have been so in default whichever shall be the later

(c) In the implementation of this Condition the Vendor shall be regarded as being the owner of the Subject Property until midnight on such date as is appropri-ate for apportionment purposes

(d) The balance of the Purchase Price shall (where appropriate) be adjusted upwards or downwards to accommodate apportionments calculated pursuant to this Condition and the expression 'balance of the Purchase Price' where used in the Conditions shall be construed accordingly

(e) To the extent that same shall be unknown at the Apportionment Date (or shall not then be readily ascertainable) amounts to be apportioned hereunder, including any amount apportionable pursuant to Condition 27(f), shall be apportioned provisionally on a fair estimate thereof, and, upon ascertainment of the actual figures, a final apportionment shall be made, and the difference between it and the provisional apportionment shall be refunded by the Vendor or the Purchaser (as the case may be) to the other within ten Working Days of the liable party becoming aware of the amount of such difference

(f) Excise and kindred duties payable in respect of the Subject Property or any licence attached thereto shall be apportioned on a day to day basis as at the Apportionment Date up to which the liability for the same shall be for the account of the Vendor and thereafter for that of the Purchaser and Condition 27 (c) shall apply for the purposes of such apportionment.

SECTION 45, LAND ACT, 1965

28. Where Section 45, Land Act, 1965 applies, the Purchaser shall, at his own expense, procure any such Certificate or Consent as may be necessary thereunder for the vesting of the Subject Property in him or his nominee and the Sale is not conditional upon such consent being obtained

COMPULSORY REGISTRATION

29. (a) If all or any of the Subject Property is unregistered land the registration of which was compulsory prior to the Date of Sale the Vendor shall be obliged to procure such registration prior to completion of the Sale

(b) If all or any of the Subject Property is unregistered land, the registration of which shall become compulsory at or subsequent to the Date of Sale, the Vendor shall not be under any obligation to procure such registration but shall at or prior to such completion furnish to the Purchaser a Map of the Subject Property complying with the requirements of the Land Registry as then recognised and further the Vendor shall, if so requested within two years after completion of the Sale, by and at the expense of the Purchaser, supply any additional information, which he may reasonably be able to supply, and produce and furnish any documents in his possession that may be required to effect such registration.

SIGNING 'IN TRUST' OR 'AS AGENT'

30. A Purchaser who signs the Memorandum 'in Trust', 'as Trustee' or 'as Agent', or with any similar qualification or description without therein specifying the identity of the principal or other party for whom he so signs, shall be personally liable to complete the Sale, and to fulfil all such further stipulations on the part of the Purchaser as are contained in the Conditions, unless and until he shall have disclosed to the Vendor the name of his principal or other such party.

FAILURE TO PAY DEPOSIT

31. The failure by the Purchaser to pay in full the deposit hereinbefore specified as payable by him shall constitute a breach of condition entitling the Vendor to terminate the Sale or to sue the Purchaser for damages or both but such entitlement shall be without prejudice to any rights otherwise available to the Vendor.

32. In case a cheque taken for the deposit (having been presented and whether or not it has been re-presented) shall not have been honoured, then and on that account the Vendor may (without prejudice to any rights otherwise available to him) elect either:

(a) to treat the Contract evidenced by the Memorandum, the Particulars and the Conditions as having been discharged by breach thereof on the Purchaser's part

or

(b) to enforce payment of the deposit as a deposit by suing on the cheque or otherwise.

DIFFERENCES—ERRORS

33. (a) In this Condition 'error' includes any omission, non-disclosure, discrepancy, difference, inaccuracy, mis-statement or mis-representation made in the Memorandum, the Particulars or the Conditions or the Non-Title Information Sheet or in the course of any representation, response or negotiations leading to the Sale, and whether in respect of measurements, quantities, descriptions or otherwise

(b) The Purchaser shall be entitled to be compensated by the Vendor for any loss suffered by the Purchaser in his bargain relative to the Sale as a result of an error made by or on behalf of the Vendor provided however that no compensation shall be payable for loss of trifling materiality unless attributable to recklessness or fraud on the part of the Vendor nor in respect of any matter of which the Purchaser shall be deemed to have had notice under Condition 16(a) nor in relation to any error in a location or similar plan furnished for identification only

(c) Nothing in the Memorandum, the Particulars or the Conditions shall:

(i) entitle the Vendor to require the Purchaser to accept property which differs substantially from the property agreed to be sold whether in quantity, quality, tenure or otherwise, if the Purchaser would be prejudiced materially by reason of any such difference

or

(ii) affect the right of the Purchaser to rescind or repudiate the Sale where compensation for a claim attributable to a material error made by or on behalf of the Vendor cannot be reasonably assessed

(d) Save as aforesaid, no error shall annul the Sale or entitle the Vendor or the Purchaser (as the case may be) to be discharged therefrom.

DOCUMENTS OF TITLE RELATING TO OTHER PROPERTY

34. (a) Documents of title relating to other property as well as to the Subject Property shall be retained by the Vendor or other person entitled to the possession thereof

(b) where the property is sold in lots, all documents of title relating to more than one lot shall be retained by the Vendor, until the completion of the Sales of all the lots comprised in such documents, and shall then (unless they also relate to any property retained by the Vendor) be handed over to such of the Purchasers as the Vendor shall consider best entitled thereto

(c) the Vendor shall give to the Purchaser (and where the property is sold in lots, to the Purchaser of each lot) certified copies of all documents retained under this Condition and pertinent to the title to be furnished (other than documents of record, of which plain copies only will be given)

(d) subject as hereinafter provided, the Vendor shall give the usual statutory acknowledgement of the right of production and undertaking for safe custody of all documents (other than documents of record) retained by him under this Condition and pertinent to the title to be furnished. Such acknowledgement and undertaking shall be prepared by and at the expense of the Purchaser

(e) if the Vendor is retaining any unregistered land held wholly or partly under the same title as the Subject Property, the Assurance shall be engrossed in duplicate by and at the expense of the Purchaser, who shall deliver to the Vendor the Counterpart thereof, same having been stamped and registered and (if appropriate) executed by the Purchaser.

DISCLOSURE OF NOTICES

35. Where prior to the Date of Sale

(a) any closing, demolition or clearance order

or

(b) any notice for compulsory acquisition or any other notice (other than such other notice, details of which are required to be entered on the Planning Register pursuant to the requirements of Planning Legislation) made or issued by or at the behest of a Competent Authority in respect of the Subject Property and affecting the same at the Date of Sale has been notified or given to the Vendor (whether personally or by advertisement or posting on the Subject Property or in any other manner) or is otherwise known to the Vendor, or where the Subject Property is, at the Date of Sale, affected by any award or grant, which is or may be repayable by the Vendor's successor in title, then if the Vendor fails to show

(i)   that, before the Date of Sale, the Purchaser received notice or was aware of the matter in question

or

(ii) that the matter in question was apparent from inspection of the Development Plan or the current or published Draft Development Plan for the area within which the Subject Property is situate

or

(iii) that same is no longer applicable or material

or

(iv) that same does not prejudicially affect the value of the Subject Property

or

(v)   that the subject thereof can and will be dealt with fully in the Apportionment Account

the Purchaser may by notice given to the Vendor rescind the Sale.

DEVELOPMENT

In cases where property is affected by an unauthorised development or a breach of Condition/Conditions in a Permission/ Approval amounting to a non-conforming development or where the Bye-Law Amnesty covered by Section 22(7), Building Control Act, 1990 is relevant, it is recommended that same be dealt with expressly by Special Condition.

36. (a) Unless the Special Conditions contain a stipulation to the contrary, the Vendor warrants:

(i)   that there has been no Development of the Subject Property since the 1st day of October, 1964, for which Planning Permission or Building Bye-Law Approval was required by law

or

(ii) that all Planning Permissions and Building Bye-Law Approvals required by law for the Development of the Subject Property as at the Date of Sale were obtained (save in respect of matters of trifling materiality), and that, where implemented, the conditions thereof in relation to and specifically addressed to such Development were complied with substantially

PROVIDED HOWEVER that the foregoing warranty shall not extend to (and the Vendor shall not be required to establish) the obtaining of approvals under the Building Bye-Laws or compliance with such Bye-Laws in respect of Development or works carried out prior to the 13th day of December, 1989 (this proviso being hereinafter in Condition 36 referred to as the 'Proviso')

(b) unless the Special Conditions contain a stipulation to the contrary, the Vendor warrants in all cases where the provisions of the Building Control Act, 1990 or of any Regulation from time to time thereunder apply to the design or Development of the Subject Property or any part of the same or any activities in connection therewith, that there has been substantial compliance with the said provisions in so far as they pertained to such design, Development or activities

(c)   the warranties referred to in (a) and (b) of this Condition shall not extend to any breach of provisions contained in Planning Legislation, which breach has been remedied or is no longer continuing at the Date of Sale.

(d)   the Vendor shall prior to the Date of Sale make available to the Purchaser for inspection or furnish to the Purchaser copies of:

(i)   all such Permissions and Approvals as are referred to in Condition 36 (a) other than in the Proviso

(ii)   all Fire Safety Certificates and (if available) Commencement Notices issued under Regulations made pursuant to the Building Control Act, 1990, and referable to the Subject Property (such Permissions, Approvals and Certificates specified in this Condition 36(d) being hereinafter in Condition 36 referred to as the 'Consents')

and

(iii) (Save where Development is intended to be carried out between the Date of Sale and the date upon which the Sale shall be completed) the documents referred to in Condition 36 (e)

(e)   the Vendor shall, on or prior to completion of the Sale, furnish to the Purchaser

(i)   written confirmation from the Local Authority of compliance with all conditions involving financial contributions or the furnishing of bonds in any such Consents (other than those referred to in the Proviso) PROVIDED HOWEVER that where

the Development authorised by such Consents relates to a residential housing estate of which the Development of the Subject Property forms part

and

such Consents relate to the initial construction of a building on the Subject Property

written confirmation from the Local Authority that the roads and services abutting on the Subject Property have been taken in charge by it shall be accepted as satisfactory evidence of compliance with such conditions, unless the said confirmation discloses a requirement for payment of outstanding moneys

(ii)   a Certificate or Opinion by an Architect or an Engineer (or other professionally qualified person competent so to certify or opine) confirming that, in relation to such Consents (save those referred to in the Proviso)

—   the same relate to the Subject Property

—   (where applicable) the design of the buildings on the Subject Property is in substantial compliance with the Building Control Act, 1990 and the Regulations made thereunder

—   the Development of the Subject Property has been carried out in substantial compliance with such Consents and (where applicable) the requirements of the Building Control Act, 1990 and regulations made thereunder

—   all conditions (other than financial conditions) of such Consents have been complied with substantially and

— in the event of the Subject Property forming part of a larger development, all conditions (other than financial conditions) of such Consents which relate to the overall development have been complied with substantially so far as was reasonably possible in the context of such development as at the date of such Certificate or Opinion

(f) (i) where the Vendor has furnished Certificates or Opinions pursuant to Condition 36 (e), the Vendor shall have no liability on foot of the warranties expressed in Condition 36(a) or 36(b) or either of them in respect of any matter with regard to which such Certificate or Opinion is erroneous or inaccurate, unless the Vendor was aware at the Date of Sale that the same contained any material error or inaccuracy

(ii) if, subsequent to the Date of Sale and prior to the completion thereof, it is established that any such Certificate or Opinion is erroneous or inaccurate, then, if the Vendor fails to show

that before the Date of Sale the Purchaser was aware of the error or inaccuracy

or

that same is no longer relevant or material

or

that same does not prejudicially affect the value of the Subject Property

the Purchaser may by notice given to the Vendor rescind the Sale.

RESCISSION

37. Upon rescission of the Sale in accordance with any of the provisions herein or in the Special Conditions contained or otherwise:

(a) the Purchaser shall be entitled to a return of his deposit (save where it shall lawfully have been forfeited) but without interest thereon

(b) the Purchaser shall remit to the Vendor all documents in his possession belonging to the Vendor and the Purchaser shall at his expense (save where Special Conditions otherwise provide) procure the cancellation of any entry relating to the Sale in any register.

38. If any such deposit as is to be returned pursuant to Condition 37 shall not have been returned to the Purchaser within five Working Days from the date upon which the Sale shall have been rescinded, the Purchaser shall be entitled to interest thereon at the Stipulated Interest Rate from the expiration of the said period of five Working Days to the date upon which the deposit shall have been so returned.

39. The right to rescind shall not be lost by reason only of any intermediate negotiations or attempts to comply with or to remove the issue giving rise to the exercise of such right.

COMPLETION NOTICES

40. Save where time is of the essence in respect of the Closing Date, the following provisions shall apply:

(a) if the Sale be not completed on or before the Closing Date either party may on or after that date (unless the Sale shall first have been rescinded or become void) give to the other party notice to complete the Sale in accordance with this condition, but such notice shall be effective only if the party giving it shall then either be able, ready and willing to complete the Sale or is not so able, ready or willing by reason of the default or misconduct of the other party

(b)   upon service of such notice the party upon whom it shall have been served shall complete the Sale within a period of twenty-eight days after the date of such service (as defined in Condition 49 and excluding the date of service), and in respect of such period time shall be of the essence of the contract but without prejudice to any intermediate right of rescission by either party

(c)   the recipient of any such notice shall give to the party serving the same reasonable advice of his readiness to complete

(d)   if the Purchaser shall not comply with such a notice within the said period (or within any extension thereof which the Vendor may agree) he shall be deemed to have failed to comply with these Conditions in a material respect and the Vendor may enforce against the Purchaser, without further notice, such rights and remedies as may be available to the Vendor at law or in equity, or (without prejudice to such rights and remedies) may invoke and impose the provisions of Condition 41

(e)   if the Vendor does not comply with such a notice within the said period (or within any extension thereof which the Purchaser may agree), then the Purchaser may elect either to enforce against the Vendor, without further notice, such rights and remedies as may be available to the Purchaser at law or in equity or (without prejudice to any right of the Purchaser to damages) to give notice to the Vendor requiring a return to the Purchaser of all moneys paid by him, whether by way of deposit or otherwise, on account of the Purchase Price. Condition 38 shall apply to all moneys so to be returned, the period of five Working Days therein being computed from the date of the giving of such last mentioned notice. If the Purchaser gives such a notice and all the said moneys and interest (if any) are remitted to him, the Purchaser shall no longer be entitled to specific performance of the Sale, and shall return forthwith all documents in his possession belonging to the Vendor, and (at the Vendor's expense) procure the cancellation of any entry relating to the Sale in any register

(f)   the party serving a notice under this Condition may, at the request of or with the consent of the other party, by written communication to the other party extend the term of such notice for one or more specified periods of time, and, in that case, the term of the notice shall be deemed to expire on the last day of such extended period or periods, and the notice shall operate as though such extended period or periods had been specified in this Condition in lieu of the said period of twenty-eight days, and time shall be of the essence in relation to such extended period

(g)   the Vendor shall not be deemed to be other than able, ready and willing to complete for the purposes of this Condition:

(i)   by reason of the fact that the Subject Property has been mortgaged or charged, provided that the funds (including the deposit) receivable on completion shall (after allowing for all prior claims thereon) be sufficient to discharge the aggregate of all amounts payable in satisfaction of such mortgages and charges to the extent that they relate to the Subject Property

or

(ii)   by reason of being unable, not ready or unwilling at the date of service of such notice to deliver vacant possession of the Subject Property provided that (where it is a term of the Sale that vacant possession thereof be given) the Vendor is, upon being given reasonable advice of the other party's intention to close the Sale on a date within the said period of twenty-eight days or any extension thereof pursuant to Condition 40 (f), able, ready and willing to deliver vacant possession of the Subject Property on that date.

FORFEITURE OF DEPOSIT AND RESALE

41. (a) If the Purchaser shall fail in any material respect to comply with any of the Conditions, the Vendor (without prejudice to any rights or remedies available to him at law or in equity) shall be entitled to forfeit the deposit and to such purpose unilaterally to direct his Solicitor to release same to him AND the Vendor shall be at liberty (without being obliged to tender an Assurance) to resell the Subject Property, with or without notice to the Purchaser, either by public auction or private treaty. In the event of the Vendor re-selling the Subject Property within one year after the Closing Date (or within one year computed from the expiration of any period by which the closing may have been extended pursuant to Condition 40) the deficiency (if any) arising on such re-sale and all costs and expenses attending the same or on any attempted re-sale shall (without prejudice to such damages to which the Vendor shall otherwise be entitled) be made good to the Vendor by the Purchaser, who shall be allowed credit against same for the deposit so forfeited. Any increase in price obtained by the Vendor on any re-sale, whenever effected, shall belong to the Vendor.

    (b) A Solicitor acting on any such direction as is referred to in Condition 41(a) shall have no further obligations as stakeholder or otherwise in respect of such deposit to the Vendor or to the Purchaser PROVIDED that he shall have given to the Purchaser notice of the receipt by him of the said direction and the Purchaser shall not within twenty one days of the giving of such notice have instituted and served proceedings disputing the rights alleged by the Vendor to forfeit the deposit.

DAMAGES FOR DEFAULT

42. (a) Neither the Vendor nor the Purchaser, in whose favour an order for specific performance has been made, shall be precluded from an award of damages at law or in equity, in the event of such order not being complied with.

    (b) Notwithstanding any rule of law to the contrary failure on the part of the Vendor to show title to the Subject Property in accordance with the Conditions shall not per se preclude the making of an award for damages to the Purchaser for loss of bargain or otherwise in relation to the Sale.

RISK

43. Subject as hereinafter provided, the Vendor shall be liable for any loss or damage howsoever occasioned (other than by the Purchaser or his Agent) to the Subject Property (and the Purchased Chattels) between the Date of Sale and the actual completion of the Sale BUT any such liability (including liability for consequential or resulting loss) shall not as to the amount thereof exceed the Purchase Price.

44. The liability imposed on the Vendor by Condition 43 shall not apply:

   (a) to inconsequential damage or insubstantial deterioration from reasonable wear and tear in the course of normal occupation and use, and not materially affecting value

   (b) to damage occasioned by operations reasonably undertaken by the Vendor in his removal from, and vacation of the Subject Property, provided that the same are so undertaken with reasonable care

   (c) where any such loss or damage has resulted from a requirement restriction or obligation imposed by a Competent Authority after the Date of Sale.

45. Nothing in Conditions 43 and 44 shall affect:

   (a) the Purchaser's right to specific performance in an appropriate case

   (b) the Purchaser's right to rescind or repudiate the Sale upon the Vendor's failure to deliver the Subject Property substantially in its condition at the Date of Sale (save where such failure shall have been occasioned by the Purchaser or his Agent)

   (c) the operation of the doctrine of conversion

   (d) the Purchaser's right to gains accruing to the Subject Property (or the Purchased Chattels) after the Date of Sale

   (e) the Purchaser's right to effect on or after the Date of Sale his own insurance against loss or damage in respect of the Subject Property or any part of the same (or the Purchased Chattels)

   (f) the rights and liabilities of parties other than the Vendor and the Purchaser

   (g) the rights and liabilities of the Purchaser on foot of any lease subsisting at the Date of Sale, or of any arrangement whereby the Purchaser shall prior to the actual completion of the Sale have been allowed into occupation of the Subject Property or any part thereof (or into possession of the Purchased Chattels).

CHATTELS

46. Unless otherwise disclosed to the Purchaser prior to the Sale the Vendor warrants that, at the actual completion of the Sale, all the Purchased Chattels shall be his unencumbered property and that same shall not be subject to any lease, rental hire, hire-purchase or credit sale agreement or chattel mortgage.

INSPECTION

47. The Vendor shall accede to all such requests as may be made by the Purchaser for the inspection on a reasonable number of occasions and at reasonable times of the Subject Property (and the Purchased Chattels).

NON-MERGER

48. Notwithstanding delivery of the Assurance of the Subject Property to the Purchaser on foot of the Sale, all obligations and provisions designed to survive completion of the Sale and all warranties in the Conditions contained, which shall not have been implemented by the said Assurance, and which shall be capable of continuing or taking effect after such completion, shall enure and remain in full force and effect.

NOTICES

49. Unless otherwise expressly provided, any notice to be given or served on foot of the Conditions shall be in writing, and may (in addition to any other prescribed mode of service) be given:

   (a) by handing same to the intended recipient, and shall be deemed to have been delivered when so handed

   (b) by directing it to the intended recipient, and delivering it by hand, or sending same by prepaid post to:

   (i) such address as shall have been advised by him to the party serving the notice as being that required by the intended recipient for the service of notices,
   or

   (ii) (failing such last mentioned advice) the address of the intended recipient as specified in the Memorandum,

   or

   (iii) (in the event of the intended recipient being a Company) its Registered Office for the time being,

   or

   (iv) the office of the Solicitor representing the intended recipient in relation to the Sale

   (c) by facsimile transmission directed to the office of the Solicitor representing the intended recipient in relation to the Sale

   and any such notice shall be deemed to have been given or served, when delivered, at the time of delivery, and, when posted, at the expiration of three Working Days after the envelope containing the same, and properly addressed, was put in the post and, when sent by facsimile transmission, at the time of its transmission.

TIME LIMITS

50. Where the last day for taking any step on foot of the Conditions or any Notice served thereunder would, but for this provision, be a day other than a Working Day, such last day shall instead be the next following Working Day provided that for the purpose of this Condition the expression 'Working Day' shall not be deemed to include (i) any Saturday, Sunday, Bank or Public Holiday nor (ii) any of the seven days immediately succeeding Christmas Day nor (iii) any day on which the registers or records wherein it shall be appropriate to make searches referable to the Sale shall not be available to the public nor (iv) any day which shall be recognised by the Solicitors' Profession at large as being a day on which their offices are not open for business.

ARBITRATION

51. All differences and disputes between the Vendor and the Purchaser as to:

   (a) whether a rent is or is not a rack rent for the purpose of Condition 10 (c), or

   (b) the identification of the Apportionment Date, or the treatment or quantification of any item pursuant to the provisions for apportionment in the Conditions, or

(c) any issue on foot of Condition 33, including the applicability of said Condition, and the amount of compensation payable thereunder, or

(d) the materiality of any matter for the purpose of Condition 36 (a), or

(e) the materiality of damage or any other question involving any of the provisions in Conditions 43, 44 and 45, including the amount of compensation (if any) payable, or

(f) whether any particular item or thing is or is not included in the Sale, or otherwise as to the nature or condition thereof

shall be submitted to arbitration by a sole Arbitrator to be appointed (in the absence of agreement between the Vendor and the Purchaser upon such appointment and on the application of either of them) by the President (or other Officer endowed with the functions of such President) for the time being of the Law Society of Ireland or (in the event of the President or other Officer as aforesaid being unable or unwilling to make the appointment) by the next senior Officer of that Society who is so able and willing to make the appointment and such arbitration shall be governed by the Arbitration Acts, 1954 to 1998 provided however that if the Arbitrator shall relinquish his appointment or die, or if it shall become apparent that for any reason he shall be unable or shall have become unfit or unsuited (whether because of bias or otherwise) to complete his duties, or if he shall be removed from office by Court Order, a substitute may be appointed in his place and in relation to any such appointment the procedures hereinbefore set forth shall be deemed to apply as though the substitution were an appointment de novo which said procedures may be repeated as many times as may be necessary.

CHAPTER 6

THE FAMILY HOME

6.1 Introduction

The Family Home Protection Act, 1976 is the first in a succession of enactments dealing with matters of family law, which have impacted greatly on Irish conveyancing practice. Since coming into force on 12 July 1976, the Family Home Protection Act, 1976 and its related enactments have done more to regulate the ownership of matrimonial property than any other piece of legislation since the foundation of the State. The purpose of this chapter is to examine the effects of this Act and its sister enactments upon conveyancing practice and to explain the best practice to be followed in light of those effects.

6.2 Protection of Spousal Rights of Residence

6.2.1 FAMILY HOME PROTECTION ACT, 1976

The Family Home Protection Act, 1976 (the 1976 Act) came into force on 12 July 1976. Prompted by a report published in 1972 by the Commission on the Status of Women, the purpose of the Act was to prevent one spouse, in whose sole name the family home (as defined in the Act) was vested, from dealing with the property without the knowledge and/or the consent of the non-owning spouse. Although the Act was principally designed to protect a wife's right to reside in the family home, it does not, in fact, make any distinction between a wife and a husband and affords the same protection to both. That protection is contained in s 3(1), which provides as follows:

> Where a spouse, without the prior consent in writing of the other spouse, purports to convey any interest in the family home to any person except the other spouse, then, subject to subsections (2) and (3) and section 4, the purported conveyance shall be void.

Rather than to confer any interest in the property on a non-owning spouse the 1976 Act seeks to protect that spouse's right to reside in the family home. It achieves this by declaring void any conveyance by the owning spouse, where the prior written consent of the non-owning spouse has not been obtained.

The operation of s 3(1) was discussed in *Barclays Bank (Ireland) Ltd v Carroll*, 10 September 1986 (unreported). In that case, a husband transferred the family home to C, without having obtained his wife's prior consent to the transfer. The transferee subsequently mortgaged the property. When C went bankrupt, his assignee in bankruptcy sought to have the mortgage set aside on the basis that the original transfer was void for non-compliance with s 3(1) and, therefore, C did not have sufficient title to create the mortgage. Hamilton P stated, however, that, as the purpose of the section was the protection of the right of residence of the non-owning spouse, only he or she could invoke the section to have an offending conveyance declared void. In the instant case, as the wife had no desire to have the original transfer avoided, there was no other person entitled to do so.

There are two, interconnected, conclusions to be drawn from this decision. First, the protection afforded by s 3(1) is personal to a spouse whose right to reside in the family home is under threat. Secondly, the stipulation that any conveyance not complying with the provisions of s 3(1) is void is to be interpreted as meaning voidable at the instigation of such a spouse.

Clearly, the introduction of the 1976 Act impacted greatly on practitioners, who were, as a result of its introduction, obliged to ensure that the prior written consent of any non-owning spouse was obtained to any conveyance of the family home executed after 12 July 1976 (this is subject to the exception expounded in *Hamilton v Hamilton* [1982] IR 466 where the Supreme Court held that the Act did not apply to conveyances executed after 12 July 1976 where the relevant contract for sale had been executed prior to that date). The consequence, subject to certain exceptions, of failing to do so was the possibility that the conveyance in question could be declared void.

6.2.2   SECTION 54 OF THE FAMILY LAW ACT, 1995

The draconian effect of s 3(1) was tempered by the introduction of s 54(8)(b) of the Family Law Act, 1995 (the 1995 Act) (the effective date of the Family Law Act, 1995 is 1 August 1995), which added a new subsection (8) to s 3 of the 1976 Act and which provides as follows:

> *Proceedings will not be instituted to have a conveyance declared void by reason only of subsection (1) [of s 3 of the 1976 Act] after the expiration of six years from the date of the conveyance.*

The section effectively introduced a six-year time limit within which proceedings to have a conveyance declared void by a non-owning spouse could be brought. The section further provides that a conveyance will not be void by virtue of s 3(1) of the 1976 Act unless declared so by a court in proceedings instituted before the passing of the 1995 Act or, if after that date, within the six-year time limit introduced by the 1995 Act.

It should be noted that the six-year rule does not apply to a conveyance which is the subject of proceedings instituted prior to 1 August 1995. In addition, the six-year rule does not apply to proceedings instituted by a spouse who has been in actual occupation of the family home from immediately before the expiration of six years from the date of the conveyance in question until the institution of the proceedings. This exception is provided for in s 54(1)(b)(ii) of the 1995 Act. The operation of this exception is illustrated by the following example. In January 1990, a husband, the sole owner of a family home, executes a mortgage, without obtaining the prior written consent of his wife. Under the normal operation of the six-year rule, the time for instituting proceedings to have the mortgage declared void elapses in 1996. However, the wife has been in actual occupation of the property since before January 1990, so that when, in March 1997, she discovers the existence of the mortgage she is still entitled to bring proceedings to have the mortgage declared void.

6.2.3   EXCEPTIONS

There are four specific exceptions to the application of s 3(1).

6.2.3.1   Agreements made in contemplation of marriage

Section 3(2) is self-explanatory and provides that s 3(1) does not apply to conveyances made in pursuance of an enforceable pre-nuptial agreement.

6.2.3.2 Conveyance to a purchaser for full value

Section 3(3) provides that 'No conveyance shall be void by reason only of subsection (1)(a) if it is made to a purchaser for full value'. Section 3(6) defines a 'purchaser' as 'a grantee, lessee, assignee, mortgagee, chargeant or other person who in good faith acquires an estate in property'. The exception contained in s 3(3) therefore applies only to a bona fide purchaser for value. Furthermore, s 3(5) provides that, for the purposes of s 3(3), 'full value' shall mean 'such value as amounts or approximates to the value of that for which it is given'.

Section 3(3) itself makes reference to the Conveyancing Act 1882, s 3, which provides that a purchaser will be held to have had notice of a fact if it was within his own personal knowledge or 'would have come to his knowledge if such enquiries and inspections had been made as ought reasonably to have been made by him'. In addition, knowledge in the possession of a purchaser's agent or solicitor will, by virtue of s 3(1) of the Conveyancing Act, be imputed to the purchaser. Section 3(3) of the 1976 Act will therefore operate to protect a purchaser where the vendor conceals the fact that the property for sale is his family home and the purchaser or his agents, having made due enquiry, do not discover this fact. In that situation, the non-owning spouse is precluded from instituting proceedings to have the conveyance declared void. However, the section will not protect the purchaser who is ignorant of the fact that the property is a family home by reason of his own failure to make proper enquiries.

A case in point is the decision in *Somers v Weir* [1979] IR 94. The property in question was a leasehold premises, the lease to which the husband of the defendant had taken in March 1961, five months before his marriage to the defendant. The defendant and her husband resided in the premises until October 1973, when the marriage broke down and the defendant left the family home and went to reside in accommodation rented from Dublin Corporation. A separation agreement was executed in November 1974, but the agreement was silent as to the ownership of the family home, which therefore remained in both the possession and ownership of the husband. On 2 August 1976 (ie after the coming into effect of the 1976 Act) the husband entered into an agreement with the plaintiff for the sale to the plaintiff of the premises. On 10 August, the plaintiff's solicitor wrote to the husband's solicitor, requesting sight of a copy of the separation agreement. The husband's solicitor replied, saying that he had not acted for the husband in relation to the separation, and, therefore, did not possess a copy of the agreement. The solicitor further stated that 'In view of the fact that the premises are not now a family home and your client is the purchaser for full value, we cannot see how your client is concerned with the matrimonial situation'. The plaintiff's solicitor completed the sale on 17 August 1976 on foot of a statutory declaration of the husband, stating that the defendant had not relied on the premises as her family home since the execution of the separation agreement and that, by virtue of the separation agreement, she now had no interest in the property. This declaration had been prepared by the plaintiff's solicitor, who had never seen the separation agreement.

The matter came to light when the plaintiff sought to resell the premises in 1977 and the lending institution for the new purchaser requested proof that the provisions of s 3 had been complied with. The plaintiff's solicitor sought the defendant's retrospective consent to the 1976 deed, which she refused. The plaintiff then applied to court to have the defendant's consent dispensed with under s 4 of the 1976 Act. On appeal to the Supreme Court, Henchy J found that the premises had, in fact, at all material times been the family home of the defendant and her husband. Having stated that a conveyance will be no less void if the purchaser for value takes a property, without having first made the proper enquiries, than if he had had actual knowledge that the wife's prior consent was required and failed to obtain it, he went on to say:

> 'In this case, the inquiries and inspections which ought reasonably to have been made as a matter of common prudence were not made. Instead, a statement which was unwarranted by any document and which falsely swept aside the defendant's rights was presented to her husband for execution as a statutory declaration and, on the basis

of that statutory declaration, the sale by him went through behind his wife's back. It was a transaction of the precise kind that s 3 of the Act of 1976 was designed to make void.'

From the practitioner's perspective, the clear implication of this decision is that the solicitor acting for the purchaser of any property is under a strict duty to carry out all necessary investigations to ascertain the position regarding the family home. Failure to do so will result in the conveyance to his client being vulnerable to challenge under s 3(1). The proper investigations to be carried out by purchasers' solicitors are discussed at **6.2.7** and **6.2.8** below.

6.2.3.3 Conveyance of an interest by a person other than a spouse

Conveyances of an interest in the family home by a person other than a spouse are specifically excluded from the ambit of s 3(1) by s 3(3)(b). In other words, the only party obliged to obtain spousal consent when purporting to alienate his or her interest in the family home is a spouse. This means, for example, that the mortgagee of the family home may convey its interest in the property without requiring the consent of a non-owning spouse to the conveyance. (Note, however, the provisions of the Bankruptcy Act, 1988, s 61(4) which oblige the official assignee of a bankrupt to obtain the consent of the High Court before disposing of the interest of a bankrupt in the family home.)

6.2.3.4 Family Law Act, 1995, s 54(3)

Section 54(3) of the 1995 Act provides that where a court, when granting a decree of judicial separation, orders that the ownership of the family home shall be vested in one or other of the spouses, it shall, unless it sees reason to the contrary, order that s 3(1) shall not apply to any conveyance by that spouse of his or her interest in the family home.

6.2.4 THE MEANING OF 'CONVEYANCE'

In order for the 1976 Act to apply, there must be a 'conveyance' within the meaning of the Act. 'Conveyance' is defined in s 1 of the 1976 Act as including:

> *a mortgage, lease, assent, transfer, disclaimer, release, and any other disposition of property otherwise than by a will or a donatio mortis causa and also includes an enforceable agreement (whether conditional or unconditional) to make any such conveyance, and 'convey' shall be construed accordingly.*

Where any of these documents relates to a family home, it is necessary to obtain the prior consent in writing of the spouse to the proposed conveyance.

By virtue of the above definition, a contract for the sale of property is as much a conveyance as is the deed of assurance. Thus, where the transaction to which the contract relates is the disposal of one spouse's interest in the family home, strictly speaking, the prior written consent of the non-owning spouse to both the contract and the deed is required in order to satisfy s 3(1). This point was discussed in the case of *Kyne v Tiernan*, July 1980 (unreported). In that case, the family home was registered in the sole name of the husband. The husband and the wife decided to put the property on the market. When a purchaser was found, the wife, although unwilling to sign a consent endorsed on the contract for sale in the usual manner, did sign an unequivocal consent to the sale, which had been printed on a separate sheet of paper. Prior to the completion of the sale, the couple experienced marital difficulties and the wife ultimately refused to endorse her consent on the deed of transfer. When the purchaser applied to court for an order for specific performance of the contract, the question arose as to whether the consent to the contract would also suffice as consent to the deed. McWilliam J was of the opinion that it would, stating ' I cannot imagine that it could have been the intention of the legislature to require two consents for the completion of one transaction, namely the sale of one house'.

Thus, it would seem that only the consent to the contract for sale is required. It is, nonetheless, good conveyancing practice to have the spousal consent endorsed on the deed, as well as the contract. This avoids any difficulties arising, should the contract for sale be lost. An alternative solution would be to bind the contract to the back of the deed, for safekeeping.

The list of documents contained in s 1 is not conclusive. Thus, in the case of *Bank of Ireland v Purcell* [1989] 2 IR 327, it was held that an equitable deposit of deeds could constitute a conveyance within the meaning of s 3(1). On the other hand, in both *Containercare (Ireland) Ltd v Wycherly* [1982] IR 143 and *Murray v Diamond* [1982] 2 ILRM 113, the court found that a judgment mortgage did not constitute a conveyance for the purposes of the Act. At p 115 of the judgment in *Murray v Diamond*, Barrington J stated:

'I do not think that the mere fact that a man has irresponsibly allowed himself to get into debt, or allowed a judgment to be obtained against him and thereby allowed a situation to develop in which his creditor registers a judgment against his interest in the family home, would justify a court in saying that he has conveyed or purported to convey his interest in the family home to the judgment mortgagee.'

6.2.5   THE MEANING OF 'FAMILY HOME'

6.2.5.1   Definition of 'family home'

It is only the purported conveyance of an interest in the 'family home' to which s 3(1) applies. In this regard, there are two questions, which should be asked:

(a)   whether the property is or was a family home for some period of time, and

(b)   whether there is a spouse whose consent is necessary.

A 'family home' is defined in s 2(1) of the 1976 Act as meaning a dwelling in which a married couple ordinarily resides. Furthermore, the definition encompasses a 'dwelling in which a spouse whose protection is in issue ordinarily resides, or, if that spouse has left the other spouse, ordinarily resided before so leaving'. Thus, as has been seen in *Somers v Weir* [1979] IR 94, where the spouse whose rights are vulnerable has been forced to leave the property in which he or she had formerly resided with his or her spouse, that former residence will remain the family home for the purposes of the 1976 Act. The rule of thumb to be followed in all cases of doubt is 'once a family home, always a family home'. The Act intends to protect the current residence of a married couple, who are living together, and the former residence of a couple, who are separated.

It should also be noted that this definition also encompasses a dwelling in which a spouse is residing, having been forced by the other spouse to leave the family home.

6.2.5.2   Definition of 'dwelling'

The definition of family home contained in s 2(1) refers to a 'dwelling'. Section 2(2), as amended by s 54(1)(a) of the 1995 Act, defines a dwelling as:

any building or part of a building occupied as a separate dwelling and includes any garden or other land usually occupied with the dwelling, being land that is subsidiary and ancillary to it, is required for amenity or convenience, and is not being used or developed primarily for commercial purposes, and includes a structure that is not permanently attached to the ground and a vehicle, or vessel, whether mobile or not, occupied as a separate dwelling.

It follows from this definition that, for example, where an agricultural holding consists of both a farmhouse, which is a family home, and land upon which the farming is carried out, it is possible to dispose of the farmland separately from the farmhouse, without the necessity of obtaining spousal consent. This is by virtue of the land being used primarily for commercial purposes and therefore not coming within the definition of 'dwelling'. On the other hand, if the land attached to the family home were merely a small garden, not used for any commercial purpose, it would not be possible to dispose of the garden separately, without obtaining spousal consent.

Another possibility, which stems from the definition, relates to the situation of an apartment above a shop or pub. Quite clearly, the apartment could be the ordinary residence of a married couple. According to the above definition, it is possible to sever the commercial premises on the ground floor from the apartment above. Thus, if the entire premises were in the sole ownership of the wife, for example, it would be in order for her to sell the commercial premises separately from the residential premises, without obtaining the husband's prior consent to the conveyance.

6.2.5.3 'Ordinarily reside'

Apart from the situation outlined in **6.2.5.1**, namely where one spouse has been forced to reside in a dwelling other than the premises occupied by both spouses, a husband and wife must use a premises as their ordinary residence, in order for it to constitute a family home. In *National Irish Bank v Graham* [1995] 2 IR 244, the Supreme Court made clear that the term 'ordinarily reside' did not apply to a premises in which a married couple *intended* to reside.

In most situations, the question of where a married couple ordinarily resides is easily answered. Sometimes, however, the answer may not be so straightforward. Take, for example, the case of a married couple with two residences, one in the city, perhaps, and the other in the country. They spend an equal amount of time in each residence. Which is their family home? Or perhaps they do not spend exactly equal amounts of time in each premises. Is it now possible to say with certainty which property is the family home? In such a situation, by far the wisest course of action for a solicitor acting for the purchaser of either residence is to obtain the wife's consent.

6.2.6 THE MEANING OF 'CONSENT'

6.2.6.1 Generally

Where the premises for sale are a family home, but the vendors are the joint owners of the property and are married to each other, no spousal consent is required to any conveyance of the property, as both spouses will be joining in the deed of assurance. Likewise, where the vendor is one spouse only, but the property for sale is not the family home of the vendor and his or her spouse, the consent of the non-owning spouse is not necessary. (In this case, however, solicitors acting for purchasers and lending institutions should be extremely careful to investigate the position regarding whether or not the premises are, in fact, a family home.)

In all other situations, where one spouse is alienating his or her interest in the family home, the consent of the non-owning spouse to at least the contract is required.

6.2.6.2 Consent must be prior and in writing

Section 3(1) is very clear that the spousal consent must be given prior to the purported conveyance and it must be in writing. A solicitor acting for the vendor must therefore take every care to ensure that this has, in fact, been done. In the case of a contract for sale, for example, the 1995 edition of the Law Society General Conditions of Sale includes the following endorsement at the top of the memorandum of agreement:

I . . . . being the Spouse of the undernamed Vendor, hereby, for the purposes of Section 3, Family Home Protection Act 1976, consent to the proposed sale of the property described in the within particulars at the price mentioned below.

SIGNED by the said Spouse
In the presence of:

Solicitors should ensure that the consenting spouse does, in fact, sign the endorsement *before* any other party to the contract. In the case of a deed, it is also usual to have the consent endorsed on the actual document. Although most practitioners insert this endorsement after the signatures of the parties to the deed, it is again *absolutely vital* that the consent is actually executed *prior* to any other party executing the deed. It is good practice to recite this fact in the endorsement. Although this is the usual method of obtaining spousal consent, it is not absolutely necessary. A case in point is *Kyne v Tiernan*, discussed at **6.2.4** above. Here, the wife had endorsed her consent on a separate sheet of paper and the court found that this was an acceptable consent to the deed of transfer. Note that the prior consent should be dated prior to the date of the deed of assurance.

Where the property is being sold at auction, the vendor's solicitor should arrange to have the non-owning spouse present to endorse consent on the contract. Where this is not possible, it is necessary to have the spouse execute a separate consent, prior to the auction. This consent should recite that the spouse consents to the sale at auction of the property and should stipulate a minimum sale price. This price will, in fact, be the reserve agreed for the auction. Should the property not achieve this price, the spouse's consent will not be valid.

6.2.6.3 Consent must be informed

Apart from the requirement that spousal consent be prior and in writing, the courts have made clear that the consent must also be informed. The question of informed consent was discussed by the Supreme Court in *Bank of Ireland v Smyth* [1996] ILRM 401. Here, the wife had given her consent to what she believed to be a charge over the land attached to the family home. In fact, the charge included both the family home and the land. Mrs Smyth had executed her consent to the charge in the presence of an employee of the plaintiff bank. It transpired that the employee had not enquired of Mrs Smyth whether she understood what was being covered by the document to which she was consenting.

The bank contended that it was not required to take into account what was in Mrs Smyth's mind. Discussing the nature of spousal consent, however, Blayney J stated that validity of Mrs Smyth's consent depended on whether she had full knowledge of what she was doing. At p 428 of the judgment he stated:

> 'The spouse giving it [consent] must know what it is he or she is consenting to. Since giving one's consent means that one is approving of something, obviously, a precondition is that one should have knowledge of what it is that one is approving of.'

In the instant case, Mrs Smyth could not give a valid consent to the conveyance in question, as she was not aware of its full import. Furthermore, the court found the bank to be on notice of Mrs Smyth's lack of knowledge, as it would have been apparent if the bank employee had made reasonable enquiry. The charge was therefore held to be invalid as no valid consent had been obtained.

Examining this judgment from the perspective of a solicitor acting for a lending institution, it should not be interpreted as placing upon banks a duty either to explain a charge fully to spouses or to advise them to seek independent legal advice. This suggestion was specifically rejected by Blayney J. However, he did state that it would have been good practice to have done so, not because the bank owed any duty to Mrs Smyth, but because, if these steps had been taken, the charge would not have been invalidated, as Mrs Smyth would have then been precluded from claiming that the exact import of the charge was unknown to her.

6.2.6.4 Consent of a minor

Although the 1976 Act does not stipulate an age limit, below which a spouse cannot give a valid consent, the question as to whether a minor could give a valid consent was rendered academic by the introduction of the Age of Majority Act, 1985 and the Family Law Act, 1995. The former lowered the age of majority from twenty-one years to either eighteen years or upon marriage. The latter, at Part V, rendered null and void any marriage contracted by a person under eighteen years, unless a court exemption has been obtained.

6.2.6.5 Dispensing with spousal consent

The requirement to obtain spousal consent in every case where there is a purported conveyance of one spouse's interest in the family home is somewhat tempered by the provisions of s 4(1) of the 1976 Act. Section 4(1) provides that '[w]here the spouse whose consent is required under s 3(1) omits or refuses to consent, the court may, subject to the provisions of this section, dispense with the consent'. The section provides for three situations in which the court may dispense with spousal consent. Before considering these situations, however, there are three preliminary points to be noted:

(a) the application to the court to dispense with the consent may be made under the 1976 Act itself;

(b) the application must be made prior to the conveyance in question. The court clearly stated in *Somers v Weir* [1979] IR 94 (discussed at 6.2.5.1) that it had no jurisdiction to dispense with spousal consent retrospectively; and

(c) the application may be made by either the spouse purporting to dispense with his or her interest in the family home, or by the intended transferee.

Turning to the circumstances in which the court may dispense with consent, the first relates to a situation where a spouse unreasonably withholds consent. This situation is covered by s 4(2), which provides:

The court shall not dispense with the consent of a spouse unless the court considers that it is unreasonable for the spouse to withhold consent, taking into account all the circumstances, including:

(a) the respective needs and resources of the spouses and of the dependent children (if any) of the family, and

(b) in a case where the spouse whose consent is required is offered alternative accommodation having regard to the respective degrees of security of tenure in the family home and in the alternative accommodation.

In the case of *R v R*, December 1978 (unreported), the court refused to dispense with the wife's consent, on the basis that her refusal was not unreasonable. Here, the husband and wife had been married in 1960 and had three daughters. The couple experienced marital difficulties for a number of years and, for a year prior to the application to court, had slept apart in separate rooms within the family home.

Prior to the application, the husband had formed an attachment with another woman and had decided to leave the family home. As he had a number of outstanding debts and wished to make a fresh start, he proposed mortgaging the family home, hoping to raise sufficient funds to discharge his debts. The wife refused her consent to the mortgage, stating that, on the husband's salary, it would not be possible for him to make the mortgage repayments, while at the same time, supporting two households. The husband therefore applied to the court to have his wife's consent dispensed with. The application was refused on the grounds that the court could not hold that the wife's refusal in this instance was unreasonable. McMahon J did comment, however, that the situation might be different, if the husband were to succeed in paying off the short-term loans over the succeeding two years.

The decision in *R v R* should be contrasted with that in *S O'B v M O'B*, December 1981 (unreported). Here, a Roman Catholic Church decree of nullity was granted, with the concurrence of both the husband and the wife. The wife continued to reside with their two children in the family home, which was in the sole ownership of the husband. The husband moved to Hong Kong, where he subsequently remarried in a church ceremony. He had a third child out of this relationship.

Some time after his second marriage, the husband wished to return to Ireland and decided to sell the family home, in order to raise enough money to do so. As the original marriage had not been annulled by the State, the first wife was still his spouse for the purposes of the 1976 Act. The first wife refused her consent to the sale and the husband applied to the court under s 4. It was the husband's proposal that, once he had disposed of the family home, a portion of the proceeds, sufficient to set the first wife up in alternative accommodation, would be handed over to the first wife. On the facts, O'Hanlon J concluded that as both parties had been responsible for the break-up of the marriage, they both had suffered the consequences in terms of attempting to maintain two households on whatever resources were available. As the husband was willing to make as much as half of the proceeds of sale available to the wife, O'Hanlon J concluded that her refusal to give consent was unreasonable and granted an order dispensing with her consent.

6.2.7 STANDARD QUERIES

6.2.7.1 Introduction

As has been seen, s 3(1) will not apply to a conveyance to a bona fide purchaser for value without notice. It has also been seen that, in order to qualify as such, a purchaser and/or his or her agents are under a duty to carry out reasonable investigations into the position regarding the family home. The enquiries which are considered reasonable in particular circumstances are set out at **6.2.8** below. However, there are some basic enquiries, which must be made in every case.

6.2.7.2 Statutory declarations

Although the 1976 Act does not require the production of a statutory declaration by way of proof as to the situation regarding the family home, it is now standard practice to require a statutory declaration from the vendor and his or her spouse, evidencing the position. The practice has also been adopted by practitioners of seeking corroboration of certain matters. It is quite usual, for example, for a declaration to exhibit a marriage or death certificate as proof of marriage or death. Similarly, a declaration might exhibit an extract of the separation agreement or a divorce decree, where appropriate.

Note carefully, that the statutory declaration should not be confused with the prior written consent of the spouse. As shall be seen, it is now normal practice to request a statutory declaration as corroborating evidence in most situations. However, this does not negate the necessity for the spouse's prior written consent to be obtained where there is a conveyance of the family home, and the spouse in question is not a joint owner.

Although the practice of seeking a statutory declaration is now the norm, this was not the case immediately after the introduction of the 1976 Act. As a result, many solicitors, in and around 12 July 1976, failed to obtain such supporting evidence. To alleviate the confusion thus caused, the Conveyancing Committee of the Law Society issued a practice note in June 1981, advising that, where, in accordance with s 3(1), a spouse's consent is endorsed on a conveyance of the family home, executed prior to 1 January 1978, a purchaser's solicitor should seek no supporting evidence, where none is available. Examples of the current Family Law Statutory Declarations are contained in the Law Society's Conveyancing Handbook.

In March 2001 the Conveyancing Committee of the Law Society issued a practice note, dealing with the practice of providing and accepting solicitors' certificates in relation to the 1976 Act and other related acts notwithstanding that such certificates are acceptable to the Registrar in Land Registry. In its practice note, the Conveyancing Committee expressed the view that the practice of giving such certificates, simply because it is more convenient than obtaining an appropriate statutory declaration from the vendor, is to be discouraged. Best conveyancing practice requires that a purchaser's solicitor should always seek the best evidence in respect of the position pertaining to the family home. Other than in exceptional circumstances, 'best evidence' is a statutory declaration of the vendor and, his or her spouse, if appropriate, together with corroborating evidence. To quote the practice note, a vendor's solicitor's certificate should only be accepted 'where the best evidence is not reasonably available and where there is good reason for its non-availability'.

6.2.7.3 Searches

A conveyance shall be deemed not to be and never to have been void by reason of s 3(1) unless it has been declared void by a court or the parties to the conveyance, or their successors in title, within six years from the date of the conveyance, make a statement in writing to the effect that the conveyance is void for lack of consent. A solicitor acting for a purchaser must therefore be satisfied both that no proceedings have been brought to have any conveyance pertaining to the property for sale declared void and that no statement declaring the conveyance void has been made. Although the precedent family law declarations contain an averment to the effect that no proceedings have been brought and the Law Society Standard Requisitions on Title also query the position, it is, nevertheless, necessary for a purchaser's solicitor (or, indeed, a solicitor acting for a lending institution) to make further enquiries. These take the form of searches to be made in either the Land Registry or the Registry of Deeds (whichever is appropriate) and in the Lis Pendens Register.

The search in the Registry of Deeds or the Land Registry will reveal whether a statement has been lodged in respect of any conveyance. This is because s 3(8)(c) (inserted by the 1995 Act, s 54) requires that a certified copy of any statement declaring a conveyance to be void be lodged in the appropriate registry.

Section 3(8)(d) requires that to have a conveyance declared void by reason of s 3(1) a person who institutes proceedings shall, as soon as may be, cause relevant particulars of the proceedings to be entered as a lis pendens in accordance with the Judgments (Ireland) Act, 1844.

Where such searches reveal the existence of proceedings, the only course of action for the solicitor acting for a purchaser is to await the outcome of the proceedings.

6.2.7.4 Requisitions on Title

The various provisions of the 1976 Act, the Family Law Act, 1981, the Judicial Separation and Family Law Reform Act, 1989 and the 1995 Act, discussed in previous paragraphs, are covered by requisitions 24, 25 and 26 of the Requisitions on Title:

— requisition 24: the Family Home Protection Act, 1976, the Family Law Act, 1995 and the Family Law (Divorce) Act, 1996

— requisition 25: the Family Law Act, 1981 and the Family Law Act, 1995

— requisition 26: the Judicial Separation and Family Law Reform Act, 1989, the Family Law Act, 1995 and the Family Law (Divorce) Act, 1996

As a result of the effects of these Acts, it is extremely important, when acting for the vendor of property that a solicitor makes proper enquiry of the vendor, to be able to reply fully to these requisitions. As with replies to all other requisitions, the vendor verifies the replies, before they are forwarded to the solicitor acting for the purchaser. Likewise, when acting for the purchaser, a solicitor should ensure that complete responses to requisitions 24,

25 and 26 have been received and those responses should be forwarded to the purchaser, so that he or she may confirm that he or she is happy with same.

The following is a brief summary of requisitions 24 to 26.

Requisition 24 deals with whether or not the premises are the family home of the vendor or *any other person*. The requisition requires the vendor to confirm requisition and to support that confirmation with a statutory declaration and appropriate corroborating evidence. The requisition also seeks evidence of spousal consent in respect of conveyances of unregistered property on or after 12 July 1976.

Requisition 25 queries the position in respect of the Family Law Act, 1981, as amended by the Family Law Act, 1995. The vendor is required to advise whether there have been any dispositions of the property to which ss 3, 4 and 5 of the 1981 Act apply. For further discussion of ss 3, 4 and 5 of the 1981 Act see **6.3** below.

Requisition 26 deals with the Judicial Separation and Family Law Reform Act, 1989, the Family Law Act, 1995 and the Family Law (Divorce) Act, 1996. The requisition is aimed at ascertaining whether or not an order in respect of the property has been made by the court, using its powers under these Acts. A statutory declaration is required confirming that no application or order has made under these Acts. The vendor is further required to confirm that the transaction is not for purposes of defeating a claim for financial relief. For further discussion of these property orders, see **6.4** below.

6.2.8 PARTICULAR ENQUIRIES

6.2.8.1 Where the vendor sells as personal representative

In December 1981, the Conveyancing Committee recommended that it was not necessary for a solicitor purchasing a property from a personal representative, selling qua personal representative, to enquire into the position in relation to the 1976 Act. This recommendation did not receive widespread acceptance, as it did not deal with the (quite common) situation where the personal representative was selling, several years after the death, albeit in his capacity as personal representative. Having consulted senior counsel, the committee issued the following guidelines:

(a) The facts in each case must ultimately determine the position.

(b) Where there is no evidence to suggest that the personal representative and his or her spouse have resided in the property, no consent should be sought. However, a declaration confirming non-residency should be obtained from the personal representative.

(c) Where there is some evidence to suggest that the personal representative and his or her spouse resided in the property for a short period, but there is evidence that the personal representative's family home is elsewhere, no consent should be sought. Again, a declaration confirming the situation should be obtained.

(d) Where the personal representative and his or her spouse have lived in the property and there is no evidence to suggest that their family home is elsewhere, it is reasonable to require the consent of the spouse. This is particularly important where the personal representative and his or her spouse are beneficially entitled under the will or intestacy.

6.2.8.2 Where the vendor is a company

In 1980, the Joint Committee of the Law Society and the Building Societies issued a recommendation that solicitors acting for purchasers, where the vendor was a company, need not concern themselves with the provisions of the 1976 Act. This was simply because the vendor, being a company, could not have a spouse whose consent was required.

This position was significantly altered by the decision in *Walpole v Jay*, November 1980 (unreported). In that case, the vendor of the property was a company, but the purchaser was on notice that a director of the company and his wife had resided in the premises for a number of years. McWilliam J held that, while there was nothing in the 1976 Act which would invalidate a conveyance by a company, the purchaser was entitled to make enquiries as to the nature of any interest held by the director. If such an investigation revealed that an interest had vested in the director, then the consent of the director's spouse was required to any alienation of that interest.

As a result of this decision, the Conveyancing Committee issued a further practice note, published in the Law Society Gazette, October 1983, recommending that, where the purchaser after enquiry is aware that a director or other employee of the vendor company has been in occupation of the premises, additional requisitions should be raised.

6.2.8.3 In cases of matrimonial dispute

As may be seen from the cases discussed above, the risk to purchasers/ mortgagees/lessees is highest in cases where there is or has been a matrimonial dispute between the spouses. In a situation where a matrimonial dispute has not been resolved, either by a separation agreement or the granting of a decree of judicial separation or divorce, a statutory declaration by the vendor only, without any corroboration, is not acceptable.

The extreme caution, which must be exercised by practitioners, in cases of matrimonial dispute was made clear in the decision handed down by the High Court in *Tesco Ireland Ltd v McGrath*, 14 June 1999, High Court (unreported). This case related to the purchase of lands by the plaintiff from the defendants. The transaction proceeded in the normal course, with the plaintiff seeking and obtaining the usual confirmation, in compliance with requisition 26 of the Law Society Requisitions and Objections on Title, that the sale was not being made for the purpose of defeating any claim for financial relief. Prior to completion, however, the plaintiff became aware that the defendant and his wife had instituted proceedings for judicial separation. The plaintiff sought sight of the proceedings but the request was refused by the defendant's solicitor on the basis that the proceedings had been held in camera and to furnish copies would, therefore, have been in contempt of court. Having failed to satisfy himself as to the precise arrangements vis-à-vis the property as a result of the proceedings, the plaintiff sought to rescind the contract for sale. The matter was referred to the court by way of special summons. The court found that the plaintiff, having been put on notice of the existence of proceedings, could no longer rely on the statutory declaration furnished by the vendor, confirming that the disposal was not for the purpose of defeating a claim for financial relief. To do so would, in the view of the court, put the plaintiff in peril of a finding that it was not a bona fide purchaser for value without notice and, in the event of a finding of the court under s 35 of the 1995 Act that the disposition was for the purpose of defeating a claim for financial relief, the disposition to the plaintiff could be set aside by the court. Thus, the plaintiff could rescind the contract. The practical effect of this decision is to place a moratorium upon either spouse dealing with matrimonial property, once proceedings have been instituted, since any prudent purchaser, once put on notice of the proceedings, should withdraw from the transaction and await the outcome of the action.

Considerable caution should also be exercised in relation to cases where the vendor is stated to be either divorced or separated. In such a situation, the vendor may either claim that the property was purchased subsequent to the court decree or separation agreement and his or her spouse never resided in the premises or that the decree or separation agreement provided that the property be vested in the vendor. In the case of separation agreements, the Conveyancing Committee, in a practice note published in the Law Society Gazette, January/February 1985, recommended that a purchaser's/mortgagee's solicitor should seek a statutory declaration from the disinterested spouse confirming that the property is not a family home. Where such a declaration is not available, the solicitor should seek either:

(a)   a corroborative declaration from the vendor's solicitor stating that he or she has read the separation agreement and quoting any relevant extracts therefrom, or

(b) a declaration from a party to the separation agreement, exhibiting a solicitor's certified copy of the relevant extracts therefrom. The committee recommends that only those sections of the agreement relating to the property should be exhibited, as it would not be proper to exhibit the entire document. In this regard, it is good practice, when drafting separation agreements, to place the paragraphs dealing with the family home just above the signatures of the parties.

The same considerations apply in relation to divorce decrees and judicial separations.

In relation to the drafting of separation agreements, practitioners should note that, since the introduction of s 3(9) of the 1976 Act, by s 54(1) of the 1995 Act, it is now possible for a spouse to give a general consent to any future conveyance of an interest in the family home, provided that the general consent is in writing. In drafting a separation agreement, which contains provisions relating to the family home, practitioners should be careful to include a general consent of the disinterested spouse. The issue of the exhibition of court orders and proceedings with statutory declarations has become a thorny issue since the decision in *Tesco Ireland Ltd v McGrath*, discussed above. In that case, the court held that the solicitors for the defendants had acted correctly in refusing to furnish the plaintiff with copies of the pleadings and orders relating to the case.

This issue was also discussed in the case of *RM v DM* [2000] 3 IR 373. In that case, one of the parties to proceedings under the Family Law (Divorce) Act, 1996 sought to adduce the proceedings relating to the family law hearing as evidence in an action brought against his barrister before the Barristers' Professional Conduct Tribunal. When the Circuit Court refused consent to allow the proceedings to be used in evidence, the matter was appealed to the High Court. In the High Court, Murphy J confirmed the decision of the lower court. Reviewing the decision of the Circuit Court, Murphy J stated:

'Having considered the authorities the court held, inter alia, that the primary reason for the in camera rule is to provide protection for minors from the harmful publicity arising out of the disclosure of evidence and other related matters in protected proceedings. There is no absolute embargo on disclosure of evidence in all circumstances.'

Whether or not the court would, in a particular case, grant consent for the dissemination of documentation relating to the proceedings, the subject of the in camera rule, depends upon whether or not the release of the information is in the interests of justice or it is crucial in the public interest that the information on the matrimonial proceedings be made public. In the instant case, neither requiremnt was satisfied. In the course of his judgment, Murphy J confirmed the decision in *Tesco Ireland Ltd v McGrath*, stating that he was in no doubt that solicitors for vendors are precluded by the in camera rule from furnishing copies of claims, orders and pleadings made in family law proceedings.

In order to deal with the practical implications of these two decisions, many practitioners, involved in litigation under either the 1989 or the 1996 Act, request the court, as part of the proceedings, to make an order allowing the exhibition of any appropriate documentation in statutory declarations, relating to subsequent transactions.

6.2.8.4 Where the property is registered property

Where the property is registered land, the Registrar of Titles is concerned with the application of the 1976 Act, as the Registrar is under a general duty to register only valid transfers. The Registrar will therefore require the best evidence available.

The Registrar will not accept a certificate in the body of the deed merely stating that the property is not a family home. The Registrar will accept a statutory declaration by the vendor setting out the basis on which the property is not a family home, or otherwise, as the case might be. The Registrar will also accept a certificate from a solicitor that the property is not a family home. In this regard, however, it should be noted that the Law Society does not advise solicitors to give such a certificate lightly. It is strongly advised that solicitors only give such a certificate in cases of the clearest possible personal knowledge and not on the basis only of information given to him or her by the client.

6.2.8.5 Where the property is unregistered property

Where the property is registered in the Registry of Deeds, the Registrar is not concerned with the validity of the deed and will register the priority of the deed, without enquiring into the position regarding the family home. Where spousal consent to the conveyance has been required and obtained, it is normal to endorse that consent on the actual deed. There is, of course, always the possibility that the deed may be lost and with it the spouse's consent. It is therefore good practice to recite, in the memorial of the deed, the fact that consent had been endorsed on the conveyance.

6.2.8.6 Where vendor is selling under a power of attorney

The situation where the vendor is selling under a power of attorney is dealt with in a practice note published by the Conveyancing Committee in the Law Society Gazette, July 1997.

The recommended practice in relation to sales, mortgages etc, where the vendor is acting under a power of attorney of the non-owning spouse, is that, where the power of attorney either relates to a specific transaction or is more general in nature, if correctly drafted, it will empower the donee to execute a consent on behalf of the donor. It is, therefore, in order for a solicitor acting for a purchaser in such a situation to accept a conveyance with the consent of the donee endorsed thereon, provided that the solicitor has satisfied himself or herself that the power of attorney is appropriately drafted.

The donee of a power of attorney is never empowered to complete a statutory declaration on behalf of the donor. A person may only make a declaration from his own personal knowledge. Thus, a solicitor acting for a purchaser, where the vendor is selling under a power of attorney, may never accept a declaration which the donee purports to make on foot of a power of attorney. A declaration of the donee, in his personal capacity, and declaring facts which are within his own personal knowledge, is acceptable, where there is no better evidence available.

These recommendations apply equally to a general power of attorney and to an enduring power of attorney, granted under the Powers of Attorney Act, 1996 with one slight difference. An enduring power of attorney will only come into effect once the donor has become mentally incapable and the power of attorney has been registered under s 10 of the Powers of Attorney Act, 1996. A solicitor acting for a purchaser/mortgagee must, therefore, check carefully that the power of attorney has, in fact, been so registered. If it has not, the donee will have no authority to execute a consent on behalf of the donor.

6.3 Family Law Act, 1981

The provisions of the Family Law Act, 1981 (the 1981 Act) which impact most upon conveyancing practice are ss 3, 4 and 5.

6.3.1 ENGAGEMENT GIFTS: SS 3 AND 4

Under s 3, where two persons agree to marry and are given any property by a third party as a wedding gift, there is a rebuttable presumption that such property was given to them as joint owners. There is a further presumption that the gift was made subject to the condition that it will be returned, should the engaged couple not marry. Section 4 deals with the situation where one party to the engagement makes a gift to the other party. Here, there is also a rebuttable presumption that the gift is made subject to the condition that it shall be returned if the marriage does not take place for any reason other than the death of the donor. Where the donor dies prior to the marriage, there is a rebuttable presumption that the gift was given unconditionally.

6.3.2 BROKEN ENGAGEMENTS: S 5

The effect of s 5 is to give parties to a broken engagement the same rights as those given to spouses in relation to property in which either or other of them has a beneficial interest. The section only relates to engagements terminated within the three years prior to the purported conveyance.

The extent to which the 'rules of law relating to the rights of spouses' pertain to engaged couples is rather uncertain. Probably, the presumption of advancement is included. By virtue of this presumption, if the property is bought in the joint names of the spouses, with money put forward by the husband only, there is a presumption of advancement in favour of the wife and she is thus entitled to half of the property.

Included also is the doctrine of resulting trust, whereby, if the property is bought in the sole name of one spouse, and there is a contribution towards the purchase price by the other spouse, the courts will apply the doctrine of resulting trust to give the contributing spouse a share based on the proportion of the contribution.

The normal conveyancing practice is to include a paragraph in the statutory declaration dealing with the Family Home Protection Act, stating that the provisions of s 5 of the Family Law Act, 1981 do not apply.

Where the vendors are joint owners, have been married to each other for more than three years and execute a statutory declaration to that effect, exhibiting a civil marriage certificate, it is not necessary to require a statement in relation to s 5: see Conveyancing Committee Practice Note, published in Newsletter January/February 1986.

Where enquiries reveal that there is a broken engagement within the past three years and the other party did, indeed, make a contribution, two possible situations may arise. The most satisfactory, from the perspective of the purchaser, is to have the other party join in the deed of assurance. For obvious reasons, this might not always be possible. As the interest of the contributing party is equitable, it is not absolutely necessary to have them join in the deed of assurance. It is, however, essential that the fiancé(e) receive his or her share of the proceeds and that he or she provides a receipt for same. In circumstances such as these, the solicitor acting for the purchaser should not only request that the receipt, or a certified copy of same, be handed over on closing, but also that a separate statutory declaration, dealing solely with the 1981 Act be furnished.

6.4 Power of the Court to Deal with Property

6.4.1 THE FAMILY HOME PROTECTION ACT, 1976

By virtue of s 5 of the 1976 Act, the court is empowered to make any order, which it considers proper, where it is of the view that one spouse is guilty of conduct which could lead to the loss of the family home. In addition, s 9 of the 1976 Act permits the court to restrict the disposal of any household chattels. Section 4 of the Act enables the court to make an order dispensing with the prior consent of the non-owning spouse. Finally, s 7 of the 1976 Act empowers the court to postpone proceedings brought by the mortgagor or lessor of the family home, where those proceedings arise as a result of late payment under either a lease or mortgage. These basic powers have been expanded by the provisions of the Judicial Separation and Family Law Reform Act, 1989 (the 1989 Act) and the Family Law (Divorce) Act, 1996.

6.4.2 THE JUDICIAL SEPARATION AND FAMILY LAW REFORM ACT, 1989

The 1989 Act must be read in conjunction with the provision of the Family Law Act, 1995, which repealed and/or amended many of the provisions of the 1989 Act. With the introduction of the 1989 Act, the State recognised the necessity to put in place a framework, whereby spouses experiencing marital breakdown could bring proceedings for judicial separation.

Section 6 of the 1995 Act deals with the situation during the period after the institution of such proceedings and before the hearing of the action. By virtue of s 6, the court is empowered to make preliminary orders under ss 5 and 9 of the 1976 Act. Once made, such a preliminary order remains in force until the hearing of the action.

On granting a decree of judicial separation, at any time during the lifetime of the respondent spouse, the court is empowered by virtue of s 9 of the 1995 Act (replacing s 15 of the 1989 Act) to make a property adjustment order. A property adjustment order made subsequent to the granting of a decree of judicial separation may be made on the application of either spouse at any time during the lifetime of the other spouse. This entitlement to apply to the court for a property adjustment order, ceases, however, in the event of the remarriage of either spouse (s 9 of the 1995 Act). The property adjustment orders, which may be made under s 9, deal with the following issues:

(a) the transfer of property from one spouse to the other spouse or to any dependent member of the family or to a third party for the benefit of such a member;

(b) the settlement of any property for the benefit of one or both spouses or for any dependent member of the family;

(c) the variation of a previous agreed settlement of any property;

(d) the extinguishment or reduction of any interest held by either spouse held under any such settlement.

By virtue of s 10 and of the 1995 Act, the court is empowered to make a variety of orders:

(a) s 10(a)(i)   order allowing one spouse to occupy the family home exclusively;

(b) s 10(a)(ii)   order for the sale of the family home; and

(c) s 10(b)   order determining any issue of ownership of property between spouses.

Like orders made under s 9, the foregoing orders may be made by the court either at the time of granting the decree of judicial separation or subsequently, on the application of either spouse during the lifetime of the other spouse.

Finally, s 18 provides for the variation by the court of any order made pursuant to ss 9(b), (c) or (d) and 10(1)(a)(i) or 10(1)(a)(ii).

6.4.3 THE FAMILY LAW (DIVORCE) ACT, 1996

The Family Law (Divorce) Act, 1996 (the 1996 Act) came into force 'on the day that is 3 months after the date of its passing', ie 27 February 1997. By virtue of s 5(1) of the 1996 Act, the court was empowered, on being satisfied in respect of certain matters, to grant a decree of divorce in respect of any marriage, the subject of an application under the Act. The effect of such a decree is set out in s 10, which states:

Where the court grants a decree of divorce, the marriage, the subject of the decree, is thereby dissolved and a party to that marriage may marry again.

Sections 14 and 19 of the 1996 Act grant the court power to make property adjustment orders and orders for the sale of property, respectively. Orders made under these sections may be subsequently varied by the court by virtue of s 22. In addition to ss 14 and 19, s 37 of the 1996 Act empowers the court to 'make such order as it thinks fit' in order to restrain one spouse from making a disposition of property, where the other spouse has instituted divorce proceedings and where the court is satisfied that the purpose of the disposition is to defeat the claim for relief of the applicant spouse. Under s 37(2)(a)(ii), the court is further empowered to set aside a 'reviewable disposition' where satisfied that the disposition has been made in order to defeat the claim for relief. 'Reviewable disposition' is defined by s 37(1) as meaning:

> *a disposition made by the other spouse concerned or any other person but does not include such a disposition made for valuable consideration (other than marriage) to a person who, at the time of the disposition, acted in good faith and without notice of an intention on the part of the respondent to defeat the claim for relief.*

6.4.4 REGISTRATION OF COURT ORDERS

Where a property adjustment order has been made by a court in respect of property under either s 14 of the 1996 Act (in the case of divorce) or s 9 of the 1995 Act (in the case of an order for judicial separation), the Registrar of that court is obliged by ss 14(4) and 9(4) respectively to lodge a certified copy of the order in the Land Registry for registration as a burden under s 69(1)(h) of the Registration of Title Act, 1964 either in the Land Registry or the Registry of Deeds. The Acts do not provide for the automatic cancellation of the burden, once the terms of the order have been satisfied. In such circumstances, practitioners should heed the practice note, issued by the Conveyancing Committee in the Law Society Gazette, May 2000, in which the committee recommends that the instrument, implementing the terms of the order, should contain the consent of the parties to the instrument to the cancellation of the burden.

In October 2001 the Conveyancing Committee issued a further practice note on this topic, advising that, when instituting proceedings under either the 1995 or the 1996 Acts, practitioners ensure that comprehensive details of title are included in the civil bill or special summons. This is to ensure that, when the order is perfected, the Registrar has sufficient information to enable registration in the correct registry.

APPENDIX 6.1

Law Society Family Law Declarations

LAW SOCIETY CONVEYACING HANDBOOK

Appendix 1   Precedent Family Law Declarations

FORM 1

STATUTORY DECLARATION OF HUSBAND AND WIFE THAT PROPERTY IS A FAMILY HOME

Precedent
(To be
adapted as
circumstances
require)

We _____

and _____

both of _____

_____

in the County of _____ both aged 18 years and upwards SOLEMNLY AND SINCERELY DECLARE as follows:

1. This Declaration relates to the property known as _____

   _____

   _____

   _____

   in the County of _____ (being the property comprised in folio _____ County _____) (hereinafter called 'the property').

2. The property is our family home within the meaning of that term in the Family Home Protection Act, 1976, as amended by the Family Law Act, 1995.

3. We have been married once and once only, namely to each other, on the ____ day of _____ 19__. We are each the lawful spouse of the other. We refer to a photocopy of our Civil Marriage Certificate upon which we have endorsed our names prior to making this Declaration.

4. None of the provisions of the Family Law Act, 1981 (hereinafter called 'the Act of 1981') applies to the property because neither of us has been party to an agreement to marry which has terminated within the past three years, and no proceedings of any kind have been threatened or instituted in relation to the property under any of the provisions of the Act of 1981.

5. No proceedings of any kind have been instituted or threatened, and no application or order of any kind has been made, in relation to the property, under any of the provisions of the Judicial Separation and Family Law Reform Act, 1989, the Family Law Act, 1995 ('the 1995 Act'), or the Family Law (Divorce) Act, 1996 ('the 1996 Act') and the assurance of the property to the party or parties mentioned in paragraph 8 hereof is not a disposal for the purposes of defeating a claim for relief (as defined in Section 35 of the 1995 Act and Section 37 of the 1996 Act).

6. The property is not subject to any trust, licence, tenancy or proprietary interest in favour of any person or body corporate arising by virtue of any arrangement, agreement or contract entered into by either of us, or by virtue of any direct or indirect financial or other contribution to the purchase thereof, or by operation of law, or otherwise, and the property is held free from encumbrances.

7. We understand the effect and import of this Declaration which has been fully explained to us by our solicitor.

8. We make this Solemn Declaration conscientiously believing it to be true for the satisfaction of _____
   and pursuant to the provisions of the Statutory Declarations Act, 1938.

LAW SOCIETY FAMILY LAW DECLARATIONS

DECLARED before me by_____

and _____

who are personally known to me (or who are identified to me by

_____

who is personally known to me)

at _____

in the County of _____

this _____ day of _____ 19/20_____.

_____

COMMISSIONER FOR OATHS/PRACTISING SOLICITOR

Form 2

STATUTORY DECLARATION OF HUSBAND AND WIFE THAT PROPERTY IS NOT A FAMILY HOME

Precedent
(To be adapted as
circumstances
require)

We, _____

and _____

both of _____

in the County of _____ both aged 18 years and upwards SOLEMNLY AND SINCERELY DECLARE as follows:-

1. This Declaration relates to the property known as _____
    _____
    in the County of _____ (being the property comprised in folio _____ County
    _____) (hereinafter called 'the property').

2. The property is not a family home within the meaning of that term in the Family Home Protection Act, 1976 as amended by the Family Law Act, 1995. Neither we, nor any other married couple, have ordinarily resided therein since we acquired an interest therein. Our family home is at _____
    _____

3. We have been married once and once only, namely to each other, on the _____ day of _____ 19__. We are each the lawful spouse of the other. We refer to a photocopy of our Civil Marriage Certificate upon which we have endorsed our names prior to making this Declaration.

4. None of the provisions of the Family Law Act, 1981 (hereinafter called 'the Act of 1981') applies to the property because neither of us has been party to an agreement to marry which has terminated within the past three years, and no proceedings of any kind have been threatened or instituted in relation to the property under any of the provisions of the Act of 1981.

5. No proceedings of any kind have been instituted or threatened, and no application or order of any kind has been made, in relation to the property, under any of the provisions of the Judicial Separation and Family Law Reform Act, 1989 , the Family Law Act 1995 ('the 1995 Act'), or the Family Law (Divorce) Act, 1996 ('the 1996 Act') and the assurance of the property to the party or parties mentioned in paragraph 8 hereof is not a disposal for the purposes of defeating a claim for relief (as defined in Section 35 of the 1995 Act and Section 37 of the 1996 Act).

6. The property is not subject to any trust, licence, tenancy or proprietary interest in favour of any person or body corporate arising by virtue of any arrangement, agreement or contract entered into by either of us, or by virtue of any direct or indirect financial or other contribution to the purchase thereof, or by operation of law, or otherwise, and the property is held free from encumbrances.

7. We understand the effect and import of this Declaration which has been fully explained to us by our solicitor.

8. We make this Solemn Declaration conscientiously believing it to be true for the satisfaction of _____
    and pursuant to the provisions of the Statutory Declarations Act, 1938.

127

LAW SOCIETY FAMILY LAW DECLARATIONS

DECLARED before me by_____

and _____

who are personally known to me (or who are identified to me by

_____

who is personally known to me)

at _____

in the County of _____

this _____ day of _____ 19/20_____

_____

Commissioner for Oaths/Practising Solicitor

FORM 3

STATUTORY DECLARATION OF HUSBAND AND WIFE THAT A SITE WITHOUT A BUILDING IS NOT A FAMILY HOME

Precedent
(To be
adapted as
circumstances
require)

We, _____

and _____

both of _____

_____

in the County of _____ both aged 18 years and upwards SOLEMNLY AND SINCERELY DECLARE as follows:-

1. This Declaration relates to the property known as _____
    _____
    _____

    in the County of _____ (being part of the property comprised in folio _____ County _____) (hereinafter called 'the property').

2. The property is not a family home within the meaning of that term in the Family Home Protection Act, 1976 as amended by the Family Law Act, 1995. Neither we, nor any other married couple, have ordinarily resided therein since we acquired an interest therein. Our family home is at _____
    _____

    The property is not a 'dwelling' within the meaning of that term in the Family Home Protection Act 1976 as amended by the Family Law Act 1995.

3. We have been married once and once only, namely to each other, on the____day of _____ 19 ____. We are each the lawful spouse of the other. We refer to a photo-copy of our Civil Marriage Certificate upon which we have endorsed our names prior to making this Declaration.

4. None of the provisions of the Family Law Act, 1981 (hereinafter called 'the Act of 1981') applies to the property because neither of us has been party to an agreement to marry which has terminated within the past three years, and no proceedings of any kind have been threatened or instituted in relation to the property under any of the provisions of the Act of 1981.

5. No proceedings of any kind have been instituted or threatened, and no application or order of any kind has been made, in relation to the property, under any of the provisions of the Judicial Separation and Family Law Reform Act, 1989, the Family Law Act 1995 ('the 1995 Act'), or the Family Law (Divorce) Act, 1996 ('the 1996 Act') and the assurance of the property to the party or parties mentioned in para-graph 8 hereof is not a disposal for the purposes of defeating a claim for relief (as defined in Section 35 of the 1995 Act and Section 37 of the 1996 Act).

6. The property is not subject to any trust, licence, tenancy or proprietary interest in favour of any person or body corporate arising by virtue of any arrangement, agree-ment or contract entered into by either of us, or by virtue of any direct or indirect financial or other contribution to the purchase thereof, or by operation of law, or otherwise, and the property is held free from encumbrances.

7. We understand the effect and import of this Declaration which has been fully explained to us by our solicitor.

LAW SOCIETY FAMILY LAW DECLARATIONS

8. We make this Solemn Declaration conscientiously believing it to be true for the satisfaction of _____ and pursuant to the provisions of the Statutory Declarations Act, 1938.

DECLARED before me by_____

and _____

who are personally known to me (or who are identified to me by

_____

who is personally known to me)

at_____

in the County of_____

this _____ day of _____ 19/20_____.

_____

COMMISSIONER FOR OATHS/PRACTISING SOLICITOR

FORM 4

STATUTORY DECLARATION OF HUSBAND AND WIFE THAT PROPERTY IS A FAMILY HOME WHERE THE PROPERTY IS OWNED BY ONLY ONE OF THEM

Precedent
(To be
adapted as
circumstances
require)

We, _____('owner spouse')

and _____('consenting spouse')

both of _____

_____

in the County of _____ both aged 18 years and upwards SOLEMNLY AND SINCERELY DECLARE as follows:

1. This Declaration relates to the property known as _____
_____
in the County of _____ (being part of the property comprised in folio _____ County _____) (hereinafter called 'the property').

2. The property is our family home within the meaning of that term in the Family Home Protection Act, 1976 as amended by the Family Law Act, 1995. The property is owned by owner spouse.

3. We have been married once and once only, namely to each other, on the _____ day of _____ 19 _____. We are each the lawful spouse of the other. We refer to a photocopy of our Civil Marriage Certificate upon which we have endorsed our names prior to making this Declaration.

4. None of the provisions of the Family Law, 1981 (hereinafter called 'the Act of 1981') applies to the property because neither of us has been party to an agreement to marry which has terminated within the past three years, and no proceedings of any kind have been threatened or instituted in relation to the property under any of the provisions of the Act of 1981.

5. No proceedings of any kind have been instituted or threatened, and no application or order of any kind has been made, in relation to the property, under any of the provisions of the Judicial Separation and Family Law Reform Act, 1989, the Family Law Act 1995 ('the 1995 Act'), or the Family Law (Divorce) Act, 1996 ('the 1996 Act') and the assurance of the property to the party or parties mentioned in paragraph 9 hereof is not a disposal for the purposes of defeating a claim for relief (as defined in Section 35 of the 1995 Act and Section 37 of the 1996 Act).

6. The property is not subject to any trust, licence, tenancy or proprietary interest in favour of any person or body corporate arising by virtue of any arrangement, agreement or contract entered into by either of us, or by virtue of any direct or indirect financial or other contribution to the purchase thereof, or by operation of law, or otherwise, and the property is held free from encumbrances.

7. I consenting spouse have given my prior written consent to the assurance of the property to the party or parties named in paragraph 9 hereof pursuant to Section 3 of the said Family Home Protection Act, 1976. I consenting spouse fully understand the nature and import of this consent. I consenting spouse have been advised that I have the right to be independently advised in connection therewith, and I have waived this right.

131

LAW SOCIETY FAMILY LAW DECLARATIONS

8. We understand the effect and import of this Declaration which has been fully explained to us by our Solicitor.

9. We make this Solemn Declaration conscientiously believing it to be true for the satisfaction of _____
and pursuant to the provisions of the Statutory Declarations Act, 1938.

DECLARED before me by _____

and_____

who are personally known to me (or who are identified to me by

_____

who is personally known to me)

at _____

in the County of_____

this _____ day of _____ 19/20_____.

_____

COMMISSIONER FOR OATHS/PRACTISING SOLICITOR

FORM 5

STATUTORY DECLARATION OF SINGLE PERSON THAT PROPERTY IS NOT A FAMILY HOME

Precedent
(To be
adapted as
circumstances
require)

I, _____

of _____

_____

in the County of _____ aged 18 years and upwards SOLEMNLY AND SINCERELY
DECLARE as follows:

1. This Declaration relates to the property known as_____
_____
_____
in the County of _____ (being the property comprised in folio _____ County
_____) (hereinafter called 'the property').

2. The property is not a family home within the meaning of that term in the Family
Home Protection Act, 1976 as amended by The Family Law Act, 1995. No married
couple has ordinarily resided therein since I acquired an interest therein.

3. I am not and never have been married to any person under the law of this or any
other jurisdiction, and no proceedings have been instituted or threatened by any
person alleging the contrary.

4. None of the provisions of the Family Law Act, 1981 (hereinafter called 'the Act of
1981') applies to the property because I have not been party to an agreement to marry
which has terminated within the past three years, and no proceedings of any kind
have been threatened or instituted in relation to the property under any of the provisions of the Act of 1981.

5. The property is not subject to any trust, licence, tenancy or proprietary interest in
favour of any person or body corporate arising by virtue of any arrangement, agreement or contract entered into by me, or by virtue of any direct or indirect financial
or other contribution to the purchase thereof, or by operation of law, or otherwise,
and the property is held free from encumbrances.

6. I understand the effect and import of this Declaration which has been fully explained
to me by my solicitor.

7. I make this Solemn Declaration conscientiously believing it to be true for the
satisfaction of _____
and pursuant to the provisions of the Statutory Declarations Act, 1938.

LAW SOCIETY FAMILY LAW DECLARATIONS

DECLARED before me by_____

who are personally known to me (or who are identified to me by

_____

who is personally known to me) at

_____

in the County of _____

this _____ day of _____ 19/20_____.

_____

COMMISSIONER FOR OATHS/PRACTISING SOLICITOR

STATUTORY DECLARATION OF LEGAL PERSONAL REPRESENTATIVE THAT PROPERTY IS NOT A FAMILY HOME

Precedent
(To be
adapted as
circumstances
require)

I, _____

of _____

_____

in the County of _____ aged 18 years and upwards SOLEMNLY AND SINCERELY

DECLARE as follows:

1. This Declaration relates to the property known as _____

    _____

    in the County of _____ (being the property comprised in folio _____ County
    _____) (hereinafter called 'the property').

2.1 The property is not a family home within the meaning of that term in the Family
    Home Protection Act, 1976 as amended by the Family Law Act, 1995. No married
    couple has ordinarily resided therein since the death of _____ (hereinafter called
    'the deceased'), who was the owner of the property, on the _____ day of _____
    19_____.

2.2 I refer to a photocopy of the Death Certificate of the deceased upon which marked
    with the letter 'A' I have endorsed my name prior to making the Declaration.

3. I am the legal personal representative of the deceased, and I am assuring the prop-
    erty to the party or parties mentioned in paragraph 8 hereof as such. My family
    home is at _____

    _____

    in the County of _____.

4. None of the provisions of the Family Law Act, 1981 (hereinafter called 'the Act of
    1981') applies to the property because the deceased was not party to an agreement
    to marry which terminated within the past three years, and no proceedings of any
    kind have been threatened or instituted in relation to the property under any of the
    provisions of the Act of 1981.

5. No proceedings of any kind have been instituted or threatened, and no application
    or order of any kind has been made, in relation to the property, under any of the
    provisions of the Judicial Separation and Family Law Reform Act, 1989, the Family
    Law Act, 1995 ('the 1995 Act'), or the Family Law (Divorce) Act, 1996 ('the 1996
    Act') and the assurance of the property to the party or parties mentioned in para-
    graph 8 hereof is not a disposal for the purposes of defeating a claim for relief (as
    defined in Section 35 of the 1995 Act and Section 37 of the 1996 Act).

6. The property is not subject to any trust, licence, tenancy or proprietary interest in
    favour of any person or body corporate arising by virtue of any arrangement, agree-
    ment or contract entered into by me or by the deceased, or by virtue of any direct
    or indirect financial or other contribution to the purchase thereof, or by operation
    of law, or otherwise, and the property is held free from encumbrances.

7. I understand the effect and import of this Declaration which has been fully explained
    to me by my solicitor.

8.   I make this Solemn Declaration conscientiously believing it to be true for the satisfaction of _____
and pursuant to the provisions of the Statutory Declarations Act, 1938.

DECLARED before me by_____

who is personally known to me (or who is identified to me by

_____

who is personally known to me)

at _____

in the County of _____

this _____ day of _____ 19/20_____.

_____

COMMISSIONER FOR OATHS/PRACTISING SOLICITOR

STATUTORY DECLARATION OF WIDOW/WIDOWER THAT PROPERTY IS NOT A FAMILY HOME

Precedent
(To be
adapted as
circumstances
require)

I, _____

of _____

_____

in the County of _____ aged 18 years and upwards SOLEMNLY AND SINCERELY

DECLARE as follows:

1. This Declaration relates to the property known as _____
_____

   in the County of _____ (being the property comprised in folio _____ County
   _____) (hereinafter called 'the property').

2. The property is not a family home within the meaning of that term in the Family Home Protection Act, 1976 as amended by the Family Law Act 1995. No married couple has ordinarily resided therein since I acquired an interest therein, apart from myself and my late spouse _____
(hereinafter called 'my late spouse').

3. I have been married once and once only, namely to my late spouse on the _____ day of _____ 19____. We were each the lawful spouse of the other. I refer to a photocopy of our Civil Marriage Certificate upon which marked with the letter 'A' I have endorsed my name prior to making this Declaration. My late spouse died on the _____ day of _____19____ and I refer to a photocopy of his/her death certificate upon which marked with the letter 'B' I have endorsed my name prior to making this Declaration. I have not married or entered into an agreement to marry any person since the death of my late spouse.

4. None of the provisions of the Family Law Act, 1981 (hereinafter called 'the Act of 1981') applies to the property because I have not been party to an agreement to marry which has terminated within the past three years, and no proceedings of any kind have been threatened or instituted in relation to the property under any of the provisions of the Act of 1981.

5. No proceedings of any kind have been instituted or threatened, and no application or order of any kind has been made, in relation to the property, under any of the provisions of the Judicial Separation and Family Law Reform Act, 1989, the Family Law Act, 1995 ('the 1995 Act'), or the Family Law (Divorce) Act, 1996 ('the 1996 Act') and the assurance of the property to the party or parties mentioned in paragraph 8 hereof is not a disposal for the purposes of defeating a claim for relief (as defined in Section 35 of the 1995 Act and Section 37 of the 1996 Act).

6. The property is not subject to any trust, licence, tenancy or proprietary interest in favour of any person or body corporate arising by virtue of any arrangement, agreement or contract entered into by me, or by virtue of any direct or indirect financial or other contribution to the purchase thereof, or by operation of law, or otherwise, and the property is held free from encumbrances.

7. I understand the effect and import of this Declaration which has been fully explained to me by my solicitor.

LAW SOCIETY FAMILY LAW DECLARATIONS

8.   I make this Solemn Declaration conscientiously believing it to be true for the satisfaction of _____ and pursuant to the provisions of the Statutory Declarations Act, 1938.

DECLARED before me by_____

who is personally known to me (or who is identified to me by

_____

who is personally known to me)

at _____

in the County of _____

this _____ day of _____ 19/20_____.

_____

COMMISSIONER FOR OATHS/PRACTISING SOLICITOR

FORM 8

STATUTORY DECLARATION THAT PROPERTY IS NOT A FAMILY HOME WHERE A HUSBAND AND WIFE HAVE SEPARATED

Precedent
(To be
adapted as
circumstances
require)

I, _____

of _____

_____

in the County of _____ aged 18 years and upwards SOLEMNLY AND SINCERELY DECLARE as follows:

1. This Declaration relates to the property known as _____

    _____

    _____

    in the County of _____ (being the property comprised in folio _____ County _____) (hereinafter called 'the property').

2. The property is not a family home within the meaning of that term in the Family Home Protection Act, 1976 as amended by the Family Law Act, 1995. No married couple has ordinarily resided therein since I acquired an interest in the property.

3.1 I have been married once and once only, namely to _____ (hereinafter called 'my estranged spouse') on the _____ day of _____ 19_____. I refer to a photocopy of our Civil Marriage Certificate upon which marked with the letter 'A' I have endorsed my name prior to making this Declaration. I separated from my estranged spouse on the _____ day of _____ 19_____ and I refer to a photocopy/ certified extracts from a Deed of Separation/Deed of Waiver which my estranged spouse and I entered into dated the _____ day of _____ 19_____ upon which marked with the letter 'B' I have endorsed my name prior to making this Declaration. I have not married or entered into an agreement to marry any person since the date of the said Deed of Separation/Deed of Waiver.

3.2 My estranged spouse never resided in the property, nor is it intended that he/she should ever reside therein. I purchased the property after the date of the said Deed of Separation out of my own resources. There has been no reconciliation between my estranged spouse and I. He/she has never made any financial or other contribution to the purchase of the property, nor to any mortgage or similar payments relating thereto. He/she has no claim whatever to the property under common law, statute law, equity or otherwise.

4. None of the provisions of the Family Law Act, 1981 (hereinafter called 'the Act of 1981') applies to the property because I have not been party to an agreement to marry which has terminated within the past three years, and no proceedings of any kind have been threatened or instituted in relation to the property under any of the provisions of the Act of 1981.

5. No proceedings of any kind have been instituted or threatened, and no application or order of any kind has been made, in relation to the property, under any of the provisions of the Judicial Separation and Family Law Reform Act, 1989, the Family Law Act, 1995 ('the 1995 Act'), or the Family Law (Divorce) Act, 1996 ('the 1996 Act') and the assurance of the property to the party or parties mentioned in paragraph 8 hereof is not a disposal for the purposes of defeating a claim for relief (as defined in Section 35 of the 1995 Act and Section 37 of the 1996 Act).

139

LAW SOCIETY FAMILY LAW DECLARATIONS

6. The property is not subject to any trust, licence, tenancy or proprietary interest in favour of any person or body corporate arising by virtue of any arrangement, agreement or contract entered into by me, or by virtue of any direct or indirect financial or other contribution to the purchase thereof, or by operation of law, or otherwise, and the property is held free from encumbrances.

7. I understand the effect and import of this Declaration which has been fully explained to me by my solicitor.

8. I make this Solemn Declaration conscientiously believing it to be true for the satisfaction of _____
and pursuant to the provisions of the Statutory Declarations Act, 1938.

DECLARED before me by_____

who is personally known to me (or who is identified to me by

_____

who is personally known to me)

at _____

in the County of _____

this _____ day of _____ 19/20_____.

_____

COMMISSIONER FOR OATHS/PRACTISING SOLICITOR

Form 9

STATUTORY DECLARATION OF SINGLE PERSON THAT PROPERTY IS NOT A FAMILY HOME WHERE A DECREE OF NULLITY HAS BEEN GRANTED

Precedent
(To be
adapted as
circumstances
require)

I, _____

of _____

_____

in the County of _____ aged 18 years and upwards SOLEMNLY AND SINCERELY DECLARE as follows:

1. This Declaration relates to the property known as _____

    _____

    _____

    in the County of _____ (being the property comprised in folio _____ County _____) (hereinafter called 'the property').

2. The property is not a family home within the meaning of that term in the Family Home Protection Act, 1976 as amended by the Family Law Act, 1995. No married couple has ordinarily resided therein since I acquired an interest therein, apart from myself and my former spouse _____
    (hereinafter called 'my former spouse').

3. I have been married once and once only, namely to my former spouse on the ____ day of _____ 19 ____ and I refer to a photocopy of our Civil Marriage Certificate upon which marked with the letter 'A' I have endorsed my name prior to making this Declaration. A Declaration of Nullity of the said marriage was granted by the High Court/Circuit Court on the _____ day of ____ 19 ____ and I refer to a photocopy thereof upon which marked with the letter 'B' I have endorsed my name prior to making this Declaration. I have not married or entered into an agreement to marry any person since the date of the said Declaration of Nullity.

4. None of the provisions of the Family Law Act, 1981 (hereinafter called 'the Act of 1981') applies to the property because I have not been party to an agreement to marry which has terminated within the past three years, and no proceedings of any kind have been threatened or instituted in relation to the property under any of the provisions of the Act of 1981.

5. No proceedings of any kind have been instituted or threatened, and no application or order of any kind has been made, in relation to the property, under any of the provisions of the Judicial Separation and Family Law Reform Act, 1989, the Family Law Act, 1995 ('the 1995 Act'), or the Family Law (Divorce) Act, 1996 ('the 1996 Act') and the assurance of the property to the party or parties mentioned in paragraph 8 hereof is not a disposal for the purposes of defeating a claim for relief (as defined in Section 35 of the 1995 Act and Section 37 of the 1996 Act).

6. The property is not subject to any trust, licence, tenancy or proprietary interest in favour of any person or body corporate arising by virtue of any arrangement, agreement or contract entered into by me, or by virtue of any direct or indirect financial or other contribution to the purchase thereof, or by operation of law, or otherwise, and the property is held free from encumbrances.

7. I understand the effect and import of this Declaration which has been fully explained to me by my solicitor.

141

8.   I make this Solemn Declaration conscientiously believing it to be true for the satisfaction of _____
     and pursuant to the provisions of the Statutory Declarations Act, 1938.

DECLARED before me by_____

who is personally known to me (or who is identified to me by

_____

who is personally known to me)

at _____

in the County of _____

this _____ day of _____ 19/20 _____.

_____

COMMISSIONER FOR OATHS/PRACTISING SOLICITOR

FORM 10

STATUTORY DECLARATION THAT PROPERTY IS NOT A FAMILY HOME WHERE IT IS OWNED BY A COMPANY AND HAS FULL COMMERCIAL USE

Precedent
(To be
adapted as
circumstances
require)

I, _____

of _____

_____

in the County of _____ aged 18 years and upwards SOLEMNLY AND SINCERELY DECLARE as follows:

1. This Declaration relates to the property known as _____

    _____

    in the County of _____ (being the property comprised in folio _____ County _____) (hereinafter called 'the property'). The property is owned by

    _____

    Limited (hereinafter called 'the company') of which I am a director.

2. The property is not a family home within the meaning of that term in the Family Home Protection Act, 1976 as amended by the Family Law Act, 1995. No married couple has ordinarily resided therein since the company acquired an interest in the property. No Lease, Letting Agreement, Tenancy Agreement, Licence or similar agreement has been made by the company which would entitle any person to reside in the property. No officer, director, member, tenant, invitee or licensee of the company has ever resided therein.

3. None of the provisions of the Family Law Act, 1981 (hereinafter called 'the Act of 1981') applies to the property because the property is owned by the company which is incapable of entering into an agreement to marry, and no proceedings of any kind have been threatened or instituted in relation to the property under any of the provisions of the Act of 1981.

4. No proceedings of any kind have been instituted or threatened, and no application or order of any kind has been made, in relation to the property, under any of the provisions of the Judicial Separation and Family Law Reform Act, 1989, the Family Law Act, 1995 ('the 1995 Act'), or the Family Law (Divorce) Act, 1996 ('the 1996 Act') and the assurance of the property to the party or parties mentioned in paragraph 7 hereof is not a disposal for the purposes of defeating a claim for relief (as defined in Section 35 of the 1995 Act and Section 37 of the 1996 Act).

5. The property is not subject to any trust, licence, tenancy or proprietary interest in favour of any person or body corporate arising by virtue of any arrangement, agreement or contract entered into by the Company, or by virtue of any direct or indirect financial or other contribution to the purchase thereof, or by operation of law, or otherwise, and the property is held free from encumbrances.

6. I understand the effect and import of this Declaration, which has been fully explained to me by the Company's solicitor, and I am authorised by the Company to make this Declaration.

7. I make this Solemn Declaration conscientiously believing it to be true for the satisfaction of _____
    and pursuant to the provisions of the Statutory Declarations Act, 1938.

LAW SOCIETY FAMILY LAW DECLARATIONS

DECLARED before me by

_____

who is personally known to me (or who is identified to me by

_____

who is personally known to me)

at _____

in the County of _____

this _____ day of _____ 19/20 _____.

_____ _____

COMMISSIONER FOR OATHS/PRACTISING SOLICITOR

Form 11

STATUTORY DECLARATION OF SINGLE PERSON THAT PROPERTY IS NOT A FAMILY HOME WHERE A DECREE OF DIVORCE HAS BEEN GRANTED

Precedent
(To be
adapted as
circumstances
require)

I, _____

of _____

_____

in the County of _____ aged 18 years and upwards SOLEMNLY AND SINCERELY DECLARE as follows:

1. This Declaration relates to the property known as _____

    _____

    _____

    in the County of _____ (being the property comprised in folio _____ County _____) (hereinafter called 'the property').

2. The property is not a family home within the meaning of that term in the Family Home Protection Act, 1976 as amended by the Family Law Act, 1995. No married couple has ordinarily resided therein since I acquired an interest therein, apart from myself and my former spouse _____ (hereinafter called 'my former spouse').

3. I have been married once and once only, namely to my former spouse on the _____ day of _____ 19___ and I refer to a photocopy of our Civil Marriage Certificate upon which marked with the letter 'A' I have endorsed my name prior to making this Declaration. A Decree of Dissolution of the said marriage was granted by the Circuit Court/High Court on the _____ day of _____ 19_____ and I refer to a photocopy thereof upon which marked with the letter 'B' I have endorsed my name prior to making this Declaration. I have not married or entered into an agreement to marry any person since the date of the said Decree of Dissolution.

4. None of the provisions of the Family Law Act, 1981 (hereinafter called 'the Act of 1981') applies to the property because I have not been party to an agreement to marry which has terminated within the past three years, and no proceedings of any kind have been threatened or instituted in relation to the property under any of the provisions of the Act of 1981.

5. Apart from the proceedings leading to the Decree of Dissolution mentioned in paragraph 3 hereof, no proceedings of any kind have been instituted or threatened, and no application or order of any kind has been made, in relation to the property, under any of the provisions of the Judicial Separation and Family Law Reform Act, 1989, the Family Law Act, 1995 ('the 1995 Act'), or the Family Law (Divorce) Act, 1996 ('the 1996 Act') and the assurance of the property to the party or parties mentioned in paragraph 8 hereof is not a disposal for the purposes of defeating a claim for relief (as defined in Section 35 of the 1995 Act and Section 37 of the 1996 Act).

6. The property is not subject to any trust, licence, tenancy or proprietary interest in favour of any person or body corporate arising by virtue of any arrangement, agreement or contract entered into by me, or by virtue of any direct or indirect financial or other contribution to the purchase thereof, or by operation of law, or otherwise, and the property is held free from encumbrances.

7. I understand the effect and import of this Declaration which has been fully explained to me by my solicitor.

145

LAW SOCIETY FAMILY LAW DECLARATIONS

8.   I make this Solemn Declaration conscientiously believing it to be true for the satisfaction of _____
and pursuant to the provisions of the Statutory Declarations Act, 1938.

DECLARED before me by_____

who is personally known to me (or who is identified to me by

_____

who is personally known to me)

at _____

in the County of _____

this _____ day of _____ 19/20_____.

_____

Commissioner for Oaths/Practising Solicitor

Form 12

STATUTORY DECLARATION OF HUSBAND AND WIFE THAT PROPERTY IS A FAMILY HOME WHERE EITHER OF THEM WAS PREVIOUSLY MARRIED, BUT THAT PREVIOUS MARRIAGE WAS DISSOLVED

Precedent
(To be
adapted as
circumstances
require)

We, _____

and _____

both of _____

in the County of _____ both aged 18 years and upwards SOLEMNLY AND SIN-
CERELY DECLARE as follows:

1. This Declaration relates to the property known as _____
    _____
    _____
    in the County of _____ (being the property comprised in folio_____ County
    _____) (hereinafter called 'the property').

2. The property is our family home within the meaning of that term in the Family
    Home Protection Act, 1976.

3. We were lawfully married to each other on the _____ day of _____ 19_____.
    We are each the lawful spouse of the other. We refer to a photocopy of our Civil
    Marriage Certificate upon which we have endorsed our names prior to making this
    Declaration. _____ (either spouse, as applicable) was never previously
    married. _____(either spouse, as applicable) was previously
    married, namely to ——— (former spouse) on the _____ day of _____ 19____. We
    refer to a photocopy of the Civil Certificate of the said earlier marriage upon which
    marked with the letter 'B' we have endorsed our names prior to making this
    Declaration. A Decree of Dissolution of the said former marriage was granted by the
    Circuit Court/High Court on the ——— day of ——— 19—— and we refer to a pho-
    tocopy thereof upon which marked with the letter 'C' we have endorsed our names
    prior to making this Declaration.

4. None of the provisions of the Family Law Act, 1981 (hereinafter called 'the Act of
    1981') applies to the property because neither of us has been party to an agreement
    to marry which has terminated within the past three years, and no proceedings of
    any kind have been threatened or instituted in relation to the property under any
    of the provisions of the Act of 1981.

5. Apart from the proceedings leading to the Decree of Dissolution mentioned in para-
    graph 3 hereof, no proceedings of any kind have been instituted or threatened, and
    no application or order of any kind has been made, in relation to the property, under
    any of the provisions of the Judicial Separation and Family Law Reform Act, 1989,
    the Family Law Act, 1995 ('the 1995 Act'), or the Family Law (Divorce) Act, 1996
    ('the 1996 Act') and the assurance of the property to the party or parties mentioned
    in paragraph 8 hereof is not a disposal for the purposes of defeating a claim for relief
    (as defined in Section 35 of the 1995 Act and Section 37 of the 1996 Act).

6. The property is not subject to any trust, licence, tenancy or proprietary interest in
    favour of any person or body corporate arising by virtue of any arrangement, agree-
    ment or contract entered into by either of us, or by virtue of any direct or indirect
    financial or other contribution to the purchase thereof, or by operation of law, or
    otherwise, and the property is held free from encumbrances.

LAW SOCIETY FAMILY LAW DECLARATIONS

7. We understand the effect and import of this Declaration which has been fully explained to us by our solicitor.

8. We make this Solemn Declaration conscientiously believing it to be true for the satisfaction of _____
    and pursuant to the provisions of the Statutory Declarations Act, 1938.

DECLARED before me by

_____

who is personally known to me (or who is identified to me by

_____

who is personally known to me)

at _____

in the County of _____

this _____ day of _____ 19/20_____.

_____

COMMISSIONER FOR OATHS/PRACTISING SOLICITOR

FORM 13

DECLARATION FOR THE PURPOSES OF SECTION 54 (1) (B) OF THE FAMILY LAW ACT 1995

Precedent
(To be adapted as circumstances require)

I, _____ ('Immediate

Vendor') of _____

_____

in the County of _____ aged 18 years and upwards SOLEMNLY AND

SINCERELY DECLARE as follows:

1. This Declaration relates to the property known as _____
    _____
    in the County of _____ (hereinafter called 'the property') and to a Deed
    of Conveyance/Assignment made the _____ day of _____ 199____
    between_____
    ('Vendor in question') of the one part and _____ of the other part (here-
    inafter called the 'Conveyance/Assignment').

2. I have no knowledge of the existence of any proceedings calling into question the
    validity of the Conveyance/Assignment.

3. The spouse of Vendor in question has not been in actual occupation of the property
    since I acquired an interest in the property on the _____ day of _____
    19_____.

4. I have no knowledge of the existence of any statement such as is referred to in
    Section 3 (8) (b) and (c) of the Family Home Protection Act 1976 as inserted by
    Section 54 of the Family Law Act 1995.

5. And I make this Solemn Declaration conscientiously believing the same to be true
    for the satisfaction of _____
    and pursuant to the provisions of the Statutory Declarations Act 1938.

DECLARED before me by

_____

who is personally known to me (or who is identified to me by

_____

who is personally known to me)

at _____

in the County of _____

this _____ day of _____ 19/20_____.

_____

COMMISSIONER FOR OATHS/PRACTISING SOLICITOR

CHAPTER 7

THE LAND ACT, 1965

7.1 Introduction

Brought into operation on 9 March 1965, the Land Act, 1965 (the 1965 Act) is one in a long series of Land Acts, Settled Land Acts and Land Purchase Acts. Although various amendments to the provisions of the 1965 Act have curtailed the scope of the Act, it is, nevertheless, not possible to practise as a conveyancing solicitor within the State, without coming across the provisions of the 1965 Act on a regular basis. Of the Act's forty-eight sections, there are four which the conveyancer will come across regularly. These are:

(a) s 12;

(b) s 13;

(c) s 18; and

(d) s 45.

By virtue of the Irish Land Commission (Dissolution) Act, 1992, the Irish Land Commission, the body in which many of the powers under the 1965 Act had been vested, was dissolved and its powers devolved to the Minister for Agriculture and Food (the Minister). In addition, with the exception of fishing rights and fisheries, all property and rights in respect of property, formerly vested in the Land Commission, are now vested in the Minister. Fishing rights and fisheries are vested in or reserved to the Central Fisheries Board. Finally, the jurisdiction of the Judicial Commissioner and Appeal Tribunal of the Commission is now vested in the High Court. The Irish Land Commission (Dissolution) Act, 1992 came into operation on 31 March 1999, by virtue of the Irish Land Commission (Dissolution) Act, 1992 (Commencement) Order, 1999 (SI 75/1999).

7.2 Agricultural Holdings: s 12

Section 12(1) of the Land Act 1965 provides:

An Agricultural Holding shall not be let, sub-let or sub-divided without the consent in writing of the Land Commission which may be either general or particular or subject to conditions.

7.2.1 'AN AGRICULTURAL HOLDING'

Section 12 relates *only* to 'agricultural holdings', that is, holdings, which are substantially agricultural and/or pastoral in character (s 12(8)). For the purposes of s 12, the classification of a holding as being agricultural depends, not on the manner of its acquisition, ie whether it was purchased by virtue of the provisions of the Land Purchase Acts, but rather on its situation or actual use at the time of the subdivision. Any subdivision of any holding, which is:

(a)   not subject to a land purchase annuity, and

(b)   either wholly situate within the boundaries of a county borough, borough, urban district or town *or* is certified by the Land Commission to be required for urban development by reason of its proximity to a county borough, borough, urban district or town

is exempt from the provisions of s 12 and the consent of the Land Commission will not be required (s 12(4)). A list of county boroughs, boroughs, urban districts and towns is provided at **7.8.** (Note also that land covered by the terms of the general consent procedure dated 8 December 1977, as extended by the general consent dated 1 July 1980, is also excluded from the necessity to obtain s 12 consent. The general consent is discussed at **7.2.4.2.**)

In the case of a subdivision of non-agricultural land, which is neither covered by the above exemption nor the general consent, a letter may be obtained from the Minister, confirming that his or her consent is not necessary by virtue of the fact that the property is non-agricultural in nature.

7.2.2   'SHALL NOT BE LET, SUB-LET OR SUB-DIVIDED'

While the meaning of this phrase is fairly clear, many practitioners forget that one of its effects is to require s 12 consent to be obtained in relation to *every* letting of agricultural land, irrespective of whether a subdivision or subletting is involved.

7.2.3   'WITHOUT THE CONSENT IN WRITING OF THE LAND COMMISSION'

Where the letting, subletting or subdivision of an agricultural holding falls within the ambit of s 12, the consent of the Minister, in writing, *must* be obtained. Where such consent is required but not obtained, s 12(3) of the Land Act provides that any such letting, subletting or subdivision is null and void as against all persons. It should be noted, however, that the Land Commission may grant its consent retrospectively, so that failure to obtain consent prior to the attempted subdivision need not be fatal (s 12(3)).

It is worth noting that the power of the Minister to withhold s 12 consent is, by virtue of s 12(2), limited to situations where the Minister seeks to prevent the creation or continuance of uneconomic holdings.

The procedure for obtaining Land Commission consent is set out at **7.2.5.**

7.2.4   'MAY BE EITHER GENERAL OR PARTICULAR OR SUBJECT TO CONDITIONS'

7.2.4.1   Particular consent

Clearly, where an application is made to the Minister in respect of a particular transaction, the consent which issues will be particular to that transaction. Often, a particular consent will issue subject to conditions. For example, where the agricultural holding in question is subject to a land purchase annuity, s 12 consent will usually only issue on condition that the annuity is apportioned between that part of the holding being partitioned and that part being retained. The consent will then require that the portion of the annuity relating to the divided plot be redeemed.

Section 12 consents will also usually stipulate a 'shelf life' for the consent. This is most commonly three years from the date of the consent.

7.2.4.2 General consent

By virtue of SR 1977/13 (Direction dated 8 December 1977 from the Department of Agriculture (Land Commission) under reference SR 13/77), originally issued in December 1977 and subsequently amended on 1 June 1980, the Land Commission amended the consent procedure in respect of certain subdivision transactions. SR 1977/13 essentially grants a general consent in respect of the subdivision of agricultural holdings, where the subdivision satisfies certain criteria. These are:

(a) the holding to be subdivided must be registered land. Thus, the subdivision of a holding, which is registered in the Registry of Deeds will never be covered by the general consent;

(b) the severed plot must not exceed one hectare (2.471 acres) in size;

(c) the purchaser of the severed plot must be a qualified person within the meaning of the 1965 Act, s 45 (see **7.5.3** below). In this regard, it is important to note that the general consent will not apply even where the purchaser of the severed plot is not a qualified person within the meaning of s 45, but subsequently obtains consent under s 45; and

(d) where the holding to be subdivided is subject to either a land purchase annuity or a land reclamation annuity, the severed plot must be discharged from payment of same. In such cases, the balance of the holding will remain charged with the entire annuity.

Paragraph 6 of SR 1977/13 stipulates certain exclusions from the general consent. These are:

(i) where the owner of the agricultural holding, or his solicitor, has received any communication from the Land Commission concerning proceedings for the acquisition under the Land Acts of whole or part of the holding;

(ii) where the balance of the holding, after severance of the plot, would have an area of less than two hectares. For the purpose of calculating the area of the remainder of the holding, any land held in undivided commonage shares should be excluded. The original version of SR 1977/13 required that the area of the remainder of the holding should exceed five hectares. This was amended in June 1980. In addition, the initial stipulation limiting the number of times a holding could be subdivided to five, was also removed in 1980;

(iii) in order to avail of the general consent, multiple subdivisions aggregating in excess of two hectares, must be to different parties;

(iv) where the severed plot contains any buildings other than:

(a) old buildings which are uninhabited and unused, or

(b) a building or buildings newly erected or in the course of erection pursuant to the current subdivision transaction;

(v) where the holding to be subdivided comprises a Land Commission trust scheme; and

(vi) where the holding to be subdivided is a registered holding which has been involved in exchange or partial exchange proceedings with the Land Commission and where the exchanged lands are awaiting revesting.

In all cases where it is sought to rely on the general consent procedure, the appropriate certificate must be furnished to the Land Registry. This certificate is incorporated in the transfer. The appropriate wording in the deed of transfer is:

It is hereby certified that Folio X County Y herein is not affected by any of the circumstances listed in para 6 of the General Consent dated 1 June 1980 SR 1977/13

Where a transfer is lodged in the Land Registry for registration and it is sought to rely on the general consent, and it subsequently transpires that the transaction is not covered by the general consent, the dealing will be rejected by the Land Registry. In such circumstances, it is open to the parties to apply for ministerial consent retrospectively.

7.2.5   OBTAINING S 12 CONSENT

Although the contract for sale does not stipulate the person whose responsibility it is to obtain s 12 consent, as a matter of practice, it is the vendor who usually does so. For the avoidance of doubt, a prudent purchaser's solicitor should ensure that a special condition, dealing with the matter, is inserted into the contract. The following is a sample special condition, which might be inserted in such circumstances:

The within contract is conditional upon the vendor obtaining, within 10 days from the date hereof, sub-division consent under section 12 of the Land Act, 1965 in respect of the lands being sold hereunder. In the event that such consent is not forthcoming within 10 days from the date hereof (unless the time shall be extended by agreement between the parties) the purchaser shall be entitled to rescind this contract and be refunded his deposit but without interest, costs or compensation thereon. Completion shall be two weeks from the date of receipt by the vendor of such consent.

Any special condition inserted into a contract for sale, whereby the vendor seeks to preclude the purchaser from raising requisitions or objections in relation to the letting, subletting or subdivision of an agricultural holding shall be null and void (s 12(7)).

Prior to 16 August 1999, applications for s 12 consent were made on foot of an application form. These forms are no longer in use, and the application is now made in the form of a covering letter, setting out the nature of the application, ie whether the application refers to a subdivision or a lease. The covering letter should be accompanied by the following:

(a)   subdivision consent:

(i)   registered land: certified up-to-date copy appropriate folio (ie a folio issued within six months of the date of the application);

(ii)   unregistered land: copy map, indicating the property affected by the subdivision;

(b)   leasing consent:

(i)   registered land: certified up-to-date copy of the appropriate folio. There is no necessity to lodge a copy of the lease;

(ii)   unregistered land: copy map, indicating the property affected by the letting. Again, there is no necessity to lodge a copy of the lease.

When acting for the vendor of a plot of land, to which s 12 applies, it is advisable to make the application for consent at the earliest possible stage in the transaction. If acting for the purchaser in such a transaction, it is worth remembering that, although the onus of obtaining the s 12 consent may not rest with the purchaser, it *is* his solicitor's obligation to register the client's title. Since the Land Registry will reject any application not accompanied by an appropriate consent, it is important that the purchaser's solicitor ensures that he or she obtains the s 12 consent on closing. An undertaking to furnish s 12 consent should neither be given nor accepted.

When investigating title, a solicitor acting for a purchaser of unregistered land should ensure that s 12 consents were obtained for all previous subdivisions, lettings or sublettings, which took place after 9 March 1965. Clearly, this warning does not apply to the purchase of registered property, as the Registrar of Titles will only register an interest if accompanied by s 12 consent (where same is required). Thus, when acting for the purchaser of registered land, one need be concerned only with the implications of s 12 for the current transaction.

If the purchaser is not a qualified person within the meaning of the Land Act, 1965, s 45 (see discussion at **7.5.3**), an application for s 45 consent should be filed contemporaneously with the application for s 12 consent.

7.2.6 Certificates and Descriptions

7.2.6.1 Where general consent is relied upon

At **7.2.4.2**, it has been seen that, where seeking to rely upon the general consent procedure, a certificate, confirming that the transaction does not fall within any of the exclusions set out in para 6 of SR 1977/13, must be furnished. This certificate is generally incorporated in the deed of assurance and takes the following form:

> *It is hereby certified that Folio X County Y herein is not affected by any of the circumstances listed in paragraph 6 of the General Consent dated 1 July 1980 (SR 1977/13).*

7.2.6.2 Where consent to the subdivision has been obtained

Where consent to subdivision has been obtained, the description of the property in the appropriate deed of assurance should make reference to the letter of consent.

A. Registered Land

ALL THAT AND THOSE that part of the lands comprised in Folio 123 of the Register of Freeholders County Clare more particularly marked on the map referred to in the Letter of Consent to Sub-Division dated 21st Samhain 1981 Ref.: PD 601/81.

B. Unregistered Land

ALL THAT AND THOSE that part of the townland of Puckcastle, Barony of Rathdown and County of Dublin comprising 10 acres or thereabouts statute measure more particularly delineated on the map annexed hereto and thereon outlined in red and marked with the letter 'B' which map is referred to in the Letter of Consent to Sub-Division dated 1st Samhain 1981 Ref.: PD 678/81.

7.3 Provisional List of Land for Compulsory Purchase: s 13

Although s 13 should not trouble the practitioner very often, it is important that a solicitor acting for the purchaser of agricultural land is aware of its application and makes appropriate enquiries. The section applies only to lands appearing on the Minister's provisional list for compulsory purchase. Any land appearing on this list may not be sold, let, sublet or subdivided without the written consent of the Minister, until such time as the proceedings for the acquisition of the lands, under the Land Purchase Acts, have been terminated (s 13(1)).

This provisional list is transmitted to the Registrar of Titles, who will make appropriate entries in the register. These entries are deleted when they cease to have effect. In the case of registered land, therefore, the usual search in the Land Registry will disclose whether or not a property is affected by the provisional list. In the case of unregistered land, the usual searches will not make a similar disclosure. It is, therefore, imperative for the solicitor acting for the purchaser of unregistered agricultural land to pay particular attention to the reply furnished by the vendor to requisition 12 of the Requisitions on Title. This requisition includes the Land Acts in its list of notices to be disclosed. Also helpful is requisition 19.3, which calls for the production of 'any Vesting Order made to provide for consolidation with the property sold'.

From the perspective of the solicitor acting for the vendor of agricultural land, it is extremely important to make careful enquiry of the vendor, to ascertain whether any notices, relating to compulsory purchase under the Land Purchase Acts, have been served on him. In this regard, the vendor's solicitor must note carefully the provisions of s 40(6) of the Land Act, 1923 and s 13(2) of the 1965 Act. The former provision enables any person appointed by the Minister to enter upon any lands to inspect them, once notice in writing has been served upon the owner or occupier of such lands. By virtue of the 1965 Act, s 13(2) any sale, letting, subletting or subdivision of land, within three months of service of such a notice, is void as against any person. This period of three months may be extended to six months by the Minister. When taking instructions in relation to the sale of agricultural land, therefore, the vendor's solicitor must bear in mind the provisions of general condition 35 of the Contract for Sale, relating to the disclosure of notices.

7.4   Sporting Rights: s 18

Section 18 applies only to registered land and deals with sporting rights reserved to a person other than the registered owner of the lands affected by the rights. Where the sporting rights have not been exercised for a period of twelve years ending on 9 March 1965 (the effective date of the 1965 Act), or for any subsequent twelve-year period, s 18 provides that these rights shall cease to exist.

In the context of s 18, sporting rights exclude (a) fishing rights, and (b) sporting rights reserved to the Land Commission (now the Minister).

Where the sporting rights have ceased to exist by operation of s 18, the registered owner or occupier of the property is entitled to make an application to the Land Registry to have the reference to the sporting rights removed from the register. The application is made on foot of an affidavit sworn by the interested party, a notice having first been placed in a local newspaper. Samples of the affidavit and advertisement to be used are set out below.

ADVERTISEMENT

_____ of _____(insert full name and address) at the expiration of fourteen days from the date hereof intends to apply pursuant to section 18 of the Land Act 1965 to the Registrar of Titles, Land Registry, Chancery Street, Dublin 7, for cancellation of certain Sporting Rights reserved to _____ on Folio

THE LAND ACT, 1965

The existence of such sporting rights is covered by requisition 7 of the Requisitions on Title.

When acting for the purchaser of such sporting rights, a solicitor should take care to ascertain whether the rights have been exercised within the twelve years prior to the transaction. If they have not, the rights will cease to exist by operation of s 18. Where the sporting rights have been exercised within the relevant period, an affidavit to that effect should be obtained from the vendor.

7.5   Section 45

Section 45(2)(a) provides:

Notwithstanding any other enactment or any rule of law but subject to paragraph (b) of this section and to subsection (3) of this section, no interest in land to which this section applies shall become vested in a person who is not a qualified person except with the written consent (whether general or particular) of the Land Commission and subject to any conditions attached to the consent having been complied with, and the determination of the application for such consent shall be an excepted matter for the purposes of section 12 of the Land Act, 1950.

7.5.1   'INTEREST IN LAND'

For the purposes of s 45, an interest in land is defined as including:

(a)   an estate;

(b)   a leasehold interest or tenancy (including an interest under a grant for a term of years whether or not reserving a rent);

(c) an interest of a mortgagee (including an equitable motgagee) or a chargeant;

(d) an interest referable to a person's having contracted to buy, or having contracted to take a lease or tenancy;

(e) an interest referable to a right to become registered as owner of the land or of a charge thereon under the Registration of Title Acts, 1891 and 1942, or the Registration of Title Act, 1964;

(f) an interest consisting of the right to ratify the contract or other transaction conferred by s 37(1) of the Companies Act, 1963; or

(g) an interest referable to a possession,

and comprises equitable and beneficial interests as well as legal interests.

7.5.2 'LAND TO WHICH THIS SECTION APPLIES'

This phrase is defined by s 45(1) and means land *not* situate in a county borough, borough, urban district or town. Thus, land entirely situated within a county borough etc is excluded from the application of s 45. Consent to the vesting of such land, even where the purchaser is not a qualified person within the meaning of the section (see **7.5.3** below), is therefore not required. It is important to remember that, in order to benefit from this exclusion, the *entirety* of the land being transferred must be so situated.

In order to assist practitioners in determining whether a property is land to which s 45 does not apply, the Conveyancing Committee published a list of county boroughs, boroughs, urban districts and towns in the Law Society Gazette, December 1993. This list is reproduced at **7.9**.

7.5.3 'QUALIFIED PERSON'

In any case where the property in question is not exempted by virtue of being situated in a county borough etc, the provisions of s 45(2)(a) will operate to prevent the property from vesting in any body (legal or natural), which is not a qualified person within the meaning of s 45.

Section 45(1) sets out ten categories of persons, who are 'qualified persons' within the meaning of the section. These categories are:

(i) *an Irish citizen,*

(ii) *a person (other than a body corporate) who has been ordinarily resident in the State continuously during the seven years ending at the material time,*

(iii) *a person who is certified by the Minister for Industry and Commerce as having shown to the satisfaction of that Minister that he is acquiring the relevant interest exclusively for the purpose of an industry other than agriculture,*

(iv) *a local authority for the purposes of the Local Government Act, 1941,*

(v) *a body corporate which, by virtue of a licence issued under or having effect by virtue of the Companies Act, 1963, is registered under the Act without the addition of the word 'limited' or the word 'teoranta',*

(vi) *a body corporate established by a Saorstat Eireann statute or an Act of the Oireachtas,*

(vii) *a body corporate incorporated in the State pursuant to a specific direction or authorisation contained in a Saorstat Eireann statute or an Act of the Oireachtas,*

(viii) *a bank named in the Third Schedule to the Central Bank Act, 1942,*

(ix) *a person who is certified by the Land Commission as having shown to their satisfaction that he is acquiring the relevant interest for private residential purposes where the land involved does not exceed five acres in extent,*

(x) *any category declared by the Minister by regulations to be an additional category for the purposes of this definition*

Originally, the effect of these categories was to exclude, inter alia, non-Irish citizens and all bodies corporate, irrespective of whether they were incorporated in the State. Fortunately for practitioners and their clients this ministerial power provided for in s 45(1)(x) has been exercised on a number of occasions, most significantly in the Land Act, 1965 (Additional Category of Qualified Persons) Regulations, 1983 (SI 144/1983), in the Land Act, 1965 (Additional Category of Qualified Persons) Regulations, 1994 (SI 67/1994) and again in the Land Act, 1965 (Additional Category of Qualified Persons) Regulations, 1995 (SI 56/1995).

7.5.3.1 Land Act, 1965 (Additional Category of Qualified Persons) Regulations, 1983 (SI 144/1983)

SI 144/1983 was introduced to implement various EC Directives on the freedom of establishment. The effect of SI 144/1983 was to extend the definition of 'qualified person' to include citizens of EC member states acquiring an interest in land for the purposes of exercising the right of establishment under the Treaty of Rome. It should be noted that SI 144/1983 relates only to self-employed persons. Furthermore, the property in question must be acquired in connection with the exercise by the self-employed person of his or her right of establishment. See the practice notes issued by the Conveyancing Committee in the Law Society Gazette, December 1980 and May 1985.

7.5.3.2 Land Act, 1965 (Additional Category of Qualified Persons) Regulations, 1994 (SI 67/1994)

In issuing SI 67/1994, the Minister excluded the 'counties' of Dublin South, Fingal and Dun-Laoghaire/Rathdown from the ambit of s 45 by extending the definition of 'qualified person' to include persons acquiring an interest in land in one of these areas.

7.5.3.3 Land Act, 1965 (Additional Category of Qualified Persons) Regulations, 1995 (SI 56/1995)

Given the limitations of SI 144/1983, and the progress made by the European Communities with regard to the free movement of persons and freedom of establishment within the EC, it is not surprising that in 1995, the Minister published SI 56/1995. By virtue of this statutory instrument, the following persons may now be described as a 'qualified person':

(a) a natural person whose principal place of residence is in a member state of either the European Communities or in a contracting party to the European Economic Area Agreement (EEAA). It should be noted that, under this heading, there is no requirement that the persons should be *citizens* of such State, and

(b) a body corporate incorporated in either a member state of the European Communities or in a contracting party to the EEAA *and* which has its registered office, central administration or principal place of business within the territory of those States.

The EEAA covers all the member states of the EU as well as Sweden, Norway, Iceland and, shortly, Liechtenstein. Switzerland, the Channel Islands and the Isle of Man are not member states of the EEAA.

7.5.4 'EXCEPT WITH THE WRITTEN CONSENT (WHETHER GENERAL OR PARTICULAR) OF THE LAND COMMISSION'

Where the property to be vested is *not* situated within one of the exempted areas and the person in whom the property is to be vested is *not* a qualified person, as defined, the consent of the Minister must be obtained.

As with s 12 consent, s 45 consent may be either particular or general.

Failure to obtain consent will prevent the interest from vesting in the purchaser/mortgagee. However, failure to obtain the consent prior to the execution of the deed of assurance need not be fatal, as the consent may be given retrospectively (s 45(9)(a)).

7.5.5 EXCLUSIONS FROM S 45

Apart from the areas exempted from s 45, discussed at **7.5.2** above, the vesting of land in the following categories of persons is excluded by s 45(2)(b) from the ambit of s 45(2)(a):

(a) a State authority;

(b) a person acting as legal representative of a deceased person; or

(c) on the distribution of the estate of a deceased person if the interest becomes vested, in the case of an interest which is real estate, in the heir or a member of the family (not being the heir) of the deceased person or, in any other case, in a member of the family of the sample person.

7.5.6 APPLYING FOR S 45 CONSENT

By virtue of general condition 28 of the Contract for Sale, it is the obligation of the purchaser to apply for and obtain s 45 consent. A solicitor acting for a purchaser in a transaction where s 45 consent is required, should note that general condition 28 provides that the sale shall not be conditional upon obtaining the consent. It is therefore a wise practice for the purchaser's solicitor to insert a special condition, countermanding general condition 28. The following is a sample condition, which might be used in this situation:

> This contract is subject to the purchaser obtaining the consent of the Minister for Agriculture pursuant to s 45 of the Land Act, 1965, to the vesting in the purchaser of the property, the subject matter of this contract. In the event of same not being forthcoming within four weeks from the date hereof or within such reasonable time thereafter as the vendor and the purchaser may agree, this agreement shall be at an end and the purchaser shall be entitled to a refund of his deposit in full but without interest, costs or compensation. General condition 28 is hereby amended.

The application for consent should be lodged by the purchaser as soon as is possible. This application must be bona fide, as was held in *Costelloe v Mahraj, Krishna Properties (Ireland) Ltd*, 10 July 1975, High Court (unreported) per Finlay P. In this case, one of the defendants contracted to purchase property to which s 45 applied. The contract was made subject to the purchaser obtaining s 45 consent. The consent was refused. On the facts of the case, the court found that the defendants, in replying to a series of questions raised by the Land Commission, had given certain replies, in an intentional effort to prevent the granting of the consent. It was, therefore, held that there is an obligation on the purchaser to make a bona fide application for s 45 consent. In the instant case, as the application had been made mala fide, the purchaser was not entitled to the return of his deposit, as provided for by the relevant special condition.

The application for s 45 consent is made on a form, which is reproduced in **Appendix 7.1.** The form should be completed carefully and should be accompanied by the following documents:

(a) copy folio (registered land);

(b) copy map (unregistered land);

159

(c) copy relevant instrument relating to transaction (eg draft transfer); and

(d) copy memorandum and articles of association (where applicant is a company).

As with s 12 consent, the parties may not contract out of their respective rights to raise requisitions pertaining to the s 45 consent (s 45(10)).

7.6 Certificates to be Included in Deeds of Assurance

Although it is not strictly necessary to include a s 45 certificate in an instrument vesting ownership in land which is wholly situated in one of the exempted areas (see **7.5.3.2** and **7.5.2** above), it is, nevertheless, good practice to include an s 45 certificate in *all* deeds of assurance. Where the appropriate certificate has been included, s 45(3)(a) provides that the instrument, in which the certificate is contained, will effectively vest the interest, passing under the instrument, in the purchaser. The certificate is contained in the body of the instrument and is given by the purchaser. In this regard, practitioners and their clients should heed the warning of the Conveyancing Committee, contained in its practice note, published in the Law Society Gazette, August 1989, regarding the veracity of such certificates. Subsequent purchasers may rely upon the certificate.

7.6.1 SAMPLE CERTIFICATES

7.6.1.1 Consent has been obtained

It is **hereby certified** by the purchaser that the consent of the Minister for Agriculture has been obtained to the vesting in him of the lands the subject of this deed and that any conditions attached thereto have been complied with.

7.6.1.2 Purchaser is a qualified person

It is **hereby certified** by the purchaser being the person becoming entitled to the entire beneficial interest in the property hereby transferred that he is an Irish citizen and as such is a qualified person within the meaning of s 45 of the Land Act, 1965.

It is **hereby certified** by the purchaser being the person becoming entitled to the entire beneficial interest in the property hereby transferred that he is a person whose principal place of residence is a Member State of the EU and as such he is a qualified person within the meaning of s 45 of the Land Act, 1965, as amended by SI 56/1995.

It is **hereby certified** by the purchaser being the person becoming entitled to the entire beneficial interest in the property hereby transferred that it is a company having its principal place of business within the EU and as such it is a qualified person within the meaning of s 45 of the Land Act, 1965, as amended by SI 56/1995.

7.6.1.3 Property is wholly situate in an exempted area (certificate of location)

It is **hereby certified** by the purchaser that the property hereby transferred is wholly situated in the urban district of Cobh.

7.6.1.4 Purchaser is excluded under s 45(2)(b)

It is **hereby certified** by the Minister for Agriculture that he is a State Authority within the meaning of s 45(1) of the Land Act, 1965.

7.7 Offences Under s 45

By virtue of s 45(6) it is an offence for any person to make any statement, which, to his knowledge, is false or misleading:

(a) in connection with an application for a certificate under paragraph (iii) or (ix) of the definition of 'qualified person';

(b) in connection with an application for a consent under s 45(2);

(c) in a certificate under s 45(3); and

(d) in reply to a requisition under s 45.

Failure to comply with a requisition under s 45 and failure to make any disclosure required by s 45 is also an offence.

An offence under s 45(6) is triable either summarily or on indictment, at the discretion of the prosecutor.

7.8 Areas Exempted From the Provisions of the Land Act, s 12

7.8.1 COUNTY BOROUGHS, BOROUGHS, URBAN DISTRICTS AND TOWNS

A town means the area comprised in a town, not being an urban district, in which the Towns Improvement (Ireland) Act, 1854 is in operation (Interpretation Act, 1937, s 12). A list of county boroughs, boroughs, urban districts and towns is appended.

7.8.1.1 County boroughs

Cork, Dublin, Galway, Limerick, Waterford.

7.8.1.2 Boroughs

Clonmel, Drogheda, Dun Laoghaire, Kilkenny, Sligo, Wexford.

7.8.1.3 Urban districts

Arklow, Athlone, Athy, Ballina, Ballinasloe, Birr, Bray, Buncrana, Bundoran, Carlow, Carrickmacross, Carrick-on-Suir, Cashel, Castlebar, Castleblayney, Cavan, Ceannanus Mor, Clonakilty, Clones, Cobh, Dundalk, Dungarvan, Ennis, Enniscorthy, Fermoy, Killarney, Kilrush, Kinsale, Letterkenny, Listowel, Longford, Macroom, Mallow, Midleton, Monaghan, Naas, Navan, Nenagh, New Ross, Skibbereen, Templemore, Thurles, Tipperary, Tralee, Trim, Tullamore, Westport, Wicklow, Youghal.

7.8.1.4 Towns

Ardee, Balbriggan, Ballybay, Ballyshannon, Bandon, Bantry, Belturbet, Boyle, Callan, Cootehill, Droichead Nua, Edenderry, Fethard, Gorey, Granard, Kilkee, Lismore, Loughrea, Mountmellick, Muine Beag, Mullingar, Newbridge, Newcastle West, Passage West, Portlaois, Rathkeale, Roscommon, Tramore, Tuam.

7.9   Areas Exempted From the Land Act, s 45

7.9.1   COUNTY BOROUGHS, BOROUGHS, URBAN DISTRICTS AND TOWNS

A town means the area comprised in a town, not being an urban district, in which the Towns Improvement (Ireland) Act, 1854 is in operation (Interpretation Act, 1937, s 12). A list of county boroughs, boroughs, urban districts and towns is appended.

7.9.1.1   County boroughs

Cork, Dublin, Galway, Limerick, Waterford.

7.9.1.2   Boroughs

Clonmel, Drogheda, Dun Laoghaire, Kilkenny, Sligo, Wexford.

7.9.1.3   Urban districts

Arklow, Athlone, Athy, Ballina, Ballinasloe, Birr, Bray, Buncrana, Bundoran, Carlow, Carrickmacross, Carrick-on-Suir, Cashel, Castlebar, Castleblayney, Cavan, Ceannanus Mor, Clonakilty, Clones, Cobh, Dundalk, Dungarvan, Ennis, Enniscorthy, Fermoy, Killarney, Kilrush, Kinsale, Letterkenny, Listowel, Longford, Macroom, Mallow, Midleton, Monaghan, Naas, Navan, Nenagh, New Ross, Skibbereen, Templemore, Thurles, Tipperary, Tralee, Trim, Tullamore, Westport, Wicklow, Youghal.

7.9.1.4   Towns

Ardee, Balbriggan, Ballybay, Ballyshannon, Bandon, Bantry, Belturbet, Boyle, Callan, Cootehill, Droichead Nua (Co Kildare), Edenderry, Fethard (Co Tipperary), Gorey, Granard, Kilkee, Lismore, Loughrea, Mountmellick, Muine Beag, Mullingar, Newcastle West, Passage West, Portlaois, Rathkeale, Roscommon, Tramore, Tuam.

7.9.1.5   Non-municipal towns

Abbeyfeale, Abbeyleix, Athenry, Bailieboragh, Ballaghadeareen, Ballinrobe, Ballybofey, Ballybunion, Ballyhaunis, Banagher, Blanchardstown, Blarney, Caherciveen, Cahir, Carndonagh, Carrick-on-Shannon, Castlecomer-Donaguile, Castleisland, Castlereagh, Celbridge, Clara, Claremorris, Clifden, Clondalkin, Dingle, Donegal, Dunmanway, Ennistimon, Gort, Graigenamanagh-Tinnahinch, Greystones-Delgany, Kanturk, Kenmare, Kildare, Killorglin, Killybegs, Kilmallock, Lucan-Doddsborough, Malahide, Maynooth, Millstreet, Moate, Mitchelstown, Monasterevin, Mountrath, Moville, Portarlington, Portlaw, Rathdrum, Rathluirc, Roscrea, Rush, Skerries, Swinford, Swords, Tallaght, Thomastown, Tullow.

APPENDIX 7.1

Section 45 Application Form

DEPARTMENT OF AGRICULTURE & FOOD

Land Act, 1965—Section 45

APPLICATION FOR

(I) CONSENT TO THE VESTING IN NON-QUALIFIED PERSON(S) OF AN INTEREST IN LAND, NOT SITUATE IN A COUNTY BOROUGH, URBAN DISTRICT OR MUNICIPAL TOWN. SECTION (2)

OR

(II) CERTIFICATION THAT THE INTEREST IS BEING ACQUIRED FOR PRIVATE RESIDENTIAL PURPOSES WHERE THE LAND DOES NOT EXCEED 2.023 HECTARES IN EXTENT. SECTION (1) (IX)

If practicable, this form should be personally completed by the person in whom the interest is proposed to be vested: if completed by an agent, the circumstances should be explained. In the case of a body corporate, it may be completed by any Director, Manager, Secretary or other duly authorised officer of the company. When completed the form should be sent to Lands Division, Department of Agriculture & Food, Farnham Street, Cavan. Tel. (049) 4368200. Failure to supply all the information indicated in the form may delay a decision.

N.B. Special attention is drawn to subsections (6) and (7) of Section 45 of Land Act, 1965. These subsections include provisions for prosecution and heavy penalties for a false or misleading statement in connection with an application for a consent, etc. On conviction of indictment, the Court may impose a fine not exceeding ten thousand pounds (£10,000) and/or imprisonment not exceeding three years.

PARTICULARS OF PROPERTY FOR WHICH CONSENT/CERTIFICATE IS APPLIED

(1)   Lands and buildings

County	Folio No.	Townland	Area (hectares)

Copy folio or, in the case of unregistered land, copy map should be furnished.

PARTICULARS OF TRANSACTION

(2)   Full details of the relevant transaction should be given hereunder and a copy of any relevant instrument should be attached:

(2)(a)   Is it intended to use the property for residential purposes: Yes ☐ No ☐

SECTION 45 APPLICATION FORM

PARTIES

Present owner of the lands

(3) Name   _____

    Address   _____

                  _____

(4) Place of permanent   _____
    residence

                  _____

Person in whom the interest is proposed to be vested

(5) Name   _____

    Address   _____

                  _____

(6) Place of permanent   _____
    residence

                  _____

In the case of a body corporate, a copy of the memorandum and articles of association should be furnished.

              SIGNATURE OF APPLICANT   _____

(Block Letters)   GIVEN NAME(S)   _____

                  FAMILY NAME   _____

                  ADDRESS   _____

                        DATE _____

              SIGNED BY APPLICANT IN THE PRESENCE OF

              SIGNATURE OF WITNESS   _____

(Block Letters)   GIVEN NAME(S)   _____

                  FAMILY NAME   _____

                  ADDRESS   _____

                               _____

                               _____

                  OCCUPATION   _____

Please ensure form is signed and witnessed

CHAPTER 8

DRAFTING

8.1 Introduction

This chapter deals with two aspects of drafting, drafting of deeds and drafting of memorials. It deals primarily with the drafting of deeds in relation to unregistered title. It deals only briefly with the drafting of transfers in relation to registered titles as these are dealt with more fully in **chapter 14**.

This chapter also outlines the procedure for registering deeds in the Registry of Deeds. It does not deal with the procedure for registering deeds in the Land Registry as this is dealt with in **chapter 14**.

Drafting is an important aspect of conveyancing practice as a poorly drafted deed may have serious consequences for the conveyancer. A deed of rectification may be required or, if the parties to the original deed cannot be located, the deed may remain a defect on the title. The deed could also be void with consequent implications for the client and the solicitor's professional indemnity insurance.

8.2 Drafting a Deed in Relation to Unregistered Title

8.2.1 INTRODUCTION

Save in certain exceptional cases (mortgage, lease, building estate grant) the deed of purchase is drafted by the purchaser's solicitor and furnished for approval to the vendor's solicitor. Its purpose is to give effect to the intention of the parties, as expressed in the contract for sale, to make, confirm or concur in an assurance of some interest in property. The purchaser's solicitor must ensure that the deed provides for his or her client to obtain everything he or she is paying for and the vendor's solicitor must ensure that the deed does not give the purchaser more than he or she is paying for.

General condition 20 of the Contract for Sale provides that subject to the legislation listed therein:

> 'On payment of all moneys payable by him in respect of the Sale, and subject to the provisions of Section 980, Taxes Consolidation Act, 1997, and (if relevant) to those contained in Section 107, Finance Act, 1993 (in relation to Residential Property Tax), the Purchaser shall be entitled to a proper Assurance of the Subject Property from the Vendor and all other (if any) necessary parties, such Assurance to be prepared by and at the expense of the Purchaser.'

This condition further provides that a draft of the deed shall be submitted to the vendor's solicitor not less than seven working days, and the engrossment (ie the final version for execution) not less than four working days, before the closing date. There are many books of precedents to assist practitioners with the drafting of deeds and many firms have, over time, build up their own precedents bank. The Land Registry has also set out precedent transfers in the Land Registration Rules, 1972 (SI 230/1972). It should be noted that over-reliance on precedents inevitably leads to errors. Every transaction is different and thus precedents should be used merely as a guide for even the most experienced of practitioners.

There are general rules of construction which govern all deeds. These provide guidelines to be followed when drafting a deed for a specific transaction and also when interpreting a deed drafted by someone else.

There are particular deeds used for particular transactions depending on the nature of the title being passed. These are listed below.

Conveyance	sale of unregistered freehold interest
Fee farm grant	creation of unregistered freehold interest subject to a rent
Lease	creation of leasehold interest (term of years and subject to a rent and covenants and conditions) carved out of a freehold interest
Sublease	creation of leasehold interest (term of years and subject to a rent and covenants and conditions) carved out of a leasehold interest (then called a head lease)
Assignment	sale of unregistered leasehold interest (residue of a term of years and subject to a rent)
Transfer	sale of registered land (both freehold and leasehold)

The generic words indenture/deed/assurance/purchase deed may be used in any given situation to refer to the purchase deed drafted by the purchaser's solicitor.

Both the purchaser's solicitor drafting the deed and the vendor's solicitor approving it should ensure that the deed correctly reflects the bargain between the parties. The essential elements of the transaction must be correctly reflected in the deed, eg the parties, the price and the property. The nature of the title must also be looked at so as to determine the correct type of deed to be drafted. If more than one type of title is passing it may be necessary to use two separate deeds or, alternatively, one deed could be drafted dealing with both titles. For example, if both freehold and leasehold unregistered title is passing a conveyance and assignment could be drafted.

8.2.2   PARTS OF THE DEED

In principle there are fifteen parts to a deed though not all them appear in every deed.

1. Commencement and date

2. Parties

3. Recital of title (narrative)

4. Recital of contract for sale (connecting)

5. Testatum

6. Consideration

7. Receipt clause

8. Operative words

9. Parcels

10. Habendum

11. Covenants and conditions/Exceptions and reservations

12. Acknowledgements and undertakings

13. Statutory certificates

14. Testimonium

15. Attestation/Execution.

8.2.3   SPECIMEN DEED OF CONVEYANCE

This is a specimen deed of conveyance. The parts of the deed have been listed in the margin for illustration purposes only.

COMMENCEMENT AND DATE	THIS INDENTURE dated the first day of May Two Thousand and Two
PARTIES	BETWEEN JOHN CITIZEN of Ballymurphy in the County of Dublin Soldier (hereinafter called 'the Vendor' which expression shall where the context so admits or requires include his executors and administrators) of the one part and PATRICK PENSIONER of Ballymurphy in the County of Dublin Retired Sailor (hereinafter called 'the Purchaser' which expression shall where the context so admits or requires include his executors, administrators and assigns) of the other part.
RECITAL OF TITLE	WHEREAS the Vendor is seised of hereditaments and premises hereinafter more particularly described and intended to be hereby assured for an estate in fee simple in possession free from encumbrances.
RECITAL OF CONTRACT	AND WHEREAS the Vendor has agreed with the Purchaser for the sale to the Purchaser of the said hereditaments and premises for an estate in fee simple free from encumbrances for the sum of One Hundred and Fifty Thousand Euro.
TESTATUM	NOW THIS INDENTURE WITNESSETH that in pursuance of the said agreement
CONSIDERATION	and in consideration of the sum of One Hundred and Fifty Thousand Euro paid by the Purchaser to the Vendor
RECEIPT CLAUSE	(the receipt whereof the Vendor doth hereby acknowledge)
OPERATIVE WORDS	the Vendor as BENEFICIAL OWNER doth hereby GRANT AND CONVEY unto the Purchaser
PARCELS	ALL THAT AND THOSE that plot of land with the buildings thereon situate at Number One Main Street in the Village of Ballymurphy Townland of Greenacre Parish of All Saints Barony of Pale and County of Dublin as the same is more particularly delineated on the map or plan thereof attached hereto and thereon shown edged red
HABENDUM	TO HOLD the same UNTO AND TO THE USE of the Purchaser IN FEE SIMPLE
STATUTORY CERTIFICATES	IT IS HEREBY CERTIFIED that the consideration (other than rent) for the sale is wholly attributable to residential property and that the transaction effected by this instrument does not form part of a larger transaction or of a series of transactions in

respect of which the amount or value, or the aggregate amount or value, of the consideration (other than rent) which is attributable to residential property or which would be so attributable if the contents of residential property were considered to be residential property exceeds €190,500.

IT IS HEREBY FURTHER CERTIFIED that this instrument gives effect to the purchase of a dwellinghouse.

IT IS HEREBY FURTHER CERTIFIED that Section 29 of the Stamp Duties Consolidation Act, 1999 does not apply to this instrument as the premises is an existing house.

IT IS HEREBY FURTHER CERTIFIED by the Purchaser that he being the person becoming entitled to the entire beneficial interest in the property hereby conveyed is an Irish Citizen and as such is a qualified person within the meaning of Section 45 of the Land Act, 1965 **AND IT IS HEREBY FURTHER CERTIFIED** . . . (additional certificates to be listed here)

TESTIMONIUM

IN WITNESS whereof the parties hereto have hereunto set their hands and affixed their seals the day and year first herein written.

ATTESTATION

SIGNED SEALED and DELIVERED by the said John Citizen in the presence of:

SIGNED SEALED and DELIVERED by the said Patrick Pensioner in the presence of:

8.2.4 ANALYSIS OF DEED

8.2.4.1 Commencement and date

The general practice is to commence a deed with the words **'THIS INDENTURE'**; however, alternative wordings are also acceptable such a **'THIS ASSIGNMENT'** if the deed is an assignment and **'THIS CONVEYANCE'** if the deed is a conveyance. When the deed is in draft form the date will be left blank. The appropriate date to insert on completion is the date of execution, that is when the deed is signed and sealed by the party giving effect to the transaction. This will usually be a vendor. Delivery may often occur after execution. In strict conveyancing theory no date is necessary provided there is alternate evidence of the date of execution. However, from a practical point of view the deed will not be stamped without the insertion of the date. A penalty is incurred for late stamping.

A deed may be delivered subject to some condition being fulfilled. The deed is stated to be held in escrow. The deed does not become effective until the condition is fulfilled and that date is then the date of execution.

8.2.4.2 Parties

The names and addresses of the parties suffice to identify them. All persons necessary to enable the deed to achieve all its objects should be joined as parties to the deed. In a straightforward deed, the parties to be joined will be obvious. Examples include: vendor and purchaser; lessor and lessee; mortgagor and mortgagee. In some circumstances it may be necessary for a spouse's prior consent to be endorsed on a deed or for the deed to be executed by a third party. Examples include a lending institution to release a loan or a liquidator to confirm a sale.

If there are only two parties to the deed the first party is generally referred to as the party 'of the one part' and the second party is referred to as the party 'of the other part'. If there are more than two parties they are generally described as the party 'of the first part', the party 'of the second part', the party 'of the third part' and so on. It is also common, after stating the names and addresses of the parties, to provide that they shall thereafter be called not by their name but by the term which indicates their capacity, for example 'the vendor', 'the purchaser' or 'the mortgagee'. This is done by inserting after the parties' name and address the words '(hereinafter called "the vendor/purchaser/mortgagee")'. This practice may also be used to describe the term of a lease, ie 'the term', the lease itself, ie 'the lease', or even the description of the property, ie 'the property'.

When listing the parties to the deed the party granting the property should always be listed first and the party taking the property listed last.

8.2.4.3   Recitals of title

Recitals are not necessary to the validity of the deed but they are to be recommended provided they are not over-used. They are designed to make the title more intelligible as they provide a history of the property from the root to the present day showing how the vendor became entitled. In conveyances they may be abbreviated to recite merely that the vendor is seised of the property for the estate in question. In assignments, the person drafting the deed may skip from the root, that is the lease, to the assignment under which the vendor acquired title, but if anything unusual has occurred on title it is customary to recite this chronologically.

Recitals may provide assistance in terms of reconstructing the title in the event that any of the title deeds are lost or mislaid. In addition s 2 of the Vendor and Purchaser Act, 1874 provides that recitals in deeds twenty years old are sufficient evidence of the truth of what is recited unless it is proved to be inaccurate. Another advantage of recitals is that the party making the recital, usually the vendor, will subsequently be estopped from denying the truth of that recital.

8.2.4.4   Recitals of contract

The practice is to recite the agreement between the parties in a general way. This introduces the rest of the deed by explaining the intention of the current deed.

8.2.4.5   Testatum

Testatum is the start of the most important part of the deed. The testatum is a declaration that what follows contains details of the operation of the deed.

8.2.4.6   Consideration

It is necessary to state the consideration in the deed in order to:

(a)   rebut any presumption of a resulting use which may arise;

(b)   show that it is not a voluntary deed;

(c)   enable a receipt clause to be included; and

(d)   enable the liability of the deed to stamp duty to be ascertained as required by law.

8.2.4.7   Receipt clause

A receipt clause is necessary in the body of the deed in order for the purchaser and his successors in title to avail of certain statutory protection.

Section 54 of the Conveyancing Act, 1881 makes a receipt in the body of a deed a sufficient discharge for the purchase money. Section 55 of the same Act provides that a receipt in the deed is sufficient evidence of the payment of the purchase money in favour of a subsequent purchaser, provided he or she is a bona fide purchaser for value without notice. Payment of the purchase money to the vendor's solicitor in exchange for the deed is authorised by s 56.

8.2.4.8 Operative words

Words of grant

Words of grant are a statement as to what the vendor does by virtue of the deed. It is important to select the words of grant appropriate to the nature of the title being passed. Appropriate words of grant are:

'Grant and/or Convey' = conveyance of an unregistered freehold interest

'Demise' = creation of a leasehold interest

'Assign' = assignment of an unregistered leasehold interest

'Transfer' = all interests registered in the Land Registry (both freehold and leasehold)

'Surrender' = surrender of lease to reversioner

'Release' = discharge of mortgage

'Appoint' = exercise of power

'Confirm' = confirmation of equitable interest supplemental to transfer of legal interest.

Capacity

It is also usual for the deed to state the appropriate capacity in which the vendor sells. If these words are omitted the validity of the deed is not affected, but the purchaser loses the benefit of various covenants for title that are implied into the deed by s 7 of the Conveyancing Act, 1881.

When the correct words are used these covenants for title are automatically implied in the deed.

In a conveyance for value, if the vendor is selling 'as beneficial owner' and this is stated in the deed, four covenants are implied (Conveyancing Act, 1881, s 7):

(a)   the vendor has full right to convey the property;

(b)   the vendor warrants a covenant for quiet enjoyment;

(c)   the vendor warrants that the property is free from encumbrances (save and except for any encumbrances which may of course be disclosed in the deed, such as that the property is subject to a leasehold interest); and

(d)   the vendor will execute further assurances to vest the interest in the purchaser if this is necessary.

Where the correct words are 'as personal representative', 'as trustee', 'as mortgagee', 'under order of court' or 'as Committee of Ward of Court' only one covenant is implied, namely a covenant that the purchaser will receive the property free from encumbrances created by that party.

8.2.4.9 Parcels

Parcels is a technical term denoting a description in words of the property being assured. It should be strictly accurate and care should be taken that a map, if attached, does not conflict with the words. It should describe only the property which the vendor has contracted to sell and which the purchaser has contracted to buy. It should be sufficient so as to ensure that someone reading the deed will be able to correctly identify the property.

The parcels clause generally commences with the words **'ALL THAT AND THOSE'** followed by a clear and accurate description of the property. The description of the property may be contained in the body of the deed or alternatively the parcels clause may refer to a schedule to the deed containing the description. If a schedule is used it should be inserted after the testimonium and before the attestation clause.

If, for some reason, a map is being attached to the deed then this should be drawn by a professional draftsman.

In the event that there is an error made in the description of the property s 6(1) and (2) of the Conveyancing Act, 1881 may assist. This section provides that a conveyance operates to convey with the land all buildings, fixtures, ditches, fences, easements, rights etc appertaining to the land and all houses, outhouses, sewers, gutters, drains etc.

Obviously, if a new easement is being created this must be expressly stated and, notwithstanding the benefits of s 6, it is also the practice to refer to existing easements in the parcels clause (see general condition 15 in **chapter 5**.)

8.2.4.10   Habendum

The main object of the habendum is to mark out, define or specify the quantum of the estate being taken by the purchaser commencing with the words **'TO HOLD'**. This is done by using appropriate words of limitation. It is crucial that the correct words of limitation are used as otherwise the deed will pass some interest in the property other than that which is intended. The correct words of limitation are:

Conveyance: 'in fee simple'
Section 51 of the Conveyancing Act, 1881 provides that 'in fee simple' are the only words of limitation required to convey a fee simple. Previously the words 'and his heirs' were essential to convey a freehold.

Lease: 'for the term of years'.

Assignment: 'for the unexpired residue of the term of years'
If the correct words of limitation are 'in fee simple' but the words 'forever' or some other incorrect words are used, the deed will only pass a life estate. A deed of rectification would be required to remedy the error.

Wylie, *Irish Conveyancing Law*, para 18.86 states:

> 'It is also common for the habendum still to contain a conveyance to uses, i.e. the time-honoured formula *'unto and to the use of'* the grantee. This is *necessary* in the case of a voluntary conveyance to prevent a resulting use in favour of the grantor coming into effect. These words are, however, not strictly necessary in the case of a conveyance for consideration, but obviously their presence may be useful in the event of a dispute as to whether or not consideration was involved.'

This formula came about as a result of the Statute of Uses (Ireland) Act, 1634 which did not apply to corporations or to leasehold interests. In these cases it is acceptable merely to state 'unto the purchaser'. Thus, if the conveyance is to a natural person, the words of limitation will be 'unto and to the use of the purchaser in fee simple' and if the conveyance is to a body corporate, the words of limitation will be 'unto the purchaser its successors and assigns'.

If there are two or more purchasers it should be stated in the habendum whether they are taking the property as joint tenants or as tenants in common. If no words of severance are included, such as 'in equal shares', 'equally' or 'as tenants in common', they will take as joint tenants.

If the sale is subject to any existing encumbrances this must be disclosed at the end of the habendum by using the words 'SUBJECT TO' followed by a description of the encumbrances. An example would be a freehold interest sold subject to a lease or if, for example, the property is subject to a right of way.

Under s 63 of the Conveyancing Act, 1881, unless a contrary intention is expressed in the deed, a conveyance shall be effectual to pass all the estate, right, title and interest vested in the conveying party to the purchaser. This provision is extremely useful in a situation where the vendor holds a leasehold and freehold interest in the same property. In the deed the vendor conveys the freehold but forgets to assign the leasehold interest. It should be noted, however, that this provision does not obviate the need for the correct words of limitation to convey the freehold.

Another interesting statutory provision is the Vendor and Purchaser Act, 1874, s 2 which provides that recitals in documents twenty years old are acceptable as sufficient evidence of the contents unless proven to be inaccurate.

8.2.4.11 Covenants and conditions/Exceptions and reservations

These will depend on the circumstances of the particular transaction and could include a covenant to build or the reservation of a right of way.

The most frequent covenant arising is a covenant to pay rent contained in a deed of assignment as follows:

> THE PURCHASERS and each of them hereby covenant with the Vendor that they the Purchasers will henceforth during the continuance of the said term pay the rent reserved by and observe the covenants on the part of the Lessee and conditions contained in the Lease and will at all times keep the Vendor effectually indemnified against all actions and proceedings, costs, damages, expenses, claims, demands and liability whatsoever by reason or on account of the non-payment of the said rent or any part thereof or the breach non-performance or non-observance of the said covenants and conditions or any of them.

It is important to note that, while all covenants will bind the parties to the deed, only negative covenants run with the land so as to bind the successors in title of the covenantor (*Tulk v Moxhay* (1848) 2 Ph 774). A positive covenant is a covenant to do something while a negative covenant is a covenant not to do something.

8.2.4.12 Statutory acknowledgement and undertaking

Where original documents of title are being retained by the vendor, under general condition 34 of the Contract for Sale, the vendor shall acknowledge the right of the purchaser to production of same and to delivery of copies thereof and undertakes to keep the documents in safe custody as provided for in the Conveyancing Act, 1881, s 9.

This usually arises where part only of a property is being sold. The purchaser will receive certified copies of the title documents and the following acknowledgement and undertaking will be included in the deed:

> The vendor hereby acknowledges the right of the purchaser to production of the title documents listed in the schedule hereto (possession of which is retained by the vendor) and to delivery of copies thereof and hereby undertakes with the purchaser for the safe custody of the said documents.

The acknowledgement imposes the following obligations on the vendor:

(a)   to produce the documents for inspection;

(b)   to produce the documents for demand for court hearings to establish title; and

(c)   to furnish copies of the documents on request.

The undertaking imposes an obligation on the vendor to keep the documents safe and whole unless destroyed by fire (Conveyancing Act, 1881, s 9).

This acknowledgement and undertaking is prepared by and at the expense of the purchaser.

8.2.4.13 Statutory certificates

Statutory certificates are mandated by legislation and include the following.

Finance Act certificate

A Finance Act certificate is required on all deeds save and except where:

(a) an s 91 SDCA (ie Stamp Duties Consolidation Act, 1999) certificate is appropriate, or

(b) the deed is to be stamped at the highest rate of stamp duty, ie 9 per cent for residential property and 6 per cent for non-residential property.

The deed will then be stamped at the appropriate rate. The wording of this certificate is:

> It is hereby certified that the consideration (other than rent) for the sale/lease is wholly attributable to residential property and that the transaction effected by this instrument does not form part of a larger transaction or of a series of transactions in respect of which the amount or value, or the aggregate amount or value, of the consideration (other than rent) which is attributable to residential property or which would be so attributable if the contents of residential property were considered to be residential property exceeds €127,000/€190,500/€254,000/€317,500/€381,000/€635,000.

Stamp Duties Consolidation Act 1999, ss 29 and 53 certificate

This certificate, which was formerly called an s 112 certificate, is required on every deed. In the case of a new house or apartment this will state that s 29 (conveyance on sale) or s 53 (lease) of the Stamp Duties Consolidation Act, 1999 applies to the instrument, ie the conveyance/lease is by way of a contract for the sale/lease of a site and building contract. If a completed house or apartment is being purchased the certificate will state that s 29 (conveyance on sale) or s 53 (lease) of the Act does not apply to the instrument. The wording of this certificate is:

> It is hereby certified that section 29/section 53 of the Stamp Duties Consolidation Act, 1999 applies/does not apply to this instrument for the reason that...

Stamp Duties Consolidation Act, 1999, s 91 certificate

This certificate, which was formerly known as an s 113 certificate, is required for the purchase of a new house/apartment with a floor area certificate to obtain exemption from stamp duty. This certificate reads as follows:

> It is hereby certified that–
>
> (a) this instrument gives effect to the purchase of a dwellinghouse/apartment on the erection of that dwellinghouse/apartment,
>
> (b) on the date of execution of this instrument, there exists a valid floor area certificate (within the meaning of section 4(2)(b) of the Housing (Miscellaneous Provisions) Act, 1979) in respect of the said dwellinghouse/apartment, and
>
> (c) the purchaser/one or more of the purchasers/a person or persons in right of the purchaser/a person or persons in right of one or more of the purchasers will occupy the dwellinghouse/apartment as his/her/their only or principal place of residence for the period specified in section 91(2)(b)(ii)(new dwellinghouse/apartment with a floor area certificate) of the Stamp Duties Consolidation Act, 1999, and that no person (other than a person who, while in such occupation, derives rent or payment in the nature of rent in consideration for the provision, on or after 6 April 2001, of furnished residential accommodation in part of the

dwellinghouse/apartment concerned or other than by virtue of a title prior to that of the Purchaser) will derive any rent or payment in the nature of rent for the use of the dwelling-house/apartment or any part of it during that period.

Certificate re occupancy

A certificate re occupancy is required on the purchase of a new house/apartment without a floor area certificate. The purchaser obtains partial relief from stamp duty provided this certificate is contained in the deed confirming that he or she will occupy it as his or her only or principal place of residence for a period of five years. The certificate states:

It is hereby certified that the purchaser/one or more of the purchasers/a person or persons in right of the purchaser/a person or persons in right of one or more of the purchasers will occupy the dwellinghouse/apartment as his/her/their only or principal place of residence for the period specified in section 91(2)(b)(ii) (new dwellinghouse/apartment with no floor area certificate) of the Stamp Duties Consolidation Act, 1999, and that no person will derive any rent or payment in the nature of rent, other than a person who, while in such occupation, derives rent or payment in the nature of rent, in consideration for the provision, on or after 6 April 2001, of furnished residential accommodation in part of the dwellinghouse/apartment concerned or (other than by virtue of a title prior to that of the purchaser) will derive any rent or payment in the nature of rent for the use of the dwellinghouse/apartment or any part of it during that period.

Land Act, 1965, s 45 certificate

This certificate is required in every deed. This is dealt with in **chapter 7** and may include a certificate of location where the property is situate in an exempted area.

Land Act, 1965, s 12 certificate

This certificate is required in the deed if there is a lease, sublease or subdivision of agricultural land. Again, this is dealt with in **chapter 7**.

Family Home Protection Act 1976, s 14 certificate

This certificate is required on a deed transferring a family home from one spouse into the joint names of both spouses in order to claim exemption from stamp duty, Land Registry fees and Registry of Deeds fees. The certificate states:

It is hereby further certified that the property hereby transferred is a family home within the meaning of the Family Home Protection Act, 1976 and that this Instrument creates a joint tenancy of a family home and is exempt from stamp duty, Land Registry fees and other Court fees by reason of Section 14 of the Family Home Protection Act, 1976.

Consanguinity certificate

A consanguinity certificate (sometimes called a relationship certificate) is required on a deed between close relatives, for example, brother and sister, to claim relief from stamp duty, ie only one-half the appropriate rate is payable. This certificate states:

It is hereby further certified by the party (or parties) becoming entitled to the entire beneficial interest in the property that the person (or each of the persons) becoming entitled to the entire beneficial interest in the property is related to the person (or each of the persons) immediately theretofore entitled to the entire beneficial interest in the property as a (state relationship(s)).

Companies Act 1990, s 29 certificate

This certificate should be included in transactions between natural persons and bodies corporate and in transactions between bodies corporate to show that the parties are not connected with one another or are connected with one another and the requisite resolution has been passed by the companies involved. Section 29 provides that a company may not enter into an arrangement with a connected person without the arrangement having been first approved by resolution of the company in general meeting. The recommended certificates are set out in Practice Note, Law Society Gazette, December 1991.

In addition, s 114 of the Finance Act, 1990 as amended by s 96 of the Stamp Duties Consolidation Act, 1999 exempts from stamp duty any transfer between spouses. To obtain the benefit of this exemption the appropriate certificate can be inserted in the deed. It is not a Revenue requirement to have such certificate in the deed and there is no statutory requirement for having such certificate in the deed.

For further information on the stamp duty certificates see Revenue Leaflet SD10 STAMP DUTY issued by the Revenue Commissioners in August 2002.

8.2.4.14 Testimonium

This part of the deed links the body of the deed to the execution thereof. The words to be used are:

> 'IN WITNESS whereof the parties hereto have hereunto set their respective hands and seals the day and year first above WRITTEN'.
>
> If the parties are companies then the testimonium will state that the parties have 'caused their common seals to be affixed hereto the day and year first above WRITTEN'.

If the deed refers to a schedule this should be inserted at this point, ie after the testimonium and before the attestation.

8.2.4.15 Execution/attestation

This is where the deed is signed, sealed and delivered. Delivery of the deed indicates an intention that the deed should become operative. A deed is deemed to be delivered on execution.

Attestation means the proper witnessing of signatures.

The type of attestation clause will depend on the parties to the transaction. The correct attestation clause for a person is:

> SIGNED SEALED and DELIVERED
> by the vendor in the presence of:

The correct attestation clause for a body corporate is:

> PRESENT when the common seal of
> the vendor was affixed hereto:

For further information on the drafting of deeds relating to unregistered land see the Continuing Legal Education (CLE) seminar on The Principles of Practical Drafting of Deeds in Conveyancing Transactions by Ms Justice Mary Laffoy on 7 December 1999.

8.3 Drafting a Transfer (a Deed in Relation to Registered Land)

In the case of both freehold and leasehold registered land the appropriate deed is a transfer. The Land Registration Rules, 1972 (SI 230/1972) prescribe the forms of transfer to be used and the forms are set out in the attached Schedule of Forms. The correct form and wording must be used, otherwise the dealing will be rejected by the Land Registry. This is discussed in more detail in **chapter 14**.

8.4 Memorials and Procedure for Registration of Deeds in the Registry of Deeds

The function of the Registry of Deeds is to provide a system of registration for deeds affecting unregistered land. Deeds which are registered in the Registry of Deeds have legal priority over unregistered deeds or deeds registered later in time.

When a deed is registered in the Registry of Deeds it is not filed there. Instead it is returned to the party who delivered it for registration. The document filed in the Registry of Deeds is a memorial which summarises the provisions of the deed and also contains other statutory requirements. A memorial of a deed may serve as evidence of the contents of a lost deed.

8.4.1 REQUIREMENT FOR REGISTRATION

The statutory enactment requiring registration of a deed in relation to the assurance of land by means of a memorial derives from the Registration of Deeds (Ireland) Act, 1707 which conferred priority on a deed on the basis of the date and time of registration of that deed in the Registry of Deeds.

8.4.2 REQUIREMENTS FOR REGISTRATION AS SET OUT IN THE 1707 ACT, S 6

The deed will be examined to ascertain that:

    (a)   it affects property;

    (b)   it has been properly executed by the grantors in the presence of at least one witness;

    (c)   it bears stamp duty or is exempt from same; and

    (d)   it bears the Revenue Particulars Delivered (PD) stamp or is exempt from same.

The memorial is addressed to the Registrar and must contain the following information:

    (i)   the date of the deed;

    (ii)   the names and descriptions of all parties to the deed;

    (iii)   the names and descriptions of all witnesses to the deed;

    (iv)   a description of the property to include the county and barony or the city or town and parish as set out in the deed; and

    (v)   the names and witnesses to the memorial.

A memorial must be presented to the Registrar, signed and sealed by one of the grantors (vendors) or grantees (purchasers).

Irish case law has held that the grantor should execute the memorial but, in practice, the Registry of Deeds will accept a memorial executed by either party to a transaction. Consequently, any purchaser carrying out proper searches in the Registry of Deeds will be on notice of any deed which has been registered irrespective of which party was the applicant for registration.

The execution of the memorial must be attested by two witnesses, one of whom must also be a witness to the deed.

The common witness must then swear an affidavit before a commissioner for oaths or practising solicitor proving the signing and sealing of the deed and memorial. This affidavit is part of the form of memorial.

8.4.3 FORMAT OF THE MEMORIAL

The memorial is always made out in the past tense. It consists of a brief summary of the deed but must contain the following particulars:

(a) the date of the deed and when it was perfected. Again, in practice, the memorial only gives particulars of the date of the deed and this is accepted by the Registrar in the Registry of Deeds;

(b) the names, addresses and occupations/descriptions of all parties and witnesses to the deed;

(c) the land affected and details of its description in the deed. A schedule must be used in the memorial if a schedule is used in the deed. The description must be identical in both deed and memorial; and

(d) following the Registry of Deeds (Ireland) Act, 1832, the Registrar requires memorials to specify the county and barony or the city or town and parish. If the property is in two different towns or counties, then both must be stated.

Most importantly, the memorial must reflect the content of the deed. It must not recite something unless that same thing is also recited in the deed, ie it must not go beyond the four corners of the deed.

8.4.4 PRACTICAL STEPS FOR REGISTRATION

The memorial and deed are lodged in the Registry of Deeds and a docket or receipt will issue to the person or firm who lodged it. The Registrar's staff will compare the deed and memorial so as to ensure that the memorial accurately reflects the deed. The Registrar is obliged to see that the deed and memorial have been properly executed and that the statutory particulars are present.

If the comparison is in order, the deed and memorial are sent from the comparison office to the registration office. The Registrar will then register and endorse on the deed a signed certificate stating the day and time of registration and the book and entry number.

For example:

Registered in the Registry of Deeds Dublin at 11 minutes after 3 o'clock on the 12th day of July 2002 Book 20 No.1037.

If the comparison shows up a defect, the deed and memorial will be returned with a Query Note from the Registry and all points set out by the Registry must be corrected before resubmission of the deed and memorial for registration. The Query Note must also be returned to the Registry. It is important to ensure that the Query Note from the Registry is not mislaid, otherwise the deed and memorial will have to be resubmitted for a full comparison once again. There is a resubmission fee of €12: Registry of Deeds (Fees) Order, 1999 (SI 346/1999). The stamp duty fee for the registration of a memorial is currently €44.

It should be noted that, other than as set out above, the Registrar does not check the correctness of the content of the deed. In the Registry of Deeds the document only is registered, as opposed to in the Land Registry where the title is registered.

8.4.5 FUNCTION OF REGISTRAR

It is important to note the difference between the functions of the Registrar of Deeds in the Registry of Deeds and the Registrar of Titles in the Land Registry. The Registrar in the Registry of Deeds will register a deed provided the statutory particulars are present. The Registrar is not concerned with any question relating to the validity of the deed. This is the function of the purchaser's solicitor. By contrast the Registrar of Titles in the Land Registry must be satisfied that any transfer which is lodged for registration is a valid transfer and, consequently, must ensure that title is validly passing to the transferee on foot of the documents which are lodged for registration.

For example, a conveyance by a husband/wife of a property which is a 'family home' within the meaning of the Family Home Protection Act, 1976 without the consent of his or her spouse may be registered in the Registry of Deeds although it is void under the Family Home Protection Act, 1976. In the Land Registry, a transfer of the same property would not be registered by the Registrar of Titles without the prior consent of the spouse and verification of the marriage by statutory declaration.

This is due to the fact that title registered in the Land Registry is guaranteed by the State.

8.4.6 COMMON REASONS FOR REJECTION OF MEMORIALS

The following are a note of some of the most frequent reasons for rejection of deeds and memorials by the Registry of Deeds:

(a) insufficient description of the property;

(b) difference of description in property between deed and memorial;

(c) incorrect setting out of names, addresses and descriptions of parties and witnesses to the deed; and

(d) date of swearing of memorial prior to the date of the deed.

Further reasons are listed in Practice Notes, Law Society Gazette, April 1980 and December 1990.

8.4.7 SPECIMEN MEMORIAL OF ASSIGNMENT

NOTE
Do not
write in
margin

To the Registrar for Registering Deeds and so forth in Ireland

A MEMORIAL of an Indenture made the 23 day of July Two this Thousand and Two BETWEEN ANDREW POORMAN of Knock Lodge, Blackrock, in the County of Dublin, Banker (therein and hereinafter called 'the Vendor') of the one part and JOE RICHMAN AND MARY RICHMAN his wife both of 2 James Gardens, Dublin 4, Income Tax Inspector and Accountant respectively (therein and hereinafter called 'the Purchasers') of the other part.

RECITING THAT By Indenture of Lease dated the 4 day of December One Thousand Nine Hundred and Seventy One (registered on the 20 day of February One Thousand Nine Hundred and Seventy Two Book 28 No. 83) and made between Blackrock Developments Limited of the one part and Edward Thomps of the other part (therein and hereinafter referred to as 'the Lease') ALL AND SINGULAR the premises thereby demised and therein described and therein and hereinafter more particularly described and intended to be thereby assured were demised unto the said Edward Thomps his executors, administrators and assigns from the 4 day of January One Thousand Nine Hundred and Seventy Two for the term of Nine Thousand Nine Hundred and Ninety Nine Years at the yearly rent of £20 thereby reserved and subject to the covenants by the Lessee and conditions therein contained AND FURTHER RECITING AS THEREIN SAID INDENTURE WITNESSED that in pursuance of an agreement and the consideration therein on or before the execution thereof paid to the Vendor by the Purchasers (the receipt whereof the Vendor did thereby acknowledge) he the Vendor as beneficial owner did thereby assign unto the Purchasers their executors administrators and assigns ALL THAT the premises demised by the Lease and therein described as 'ALL THAT AND THOSE part of the lands of Currygrange otherwise Newtowncross containing 3 roods and 12 perches or thereabouts statute measure situate in the Barony of Blackrock and County of Dublin as are more particularly delineated on the

178

map hereto annexed and thereon edged with a red verge line' together with the dwelling-house erected thereon which said premises were then known as Knock Lodge Blackrock in the County of Dublin TO HOLD the said premises unto the Purchasers their executors administrators and assigns for the residue of the said term of Nine Thousand Nine Hundred and Ninety Nine Years subject to the payment of the said rent reserved by said Indenture of Lease and to the covenants and conditions therein contained and henceforth on the part of the Lessee to be performed and observed **AND FURTHER COVENANTS AND CERTIFIES AS THEREIN.**

Which said Deed as to the due Execution thereof by Andrew Poorman was witnessed by: Michael Brown

Which said Deed as to the due Execution thereof by Joe Richman was witnessed by: Patricia Mason

Which said Deed as to the due Execution thereof by Mary Richman was witnessed by: James Ronan

SIGNED AND SEALED by	ANDREW
the said ANDREW POORMAN	POORMAN
in the presence of:	(SIGNATURE)

Michael Brown,
4 Muster Place,
Dublin 6.
Clerk.

Peter Brown,
4 Munster Place,
Dublin 6.
Clerk.

The above named Michael Brown Maketh Oath and Saith that he is a Subscribing Witness to the Deed, of which the above writing is a Memorial, and also to said Memorial; and that he saw said Deed and Memorial duly executed by the said Andrew Poorman and the name Michael Brown subscribed as Witness to said Deed and Memorial, respectively, is this Deponent's property name and handwriting.

Sworn before me this 23 day of July 2002	
at 20 Nassau Street,	MICHAEL
in the County of the City of Dublin	BROWN
and I know the Deponent	

JOSEPH SMITH
Practising Solicitor/Commissioner for Oaths

8.5   Sample Deeds and Memorials

8.5.1   FREEHOLD CONVEYANCE

THIS INDENTURE made the   day of   Two Thousand and   BETWEEN
of   (hereinafter called 'the Vendor(s)' which expression shall where the context so admits or
requires include his/her/their executors and administrators/its successors) of the One Part
and   of   (hereinafter called 'the Purchaser(s)' which expression shall where the
context so admits or requires include his/her/their executors administrators and assigns/its successors
and assigns) of the Other Part.

WHEREAS:

1.   The Vendor(s) is/are seised of the hereditaments and premises more particularly described in the
       Schedule hereto (hereinafter called 'the scheduled property') and expressed to be hereby assured
       for an estate in fee simple in possession free from encumbrances.

2.   The Vendor(s) has/have agreed with the Purchaser(s) for the sale to him/her/them of the
       scheduled property for an estate in fee simple in possession free from encumbrances for
       the sum of €   .

NOW THIS INDENTURE WITNESSETH that in pursuance of the said agreement and in consideration of
the sum of €   now paid by the Purchaser(s) to the Vendor(s) (the receipt whereof the
Vendor(s) hereby acknowledge(s)) the Vendor(s) as beneficial owner(s) hereby GRANT(S) and CON-
VEY(S) unto the Purchaser(s) ALL THAT AND THOSE the scheduled property TO HOLD the same unto
and to the use of the Purchaser(s) as joint tenants/as tenants in common (insert shareholding i.e. in
equal shares) in fee simple.

IT IS HEREBY CERTIFIED. . . (include appropriate certificates for example)

IT IS HEREBY CERTIFIED by the Purchaser(s) that he/she/they being the person(s) becoming entitled to
the entire beneficial interest in the property hereby conveyed is/are and each to them is an Irish
Citizen and as such is/are a qualified person within the meaning of Section 45 of the Land Act, 1965.

IT IS HEREBY FURTHER CERTIFIED that the consideration (other than rent) for the sale is wholly attributable to residential property and that the transaction effected by this instrument does not form part of
a larger transaction or of a series of transactions in respect of which the amount or value or the aggregate amount or value of the consideration (other than rent) which is attributable to residential property
or which would be so attributable if the contents of residential property were considered to be residential property exceeds €   .

IT IS HEREBY FURTHER CERTIFIED that section 29 of the Stamp Duties Consolidation Act, 1999 does
not apply to this instrument as the premises is an existing house.

IN WITNESS whereof the parties hereto have hereunto set their hands and affixed their Seals the day
and year first herein WRITTEN.

SCHEDULE

(Description of premises)

SIGNED SEALED AND DELIVERED
by the Vendor(s) in the
presence of:

SIGNED SEALED AND DELIVERED
by the Purchaser(s) in the
presence of:

I,   being the lawful spouse of the within named Vendor in pursuance of the provisions
of the Family Home Protection Act, 1976 HEREBY CONSENT to the assurance of the within property
to the Purchaser for the sum of €   .

SIGNED by the said
in the presence of:

Dated the   day of   20

One Part

And

Other Part

INDENTURE OF CONVEYANCE

Solicitors

8.5.2   ASSIGNMENT OF ENTIRE LEASEHOLD INTEREST

THIS INDENTURE made the   day of   Two Thousand and   BETWEEN
            of   (hereinafter called 'the Vendor(s)' which expression shall where the
context so admits or requires include his/her/their executors and administrators/its successors) of the
One Part and   of   (hereinafter called 'the Purchaser(s)' which expression
shall where the context so admits or requires include his/her/their executors administrators and
assigns/its successors and assigns) of the Other Part.

WHEREAS:

1.   By Indenture of Lease (hereinafter called 'the Lease') dated   the day of   and
      made between   of the One Part and of the Other Part the premises therein and
      in the Schedule hereto described and intended to be hereby assured (hereinafter called 'the
      scheduled property') were demised by the said   to the said   for a
      term of   years from the   day of   subject to the yearly
      rent of €   thereby reserved and to the covenants on the part of the Lessee and con-
      ditions therein contained.

2.   Pursuant to the covenant in that behalf contained in the Lease the Lessee duly erected the
      dwellinghouse and premises now standing on the scheduled property and intended to be
      hereby assigned.

3. By divers mesne assurances acts in the Law events and ultimately by Indenture of Assignment dated the   day of   and made between of   the One Part and the Vendor of the Other Part the scheduled property became vested in the Vendor for the residue of the term of years granted by the Lease subject to the yearly rent thereby reserved and to the covenants on the part of the Lessee and conditions therein contained.

4. The Vendor(s) has/have agreed with the Purchaser(s) for the sale to the Purchaser(s) subject to the covenants and conditions in the Lease but otherwise free from encumbrances for the sum of €   of the scheduled property.

NOW THIS INDENTURE WITNESSETH that in pursuance of the said agreement and in consideration of the sum of €   now paid by the Purchaser(s) to the Vendor(s) (the receipt of which the Vendor(s) hereby acknowledge(s)) the Vendor(s) as beneficial owner(s) HEREBY ASSIGN(S) to the Purchaser(s) ALL AND SINGULAR the scheduled property TO HOLD the same unto the Purchaser(s) as joint tenants/tenants in common (insert shareholding i.e. in equal shares) henceforth for all the residue now unexpired of the said term granted by the Lease and subject to the yearly rent thereby reserved and to the covenants on the part of the Lessee and conditions therein contained.

AND THE PURCHASER(S) hereby covenant(s) with the Vendor(s) that he/she/they the Purchaser(s) will henceforth during the continuance of the said term pay the rent reserved by and observe the covenants on the part of the Lessee and conditions contained in the Lease and will at all times keep the Vendor(s) effectually indemnified against all actions and proceedings costs damages expenses claims demands and liability whatsoever by reason or on account of the non payment of the said rent or any part thereof or the breach non performance or non observance of the said covenants and conditions or any of them.

IT IS HEREBY CERTIFIED. . . (include appropriate certificates for example)

IT IS HEREBY FURTHER CERTIFIED by the Purchaser(s) that the scheduled property is situate in the City of Dublin.

IT IS HEREBY FURTHER CERTIFIED that the consideration (other than rent) for the sale is wholly attributable to residential property and that the transaction effected by this instrument does not form part of a larger transaction or of a series of transactions in respect of which the amount or value or the aggregate amount or value of the consideration (other than rent) which is attributable to residential property or which would be so attributable if the contents of residential property were considered to be residential property exceeds €   .

IT IS HEREBY FURTHER CERTIFIED that Section 29 of the Stamp Duties Consolidation Act 1999 does not apply to this instrument as the premises is an existing house.

IN WITNESS whereof the parties hereto have hereunto set their hands and affixed their Seals the day and year first herein WRITTEN.

SCHEDULE

(Description of premises)

SIGNED SEALED AND DELIVERED
by the Vendor(s) in the
presence of:

SIGNED SEALED AND DELIVERED
by the Purchaser(s) in the
presence of:

I,   being the lawful spouse of the within named Vendor in pursuance of the provisions of the Family Home Protection Act, 1976 HEREBY CONSENT to the assurance of the within property to the Purchaser for the sum of € .

SIGNED by the said
in the presence of:

Dated the   day of   20

One Part

And

Other Part

INDENTURE OF ASSIGNMENT

Solicitors

8.5.3 ASSIGNMENT OF PART OF A LEASEHOLD INTEREST

THIS INDENTURE made the   day of   Two Thousand and   BETWEEN of   (hereinafter called 'the Vendor(s)' which expression shall where the context so admits or requires include his/her/their executors and administrators/its successors) of the One Part and   of   (hereinafter called 'the Purchaser(s)' which expression shall where the context so admits or requires include his/her/their executors administrators and assigns/its successors and assigns) of the Other Part.

WHEREAS:

1.   By Indenture of Lease (hereinafter called 'the Lease') dated the   day of and made between   of the One Part and   of the Other Part the premises therein and in the First Schedule hereto described and portion of which is intended to be hereby assured more particularly described in the Second Schedule hereto were demised by the said   to the said   for a term of   years from the day of   subject to the yearly rent of €   (hereinafter called 'the rent') thereby reserved and to the covenants on the part of the Lessee and conditions therein contained.

2.   By divers mesne assurances acts in the Law events and ultimately by Indenture of Assignment (hereinafter called 'the Assignment') dated the day of   and made between   (hereinafter called 'the previous Assignor') of the One Part and the Vendor of the Other Part the premises intended to be hereby assured more particularly described in the Second Schedule hereto became vested in the Vendor for the residue of the term of years granted by the Lease subject to the apportioned yearly rent thereby reserved as hereinafter recited and to the covenants on the part of the Lessee and conditions therein contained but otherwise free from encumbrances.

3.   By the Assignment the rent was apportioned so that €   portion thereof was charged exclusively on the premises intended to be hereby assured more particularly described in the Second Schedule hereto and the balance thereof amounting to €   was charged upon the remainder of the premises described in the Lease which was retained by the previous Assignor and the Vendor and the previous Assignor mutually covenanted to pay the apportioned part of the rent which ought to be paid by each of them as set out in the Assignment and to perform and observe the covenants on the part of the Lessee other than the covenant for payment of the entire of the rent and the conditions contained in the Lease in so far as same relate to their portion of the premises and to indemnify each other in respect of the apportioned part of the rent borne by each of them and the previous

Assignor and the Vendor declared that all monies which might become payable to either of them under the respective covenants for indemnity contained in the Assignment were charged on the portion of the premises belonging to the other of them.

4. The Vendor(s) has/have agreed with the Purchaser(s) for the sale to the Purchaser(s) subject to the apportioned yearly rent and to the covenants and conditions in the Lease but otherwise free from encumbrances for the sum of €   of the property in the Second Schedule hereto.

NOW THIS INDENTURE WITNESSETH that in pursuance of the said agreement and in consideration of the sum of €   now paid by the Purchaser(s) to the Vendor(s) (the receipt of which the Vendor(s) hereby acknowledge(s)) the Vendor(s) as beneficial owner(s) HEREBY ASSIGN(S) to the Purchaser(s) ALL AND SINGULAR the property described in the Second Schedule hereto TO HOLD the same unto the Purchaser(s) as joint tenants/tenants in common (insert shareholding i.e. in equal shares) henceforth for all the residue now unexpired of the said term granted by the Lease and subject to the apportioned yearly rent of £   thereby reserved and to the covenants on the part of the Lessee and conditions therein contained

AND THE PURCHASER(S) hereby covenant(s) with the Vendor(s) that he/she/they the Purchaser(s) will henceforth during the continuance of the said term pay the apportioned rent reserved by and observe the covenants on the part of the Lessee and conditions contained in the Lease and will at all times keep the Vendor(s) effectually indemnified against all actions and proceedings costs damages expenses claims demands and liability whatsoever by reason or on account of the non payment of the said rent or any part thereof or the breach non performance or non observance of the said covenants and conditions or any of them.

AND THE VENDOR(S) hereby assign(s) the benefit of the indemnity in respect of the balance of the rent contained in the Assignment and the statutory acknowledgement and undertaking for production of the title documents contained in the Third Schedule of the Assignment TO HOLD the same unto the Purchaser(s) absolutely.

IT IS HEREBY CERTIFIED . . . (include appropriate certificates for example)

IT IS HEREBY CERTIFIED by the Purchaser(s) that he/she/they being the person(s) becoming entitled to the entire beneficial interest in the property hereby assigned is/are and each to them is an Irish Citizen and as such is/are a qualified person within the meaning of Section 45 of the Land Act, 1965.

IT IS HEREBY FURTHER CERTIFIED that the consideration (other than rent) for the sale is wholly attributable to residential property and that the transaction effected by this instrument does not form part of a larger transaction or of a series of transactions in respect of which the amount or value or the aggregate amount or value of the consideration (other than rent) which is attributable to residential property or which would be so attributable if the contents of residential property were considered to be residential property exceeds €   .

IT IS HEREBY FURTHER CERTIFIED that section 29 of the Stamp Duties Consolidation Act, 1999 does not apply to this instrument as the premises is an existing house.

IN WITNESS whereof the parties hereto have hereunto set their hands and affixed their Seals the day and year first herein WRITTEN.

FIRST SCHEDULE

(Description of premises in Lease)

SECOND SCHEDULE

(Description of premises being assigned)

SIGNED SEALED AND DELIVERED
by the Vendor(s) in the
presence of:

SIGNED SEALED AND DELIVERED
by the Purchaser(s) in the
presence of:

I,   being the lawful spouse of the within named Vendor in pursuance of the provisions
of the Family Home Protection Act, 1976 HEREBY CONSENT to the assurance of the within property
to the Purchaser for the sum of €   .

SIGNED by the said
in the presence of:

Dated the   day of   20

One Part

And

Other Part

INDENTURE OF ASSIGNMENT

Solicitors

8.5.4   SPECIMEN ASSIGNMENT AND CONVEYANCE (ASSURANCE)

THIS INDENTURE made the   day of   Two Thousand and Two BETWEEN   of
(hereinafter called 'the Vendors' which expression shall where the context so admits or requires
include their executors and administrators) of the One Part and   of
(hereinafter called 'the Purchasers' which expression shall where the context so admits or requires
include their assigns and the executors, administrators and assigns of the survivor of them) of the
Other Part.

WHEREAS:

1.   By Indenture of Lease dated the   day of   and made between the
          of the One Part and   of the Other Part (hereinafter called 'the
     said Lease') ALL THAT AND THOSE the premises described in the Schedule hereto and
     intended to be hereby assured (hereinafter called 'the premises') were demised unto the said
     for a term of   years from the day of   (hereinafter called 'the term') subject
     to the yearly rent of (hereinafter called 'the rent') thereby reserved and to the covenants on
     the part of the Lessee and conditions therein contained.

2. By divers mesne assurances acts in the law and events and ultimately by Indenture of Assignment dated the   day of   and made between of the One Part and the Vendors of the Other Part the premises therein and hereinafter more particularly described in the Schedule hereto and intended to be hereby assured were assigned to the Vendors for all the residue then unexpired of the term of years subject to the rent reserved by the Lease and to the performance and observance of the covenants and conditions contained therein.

3. By Vesting Certificate dated the   day of   (Reference No. GR.) the Registrar of Titles in exercise of the powers conferred on him by Section   of the Landlord and Tenant (Ground Rents) (No. 2) Act, 1978 vested the fee simple in the premises therein and hereinafter more particularly described in the Schedule hereto and intended to be hereby assured in the Vendors free from encumbrances and any intermediate interests.

4. The Vendors have agreed with the Purchasers for the sale to them at the price or sum of Euro (€   ) of all their interest in the premises described in the Schedule hereto and intended to be hereby assured.

NOW THIS INDENTURE WITNESSETH as follows-

1. In pursuance of the said agreement and in consideration of the said sum of Euro (€   ) now paid by the Purchasers to the Vendors (the receipt whereof the Vendors hereby acknowledge) the Vendors as beneficial owners HEREBY FIRSTLY GRANT AND CONVEY unto the Purchasers ALL THAT AND THOSE the premises comprised in and demised by the said Lease as described in the Schedule hereto TO HOLD the same unto and to the use of the Purchasers as joint tenants/tenants in common (insert sharehold-ing i.e. in equal shares) in fee simple AND HEREBY SECONDLY ASSIGN unto the Purchasers ALL THAT AND THOSE the premises comprised in and demised by the said Lease as described in the Schedule hereto TO HOLD the same unto the Purchasers as joint tenants/tenants in common for all the residue of the term of years granted by the Lease subject to the covenants by the Lessee and conditions therein contained save for payment of the rent insofar as the Lease still subsists.

IT IS HEREBY CERTIFIED... (include appropriate certificates for example)

IT IS HEREBY CERTIFIED that the consideration (other than rent) for the sale is wholly attributable to residential property and that the transaction effected by this instrument does not form part of a larger transaction or of a series of transactions in respect of which the amount or value, or the aggregate amount or value, of the consideration (other than rent) which is attributable to residential property, or which would be so attributable if the contents of residential property were considered to be residential property, exceeds €   .

IT IS HEREBY FURTHER CERTIFIED by the Purchasers as the parties becoming entitled to the entire beneficial interest in the property hereby assured that they are and each of them is an Irish Citizen and as such is a qualified person within the meaning of Section 45, of the Land Act, 1965.

IT IS HEREBY FURTHER CERTIFIED that Section 29 of the Stamp Duties Consolidation Act, 1999 does not apply to this instrument as the premises is an existing house.

IN WITNESS whereof the parties hereto have hereunto set their hands and affixed their seals the day and year first herein WRITTEN.

SCHEDULE

ALL THAT AND THOSE the premises comprised in the said Lease and therein described as   .

SIGNED SEALED AND DELIVERED by
the said   in
the presence of:

SIGNED SEALED AND DELIVERED by
the said   in
the presence of:

SIGNED SEALED AND DELIVERED by
the said   in
the presence of:

SIGNED SEALED AND DELIVERED by
the said   in
the presence of:

Dated the   day of   20

One Part

AND

Other Part

DRAFT/ASSURANCE

Solicitors

8.5.4.1 Declaration of merger

If the freehold and leasehold titles are to be merged the following paragraph should be included in the deed after the recital of title and before the recital of the contract for sale:

In so far as the same has not already merged the vendors hereby declare that the term shall forthwith merge in the freehold reversion thereof and thereby become extinguished.

The deed will then become a deed of conveyance and the only operative words required are those appropriate to a freehold title, ie 'GRANT AND CONVEY'.

8.5.5 MEMORIAL OF DEED OF CONVEYANCE

To the Registrar for Registering Deeds and so forth in Ireland.

A MEMORIAL of an Indenture of Conveyance made the   day of   Two Thousand
BETWEEN   of   (therein and hereinafter called 'the Vendor') of the One Part
and   of   (therein and hereinafter called 'the Purchaser') of the Other Part.

WHEREBY AFTER RECITING that the Vendor was seised of an estate in fee simple IT WAS WITNESSED that for the consideration therein (the receipt of which was thereby acknowledged) the Vendor as beneficial owner thereby granted and conveyed unto the Purchaser ALL THAT AND THOSE the hereditaments and premises comprised in the Schedule thereto and hereto TO HOLD the same unto and to the use of the Purchaser in fee simple.

WHICH SAID INDENTURE as to the execution thereof by the Vendor was witnessed by:

WHICH SAID INDENTURE as to the execution thereof by the Purchaser was witnessed by:

SCHEDULE

(Description of premises)

SIGNED AND SEALED by the said
in the presence of:

The above named   Maketh Oath and Saith that he is a subscribing Witness to the Deed, of which the above writing is a Memorial, and also to said Memorial; and that he saw said Deed and Memorial duly executed by the said   and the name   subscribed as a Witness to said Deed and Memorial respectively, is this Deponent's proper name and handwriting.

Sworn before me this   day of   20

At

in the County of

and I know the Deponent.

_____

Commissioner for Oaths/Practising Solicitor

8.5.6   MEMORIAL OF DEED OF ASSIGNMENT

To the Registrar for Registering Deeds and so forth in Ireland.

A MEMORIAL of an Indenture of Assignment made the   day of   Two Thousand   BETWEEN   of   (therein and hereinafter called 'the Vendor') of the One Part and   of   (therein and hereinafter called 'the Purchaser') of the Other Part.

WHEREBY AFTER RECITING the provisions of an Indenture of Lease dated the   day of   and made between   of the One Part and   of the Other Part whereby the premises comprised in the Memorialised Indenture were demised to the said   for the term of   years from the   day of   subject to payment of the yearly rent of   and to the covenants on the Lessees part therein contained.

AND WHEREBY after further reciting as therein IT WAS WITNESSED that for the consideration therein (the receipt of which was thereby acknowledged) the Vendor as beneficial owner thereby assigned unto the Purchaser ALL AND SINGULAR the hereditaments and premises comprised in the Schedule thereto and hereto TO HOLD the same unto the Purchaser for all the residue then unexpired of the said term of years granted by the said Lease and subject to the said rent covenants and conditions in the said Lease reserved and contained.

WHICH SAID INDENTURE as to the execution thereof by the Vendor was witnessed by:

WHICH SAID INDENTURE as to the execution thereof by the Purchaser was witnessed by:

SCHEDULE

(Description of premises)

SIGNED AND SEALED by the said
in the presence of:

The above named   Maketh Oath and Saith that he is a subscribing Witness to the Deed, of which the above writing is a Memorial, and also to said Memorial; and that he saw said Deed and Memorial duly executed by the said   and the name subscribed as a Witness to said Deed and Memorial respectively, is this Deponent's proper name and handwriting.

Sworn before me this   day of   20

At

in the County of

and I know the Deponent.

_____

Commissioner for Oaths/Practising Solicitor

8.5.7   LAND REGISTRY TRANSFER (FREEHOLD FOLIO)

LAND REGISTRY

County   Folio

TRANSFER dated the   day of   20   the Registered Owner(s) in consideration of €   (the receipt of which is hereby acknowledged) as beneficial owner(s) HEREBY TRANS-FER(S) all the property described in Folio   of the Register County   to   as joint tenants/tenants in common.

The address(es) of the Purchaser(s) in the State for the service of notices and his/her/their description(s) is/are:

IT IS HEREBY CERTIFIED . . . (include appropriate certificates for example)

IT IS HEREBY CERTIFIED by the Purchaser(s) that he/she/they being the person(s) becoming entitled to the entire beneficial interest in the property hereby transferred is/are and each of them is an Irish Citizen and as such is/are a qualified person within the meaning of Section 45 of the Land Act, 1965.

IT IS HEREBY FURTHER CERTIFIED that the consideration (other than rent) for the sale is wholly attributable to residential property and that the transaction effected by this instrument does not form part of a larger transaction or of a series of transactions in respect of which the amount or value or the aggregate amount or value of the consideration (other than rent) which is attributable to residential property or which would be so attributable if the contents of residential property were considered to be residential property exceeds €   .

IT IS HEREBY FURTHER CERTIFIED that Section 29 of the Stamp Duties Consolidation Act, 1999 does not apply to this instrument as the premises is an existing house.

SIGNED SEALED AND DELIVERED
by the said
in the presence of:

SIGNED SEALED AND DELIVERED
by the said
in the presence of:

I,   being the lawful spouse of the within named   hereby give my prior
consent to the sale of the within described premises at the price of €   and I hereby endorse
my said consent pursuant to Section 3 of the Family Home Protection Act, 1976.

SIGNED by the said
in the presence of:

8.5.8   LAND REGISTRY TRANSFER (TRANSFER OF PART OF FOLIO)

LAND REGISTRY

County   Part of Folio

TRANSFER dated the   day of   20   the Registered Owner(s) in consideration
of €   (the receipt of which is hereby acknowledged) as beneficial owner(s) HEREBY TRANS-
FER(S) the property described in the Schedule hereto (hereinafter called 'the Scheduled Property')
being part of the property described in Folio   of the Register County   to   as
joint tenants/tenants in common.

The address(es) of the Purchaser(s) in the State for the service of notices and his/her/their descrip-
tion(s) is/are:

IT IS HEREBY CERTIFIED... (include appropriate certificates for example)

IT IS HEREBY FURTHER CERTIFIED by the Purchaser(s) that the Scheduled Property is
situate in the City of Dublin.

IT IS HEREBY FURTHER CERTIFIED that the consideration (other than rent) for the sale is wholly attributable to residential property and that the transaction effected by this instrument does not form part
of a larger transaction or of a series of transactions in respect of which the amount or value or the
aggregate amount or value of the consideration (other than rent) which is attributable to residential
property or which would be so attributable if the contents of residential property were considered to
be residential property exceeds €   .

IT IS HEREBY FURTHER CERTIFIED that Section 29 of the Stamp Duties Consolidation Act, 1999 does
not apply to this instrument as the premises is an existing house.

SCHEDULE

(Description of premises)

SIGNED SEALED AND DELIVERED
by the said
in the presence of:

SIGNED SEALED AND DELIVERED
by the said
in the presence of:

I,   being the lawful spouse of the within named   hereby give my prior consent to the sale of the within described premises at the price of €   and I hereby endorse my said consent pursuant to Section 3 of the Family Home Protection Act, 1976.

SIGNED by the said
in the presence of:

8.5.9   LAND REGISTRY TRANSFER (LEASEHOLD FOLIO)

LAND REGISTRY

County   Folio

TRANSFER dated the   day of   20   the Registered Owner(s) (hereinafter called 'the Transferor(s)') in consideration of €   (the receipt of which is hereby acknowledged) as beneficial owner(s) HEREBY TRANSFER(S) the property described in Folio   of the Register   of Leaseholders County   to   (hereinafter called 'the Transferee(s)') as joint tenants/tenants in common.

The Transferee(s) hereby covenant(s) with the Transferor(s) that he/she/they will henceforth during the continuance of the term pay the rent reserved by and perform and observe the covenants conditions and stipulations contained in the Lease dated the day of   made between   of the One Part and   of the Other Part and on the part of the Lessee to be performed and observed and will indemnify and keep indemnified the Transferor(s) from and against all actions and proceedings costs damages expenses claims demands and liabilities whatsoever by reason or on account of the non payment of the said rent or any part thereof or the breach non performance or non observance of the said covenants and conditions or any of them.

The address(es) of the Transferee(s) in the State for the service of notices and his/her/their description(s) is/are:

IT IS HEREBY CERTIFIED . . . (include appropriate certificates for example)

IT IS HEREBY CERTIFIED by the Transferee(s) that he/she/they being the person(s) becoming entitled to the entire beneficial interest in the property is/are and each of them is an Irish Citizen and as such is/are a qualified person(s) within the meaning of Section 45 of the Land Act, 1965.

IT IS HEREBY FURTHER CERTIFIED that the consideration (other than rent) for the sale is wholly attributable to residential property and that the transaction effected by this instrument does not form part of a larger transaction or of a series of transactions in respect of which the amount or value or the aggregate amount or value of the consideration (other than rent) which is attributable to residential property or which would be so attributable if the contents of residential property were considered to be residential property exceeds € .

IT IS HEREBY FURTHER CERTIFIED that Section 29 of the Stamp Duties Consolidation Act, 1999 does not apply to this instrument as the premises is an existing house.

SIGNED SEALED AND DELIVERED
by the said
in the presence of:

SIGNED SEALED AND DELIVERED
by the said
in the presence of:

I, being the lawful spouse of the within named hereby give my prior consent to the sale of the within described premises at the price of € and I hereby endorse my said consent pursuant to Section 3 of the Family Home Protection Act, 1976.

SIGNED by the said
in the presence of:

8.5.10 LAND REGISTRY TRANSFER (LEASEHOLD FOLIO WITH VESTING CERTIFICATE CONTAINING DECLARATION OF MERGER)

LAND REGISTRY

County   Folio

TRANSFER dated the day of 20 the Registered Owner(s) in consideration of € (the receipt of which is hereby acknowledged) as beneficial owner(s) HEREBY TRANSFER(S) all the leasehold interest and the freehold interest in the property described in Folio of the Register of Leaseholders County being the property also described in Vesting Certificate No. dated the day of to (hereinafter called 'the Transferee(s)') as joint tenants/tenants in common and the Transferee(s) being the person(s) becoming entitled to the entire beneficial interest in the said property HEREBY DECLARE(S) that the leasehold interest in the said Folio of the Register of Leaseholders County shall merge with and be extinguished in the fee simple interest vested by the said Vesting Certificate.

The address(es) of the Transferee(s) in the State for the service of notices and his/her/their description(s) is/are:

IT IS HEREBY CERTIFIED... (include appropriate certificates for example)

IT IS HEREBY CERTIFIED by the Transferee(s) that he/she/they being the person(s) becoming entitled to the entire beneficial interest in the property is/are and each of them is an Irish Citizen and as such is/are a qualified person(s) within the meaning of Section 45 of the Land Act, 1965.

IT IS HEREBY FURTHER CERTIFIED that the consideration (other than rent) for the sale is wholly attributable to residential property and that the transaction effected by this instrument does not form part of a larger transaction or of a series of transactions in respect of which the amount or value or the aggregate amount or value of the consideration (other than rent) which is attributable to residential property or which would be so attributable if the contents of residential property were considered to be residential property exceeds € .

IT IS HEREBY FURTHER CERTIFIED that Section 29 of the Stamp Duties Consolidation Act, 1999 does not apply to this instrument as the premises is an existing house.

SIGNED SEALED AND DELIVERED
by the said
in the presence of:

SIGNED SEALED AND DELIVERED
by the said
in the presence of:

I, being the lawful spouse of the within named hereby give my prior consent to the sale of the within described premises at the price of € and I hereby endorse my said consent pursuant to Section 3 of the Family Home Protection Act, 1976.

SIGNED by the said
in the presence of:

8.5.11 LAND REGISTRY VOLUNTARY TRANSFER RETAINING RIGHT OF RESIDENCE

LAND REGISTRY

County   Folio

TRANSFER dated the day of 20 the Registered Owner(s) in consideration of the natural love and affection which he bears towards his son as beneficial owner(s) HEREBY TRANSFER(S) all the property described in Folio of the Register County to the said subject to and charged with a right of residence maintenance and support in favour of the said (and his wife) for the duration of their natural lives.

The address of in the State for the service of notices and his description is:

hereby consents to the registration of the aforementioned right of residence mainte-nance and support as a burden on the property hereby transferred.

IT IS HEREBY CERTIFIED... (include appropriate certificates for example)

IT IS HEREBY CERTIFIED by that he being the person becoming entitled to the entire beneficial interest in the property hereby transferred is an Irish Citizen and as such is a qualified person within the meaning of Section 45 of the Land Act, 1965.

IT IS HEREBY FURTHER CERTIFIED that the consideration (other than rent) for the sale is wholly attrib-utable to residential property and that the transaction effected by this instrument does not form part of a larger transaction or of a series of transactions in respect of which the amount or value or the aggre-gate amount or value of the consideration (other than rent) which is attributable to residential property or which would be so attributable if the contents of residential property were considered to be residen-tial property exceeds € .

IT IS HEREBY FURTHER CERTIFIED by the party (or parties) becoming entitled to the entire beneficial interest in the property that the person (or each of the persons) becoming entitled to the entire beneficial interest in the property is related to the person (or each of the persons) immediately theretofore entitled to the entire beneficial interest in the property as lawful son.

IT IS HEREBY FURTHER CERTIFIED that Section 29 of the Stamp Duties Consolidation Act, 1999 does not apply to this instrument as the premises is an existing house.

SIGNED SEALED AND DELIVERED
by the said
in the presence of:

SIGNED SEALED AND DELIVERED
by the said
in the presence of:

I,   being the lawful spouse of the within named   hereby give my prior consent to the transfer of the within described property for the purposes of the Family Home Protection Act, 1976 and Section 121 of the Succession Act, 1965 and I hereby endorse my said consent pursuant to Section 3 of the Family Home Protection Act, 1976.

SIGNED by the said
in the presence of:

8.5.12 LAND REGISTRY TRANSFER OF FAMILY HOME INTO JOINT NAMES OF SPOUSES

LAND REGISTRY

County   Folio

TRANSFER dated the   day of   20   the Registered Owner in consideration of the natural love and affection which he bears towards his wife as beneficial owner HEREBY TRANSFERS all the property described in Folio   of the Register County   to the said and himself as joint tenants.

The address of   and   in the State for the service of notices and their descriptions are:

IT IS HEREBY CERTIFIED... (include appropriate certificates for example)

IT IS HEREBY FURTHER CERTIFIED by   and   that the property is situate in the City of Dublin.

IT IS HEREBY FURTHER CERTIFIED that the property hereby transferred is a family home within the meaning of the Family Home Protection Act, 1976 and that this Instrument creates a joint tenancy of a family home and is exempt from stamp duty, Land Registry fees and other Court fees by reason of Section 14 of the Family Home Protection Act, 1976.

IT IS HEREBY FURTHER CERTIFIED that Section 29 of the Stamp Duties Consolidation Act, 1999 does not apply to this instrument as the premises is an existing house.

IT IS HEREBY FURTHER CERTIFIED by the party (or parties) becoming entitled to the entire beneficial interest in the property that the person (or each of the persons) becoming entitled to the entire beneficial interest in the property is related to the person (or each of the persons) immediately theretofore entitled to the entire beneficial interest in the property as lawful spouse.

SIGNED SEALED AND DELIVERED
by the said
in the presence of:

SIGNED SEALED AND DELIVERED
by the said
in the presence of:

8.5.13 LAND REGISTRY TRANSFER OF DUBLIN CORPORATION HOUSE HELD UNDER TRANSFER ORDER (LEASEHOLD FOLIO)

LAND REGISTRY

County   Folio

TRANSFER dated the   day of   20   the Registered Owner(s) in consideration of €   (the receipt of which is hereby acknowledged) as beneficial owner(s) with the consent of The Right Honourable The Lord Mayor Aldermen and Burgesses of Dublin (hereinafter called 'the Corporation') HEREBY TRANSFER(S) all the property described in Folio   of the Register of Leaseholders County   to   as joint tenants/tenants in common subject to the terms conditions and special conditions affecting the same contained in a Transfer Order dated the   day of   and under the Housing Act, 1966.

The said   hereby covenant(s) with the said   that he/she/they will henceforth pay the rent reserved by the Transfer Order and will perform and observe all the covenants on the part of the Transferee and conditions therein contained and will indemnify and keep indemnified the said   his/her/their executors administrators and assigns from and against all actions and proceedings costs damages expenses claims demands and liabilities whatsoever by reason or on account of the non-payment of the said rent or any part thereof of the breach non performance or non observance of the said covenants and conditions or any of them. The address(es) of the said   in the State for the service of notices and his/her/their description(s) is/are:

IT IS HEREBY CERTIFIED . . . (include appropriate certificates for example)

IT IS HEREBY CERTIFIED by the Purchaser(s) that he/she/they being the person(s) becoming entitled to the entire beneficial interest in the property hereby transferred is/are and each to them is an Irish Citizen and as such is/are a qualified person within the meaning of Section 45 of the Land Act, 1965.

IT IS HEREBY FURTHER CERTIFIED that the consideration (other than rent) for the sale is wholly attributable to residential property and that the transaction effected by this instrument does not form part of a larger transaction or of a series of transactions in respect of which the amount or value or the aggregate amount or value of the consideration (other than rent) which is attributable to residential property or which would be so attributable if the contents of residential property were considered to be residential property exceeds €   .

IT IS HEREBY FURTHER CERTIFIED that Section 29 of the Stamp Duties Consolidation Act, 1999 does not apply to this instrument as the premises is an existing house.

SIGNED SEALED AND DELIVERED
by the said
in the presence of:

SIGNED SEALED AND DELIVERED
by the said
in the presence of:

The Right Honourable The Lord Mayor Aldermen and Burgesses of Dublin hereby consent to the within transfer:

8.5.14 DEED ENLARGING LONG TERM LEASE INTO A FEE SIMPLE UNDER SECTION 65 OF THE CONVEYANCING ACT, 1881

TO ALL TO WHOM THESE PRESENTS SHALL COME

                of   (hereinafter called 'the owner')

SENDS GREETINGS

WHEREAS:

A.   By a Lease (hereinafter called 'the Lease') dated the   day of   made between   of the one part and   of the other part the premises described in the Schedule hereto (hereinafter called 'the Premises') were demised to the said   for the term of 999 years from the   day of   (hereinafter called 'the term') subject to the yearly rent of one peppercorn (hereinafter called 'the peppercorn rent') thereby reserved and the covenants on the part of the lessee contained in the Lease.

B.   By divers mesne assignments acts in the law and events and ultimately by an Assignment dated the   day of   between   of the one part and the Owner of the other part the Owner became and is now entitled to the Premises for all the residue unexpired of the term subject to the peppercorn rent and the covenants on the part of the lessee and the conditions contained in the Lease but otherwise free from encumbrances.

C.   The owner is desirous of enlarging his leasehold interest in the Premises derived from the Lease into a fee simple interest in the manner hereinafter appearing.

NOW THESE PRESENTS WITNESS as follows:

1.   By virtue of the powers of the Conveyancing Act, 1881 and 1882 the Owner hereby DECLARES that from and after the execution of these presents the residue unexpired of the term created by the Lease in the Premises shall be   and the same is hereby enlarged into a fee simple.

2.   The owner being the person becoming entitled to the entire beneficial interest in the Premises hereby created hereby certifies that he/she is an Irish citizen and as such a qualified person within the meaning of Section 45 of the Land Act, 1965.

IT IS HEREBY CERTIFIED . . . (include appropriate certificates for example)

IT IS HEREBY CERTIFIED by the Purchaser(s) that he/she/they being the person(s) becoming entitled to the entire beneficial interest in the property hereby transferred is/are and each to them is an Irish Citizen and as such is/are a qualified person within the meaning of Section 45 of the Land Act, 1965.

IT IS HEREBY FURTHER CERTIFIED that the consideration (other than rent) for the sale is wholly attributable to residential property and that the transaction effected by this instrument does not form part of a larger transaction or of a series of transactions in respect of which the amount or value or the aggregate amount or value of the consideration (other than rent) which is attributable to residential property or which would be so attributable if the contents of residential property were considered to be residential property exceeds € .

IT IS HEREBY FURTHER CERTIFIED that Section 29 of the Stamp Duties Consolidation Act, 1999 does not apply to this instrument as the premises is an existing house.

IN WITNESS whereof the Owner has hereunto set his/her hand and seal this the day of

SCHEDULE

(The Premises)

ALL THAT AND THOSE

SIGNED SEALED and DELIVERED
by the OWNER
in the presence of:

NOTES

Purpose

This precedent may be used by a person who holds land under a lease which comes within s 65 of the Conveyancing Act, 1881 (as amended by s 11 of the Conveyancing Act, 1882) and wishes to enlarge the leasehold term into a fee simple by a deed under that section.

Recitals

Sufficient details of the lease under which the property is held should be recited to show that the lease comes within the scope of s 65.

Section 65

Where land is held under a lease for a term of not less than three hundred years of which not less than two hundred years remain, without any trust or right of redemption affecting the term in favour of the freeholder, or other person entitled in reversion expectant on the term, and without any rent, or with merely a peppercorn rent or other rent having no money value, incident to the reversion, or having had a rent, not being merely a peppercorn rent or other rent having no money value, originally so incident which subsequently has been released, or has become barred by lapse of time, or has in any other way ceased to be payable, then the term may be enlarged into a fee simple in the manner provided in s 65 of the Conveyancing Act, 1881 as amended by s 11 of the Conveyancing Act, 1882 whether the land now held by the owner is all or part of the land originally demised by the lease.

Section 65(2) provides that any person beneficially entitled in right of the term, whether subject to any encumbrances or not, to possession of any land comprised in the term of any person being in receipt of income as trustee, in right of the term, or having the term vested in him or her in trust for sale whether subject to any encumbrances or not or any person in whom as personal representative of any deceased person the term is vested, whether subject to any encumbrance or not, shall have power by deed to declare that from and after the execution of the deed the term shall be enlarged into a fee simple and thereupon by virtue of the deed and the statute the term is enlarged accordingly and the person in whom the term was previously vested holds the land in fee simple instead of for the term. However, s 11 of the Conveyancing Act, 1882 excluded lands held for a term liable to be determined by re-entry for condition broken or for any term created by sub-demise out of a superior term incapable of being enlarged into a fee simple.

Where a person declares by a deed that the term under which he or she holds land shall be enlarged into a fee simple so that the fee simple thus vests in him or her, that estate in fee simple so acquired by enlargement is subject to all the same trusts, powers, executory limitations over, rights and equities, and to all the same covenants and provisions relating to user and enjoyment, and to all the same obligations of every kind, as the term would have been subject to if it had not been so enlarged.

8.5.15 CONVEYANCE OF A FAMILY HOME SUBJECT TO A MORTGAGE, BY A HUSBAND TO HIMSELF AND HIS WIFE AS JOINT TENANTS, THE MORTGAGEE PARTICIPATING TO RELEASE THE HUSBAND FROM HIS SOLE COVENANT TO PAY THE MORTGAGE DEBT AND TO OBTAIN A JOINT AND SEVERAL COVENANT FROM THE HUSBAND AND THE WIFE

THIS INDENTURE made the   day of   BETWEEN   of   (hereinafter called 'the Husband') of the first part   a Building Society incorporated under the Building Societies Acts, 1976 to 1989 having its chief office at   (hereinafter called 'the Mortgagee') of the second part and the said   and   of   (hereinafter called 'the Wife') (both of whom are hereinafter collectively called 'the Husband and the Wife') of the third part.

WHEREAS:

A. The Husband is seised of the premise described in the Schedule hereto (hereinafter called 'the Premises') for an estate in fee simple in possession subject to the Mortgage next hereinafter recited but otherwise free from incumbrances.

B. By a Mortgage (hereinafter called 'the Mortgage') dated the   day of   made between the Husband of the one part and the Mortgagee of the other part the Premises were conveyed unto the Mortgagee in fee simple by way of Mortgage to secure payment to the Mortgagee of the principal sum of €   (hereinafter called "the Mortgage debt") and interest thereon as therein provided.

C. The Mortgage debt remains owing to the Mortgagee on the security of the Mortgage but all interest thereon accrued due at the date hereof has been paid.

D. The Premises constitute the family home within the meaning of the Family Home Protection Act, 1976 (hereinafter called 'the Act of 1976') of the Husband and the Wife who are married to each other.

E.   The Husband is desirous of vesting the Premises in the Husband and the Wife as joint tenants subject to the Mortgage.

F.   The Mortgagee at the request of the Husband and the Wife and in consideration of the joint and several covenant by the Husband and the Wife with the Mortgagee hereinafter contained has agreed to join in these presents for the purpose of signifying its consent to the vesting in the Premises in the Husband and the Wife as joint tenants in the manner hereinafter appearing.

NOW THIS INDENTURE WITNESSETH as follows:

1.   For effectuating the said desire and in consideration of his natural love and affection for the Wife the Husband as settlor with the consent of the Mortgagee as signified by its execution of these presents hereby conveys unto the Husband and the Wife ALL THAT AND THOSE the Premises TO HOLD the same unto and to the use of the Husband and the Wife in fee simple as joint tenants subject to the Mortgage and the Mortgage debt and the interest hereafter to accrue due thereon.

2.   The Husband and the Wife hereby jointly and severally covenant with the Mortgagee to pay to the Mortgagee the Mortgage debt and interest thereon and all other monies now due or henceforth to become due to the Mortgagee under the Mortgage in the manner and at the times stipulated in the Mortgage and henceforth to perform and observe all covenants conditions provisos and agreements expressed or implied in or by the Mortgage and on the part of the Husband to be performed and observed as if the same were herein set forth at length and as if the names of the Husband and the Wife were substituted for the same of the Husband in the Mortgage.

3.   Nothing herein contained shall prejudice or affect the power of sale and the other powers contained or implied in the Mortgage or the remedies for recovering payment of the monies thereby secured or any part thereof all of which powers and remedies shall continue in full form and effect.

4.   It is hereby certified by the Husband and the Wife being the persons becoming entitled as joint tenants to the entire beneficial interest in the Premises hereby conveyed that each of them is an Irish citizen and as such a qualified person within the meaning of Section 45 of the Land Act, 1965.

5.   It is hereby further certified for the purposes of Section 14 of the Act of 1976 that the Husband and the Wife are lawfully married to each other and that the Premises constitute their family home within the meaning of the Act of 1976.

IT IS HEREBY CERTIFIED . . . (include appropriate certificates for example)

IT IS HEREBY CERTIFIED by the Purchaser(s) that he/she/they being the person(s) becoming entitled to the entire beneficial interest in the property hereby transferred is/are and each to them is an Irish Citizen and as such is/are a qualified person within the meaning of Section 45 of the Land Act, 1965.

IT IS HEREBY FURTHER CERTIFIED that the consideration (other than rent) for the sale is wholly attributable to residential property and that the transaction effected by this instrument does not form part of a larger transaction or of a series of transactions in respect of which the amount or value or the aggregate amount or value of the consideration (other than rent) which is attributable to residential property or which would be so attributable if the contents of residential property were considered to be residential property exceeds € .

IT IS HEREBY FURTHER CERTIFIED that Section 29 of the Stamp Duties Consolidation Act, 1999 does not apply to this instrument as the premises is an existing house.

IN WITNESS whereof the Husband and the Wife have hereunto set their respective hands and seals and the common seal of the Mortgagee has been affixed hereto the day and year first above WRITTEN.

SCHEDULE

(The Premises)

ALL THAT AND THOSE

SIGNED SEALED and DELIVERED
by the HUSBAND
in the presence of:

SIGNED SEALED and DELIVERED
by the MORTGAGEE
in the presence of:

SIGNED SEALED and DELIVERED
by the HUSBAND
in the presence of:

SIGNED SEALED and DELIVERED
by the WIFE
in the presence of:

8.5.16 ASSIGNMENT OF AN UNENCUMBERED LEASEHOLD INTEREST IN A FAMILY HOME BY A HUSBAND TO HIMSELF AND HIS WIFE AS JOINT TENANTS

THIS INDENTURE made the   day of   BETWEEN   of   (hereinafter called 'the Husband') of the one part and the said   and   of   (hereinafter called 'the Wife') (both of whom are hereinafter collectively called 'the Husband and the Wife') of the other part.

WHEREAS:

A.   By a Lease (hereinafter called 'the Lease') dated the   day of   made between   of the one part and   of the other part the premises described in the Schedule hereto (hereinafter called 'the Premises') were demised to the said   for the term of   years from the day of   (hereinafter called 'the term') subject to the yearly rent of €   (hereinafter called 'the rent') thereby reserved and the covenants on the part of the lessee and the conditions therein contained.

B.   By divers mesne assignments acts in the law and events and ultimately by an Assignment dated the   day of   made between   of the one part and the Husband of the other part the Premises became and are now vested in the Husband for all the residue of the term subject to the rent and the covenants on the part of the lessee and the conditions contained in the Lease but otherwise free from incumbrances.

C.   The Premises are the family home within the meaning of the Family Home Protection Act, 1976 (hereinafter called 'the Act of 1976') of the Husband and the Wife who are married to each other.

D.   The Husband is desirous of vesting the Premises in himself and the Wife as joint tenants in the manner hereinafter appearing.

NOW THIS INDENTURE WITNESSETH as follows:

1.   For effectuating the said desire and in consideration of his natural love and affection for the Wife the Husband as settlor hereby assigns unto the Husband and the Wife ALL THAT AND THOSE the Premises TO HOLD the same unto the Husband and the Wife as joint tenants for all the residue now unexpired of the term subject to the rent and the covenants on the part of the lessee and the conditions contained in the Lease.

2.   The Wife hereby covenants with the Husband that she the Wife will henceforth during the continuance of the term jointly with the Husband pay the rent and perform and observe the covenants on the part of the lessee and the conditions contained in the Lease and will at all times keep the Husband his executors and administrators effectually indemnified against all actions and proceedings costs damages expenses claims and demands whatsoever by reason or on account of her failure to pay the rent or any part thereof as aforesaid or the breach non-performance or non-observance by her of the said covenants and conditions or any of them.

3.   It is hereby certified by the Husband and the Wife being the persons becoming entitled as joint tenants to the entire beneficial interest in the Premises hereby assigned that each of them is an Irish citizen and as such a qualified person within the meaning of Section 45 of the Land Act, 1965.

IT IS HEREBY CERTIFIED for the purposes of Section 14 of the Act of 1976 that the Husband and the Wife are lawfully married to each other and that the Premises constitute their family home within the meaning of the Act of 1976.

IT IS HEREBY FURTHER CERTIFIED . . . (include appropriate certificates for example)

IT IS HEREBY FURTHER CERTIFIED by the Purchaser(s) that he/she/they being the person(s) becoming entitled to the entire beneficial interest in the property hereby transferred is/are and each to them is an Irish Citizen and as such is/are a qualified person within the meaning of Section 45 of the Land Act, 1965.

IT IS HEREBY FURTHER CERTIFIED that the consideration (other than rent) for the sale is wholly attributable to residential property and that the transaction effected by this instrument does not form part of a larger transaction or of a series of transactions in respect of which the amount or value or the aggregate amount or value of the consideration (other than rent) which is attributable to residential property or which would be so attributable if the contents of residential property were considered to be residential property exceeds €   .

IT IS HEREBY FURTHER CERTIFIED that Section 29 of the Stamp Duties Consolidation Act, 1999 does not apply to this instrument as the premises is an existing house.

IN WITNESS whereof the parties hereto have hereunto set their respective hands and seals the day and year first above WRITTEN.

SCHEDULE

(The Premises)

ALL THAT AND THOSE

SIGNED SEALED and DELIVERED
by the HUSBAND
in the presence of:

SIGNED SEALED and DELIVERED
by the WIFE
in the presence of:

CHAPTER 9

MORTGAGES

9.1 Introduction

The most commonly used manner of raising money to buy any building or property is by arranging a loan from a bank or lending institution and securing that loan by way of mortgage over the asset to be acquired. Usually the loan cheque will be released, the purchase of the asset completed and the mortgage put into place contemporaneously. In this way the lending institution knows that the day it releases the proceeds of the loan to the borrower it has secured the loan against a tangible asset of real value. Thus the lender can be satisfied that if the borrower defaults in terms of its commitment to repay, there will be a significant asset to be targeted in terms of a resale, in addition to all of the usual remedies which would lie directly against the borrower in terms of forcing him to repay the loan money and any interest accruing thereon. Although this is the most usual scenario it is certainly not the only instance under which a mortgage is put in place.

Mortgages also are widely used as a means of securing loans which have been sanctioned for other purposes, such as home improvements or extensions, car purchases, financing the education fees of children and so forth. Borrowers raise money for a variety of purposes and, if the amount of the loan is in any way significant, the lender invariably looks for some form of security by way of mortgage over land or buildings. Although a borrower is frequently reluctant to encumber assets in this way, the temptation to do so usually is that the rate of interest charged by the lender will be significantly lower on a loan which is secured by way of mortgage over real property than on a loan which is unsecured or secured over an asset through some form of leasing or hire-purchase agreement.

The term negative equity is used when the amount secured by the mortgage exceeds the value of the property.

This chapter primarily focuses on mortgages in the context of residential conveyancing (home loans) as it is this type of mortgage most often encountered by practitioners.

9.2 What is a Mortgage?

9.2.1 INTRODUCTION

A 'mortgage' is commonly understood to be a 'conditional transfer' of property to a lending institution or bank that may become absolute if the borrower/mortgagor falls into arrears and is unable to make the repayments which it covenants to make.

In legal terms there is a difference between 'mortgaging' a property the title to which is registered in the Land Registry and 'mortgaging' an unregistered property. In fact an unregistered property is mortgaged and a registered property is charged.

A mortgage may also be created by equitable deposit of title deeds with a bank or building society.

9.2.2 UNREGISTERED PROPERTY

The distinction is that unregistered property is conveyed, leased or assigned by the borrower (the mortgagor) to the lending institution (the mortgagee) subject to the mortgagor's equity of redemption in the property. The equity of redemption describes the rights retained by the mortgagor in relation to the property and includes the borrower's equitable right to get the title back and have it vested in him or her once more when the loan is repaid.

Title formally passes under the mortgage deed from the borrower to the lending institution. Therefore in any subsequent sale or deed which deals with title to the property the correct 'moving party' is the lending institution rather than the borrower. For as long as the loan is extant and the mortgage is in place, the title is vested in the lending institution and the borrower has only an equity of redemption.

Notwithstanding the foregoing, it is common to see property being sold by borrowers even where the property is subject to an existing mortgage. This is a practice that has grown up over many years to facilitate conveyancers and to facilitate the transferral of title. If the borrower contracts to sell the property and executes a deed selling the property as beneficial owner free from encumbrances, and if the mortgage securing the loan on that property is released when the sale is completed or thereafter, the lender/mortgagee, having been repaid in full, is estopped from challenging the deed or the transferral of title by the borrower to the purchaser. By repaying the loan out of the proceeds of sale a borrower can essentially force the situation and transfer title to a third party using a principle of law called 'feeding the estoppel'. Once the loan has been repaid, the lender will be obliged to reassure the property to the borrower or the nominee of the borrower and the lender is prohibited from relying on the terms of the mortgage to defeat or prejudice the deed of assurance in favour of a third party.

Typically when the sale of a property subject to an existing mortgage takes place the existing loans are redeemed as soon as possible after closing out of the proceeds of sale and in return the mortgage is released by the lending institution. The vendor's solicitor obtains the necessary vacate and furnishes it to the purchaser's solicitor on foot of an undertaking to do so which was furnished on closing. Once this has occurred any outstanding estate which might not have been technically transferred on the closing of the sale will vest automatically in the purchaser.

In *Santley v Wilde* [1899] 2 Ch 474 a mortgage was defined by Lindley MR as 'a conveyance of land . . . as a security for the payment of a debt or the discharge of some other obligation for which it is given'.

9.2.3 REGISTERED PROPERTY

Under the Registration of Title Act, 1964, s 62 registered land may be 'mortgaged' only by the registered owner by means of a registered charge. Unlike a mortgage a charge involves no transfer of ownership to the lender. Ownership remains with the registered owner and the lender only acquires rights over the property.

The standard deed of mortgage deals with both registered and unregistered property and in this chapter the term 'mortgage' is used to denote both a mortgage and charge.

9.3 Vacate of a Mortgage

The vacate will take the form of a release in the case of unregistered land and a discharge in the case of registered land. In the case of unregistered land a memorial of the release will also be required. Under the Housing Act, 1988, s 18 the vacate may also take the form of a receipt endorsed on the back of the original mortgage. All lenders may issue a receipt but it is compulsory for local authority lenders. If such a receipt is provided then a release and memorial or discharge is not required. The receipt is sufficient for the purposes of registration both in the Land Registry and the Registry of Deeds. The term vacate is commonly used to refer to a discharge, release or receipt.

9.4 Content of the Mortgage Deed

9.4.1 INTRODUCTION

In general terms, the mortgage document is very simple. It recites the fact that the lender has made a loan available to the owner of the property and that the owner of the property has agreed to guarantee that the loan will be repaid by securing the loan against his or her property. This security is put in place by way of a mortgage over the property in question. The mortgage document contains a number of covenants made by the mortgagor. The first and most significant of these is a covenant to repay the loan coupled with an acknowledgement of indebtedness. The covenant will always extend to repay the loan and any interest which accrues thereon, together with any costs associated with the repossession of the property and the ultimate enforcement of the security, if this proves to be necessary.

9.4.2 ADDITIONAL COVENANTS

Although mortgage documents vary in substance and form from one institution to another, it is usual to find the following additional covenants in every mortgage document.

(a) There will be a covenant to the effect that the mortgaged property must be used by the borrower (in cases involving residential lending) as the borrower's principal private residence. The covenant will confirm that the property will not be rented or sublet and, in the event of the borrower breaking this covenant, the lending institution may elect between forfeiture on the one hand and charging a penalty rate or commercial rate of interest on the other hand. The commercial rate of interest which is applicable is normally somewhat higher than the residential lending rate.

(b) In addition, there will be a covenant by the owner of the property to the effect that he or she will not carry out any development whatsoever (as defined in the Local Government (Planning and Development) Act, 1963 and subsequent amendments thereto) without the consent in writing of the lender. In practice, this means that the borrower may not carry out any extension, improvements or work to the property which would require planning permission or be an infringement of the building regulations without the lender's consent in writing. The lender will invariably have no difficulty with any work undertaken which enhances the value of the property. The lender will, however, strive to ensure that the work is done in a proper and workmanlike manner. Naturally, the lending institution will be anxious to ensure that the work is not done in a poor fashion or in a way which might result in difficulties in a sale in the event of a foreclosure situation arising.

(c) There will also be a covenant by the borrower to the effect that the property must be kept insured at all times and the interest of the lender is always noted on the insurance policy in question. The lender will frequently be given rights to insure the property and to charge the premium to the borrower in the event of the property owner/borrower allowing the existing policy of insurance to lapse or be cancelled.

In practice most mortgage documents have quite a number of additional clauses, principally comprising covenants by the mortgagor, such as a covenant to keep the property insured, a covenant to repay the money which he or she has obtained promptly and on time, a provision allowing the mortgagor to apply a variable interest rate to the loan, unless the rate of interest has been fixed by agreement between the parties, and covenants that the mortgagor may not deal with his or her property in any way without the prior consent in writing of the mortgagee and so forth. It is, however, very important to read every mortgage document carefully, particularly when dealing with lenders who are not market leaders. Some mortgage documents contain clauses incorporating very penal methods of computation of interest, penalties for early redemption and the like.

9.4.3   LETTER OF LOAN OFFER

A mortgage document frequently refers back to the letter of a loan offer, which has been issued by the lender and accepted by the borrower. The letter of loan offer frequently has many additional covenants, conditions and assurances by the borrower. It also often has additional elements of default, most notably in commercial loan transactions. The letter of loan offer may also underline and set out the circumstances under which the lending institution has power to appoint a receiver and may contain provisions under which the borrower irrevocably appoints the lending institution as its attorney for certain purposes connected with the realisation of the security, should the need so occur.

In instances where property subject to a mortgage is being transferred from one spouse to another, whether on foot of a court order or otherwise, the consent of the mortgagee is required and a letter of loan offer will issue to the transferee unless the mortgage is being discharged during the course of the transaction. It is often the case that the transferee will be taking on sole obligation for meeting the terms of the mortgage. In that instance it is vital that the mortgagee is contacted at an early stage as it may take the view that the transferee does not have the necessary means to meet the repayments and thus may not consent to the transfer. Provided such consent is forthcoming the mortgagee should be joined as a party to the deed.

9.5   Types of Mortgages

9.5.1   'PRINCIPAL SUMS'

Historically, mortgages were always created to secure a fixed amount of indebtedness together with interest running on that particular loan and, if the borrower wanted a supplemental mortgage or a 'top up' loan, he had to create a second mortgage over his property. However, the commercial lending institutions are now more often than not using 'all sums due' mortgages.

9.5.2   'ALL SUMS DUE'

As a general rule the lending institutions are now writing into their mortgage document an 'all sums due' clause. This clause results in the mortgagor pledging his or her property to the lending institution, not only for the loan he or she was taking out at that time, but for all indebtedness which he might have to the lending institution at the time or which he or she may incur into the future, eg car loan or credit card bill. This clause covers potential indebtedness to the lending institution as well as actual indebtedness, including contingent liabilities, which may arise in the future on the strength of an obligation undertaken pursuant to a guarantee. Most of the lenders have now introduced this clause into their standard mortgage document.

The existence of this type of charging clause is very significant. The clause must be explained in detail to potential purchasers who may not be aware of the impact of same. Many house buyers take the view that they do not want to have 'all of their lending eggs in one basket'. In other words, they want to have their indebtedness in relation to the house with one institution and their day-to-day indebtedness (such as overdraft facilities, term loan facilities, car loans and so forth) with some other institution. However, if a borrower signs a mortgage which has an 'all sums due' charging clause in it, the property is charged to the lending institution not only to secure the repayment of the home loan but also to secure all of the borrower's indebtedness to that lending institution (or its subsidiaries) both actual and contingent and howsoever arising, for example the credit card bill or car loan.

9.5.3   THE ANNUITY MORTGAGE

The annuity mortgage is one which requires the borrower to repay the entire principal, which he or she is borrowing from the lending institution, and all of the interest throughout the term of the mortgage. The rate of repayment is set by the lending institution, having regard to the fact that both principal and interest are repaid over the term of years and the amount of the repayment is calculated to ensure that, at the end of the term, the entire amount of the principal and interest will have been repaid. Normally, the mortgage document provides for a variable rate of interest and allows the lending institution to increase and decrease the rate in line with mortgage interest changes in the mortgage market. Annuity mortgages are invariably backed up by a mortgage protection policy which is a life policy taken out by the lender at the borrower's cost on the borrower's life to secure the amount of the loan. In the event of the borrower dying 'in harness' during the currency of the mortgage, the life assurance policy falls into place and the amount due is paid by the insurance company to the lending institution whereupon the mortgage is immediately redeemed and the borrower's personal representative/beneficiary may take the mortgaged property freed and discharged from the mortgage. A mortgage protection policy is now a statutory requirement under the Consumer Credit Act, 1995, s 126 if the mortgagor is a 'consumer' and is obtaining a 'housing loan' as defined in the Act.

The mortgage protection policy is a fixed-term policy which survives only for the duration of the mortgage and expires as soon as the last payment has been made to the lending institution. In every case when a client purchases a house using an annuity loan which is backed up by a mortgage protection policy the solicitor should advise the client to make a will and to be aware of the provisions of the capital acquisitions tax legislation as the purchaser will, on death, be leaving a very valuable asset to his next of kin freed and discharged from the mortgage.

9.5.4   ENDOWMENT MORTGAGE

9.5.4.1   Generally

An endowment mortgage, by contrast, operates on the basis that the borrower will repay only interest on the money which he has borrowed from the lending institution and never pays a penny of the capital amount. In lieu of repaying the capital, the borrower takes out an endowment life policy on his own life with an insurance company. The mortgage is repaid out of the proceeds yielded by the insurance policy on its maturity or on the borrower's death. The policy itself is drafted to ensure that the amount of the loan will be paid to the lending institution on the occasion of the borrower's death (in harness) or on the occasion of the expiry of the term of years for which the loan was granted. The borrower will be allowed to complete the mortgage with the lending institution only when this policy has been taken out and when he or she has assigned the benefit of the life policy in question to the lending institution. Once the life policy has been signed over to the lending institution, it recovers the capital amount which it had advanced either on the occasion of the borrower's death during the currency of the loan or, in any event, on the last day of the term of the mortgage. Accordingly, there is no risk to the lending institution and it is quite happy to accept ongoing repayments of interest alone. Most endowment mortgages provide that in the event of the borrower failing to meet the repayments which he or she owes to the life assurance agency, the mortgage is automatically converted to an annuity mortgage whereupon the borrower becomes liable to the lending institution for principal and interest alike.

With an endowment mortgage there may be no guarantee that the proceeds of the insurance policy will be sufficient to repay the loan in full at the end of the term. The Consumer Credit Act, 1995 contains a number of provisions which attempt to protect consumers securing loans for the purchase of residential property. One of these provisions is s 133 which provides that the borrower must be warned that there is no guarantee that the proceeds of the policy will be sufficient to repay the loan in full when it becomes due for repayment.

In contrast the proceeds of the insurance policy could far exceed the amount payable to the lending institution. Whether or not this extra is passed to the borrower depends on the type of endowment policy taken out.

9.5.4.2 Annuity mortgage contrasted

To contrast an annuity and an endowment one must have regard to the following factors:

(a) When a borrower takes out an annuity mortgage the principal amount which he or she owes to the lending institution decreases continuously over the term of the mortgage. In contrast, the capital amount which the borrower owes to the lending institution when he or she takes out an endowment mortgage never changes until it is cleared when the endowment insurance policy falls into place.

(b) The rate of interest payable in respect of an annuity mortgage may be lower than that payable for an endowment mortgage.

(c) As limited income tax relief is available in respect of the premium for the endowment life policy and, in contrast, no income tax relief is available in respect of capital amounts repaid to a lending institution, the endowment mortgage is generally favoured by those on high incomes or with a high income tax bill each year.

(d) Endowment mortgages are more volatile than annuity mortgages as the endowment policy is linked to performance of a portfolio of various stocks and shares, whereas the annuity mortgage is linked to fluctuations in the property market and to inflation.

9.5.4.3 Categories of endowment mortgage

Within the general category of endowment mortgage there are many variations on the same theme. The two most common endowment mortgages which a solicitor will meet are the 'full endowment', otherwise known as the 'with profits endowment', and, in contrast, the 'low cost endowment'. In each case, the capital due to the lending institution is secured by the assignment of an endowment life policy but in each case the policy document itself differs. In the case of the 'low cost endowment' the life policy has a guaranteed yield in the amount of the loan. Accordingly, if the mortgage is for €30,000 the policy will definitely yield €30,000 on its maturity date. Any profits which the life assurance company makes will be retained by the life assurance agency and will not be passed to the insured borrower.

In contrast, the 'with profits endowment' is based on a life policy under which the life assurance company passes on any profits which accrue above and beyond the sum of €30,000 to the borrower. This may work favourably for the borrower and, on the maturity date when his mortgage is redeemed, he may (if the assurance company has prudently invested his money) receive a tax-free lump sum amount of money for his own use and benefit. The premiums payable to the life assurance company for the 'low cost endowment' policy are lower than those payable for the 'with profits endowment' policy as the life assurance company is confident of its own ability to make money and accepts a lower premium in return for the freedom to retain any profits which its investment may make over the term of the mortgage itself.

9.6   Sale

9.6.1   ACCOUNTABLE TRUST RECEIPT

Under normal circumstances, when a solicitor receives instructions in relation to the sale of a property, the first thing he or she does is obtain the client's retainer and authority so that he or she may apply to the lending institution holding the deeds and documents of title for permission to collect same so as to peruse the title and draft the contract for sale. The deeds will be released to the solicitor subject to him or her signing an accountable trust receipt and proving to the lending institution that he or she has the client's written authority to take up the title deeds on such accountable trust receipt. The accountable trust receipt is a commitment to the effect that the solicitor will hold the deeds safely, on trust and to the order of the lending institution and that he or she will not part with same or use the deeds in any way which might prejudice the lender until such time as he or she is in a position to repay all of the borrower's indebtedness as secured against the deeds themselves. Thus, a solicitor must not release the title deeds until he or she is in a position to comply with the trust. In default of honouring this commitment, the solicitor undertakes to be personally responsible for the indebtedness in question.

It is important for the solicitor to check that the sale proceeds, after payment of costs and outlay, are sufficient to cover the amount owing to the lending institution. Thus, the solicitor must determine the exact amount of indebtedness secured against the deeds and not simply the amount of the home loan which is outstanding. If the sale proceeds are not sufficient to vacate the mortgage the vendor will need to pay the difference prior to completion of the sale. If a shortfall arises after completion and after the title deeds are released and the vendor does not pay up then the solicitor is personally liable on foot of the accountable trust receipt. Thus it is vital that the exact amount due to the lending institution on foot of the mortgage is determined at an early stage in the transaction.

In recent years solicitors have found it difficult to obtain accurate figures for the total amount due from the lending institutions. Solicitors who have requested the total amount due from their client's local branch of the lending institution have sometimes discovered that the information furnished did not include figures for loans held with other branches of the same lending institution. As a result the Law Society has recently issued a practice note (Law Society Gazette, November 1999) setting out a standard letter which should be used by solicitors when requesting redemption figures from lending institutions. In the opinion of the Conveyancing Committee a borrower is entitled to be given a redemption figure which the lender will stand over, ie one which is not stated to be provisional.

9.6.2 SPECIAL CONDITION

When drafting the contract for sale a vendor's solicitor will insert a special condition in the contract to the effect that the property is subject to a mortgage which will be discharged on closing. The Law Society has recommended the wording of this type of special condition (see Practice Note, Law Society Gazette, June 1979) which provides that prior to closing:

> 'the vendor's solicitors will furnish to the purchaser's solicitors a statement from the vendor's mortgagees setting out the amount required to redeem the mortgage as at the closing date together with the accruing daily rate of interest thereafter and, on closing, the purchaser will furnish to the vendor separate lending institution drafts for the amount required to redeem the vendor's mortgage and for the balance of the purchase monies respectively and the vendor will forthwith discharge the mortgage debt to the vendor's mortgagees and will furnish to the purchaser proper evidence of such discharge and will furnish to the purchaser such release of the mortgage as may be appropriate'.

See also Practice Notes, Law Society Gazette, September 1983 and July 1995. In this way the property is sold and the mortgage cleared from the title. It should be noted that this special condition does not state which party is to bear the cost, if any, of splitting the purchaser's loan cheque or of registering the vacate. The Law Society Conveyancing Committee takes the view that the vendor's mortgage is not discharged off the title until the discharge/vacate is registered and therefore the cost of registering same should be borne by the vendor.

In order that the amount of the lending institution drafts may be determined the vendor's solicitor must obtain accurate details of the amount required to redeem the vendor's home loan and forward those details to the purchaser's solicitor. When the purchaser's solicitor receives the figures, he or she can obtain the lending institution drafts and proceed to close the sale. Subsequently the vendor's solicitor will pay the first lending institution draft to the lending institution requesting a vacate of the mortgage. What has happened occasionally in recent times is that the lender acknowledges safe receipt of the money but indicates that it is not prepared to seal a vacate of the mortgage until further indebtedness is discharged in full. This indebtedness may be captured by the all sums due charging clause or may arise as a result of other loans secured by way of a deed of further charge or an equitable deposit of title deeds. The vendor's solicitor will at this point have closed the sale, released the loan cheque and furnished an undertaking to discharge the mortgage. If the client refuses to pay the additional money then the solicitor would be forced to do so out of his or her own pocket in order to obtain the vacate and thus comply with his or her undertaking. This clearly can give rise to great difficulties for the unwary practitioner. As a result the Conveyancing Committee has issued a number of practice notes on this topic (see Practice Notes, Law Society Gazette, November 1990 and May 1989). As already stated the most recent one (Practice Note, Law Society Gazette, November 1999) sets out a recommended letter to be used when seeking redemption figures from lending institutions. It is vital in the case of an all sums due mortgage to ask for redemption figures, not just for the home loan, but also for details of all indebtedness by the client to that lending institution.

When a mortgage is redeemed, the solicitor is released from his accountable trust receipt.

It should be noted that if the redemption is not occurring because of a sale and the title documents were not already released to the solicitor on accountable trust receipt then, on redemption of the mortgage, the title documents will automatically be released to the mortgagor not to the solicitor. In these circumstances the solicitor should include with the redemption money an authority from his client authorising the release of the title documents to him or her (Practice Note, Law Society Gazette, October 1990). Solicitors must be careful about the wording of accountable trust receipts and undertakings which they execute in relation to title deeds or vacates. A solicitor's undertaking is a personal obligation assumed by the solicitor or firm of solicitors in question to the effect that something will be done, irrespective of the wishes of the client. Once the solicitor, having received appropriate authority from his or her client, issues an undertaking to a colleague, he or she is bound by the terms of that undertaking. For example, an undertaking to procure a vacate in respect of a mortgage is binding on the solicitor even if the solicitor does not have adequate client funds available to redeem the mortgage in question.

General condition 15 of the Contract for Sale provides that the vendor shall disclose before the sale, in the particulars, the special conditions or otherwise, all easements, rights, reservations, privileges, taxes and other liabilities (not already known to the purchaser or apparent from inspection) which are known by the vendor to affect the subject property or which are likely to affect it.

General condition 8(c) of the Contract for Sale provides that

'Save as stipulated in the Special Conditions the Vendor shall, prior to or at the completion of the Sale, discharge all mortgages and charges for the payment of money . . . which affect the Subject Property.'

The vendor is obliged to give an unencumbered title to the purchaser save and except where otherwise provided for in the contract for sale. He or she is obliged to ensure that all mortgages which affect the subject property are discharged and vacates handed over on closing.

9.6.3 MORTGAGEE SELLING UNDER POWER OF SALE

This obviously does not apply when a mortgagee is selling under a power of sale. This power of sale will arise under the terms of the mortgage and the mortgage deed will form part of the vendor's title. The mortgage will not be vacated and the original of the mortgage will be handed over to the purchaser.

If there is more than one mortgage on the property a purchaser need not concern himself with the other mortgages provided the power of sale is being exercised by the mortgagee holding in priority to the other mortgagees, ie the first mortgagee. Under the Conveyancing Act, 1881, s 21:

a mortgagee exercising the power of sale conferred by this Act shall have power, by deed, to convey the property sold, for such estate and interest therein as is the subject of the mortgage, freed from all estates, interests and rights to which the mortgage has priority but subject to all estates, interests and rights which have priority to the mortgage . . .

The first mortgagee will hold the proceeds of sale on trust for the subsequent mortgagees. The purchaser need not concern himself or herself with obtaining vacates in respect of the other mortgages and he or she obtains an unencumbered title.

The position is different if a subsequent mortgagee is selling under a power of sale. In that circumstance a purchaser will require that the prior mortgage be released and a vacate furnished on closing. Thus the mortgages which have priority to the mortgage under which the power of sale is being exercised (ie the mortgages above but not below) must be redeemed.

9.6.4 REQUISITIONS ON TITLE

Requisition 14 of the Law Society Requisitions on Title deals with proceedings and encumbrances including mortgages and charges. This requisition requires the vendor to confirm if the property is subject to any mortgage or charge. If there is a mortgage or charge full particulars must be furnished and the vendor is reminded that evidence of vacate must be furnished on closing.

9.7 Purchase

9.7.1 SPECIAL CONDITION

If a purchaser is obtaining a mortgage and using the loan cheque to make up the purchase money then he will need to make the contract for sale subject to him obtaining loan approval for the required amount. Loan approval of itself does not guarantee him or her the loan cheque as such approval will be subject to conditions. Thus, prior to entering into an unconditional contract to purchase the property, a purchaser must be sure not only that loan approval issues but also that he or she is in a position to comply with all of the conditions therein laid down by the lending institution. If a purchaser allows the contract to become unconditional and subsequently loan approval does not issue or the purchaser is unable to comply with the lending institution's requirements, then the loan cheque will not issue and he or she may be committed to a contract that he or she cannot complete.

The Law Society has recommended a standard special condition making a contract for sale subject to loan approval (see Practice Note, Law Society Gazette, December 1979). It provides for the contract for sale to be subject to the purchaser obtaining approval for a loan of a specified amount from a specified lending institution on the security of the premises within a certain period of time. It provides for the contract to be rescinded by either party if written loan approval does not issue within the time specified and the purchaser is to be repaid his or her deposit without interest, costs or compensation.

The special condition also states that if

'the loan approval is conditional on a survey satisfactory to the lending institution or a mortgage protection or life assurance policy being taken out or some other condition compliance with which is not within the control of the purchaser the loan shall not be deemed to be approved until the purchaser is in a position to accept the loan on terms which are within his reasonable power or procurement'.

Problems arise when the agreed time frame is about to pass and the purchaser has not yet received his or her loan approval or has received his or her loan approval but is in difficulty in relation to complying with the conditions set out therein. The vendor will seek to have the special condition deleted so as to make the contract unconditional and in order to avoid losing the property, the purchaser may agree.

If the purchaser agrees to the deletion of the special condition, even though loan approval has not issued or has issued with onerous conditions attached, then it would be advisable to obtain his or her instructions in writing. It would also be wise to advise him or her in writing that the contract is no longer unconditional and he or she will be required to complete even if he or she cannot obtain a mortgage.

9.7.2 CERTIFICATE OF TITLE SYSTEM (1999 EDITION)

9.7.2.1 Introduction

In part due to the fact that lending institutions are unable to pass to the borrower any legal fees which they incur in connection with putting a mortgage in place (Consumer Credit Act, 1995), it is normal in the case of home loans for the lending institution not to engage its own solicitor to check the title. It should be noted that this applies only in the case of residential lending and does not prohibit lenders from 'charging on' security fees in the context of commercial lending.

In residential lending, the purchaser's solicitor is required to furnish an undertaking and certificate of title in the format agreed by the Law Society with the legal advisers of the various financial institutions (1999 edition). This latest edition of the Undertaking and Certificate of Title is to be utilised for all residential mortgage loans approved after 1 April 1999. This documentation ensures that the obligation of the solicitor to the lending institution is confined to the terms agreed in the undertaking, certificate of title and approved guidelines. No other documentation should be accepted or used by practitioners and solicitors 'should reject any documentation which does not conform with the agreed package' (letter circulated to the profession on 3 June 1998). The Law Society's recommendations in this regard are endorsed by the Solicitors Mutual Defence Fund Limited and, in a letter circulated to the profession on 9 March 1999, the Law Society stated: 'Solicitors are advised that failure to utilise the agreed documents may engender difficulty with their Professional Indemnity Insurance Cover.'

The purchaser's solicitor does not act for the lender (see Practice Note, Law Society Gazette, April 1998) and thus is not paid by the lender for this work as this would lead to a conflict of interest. The undertaking and certificate of title reflect this by stating that both are given by the solicitor in his or her sole capacity as solicitor for the borrower and not as solicitor for, or as agent/quasi-agent of, the lender.

The certificate of title and undertaking form part of the mortgage documentation which is sent by the lending institution to the purchaser's solicitor once the mortgage is approved. The pack also includes details of the terms of the loan offer and the mortgage deed. In the past, lending institutions have used the terms of the loan offer to place additional obligations on the solicitor, for example, to check the creditworthiness of the borrower. The solicitor should always check the terms of the loan offer so as to ensure that no such obligations are placed upon him or her. The solicitor is, however, now protected by the terms of the undertaking which provide that the undertaking relates to matters of title and represents the sum of the solicitor's obligations to the lender in relation to the loan transaction. It further states that the solicitor has no responsibility for any matter of a non-title nature except in so far as any of the matters set out in the undertaking may be deemed to be matters of a non-title nature. The solicitor should ensure that only the agreed mortgage package is used so as to avoid other obligations being placed on him or her.

9.7.2.2 Undertaking

Having agreed the contract for sale and perused the title, the purchaser's solicitor completes the undertaking (having been authorised in writing to do so by the borrower/purchaser and having obtained the spouse's prior consent in writing (where applicable)) and returns this to the lender with evidence of the solicitor's professional indemnity insurance. The solicitor signing the undertaking should be a partner, principal or other solicitor duly authorised in writing on behalf of the firm, though the firm would be liable on foot of an undertaking signed by an authorised member of staff even if the staff member was not authorised in writing. On foot of this signed undertaking, the lending institution will then release the loan cheque to the solicitor to enable him or her to complete the purchase transaction.

On foot of the undertaking and prior to negotiating, ie releasing the loan cheque, the solicitor must ensure that:

(a) the borrower is acquiring good marketable title (as defined in the undertaking and certificate of title) to the property;

(b) the mortgage documentation is completed and properly executed by the purchaser/borrower;

(c) a deed of confirmation is executed by any other party perceived to have, possibly or actually having, an interest in the property;

(d) the provisions of the Family Home Protection Act, 1976 as amended are complied with;

(e) the mortgage ranks as a first legal mortgage/charge on the property; and

(f) the solicitor is put in sufficient funds to enable him or her to discharge all stamp duty, registration fees and other outlays payable in connection with the purchase.

After releasing the loan cheque the solicitor must ensure that:

(i) all necessary documentation is properly stamped and registered in the appropriate Registry as soon as practicable, and

(ii) all deeds and documents together with the original mortgage and certificate of title are lodged with the lender as soon as practicable thereafter.

After completion, and pending the lodging of the documents with the lender, the solicitor holds the title documents in trust for the lender.

It should be noted that once this undertaking has been given to the lending institution the solicitor will be unable to exercise a lien over the title documents in the event of his or her fees not being paid.

9.7.2.3   Qualifying the undertaking

It is important to note that the undertaking specifically provides for the possibility of the solicitor not being able to certify the title without qualification. This will arise where the purchaser is not obtaining good marketable title to the property; for example, if there is an unauthorised development on the property or if the purchase is not effected on foot of the Law Society Contract for Sale. If qualifications are required to be made, they must be cleared in advance in writing with the lending institution. In such cases, the lending institution reserves the right to either withdraw the loan approval or to appoint its own solicitor to consider the matter.

After reading the draft contract furnished by the vendor's solicitor and after examining the title, it should be apparent to a purchaser's solicitor if he or she will be seeking to qualify the certificate of title. If a qualification is necessary the purchaser's solicitor should ensure, not only that the relevant qualification is notified to the lending institution at a very early date to give the lending institution time to consider the matter and comment thereon, but also that unconditional contracts are not exchanged until it is clear that the lending institution will accept the qualification on title. The lending institution has complete discretion as to whether or not it will accept a qualification on title. Particularly if the loan equity ratio is high, the lending institution may refuse to accept the qualification and to proceed with the loan unless the title is absolutely in order.

9.7.2.4   Certificate of title

When the purchase has been completed and the mortgage documentation executed, there is an obligation on the solicitor to stamp and register all of the documents and thereafter to return the documents to the lending institution with the certificate of title confirming that the purchaser/borrower has good marketable title to the premises in question free from encumbrances.

The solicitor for the purchaser is responsible to the purchaser who is acquiring the property and also to the lending institution on the strength of the certificate of title. In theory, this dual responsibility should not present a problem. After all, if the title to the premises which is being purchased is good and marketable, one can safely certify this to any party including the lending institution.

However, complications may arise where there is a fault or defect on the title being offered. When the fault or defect is brought to the attention of the purchaser he or she may instruct that the transaction proceed in any event as he or she is acquiring the property at the 'right price'. In this event the solicitor must inform the purchaser that, as he or she is required to certify the title to the lending institution, the fault or defect must be brought to its attention and the certificate of title qualified accordingly. The purchaser may realise this could preclude him or her from getting the loan which he or she requires to complete the purchase. Clients have been known to exert pressure on solicitors to forgo mentioning or drawing attention to a problem and to issue a certificate of title in cases where an unqualified certificate should not be issued. To do this leaves the solicitor exposed to a negligence action at the hands of the lending institution. In the event that the client falls into arrears with his or her repayments and the property is repossessed, the problem with the title will come to light and the solicitor will be liable to the lending institution for any loss suffered as a result of the problem. This situation may also arise if a solicitor issues a certificate of title in reliance on a colleague's undertaking. If the colleague fails to comply with the undertaking then the solicitor is also in difficulty. Thus, undertakings given and received on the completion of a transaction should be scrutinised carefully.

Once the lender receives the title documents and the signed certificate of title the undertaking will be released and the lender will instead rely on the certificate of title. The lender or lender's solicitor, as the case may be, should not go behind a properly completed certificate of title unless the title is being qualified in some way (Practice Note, Law Society Gazette, March 1995). A lender's solicitor who does go behind a certificate of title would be putting himself or herself on notice. The lender might subsequently have difficulty holding the borrower's solicitor liable on foot of the certificate of title. Since the activation of the certificate of title procedure, no major litigation has arisen in the courts concerning the matter. This means that practitioners are unclear as to how a court will react to a certificate of title in any particular circumstance. Statistically, this is not too surprising as, for every hundred mortgages, perhaps over ninety-five of the borrowers repay with no difficulty.

As a result of the certificate of title system the onus and responsibility for the correct preparation, execution, stamping and registration of the mortgage document itself now lies with the borrower's solicitor. Thus, it is important that the solicitor follows the instructions received from the lending institution to the letter and if not in a position to comply with the lending institution's requirements the solicitor must refuse to utilise the loan cheque for the borrower's benefit or to part with it until the matter has been clarified or the lending institution has waived the offending requirement.

9.8 Acting for the Lending Institution

9.8.1 GENERALLY

It is more usual in commercial transactions for lending institutions to engage their own solicitor to investigate title. This is mainly because the sums of money in question are significantly larger than in the case of residential lending and because the lending institution is not precluded by law from passing on all of its legal costs and outlay to the borrower in the context of the transaction. It is important to read the terms of any letter of loan offer very carefully, particularly with a commercial loan, as, in addition to the usual conditions, the letter often contains a specific paragraph to the effect that all legal fees in relation to the creation of the security as well as the enforcement of same, if this becomes necessary, will be paid by the borrower. In this manner, the lender ensures that it does not have to carry any of its own legal costs. If such a condition is included in the loan offer it is important for the borrower and the borrower's solicitor to quantify the costs and to factor them into the overall cost of the transaction as these costs will invariably have to be discharged on completion.

If the lender has engaged its own solicitor, then that solicitor is invariably given very specific instructions as to how to act in relation to the mortgage and the security. The solicitor may be required to carry out a full investigation of the title or alternatively to rely on a certificate of title from the borrower's solicitor.

9.8.2   NO INVESTIGATION OF TITLE

The lender's solicitor may be told by the lender to accept a certificate of title from the borrower's solicitor and not to enquire further in relation to the title. The lender's solicitor will attend completion with the loan cheque and obtains the certificate of title and title documents in return. At completion the lender's solicitor will only examine the certificate of title to ensure that:

(a)   it has been properly completed, is absolute and unqualified (unless otherwise agreed) and has not been altered, and

(b)   the certifying solicitor is covered by professional indemnity insurance.

After completion, the lender's solicitor will attend to stamping and registration.

It should be remembered that the Certificate of Title System (1999 edition) has been agreed in respect of residential lending only. Generally, each lending institution has its own standard certificate of title for commercial transactions. This certificate of title will usually be more detailed and onerous than the Law Society Certificate of Title agreed for residential lending.

The lender's solicitor may also ensure that the borrowers have complied with the provisions of the Family Home Protection Act, 1976, as amended in relation to the creation of the mortgage, and that the deed in the purchaser's/borrower's favour is properly executed and should be registered in the Land Registry or Registry of Deeds without difficulty.

Some supplemental documents may be required by a particular lender such as an undertaking to answer Land Registry queries, a power of attorney from the borrower etc and these will be requested by the lender's solicitor. The lender's solicitor will also require a cheque or lending institution draft to cover the stamp duty and registration fees payable and, in some cases, his own fees and outlay. Once this cheque has been tendered, and on receipt of all of the title documents and certificate of title, he will release the loan cheque to the borrower's solicitor and no further examination or investigation of the documents will be carried out.

9.8.3   INVESTIGATION OF TITLE

Alternatively, a lender's solicitor may be instructed to carry out a full and detailed investigation of the title offered as security. Normally this will result in a three-way closing involving the solicitor for the vendor, solicitor for the borrower and solicitor for the lending institution.

9.9   Borrowing by a Company

When acting on behalf of a borrowing company or for a lender in a commercial loan transaction it is crucial to remember the provisions of the Companies Act, 1963, s 99 which dictates that unless a notice of the charge created by a company is lodged within twenty-one days of the date of its creation with the Companies Office the charge will be void against the liquidator or any creditor of the company. Accordingly, it is essential to ensure that a Companies Office Form C1 (previously Form 47) is completed by the borrowing company on the occasion of completing the loan transaction and that the Form

C1 is filed with the Companies Office as quickly as possible after the completion of the transaction and, in any event, within twenty-one days. The Land Registry frequently insists upon the production of a note from the Companies Office verifying that the provisions of the Companies Act, 1963, s 99 have been complied with before it will complete the registration of any charge created by a limited liability company as a burden on a folio. This procedure serves as a useful reminder to comply with the provisions of the Companies Act, 1963 but, unfortunately, it cannot be relied upon as the reminder will often come outside the twenty-one-day period and accordingly, too late to be of any real help. A court application can be made for an extension of time but it is by no means certain that the court would grant such an application. Another option is to have the charge re-executed and to lodge the C1 relating to that new charge within the correct period. When acting for a borrower company it is essential to ensure that the company has the requisite power under its memorandum and articles of association to borrow money and to give security in respect of the borrowing and loans. The solicitor should also ensure that the company seal is brought to the completion ceremony along with the requisite number of authorised signatories who must be in attendance to countersign the seal. It is not unusual to find that the various company resolutions which are required to give effect to the borrowing and to the sealing of the mortgage documentation will be passed at the closing ceremony itself and, accordingly, when the mortgage is being completed, it is wise to ensure that a quorum of the company is present so that the requisite resolutions may be passed.

It should be noted that there are many provisions in the Companies Acts and other provisions which arise under company law in general which restrict the power of companies to secure loans, the most notable of which are the 1963 Act, s 60 and the 1990 Act, s 31.

9.10   Insuring the Property

In every case where a lending institution is advancing money on the strength of a premises it will insist on being satisfied that the premises have been covered for structural insurance. It will also insist that its interest has been noted on the insurance policy and that the policy will not fail, lapse or be allowed to be cancelled unless it (the institution) receives advance notice in writing of the cancellation which is pending and an opportunity to put its own insurance in place or to call in the loan. In general, the lending institution will only oblige the borrower to insure the structure. Once the structural integrity of the premises has been secured, the lending institution will not oblige the borrower to insure his contents or to insure against flooding or personal injury or accident. As a result of this it is important that the solicitor points out to the borrower that the insurance which the lending institution requires is basic insurance alone and it is not necessarily comprehensive enough to meet or satisfy the requirements of the borrower himself or herself. The solicitor should also advise borrowers of the workings of the 'average' clause under which an insurance company may claim that because the borrower is under-insured, it will only make payment of a proportionate amount of any claim which is made on the policy, such proportion being directly equivalent to the proportionate amount of underinsurance as assessed by the institution.

9.11   Indemnity Bond

One further element of insurance which frequently arises is the indemnity bond. In situations where a borrower is obtaining a loan in excess of 75–80 per cent of the value of the property being offered as security (and irrespective of whether the mortgage in question is an annuity mortgage or an endowment mortgage) the lending institution may oblige the borrower to take out an indemnity bond to cover the excess. This is an insurance company bond which guarantees to the lending institution that it will not suffer or be at a loss as a result of the fact that the loan being granted exceeds 75–80 per cent of the purchase price and is for an amount higher than the institution would ordinarily advance. In times of property recession when the value of real property is not rising and interest rates are high, an institution may find that it has advanced too big a loan to a borrower who cannot meet the repayments. By the time the lending institution has succeeded in repossessing the property, selling and paying all of the fees and outlays which it had incurred in doing so, the proceeds of sale may be insufficient to repay the mortgage with accrued interest and to cover all of the legal costs of the repossession and the costs of the sale. This may result in the lending institution suffering an overall loss on the transaction and in such cases it calls on the insurance company under the indemnity bond to make good that loss. The premium payable for an indemnity bond is invariably charged to the borrower. It is a once-off premium and the borrower receives no direct benefit for the fact that the indemnity bond has issued other than that he or she would not receive a loan in excess of 75–80 per cent of the purchase price if the indemnity bond was not in place.

9.12 Bridging Finance

If the loan cheque will not be available for completion the purchaser may require a bridging loan. This loan will 'bridge' the gap between completion and the issue of the loan cheque. The purchase may be completed and when the loan cheque issues the bridging loan is discharged.

In such circumstances, the borrower's solicitor will issue an undertaking to the bank/building society giving the bridging loan to the effect that he or she will hold all of the deeds and documents of title relating to the property on trust and to the order of the bank/building society once the sale has been completed. The undertaking will also confirm that he or she will use all money obtained from the bank/building society solely with the aim of acquiring a good and marketable title to the premises in question, and it will also contain a provision to the effect that, as soon as the loan cheque becomes available and the mortgage is completed, the bridging account will be cleared out of the proceeds of the loan cheque itself. The undertaking which is required varies from case to case depending on the lending institution one is dealing with, the creditworthiness of the borrower and the amount of the loan relative to the purchase price. Some lending institutions require an undertaking to furnish the net process of the loan, allowing the solicitor to deduct his or her fees and outlays from the loan cheque before making the necessary payment.

If a solicitor is being pressed to furnish an undertaking in relation to the full amount of the loan it is important for him or her to check that the full amount of the loan will issue. On occasions, the lending institution makes certain deductions from the loan cheque and these will result in a situation where the solicitor is unable to comply with his or her undertaking. He or she should ensure that his or her client puts him or her in funds for the stamp duty and registration fees, as these may not be deducted from the loan cheque in such circumstances.

Never allow a borrower to take up a bridging loan or a bridging facility unless absolutely certain that he or she will be in a position to obtain the loan cheque in the reasonably foreseeable future and repay the bridging loan to the lending institution. It is important for the borrower's solicitor to check that the borrower is in a position to comply with all of the requirements of the lending institution before the bridging facility is drawn down or that he or she will be a position to comply with such requirements in the immediate future.

In the current lending climate it is rare that a loan cheque will not be available for completion and thus it is more usual for bridging to be obtained to bridge the gap between the purchase of a new house and subsequent sale of the old house.

Most borrowers have nightmares when they hear the word 'bridging loan'. However, it is fair to say that bridging finance is a useful facility and when used correctly by a solicitor is an important tool of his or her trade. With the advent of the certificate of title system bridging loans are rarely required.

9.13 Stamp Duty and Registry Fees

A mortgage must be stamped before it may be registered in either the Land Registry or the Registry of Deeds. A mortgage securing a loan of less than €254,000 is exempt from stamp duty. Where the total amount secured exceeds €254,000 the stamp duty is 0.1 per cent of the entire loan but this is limited to a maximum amount of €630. The Land Registry fee for registering a mortgage is €125 and for registering a vacate €25 (Land Registration (Fees) Order, 1999 SI 343/1999). The Registry of Deeds fee for registering a mortgage is €44 and registering a vacate is €12 (Registry of Deeds (Fees) Order, 1999 SI 346/1999).

9.14 Enforcement

9.14.1 INTRODUCTION

The most obvious remedy available to a mortgagee when the mortgagor falls behind in his or her repayments is to sue him or her for the amount outstanding. This remedy, however, does not provide satisfactory relief where a mortgagor becomes unable to meet the repayments and the amount outstanding continues to grow.

The following is a very brief outline of some of the other remedies available to mortgagees in the event that the mortgagor defaults on the terms of the mortgage.

9.14.2 FORECLOSURE

Foreclosure involves the mortgagee taking court proceedings so as to have the mortgagor's equity of redemption extinguished. Thus, the mortgagor ceases to have an interest in the property and the mortgagee becomes full owner. Foreclosure is uncommon in Ireland as it is more usual for mortgagees to realise their security by a sale of the property or by the appointment of a receiver: see *Antrim County Land, Building and Investment Co Ltd v Stewart* [1904] 2 IR 357 at pp 369–370.

9.14.3 COURT ORDER FOR POSSESSION FOLLOWED BY SALE OR SALE

The mortgagee has power to sell the property without the intervention of the court; however, if the mortgagee is unable to gain vacant possession it will need to obtain a court order for possession. In *Irish Permanent Building Society v Ryan* [1950] IR 12 the High Court felt that an order that the mortgagor give up possession to the mortgagee should be made as property would realise more if sold with vacant possession. The mortgagee's statutory power of sale arises under the Conveyancing Act, 1881, s 19 which applies to all mortgages created by deed unless the terms of the mortgage indicate a contrary intention. As we have already stated, the Conveyancing Act, 1881, s 21 provides that:

> *a mortgagee exercising the power of sale conferred by this Act shall have power, by deed, to convey the property sold, for such estate and interest therein as is the subject of the mortgage, freed from all estates, interests and rights to which the mortgage has priority but subject to all estates, interests and rights which have priority to the mortgage . . .*

It should be noted, however, that the power of sale provided for in s 19 cannot arise until the money owed has become due.

If the mortgagee cannot sell under s 19 because the mortgage was not created by deed and there is no express power of sale then he or she will have no alternative but to apply to the court for an order of sale.

9.14.4 APPOINTMENT OF A RECEIVER

It is common for mortgages to contain provisions giving the mortgagee the right to appoint a receiver. The duty of the receiver is to manage the property so as to protect the mortgagee's interest therein. The receiver would also apply the rents and profits from the property towards discharging the debt owed to the lending institution. This remedy is most usually adopted when the property is a business, for example, a shop or restaurant.

APPENDIX 9.1

The Society's Certificate of Title System (1999 edition)

Law Society of Ireland
Blackhall Place
Dublin 7
Telephone 01-6710711
Fax 01-6710704
DX 79 Dublin

The Law Society

TO ALL SOLICITORS

9th March 1999

Dear Colleague,

The Conveyancing Committee in conjunction with the Legal Advisers of the under-mentioned Financial Institutions is pleased to inform you that agreement has been reached on revised standard forms of Solicitor's Undertaking, Certificate of Title and Approved Guidelines ('the agreed documents') for future use in residential property mortgage transactions.

Specimen copies of the agreed documents are enclosed. It is proposed that the agreed documents be used for all residential property mortgage loan transactions approved on or after **1st April 1999**.

The Committee unhesitatingly recommends practitioners to utilise the agreed documents for all residential mortgage loans approved after **1st April 1999. No alternative documentation should be used**. This recommendation is endorsed by the Solicitors Mutual Defence Fund Limited and Solicitors are advised that failure to utilise the agreed documents may engender difficulty with their Professional Indemnity Insurance Cover. Henceforth any alterations to or revisions of the agreed documents necessitated either by future legislation or changes in conveyancing practice shall be introduced only by the Committee in consultation with the Lending Institutions.

The revisions of and the alterations to the existing Certificate of Title documentation were sought by the Committee in the light of the terms of Opinions procured by the Committee from two eminent Senior Conveyancing Counsel, both of whom advised that it was highly desirable that the respective roles and responsibilities of Borrowers' Solicitors and Lenders should be re-stated and clarified so as to

    (a)   define and absolutely limit the responsibility of certifying solicitors to matters of title only and

    (b)   establish that Borrowers' Solicitors do not act for Lenders.

All matters which are not related to title, such as credit worthiness of Borrowers, loan repayment arrangements, property valuations and all insurance matters shall be the responsibility of the Lenders and not of Borrowers' Solicitors save as directed by the

Approved Guidelines. While the Approved Guidelines acknowledge that the Borrowers' Solicitors have no responsibility to the Lender to explain the conditions of the Facility Letter to the Borrower this does not affect the Solicitor's duty to his/her client in that regard.

In general terms, the agreed documents require that certifying Solicitors will carry out proper investigation of title to the Borrower's property, attend to the execution of the relevant purchase and mortgage documentation including, where applicable, guarantees and assignments of Life Policies and stamp and register the Borrower's deeds of purchase and mortgage prior to furnishing to the Lending Institution a properly completed Certificate of Title together with all relevant documents as soon as practicable.

Practitioners are earnestly advised to read the Approved Guidelines carefully as they set out requirements, inter alia, in relation to non-owning spouses, Deeds of Confirmation and Rights of Residence. Practitioners particularly should note that because of the nature of an exclusive right of residence, a Deed of Release will be required.

When utilising the agreed documents, practitioners should ensure compliance with the following practice recommendations viz:

(a)   all security documents should be signed in the presence of and witnessed by a Solicitor.

(b)   all Solicitor's Undertakings should be signed either by a partner or principal or a Solicitor duly authorised in writing by a partner or principal for that purpose. (Note: The foregoing has been specifically agreed with the Lenders to facilitate instances where the Partner or Principal is unavailable).

(c)   before signing Undertakings, Borrowers' Solicitors should ensure that their clients sign the Form of Retainer and Authority endorsed on such Undertakings and obtain a spouse's prior consent to the giving of the Retainer and Authority and Undertaking when applicable.

(d)   all intended qualifications to the Certificate of Title must be previously agreed in writing with the Lender and should be set out in the Schedule to the Solicitor's Undertaking.

(e)   before negotiating the loan cheque Borrower's Solicitors should ensure that all security documents have been executed and should be in funds to discharge all stamp duty and registration outlays in connection with the purchase and mortgage transaction.

(f)   all Certificates of Title should be signed by a partner or principal. Practitioners particularly should note that the Documents Schedules comprised in their Certificates of Title should be properly completed.

It should be noted that some Lenders may offer an Electronic Funds Transfer Facility for payments of the loan funds. In such cases the Lender will include the approved wording in the Letter of Undertaking requiring the insertion of the relevant Solicitor's client account details.

In relation to transactions involving stage payment purchases of new houses, practitioners are reminded of the terms of the various practice notices issued by the Committee expressing its disapproval of such form of house purchases and warning Solicitors of the potential risks both for their clients and themselves in allowing their clients to enter into such transactions.

The following Lending Institutions participated in negotiations with the Committee in reaching agreement on the enclosed agreed documents viz:

A.I.B. Bank

Irish Permanent plc

Bank of Ireland

EBS Building Society

ACC Bank

AIB Finance

First Active plc

ICS Building Society

Irish Life Homeloans

Irish Nationwide Building Society

National Irish Bank

TSB Bank

Ulster Bank Limited

The negotiations which led to agreement being reached on the enclosed documentation were very protracted and time consuming and, on behalf of the Profession, the Committee wishes to record its sincere appreciation of the huge commitment of time and effort contributed by the Members of its own Task Force and of the Lenders' Legal Advisers which resulted in the creation of the enclosed documentation which the Committee genuinely believes will be in the best interests of practitioners, their clients and the Lenders.

THE CONVEYANCING COMMITTEE

APPENDIX 9.2

Solicitor's Undertaking

Law Society of Ireland

RESIDENTIAL MORTGAGE LENDING
SOLICITOR'S UNDERTAKING
LAW SOCIETY APPROVED FORM (1999 EDITION)

To:_____

('the Lender' its transferees, successors and assigns)

MY/OUR CLIENT(S) _____

('the Borrower')

ADDRESS(ES) _____

_____

PROPERTY_____

_____

('the Property')

YOUR REF/ACCOUNT NO. _____

In consideration of the Lender agreeing to the drawdown of a loan facility in respect of the Property before the Lender's mortgage security has been perfected and subject to the payment through me/us of the loan cheque(s), unless I/we have consented in writing to *another mode of payment, I/we, the undersigned Solicitor for the Borrower, HEREBY UNDERTAKE with the Lender as follows:

1. **Good Title**

    Save for any qualification on title as agreed in writing with the Lender as set out in the Schedule hereto, to ensure, where the Borrower is acquiring the Property, that the Borrower will acquire good marketable title to it, or, where the Borrower already owns the Property, to satisfy myself/ourselves that such Borrower has good marketable title to it. (Note 1).

2. **Execution of Security Documents**

    To ensure, prior to negotiating the loan cheque(s) or the proceeds thereof that:

    (a)   the Borrower has executed a Mortgage Deed/Charge in the Lender's standard form as produced by the Lender (the 'Mortgage') over the Property (and, if required by the Lender, that any non-owning Borrower has joined in the Mortgage),

(b)   a Deed of Confirmation is executed by all necessary parties where the circumstances render such a Deed appropriate, and

(c)   all the provisions of the Family Home Protection Act, 1976 and any Act amending, extending or replacing that Act are complied with in respect of the Mortgage and any such Deed of Confirmation.

such that the Mortgage ranks as a first legal Mortgage/Charge on the Property. (Note 2)

(d)   the Borrower has executed the Lender's Standard Form of Life Policy Assignment, if specified in the Facility Letter/Letter of Offer (the 'Facility Letter')

(e)   a Guarantee in the Lender's Standard Form is executed, if specified in the Facility Letter

(f)   I am/we are in funds to discharge all Stamp Duty and Registration Fees.

3. Stamping, Registration & Lodgment with the Lender

As soon as practicable, to stamp (if exigible) and to register the Mortgage in the appropriate Registry so as to ensure that the Lender obtains a first legal Mortgage/Charge on the Property and expeditiously, as soon as practicable thereafter, to lodge the following with the Lenden:

(a)   all Deeds and documents to the Property, stamped and registered as appropriate, including, if applicable, the Assignment of the Life Policy, stamped collateral to the Mortgage

(b)   the original Mortgage (with Certificate of Charge endorsed thereon, under Rule 156 of Land Registry Rules, 1972, if Land Registry title)

(c)   if Land Registry title, the Land Certificate or, if not issued, an up-to-date Certified Copy Folio of the Property showing the Mortgage registered as a burden thereon, and

(d)   my/our Certificate of Title in the Law Society's standard form.

To the extent to which the Lender has indicated that it will attend to stamping and registration or any other work referred to above this part of the Undertaking shall be deemed to be amended accordingly.

4. Documents in Trust

Pending compliance with paragraph 3, to hold all title documents of the Property in trust for the Lender.

Authority

I/We confirm that I/we have the Borrower's irrevocable authority to give this undertaking and, where applicable, the Borrower's spouse's prior consent to give this undertaking.

Extent of Undertaking

This Undertaking is given by me/us in my/our sole capacity as Solicitor(s) for the Borrower and not as Solicitor(s) for or as agent/quasi agent of the Lender. It relates to Matters of Title and represents the sum of my/our obligations to the Lender in relation to this loan transaction. I/We have no responsibility for any matter of a non-title nature except insofar as any of the matters set out in this Undertaking may be deemed to be matters of a non-title nature.

SOLICITOR'S UNDERTAKING

SCHEDULE

Qualifications on Title (if any) agreed in writing with the Lender.

Dated this _____**day of** _____

SIGNATURE _____

NAME OF SOLICITOR SIGNING _____

(See Note 3)

**STATE WHETHER PRINCIPAL/ PARTNER
OR AUTHORISED SOLICITOR** _____

NAME OF FIRM _____

ADDRESS OF FIRM _____

_____

  *   Where it has been specifically agreed with the Lender that the funds shall issue by way of electronic funds transfer direct to the client account of the Borrower's Solicitor(s), please tick (and initial) the boxes and insert the details of that account

Name & Address of Bank   _____

_____ | Tick | | Initial |

Bank Sort Code   _____

Solicitor's Client Account Name   _____

Solicitor's Client Account No.   _____

NOTES:

1. In this Undertaking **'good marketable title'** means a title of a quality commensurate with prudent standards of current conveyancing practice in Ireland. The latter entails, where the Property is being acquired, that the purchase was effected on foot of the current Law Society's Conditions of Sale and/or Building Agreement. It also entails that the investigation of the title to the Property was made in accordance with the current Law Society Requisitions on Title together with any additional Requisitions appropriate to the Property and that satisfactory Replies have been received. When the Property is already owned by the Borrower, the title shall be so investigated that if the said Requisitions had been raised, satisfactory Replies would have been obtained.

    In this Undertaking **'Matters of Title'** means only such matters as relate to the title to the Property in the context of a conveyancing transaction and does not include any matters relating to the condition of the Property, the suitability or otherwise of the Borrower or any other matter (including the form or efficacy of the Mortgage).

    Any dispute as to the quality of any title or as to whether or not any matter constitutes a Matter of Title (within the foregoing definitions) may be referred for a ruling to the Conveyancing Committee of the Law Society of Ireland, but without prejudice to the right of either party to seek a determination by the Court on the issue.

2. Where the Lender is a Building Society within the meaning of the Building Societies Act, 1989 and any Act amending, extending or replacing that Act, any prior Mortgage or Charge *must* be redeemed prior to or contemporaneously with the creation of the Mortgage.

3. The Undertaking must be signed by a **Partner** or, in the case of a sole practitioner, by the **Principal** or other Solicitor duly authorised in writing on behalf of the firm by either of the foregoing. (**Note**: Where signed by the latter, the original or a Solicitor's certified copy of the written authority in question *MUST* be attached to this Undertaking.)

SOLICITOR'S UNDERTAKING

CLIENT(S) RETAINER AND AUTHORITY

To _____

_____ Solicitor(s)

of _____

I/We irrevocably authorise and direct you to give an undertaking in the form and containing the information set out overleaf (including an undertaking to lodge with the Lender the Title Deeds of the Property including any Land Certificate which has issued in relation to the Property) to

(Name of Lender) _____

and in consideration of your giving the foregoing undertaking, I/we hereby undertake that I/we will not discharge your retainer as my/our Solicitor(s) in connection with the foregoing matter unless and until I/we have procured from the Lender your effective release from the obligations imposed by such undertaking and I/we hereby indemnify you and all your partners and your and their Executors, Administrators and Assigns against any loss arising from my/our act or default.

Dated the _____ **day of** _____

Signed by the Borrower _____

_____

in the presence of _____

FAMILY HOME PROTECTION ACT CONSENT

I, _____

the lawful spouse of the above named Borrower

DO HEREBY GIVE MY PRIOR IRREVOCABLE CONSENT for the purposes of the Family Home Protection Act, 1976 (as amended) to the foregoing Retainer and Authority of my said spouse and to the within undertaking to be given by my spouse's Solicitor.

I acknowledge that it has been recommended to me that I should obtain independent legal advice with regard to the legal implications of giving this irrevocable consent. Where I have chosen not to take such advice, I declare that I did so voluntarily.

The Property is not adversely affected by section 5 of the Family Law Act, 1981, the provisions of the Judicial Separation and Family Law Reform Act, 1989, the Family Law Act, 1995 or the Family Law (Divorce) Act, 1996.

Dated the _____ **day of** _____

Signature of Spouse _____

Spouse's name in BLOCK CAPITALS _____

Witness _____

(Solicitor)

Address of Witness _____

_____

APPENDIX 9.3

Certificate of Title

Law Society of Ireland

RESIDENTIAL MORTGAGE LENDING

CERTIFICATE OF TITLE

LAW SOCIETY APPROVED FORM (1999 EDITION)

To: _____

('the Lender' its transferees, successors and assigns)

NAME(S) OF MY/OUR CLIENT(S) _____

('the Borrower')

ADDRESS OF PROPERTY _____

_____

('the Property')

YOUR REF/ACCOUNT NO. _____

As Solicitor(s) for the Borrower, I/We have investigated the title to the Property and I/We hereby certify that the Borrower has good marketable title to the Property (save as set out in the First Schedule hereto), the description of which agrees with that stated in the Facility Letter/Letter of Offer for the tenure specified in the Second Schedule hereto, free from any mortgage, charge, lien or encumbrance and any lease or tenancy, except for your Mortgage which is in the form prescribed by you (the 'Mortgage').

We hereby certify that your Mortgage ranks as a first Legal Mortgage/Charge over the Property.

All the documents evidencing the Borrower's title to the Property including your Mortgage are properly listed in the Third Schedule hereto and are furnished herewith.

My/Our Firm currently holds Professional Indemnity Insurance Cover with a qualified Insurer as defined under Statutory Instrument No. 312 of 1995 for a sum which is in excess of the amount being advanced to the Borrower.

I/We as Solicitor(s) for the Borrower, am/are giving this Certificate for the benefit of the Lender, having regard to (1) the current guidelines published by the Law Society to be followed when completing Certificates of Title for Lenders and (2) the current conveyancing recommendations of the Law Society.

This Certificate is being given by me/us in my/our sole capacity as Solicitor(s) for the Borrower and (other than as specifically set out herein) it relates only to Matters of Title.

This Certificate does not purport to certify anything in relation to the standard contents of the Mortgage executed by the Borrower. In particular, it does not certify that the

229

CERTIFICATE OF TITLE

Mortgage or any other document produced by the Lender in connection with the Loan complies with the requirements of the Consumer Credit Act, 1995 or the European Communities (Unfair Terms in Consumer Contracts) Regulations, 1995.

Signature _____

Name of Solicitor signing _____

State whether Principal/Partner._____

Name of Firm _____

Address of Firm _____

_____

Dated this _____ **day of** _____

In this Certificate of Title **'good marketable title'** means a title of a quality commensurate with prudent standards of current conveyancing practice in Ireland. The latter entails where the Property is being acquired, that the purchase was effected on foot of the current Law Society's Conditions of Sale and/or Building Agreement. It also entails that the investigation of the title to the Property was made in accordance with the current Law Society Requisitions on Title together with any additional Requisitions appropriate to the Property and that satisfactory Replies have been received. When the Property is already owned by the Borrower, the title shall be so investigated that if the said Requisitions had been raised, satisfactory Replies would have been obtained.

In this Certificate of Title **'Matters of Title'** means only such matters as relate to the title to the Property in the context of a conveyancing transaction and does not include any matters relating to the condition of the Property, the suitability or otherwise of the Borrower or any other matter (including the form or efficacy of the Mortgage).

Any dispute as to the quality of any title or as to whether or not any matter constitutes a Matter of Title (within the foregoing definitions) may be referred for a ruling to the Conveyancing Committee of the Law Society of Ireland but without prejudice to the right of either party to seek a determination by the Court on the issue.

FIRST SCHEDULE

Qualifications on Title (if any)
(as previously agreed in writing with the Lender)

SECOND SCHEDULE

Tenure

THIRD SCHEDULE

See Schedule of Documents attached hereto.

Law Society Approved Guidelines

Law Society of Ireland

RESIDENTIAL MORTGAGE LENDING

LAW SOCIETY APPROVED GUIDELINES (1999 EDITION)

GUIDELINES TO BE FOLLOWED BY SOLICITORS WHEN COMPLYING WITH SOLICITOR'S UNDERTAKING AND COMPLETING CERTIFICATE OF TITLE (LAW SOCIETY APPROVED FORMS (1999 EDITION))

1. The Solicitor should ensure that there should be compliance with any requirements specified in the Conditions in the Lender's Facility Letter/Letter of Offer (the 'Facility Letter') insofar as they relate to Matters of Title.

2(a) It is a matter for the Borrower to comply with all conditions in the Facility Letter before the loan cheque is requisitioned. The Borrower will be instructed by the Lender to contact the Lender direct regarding insurance, valuation and any other matter not of a title nature.

2(b) In those cases where it is a Lender's practice to furnish the Facility Letter direct to the Solicitor, or to the client with a recommendation that it be completed in the Solicitor's presence, it is acknowledged by the Lender that the Solicitor shall have no responsibility to the Lender to explain the conditions to his/her client. This however does not affect the Solicitor's duty to his/her client to explain the said conditions.

3. The title must be Freehold, or Leasehold with an unexpired term of at least 70 years, unless you are satisfied that the Lessee has a statutory right to purchase the Fee Simple under the Ground Rents legislation. If Land Registry title, it must be either Absolute or Good Leasehold.

4. The Property must be free from encumbrances to ensure that the Lender shall have a first legal Mortgage/Charge.

5. The Law Society has already advised Solicitors that Stage Payment transactions are undesirable in view of the potential difficulties they create for both Purchasers and their Solicitors. If, however, despite this advice, the Borrower is willing to make such payments to a Builder/Developer who is registered with HomeBond, in advance of title vesting in the Borrower, and the Lender has specifically agreed to advance funds for the purpose of making such Stage Payments, the following qualification should be inserted in the Schedule to the Undertaking:

   'The Property is being purchased by Stage Payments. Stage Payments up to the limits covered by the HomeBond scheme are to be released in advance

of title vesting in the Borrower and the Supplemental Stage Payments Undertaking set out in the LAW SOCIETY APPROVED GUIDELINES (1999 EDITION) shall be deemed to be incorporated in this Undertaking'.

The Supplemental Stage Payments Undertaking reads as follows:

'Property being Acquired—Stage Payments to Builder/Developer

Where stage payments are being paid to the Builder/Developer, to ensure:

(a) that a valid and enforceable fixed price contract has been exchanged to obtain good marketable title to the Property upon completion of the construction thereof and the completion of the purchase formalities

(b) that the Property is registered with HomeBond, and

(c) that prior to payment of any stage payment which the Lender may agree to lend in excess of the amount covered by the HomeBond scheme, title to the Property (including the right to immediate possession) is unconditionally vested in the Borrower and that there is compliance with all the requirements of paragraph 2 of the SOLICITOR'S UNDERTAKING LAW SOCIETY APPROVED FORM (1999 EDITION)'

N.B. Not all lenders will advance stage payments on the basis of the foregoing, Solicitors are cautioned to check with the individual lenders.

6. The consideration expressed in the Purchase Deed/Building Agreement must be as stated in the Facility Letter. If there is any discrepancy, this must be brought to the attention of the Lender prior to drawing down the cheque. The amount of the loan may be reduced in the event of such a discrepancy.

7. There must be no restrictions on mortgaging the Property. Any necessary consent from a Housing Authority, for example, must be obtained and compliance with any condition procured.

8. The Borrower's signature on the Mortgage (including any non-owning spouse or other person who may be required to join in the Mortgage) must be made in the presence of and witnessed by a Solicitor.

9. For 'once off' properties or those not forming part of a housing estate, there must be with the title a Declaration of Identity declaring that the Property and its essential services (e.g. septic tank and well etc.) are entirely within the boundaries of the lands the subject matter of the Lender's security. If any such services are not within the boundaries of such lands, then a Grant of Easement must be furnished unless a prescriptive right thereto is established and this is verified by an appropriate Statutory Declaration.

10. Any qualification of the Certificate of Title must be specifically agreed in writing with the Lender prior to furnishing the Undertaking. It may or may not be acceptable to the Lender. Where the Lender agrees to accept any qualification it shall be understood that the responsibility for explaining the nature of the subject matter of the qualification to the Borrower rests with the Solicitor and the acceptance of the qualification shall not be taken to imply any responsibility or liability to the Borrower on the part of the Lender.

11. If Title to the Property vests in the sole name of one spouse, and if the Family Home Protection Act, 1976 applies, a prior consent to the Mortgage must be completed, signed and dated by the Mortgagor's spouse.

(Note: Even if the Property will not become a Family Home vesting in sole name until immediately after completion it is, nonetheless, recommended that the prior consent is signed by the relevant spouse as possession may have been taken informally or partially beforehand. To avoid doubt, it is prudent to get the consent completed in any such case).

12. (a) There must be no person other than the Borrower with any estate or interest, beneficial or otherwise in the Property and this must be confirmed by a Statutory Declaration of the Borrower. (Some Lenders may require such a Declaration prior to drawdown.)

    (b) If there is any such person with any such estate or interest by reason of making a contribution to the purchase price or otherwise howsoever, that person should, after the Mortgagor signs the Mortgage, execute a Deed of Confirmation so as to supplementally mortgage any such estate or interest to the Lender. (The confirmation is non recourse i.e. it does not of itself impose a liability on the beneficiary to repay.) Where appropriate the beneficiary's spouse should sign his/her prior consent to the Deed of Confirmation.

    (c) If there is a right of residence the person entitled thereto must sign a Deed of Confirmation except in the event of such right being an exclusive right – in which event the right of residence must be released prior to the execution of the Mortgage (but such right may be reconstituted thereafter).

    (d) It should be noted that a sole Mortgagor's spouse although signing the prior Family Home Protection Act 'Consent to Mortgage' may be a beneficiary nonetheless because of e.g. direct or indirect financial contribution/s. If there is any doubt in this respect, the beneficiary should, after the Mortgagor signs the Mortgage, execute a Deed of Confirmation so as to supplementally mortgage any such estate or interest to the Lender. (The confirmation is non recourse i.e. it does not of itself impose personal liability on a beneficiary to repay.)

13. If the Lender requires that the non-owning spouse joins the Mortgage there should be compliance with this requirement.

14. Any spouse signing the Family Home Protection Act consent or any non-owning spouse joining in the Mortgage or any person signing the Deed of Confirmation or consent thereto must receive independent legal advice (or, after receiving legal advice from the Borrower's Solicitor of the serious implication of not taking such advice, must sign an explicit waiver of the right to be so advised which waiver must be placed with the title deeds).

15. Searches must include those against the Borrower and, when a purchase is completed in advance of the Mortgage, searches must be updated to the date of the Mortgage.

16. The Certificate of Title together with all the Title Documents when stamped and registered must be lodged with the Lender within a reasonable time. All documents accompanying the Certificate of Title should be properly scheduled in the interest of efficiency and a quick response from the Lender.

CHAPTER 10

SEARCHES

10.1 Introduction

10.1.1 WHAT ARE SEARCHES?

Searches are enquiries carried out, usually by a purchaser's or mortgagor's solicitor, on the transfer of an interest in property. Generally, they take the form of enquiries in government departments so as to check ownership of the interest, planning, environmental and related matters, any liabilities or charges affecting that ownership and enquiries into the status of the vendor or mortgagor which might affect ownership of the interest being transferred.

Any items disclosed as a result of the searches which adversely affect the property, its ownership or the status of the vendor/purchaser will need to be brought to the attention of the purchaser/mortgagee.

10.1.2 WHY CARRY OUT SEARCHES?

10.1.2.1 Introduction

The basic conveyancing principle of the bona fide purchaser for value without notice is circumscribed by the terms of the Conveyancing Act, 1882, s 3(1) which, inter alia, provide that this doctrine can only apply after such enquiries and inspections have been made as ought reasonably to have been made by the purchaser.

Section 3(1) states as follows:

A purchaser shall not be prejudicially affected by notice of any instrument, fact, or thing unless—

(i)   It is within his own knowledge, or would have come to his knowledge if such inquiries and inspections had been made as ought reasonably to have been made by him; or

(ii) In the same transaction with respect to which a question of notice to the purchaser arises, it has come to the knowledge of his counsel, as such, or of his solicitor, or other agent, as such, if such inquiries and inspections had been made as ought reasonably to have been made by the solicitor or other agent.

Thus, in order for a purchaser to have the protection afforded by the law to a bona fide purchaser for value the purchaser must carry out reasonable enquiries. It follows without question that there is a clear obligation on solicitors acting for purchasers and lenders in conveyancing transactions to carry out all searches relevant to the transaction in question.

An additional reason why searches are carried out is to ensure that the purchaser obtains 'good marketable title' to the property in accordance with the contract for sale.

10.1.2.2 Law Society standard conditions

The standard Law Society General Conditions of Sale (2001 edition) and Objections and Requisitions on Title (2001 edition) contain clauses relevant to searches.

The Searches Schedule of the Contract for Sale provides for the listing of any negative searches (dealt with at **10.2.8.2**) which are being furnished by the vendor's solicitor to the purchaser. It is the recommended practice for the vendor's solicitor to furnish an up-to-date negative search, which relates only to unregistered property, on the vendor covering the period from when he acquired an interest in the property up to the current date.

General condition 19 provides that the purchaser shall be furnished with the searches (if any) listed in the Searches Schedule and any searches already in the vendor's possession which are relevant to the title on offer.

General condition 19 of the Contract for Sale also provides that the vendor must explain and discharge any acts appearing on searches covering the period from the date stipulated or implied in the contract for the commencement of the title to the date of actual completion. However, where the special conditions in the contract provide that the title shall commence with a particular instrument and then pass to a second instrument or to a specified event, the vendor shall not be obliged to explain and discharge any act which appears on a search covering the intermediate period (between such particular instrument and the date of the second instrument or specified event) unless same goes to the root of the title.

Requisition 13 of the standard Law Society Objections and Requisitions on Title provides that a purchaser will make searches where necessary in the following offices and registers:

(a) Registry of Deeds;

(b) Land Registry;

(c) judgments;

(d) bankruptcy;

(e) sheriff;

(f) Companies Office; and

(g) Planning Office.

Any act appearing on the result thereof must be explained and/or discharged by the vendor prior to completion.

While it is extremely important to carry out such searches it is equally important, having regard to the increasing cost of such searches, that solicitors do not make or require unnecessary searches for any transaction. All searches are becoming more expensive, particularly computer planning searches. Thus, it is vital that solicitors know the appropriate searches for each type of transaction.

10.2 Types of Searches

The following sets out the most likely searches to be made in a typical conveyancing transaction. Law searchers are usually engaged to do this work.

10.2.1 JUDGMENTS OFFICE SEARCH

10.2.1.1 Introduction

A judgment search involves a search on two registers in the central office of the High Court. It will show any judgment against the vendor in the last five years (Money

Judgments Register) and any lis pendens (Lis Pendens Register), ie proceedings to recover or charge the land which may be pending.

It should be noted that when a Judgments Office search is sought law searchers may search only against the Lis Pendens Register and may not search against the Money Judgments Register unless specifically requested to do so.

10.2.1.2 Money Judgments Register

Where a judgment appears it presents the possibility of a judgment mortgage being registered against the property under the Judgment Mortgage (Ireland) Act, 1850. The judgment itself does not affect the lands until a judgment mortgage is registered. A judgment mortgage registered after the closing of the sale will not catch any interest of the former owner as he or she has none. All his interest in the property will pass to the purchaser on payment of the balance of the purchase money on completion (see *Tempany v Hynes* [1976] IR 101). The procedure for applying to the Registrar of Titles to remove a judgment mortgage in such circumstances is quite simple (see Land Registry Rules 121 and 122). In relation to unregistered title, if there is any doubt about the creditworthiness of the client and there is the danger of a judgment mortgage being registered, it is possible to have someone on hand in the Registry of Deeds to record the fact of the sale closing on a particular date. It is also possible for that person to obtain a letter from the Registry of Deeds confirming that that deed will have priority from the date of closing.

In *Tempany v Hynes* [1976] IR 101 the Supreme Court held that a purchaser of registered land took the land free of a judgment mortgage registered against the vendor post-contract. This was because the Registration of Title Act, 1964, s 71(4) provides that such a charge is subject to 'all unregistered rights' affecting the vendor's interest at the time of registration of the judgment mortgage. The purchaser, it was held, had such an unregistered right under the contract.

10.2.1.3 Lis Pendens Register

Where a lis pendens is disclosed the purchaser is on notice of the proceedings and if he proceeds with the transaction he or she will be bound by the outcome of such proceedings. Thus, any lis pendens must be dealt with prior to completion. A lis pendens against unregistered land must be reregistered every five years and thus a search should be made for the five years prior to the sale. A lis pendens against registered land will remain on the register until cancelled. It would be highly inadvisable to close a transaction where a lis pendens appears on a search at closing unless the litigation in respect of which the lis pendens is registered does not affect the land.

It is difficult to ascertain the precise legal position in relation to lis pendens and registered land. It appears that a lis pendens may affect Registry of Deeds property only. The reason for this is as follows. Section 69 of the Registration of Title Act, 1964 sets out the burdens that affect registered land, if registered on the folio, and these include lis pendens (s 69(i) and (ii)). The logical consequence is that if a lis pendens is not registered on the folio it cannot affect registered land. It is, however, the practice to make a search on the Lis Pendens Register when buying or lending on registered land.

The statute that governs the Index of Lis Pendens in the Central Office of the High Court is the Judgments (Ireland) Act, 1844. Section 10 of that Act is as follows:

No lis pendens shall bind or affect a Purchaser or Mortgagee, without express notice thereof, unless and until a memorandum or minute containing the name and the usual or last known place of abode, and the title, trade or profession of the person whose estate shall be intended to be affected thereby, and the Court of Equity and the title of the cause or information, and the day when the Bill or information was filed, shall be left with such officer so to be appointed as aforesaid, who shall forthwith enter the same particulars in a book as aforesaid, in alphabetical order, by the name of the person whose estate is intended to be affected by such lis pendens, and which book is to be entitled 'the index to lis pendens'.

This is clearly a requirement that to affect a purchaser or lender, a lis pendens must be registered on the Index. For obvious reasons it makes no reference to registered or unregistered land.

It is important to remember when considering this that lis pendens means just what it says, ie a pending action. It does *not* mean a pending action, which has been registered on the Index of Lis Pendens.

10.2.2 SHERIFF'S OFFICE SEARCH

There are two types of Sheriff's Office search; bills of sale Sheriff's Office search and revenue Sheriff's Office search. These searches need only be carried out in respect of leasehold property.

The sheriff has a legal right to seize the goods of a debtor on foot of a decree Fi Fa or equivalent. This does not include real (freehold) property. The sheriff does not have a right to obtain possession. He merely has a right to sell. It is the purchaser from a sheriff who obtains a right to possession. A purchaser from a sheriff might have to sue for possession. The sheriff's right to execute relates only to the legal estate in a property. If the property is subject to a legal mortgage the owner has parted with the legal estate and holds only an equity of redemption. It has been held that in such circumstances the sheriff cannot execute.

It is not surprising therefore that we cannot trace any case where a sheriff has sold leasehold property in recent times. From a pragmatic view it could be argued that it is possible to dispense with a sheriff's search even on leasehold property, provided the vendor's title is subject to a mortgage as it is hard to imagine a sheriff succeeding in carrying out a valid sale in the short period between the time the first mortgage is cleared and the new mortgage is completed.

There appears to be no justification for the practice of lenders' solicitors insisting on a borrower's solicitor furnishing sheriff's searches in relation to freehold property. For further information on sheriff's searches see the Continuing Legal Education (CLE) Seminar on Practical Conveyancing: Investigation of Unregistered Title by Brid Brady and Judge Catherine Murphy, dated 20 May 1996.

10.2.3 BANKRUPTCY OFFICE SEARCH

A Bankruptcy Office search is only appropriate in the case of individuals, as a company cannot be made bankrupt. If the vendor has been made bankrupt he cannot deal with the property, as all his property will have vested in the Official Assignee. The certificate of the vesting of his estate in the Official Assignee must be registered in the Registry of Deeds or the Land Registry. If there is a voluntary deed on title a bankruptcy search must be made against the donor if the deed is less than five years old. If the donor is declared bankrupt within two years of a disposition that disposition is void as against the Official Assignee. If the donor is declared bankrupt within five years there is a presumption that it is void unless it can be shown that the donor was, at the date of the disposition, able to meet his debts without recourse to the property (Bankruptcy Act, 1988).

10.2.4 PLANNING OFFICE SEARCH

A Planning Office search is carried out on the property. This search must always be carried out regardless of the type of property being sold or the title. It should be carried out by both the vendor and purchaser prior to contract; the vendor so as to provide assistance in determining if the warranty in general condition 36 of the contract needs to be limited, and the purchaser so as to determine, inter alia, if the planning history of the property is in order. The planning search will generally reveal, inter alia, the zoning of the area, any prior applications for planning permission in respect of the property, any refusals of permission, any application for building bye-law approval and any other entries in the Planning Register in respect of the property. It may also reveal any road-widening proposals which affect the property (in some areas this information can only be obtained from the roads department). In addition any compensation awards, enforcement notices, warning notices, conservation orders, sterilisation agreements etc will be revealed. It is extremely important that this search is carried out pre-contract and the purchaser told of the results. The search should then be updated for closing. It should be noted that some law searchers only search back five years unless instructed otherwise. It is vital that a planning search cover the planning history of the property since 1 October 1963, the date of the coming into force of the Local Government (Planning and Development) Act, 1963.

A computer planning search may now be done in some areas. It is necessary to be careful doing this type of search as the computer will only search against the exact information furnished, eg if searching against Anne Ryland it will not automatically search against Ann Ryland. The name must be precise as there is a double charge for each name check which makes the search expensive.

A planning search, however, will not disclose the existence of any unauthorised developments unless the local authority has served an enforcement or warning notice or unless an application has been made for retention permission. The assistance of an architect or engineer will be required to determine if the position on the ground corresponds with what is in the planning office.

The search will only reveal the planning history of the specific property in question. It will not disclose details about other developments in the area where the property is situate. For example, it will not reveal that a factory is being built next door or that a planning application has been made to convert the premises across the road into a chip shop. As a result a purchaser should always be advised to personally attend the local authority offices to carry out an inspection of the Planning Register. This will allow the purchaser to determine if there are any proposed developments, for example a meat factory, in the immediate area of the property that might affect his decision to purchase. Alternatively it may disclose restrictions on the future development of the property that might affect his decision to purchase (see Practice Note, Law Society Gazette, November 1984).

For further information on planning searches see the CLE Series of Seminars on Planning Law by John Gore-Grimes and Patrick Sweetman, dated 2 December 1998.

10.2.5 BUILDING CONTROL REGISTER SEARCH

A Building Control Register search should be carried out in conjunction with a Planning Office search. This register will disclose details of commencement notices, fire safety certificates, enforcement notices and any order of the district court made in respect of an enforcement notice.

10.2.6 ENVIRONMENTAL SEARCHES

Purchasers are advised to carry out searches to establish if the property is listed as a proposed special area of conservation or national heritage area. Lists of all proposed sites are maintained by each local authority. An examination of these searches is outside the scope of this chapter. For further information on planning searches see the CLE Series of Seminars on Planning Law by John Gore-Grimes and Patrick Sweetman, dated 2 December 1998.

10.2.7 COMPANIES OFFICE SEARCH

A Companies Office search arises when the vendor is a company. It also arises in the case of apartments, as the management company will need to be searched against. It is not necessary to carry out such searches on companies which appear on prior title. A Companies Office search will disclose the status of the company, ie has it been struck off the register or does it still exist. It will disclose all charges on the assets of the company and whether it is in receivership, examinership or liquidation. The end of the search is as important as the body of the search itself because this lists unregistered and recently registered documents. An entry of 'C.1.' or 'CHC' must be noted as they disclose that the company has created a charge and a certificate of registration of the charge has been received by the Companies Office but has not yet been registered. Confirmation should be sought that the charges do not affect the property being sold. Alternatively, confirmation that the charges have been discharged is required. If a floating charge is disclosed a purchaser will require a certificate from the company secretary that the charge has not crystallised, in other words, that it has not attached itself to the property.

On the purchase of a new house it is vital that a search be carried out against the builder/vendor in the Companies Office. If the property is subject to a mortgage this must be brought to the attention of the purchaser (see *Roche v Peilow* [1985] IR 232 and Practice Note, Law Society Gazette, October 1985).

The Companies Office search should be carried out before contracts are exchanged to ensure that the company has not been struck off the register. The Companies Office has recently been striking off many companies, including some very prominent ones, for failure to make annual returns.

10.2.8 REGISTRY OF DEEDS SEARCH

10.2.8.1 Generally

A Registry of Deeds search is carried out when the title being offered is unregistered, ie registered in the Registry of Deeds. It is a search to find out what deeds have been registered affecting the particular property. The name of the person to be searched against, the premises affected and the dates to be searched must be furnished. There are a number of Registry of Deeds searches: negative search, common search, hand search, search on the Index of Names. All are broadly similar in that previously the Registry of Deeds had a Names Index and a Lands Index. Now the only index operating is the Names Index and thus it is on this index that searches are made. These searches may be either negative or common or hand.

10.2.8.2 Negative and common searches

A negative search is made by an official Registry of Deeds searcher and checked by a second one and the results are guaranteed by the Registry as accurate. A common search is made by only one official searcher and the results are not warranted. They are generally accurate and a common search will be accepted by the Land Registry as sufficiently accurate for its purposes when applications are made for first registration. The fees for a common search are lower than for a negative search. Negative searches are obviously preferable as they are guaranteed and thus should always be used by a solicitor acting for a purchaser or any other party acquiring an interest in land.

It has been the tradition in many parts of the country, and it is currently the recommended practice of the Law Society (see Practice Notes, Law Society Gazette, July/August 1978 and December 1988), that the vendor of unregistered property furnish a negative search against the vendor and against all parties on title for the duration of the title being shown. Under general condition 19 of the Contract for Sale the purchaser agrees to furnish the searches (if any) listed in the Searches Schedule and any searches already in the vendor's possession, which are relevant to the title or titles on offer. Generally, when following this practice, solicitors list the search in the Searches Schedule and furnish a draft of the requisition for negative search to the purchaser's solicitor for approval with the draft contract for sale. Unfortunately, there was a time when substantial delays in the Registry of Deeds meant that the result of the negative search would not have been available for closing. As a result the practice of the vendor's solicitor ordering a negative search at contract stage fell into disuse and is no longer adhered to by some practitioners. Due to computerisation these delays no longer arise and the recommended practice should now be followed.

10.2.8.3 Draft requisition for negative search

The following is a draft requisition for negative search which should be sent with the contract for sale for approval by the purchaser's solicitor:

To the Registrar of Deeds Wills & Soforth in Ireland

We require an abstract of every memorial registered in the Office for registering deeds and soforth in Ireland appearing on a search on the Index of Names only for all acts by Thomas William Thornton from the 5 March 1994 to date of certificate hereon to affect premises situate at Pinewood Drive, Ballymun being part of the lands of Clonmel in the Barony of Coolock and County of the City of Dublin.

Dated this   day of   2002.

Solicitors,
Fitzwilliam Square,
Dublin 2.

A similar practice is recommended by the Law Society in the case of new houses where the obligation to provide a negative search rests with the solicitor acting for the builder. See Practice Note, Law Society Gazette, December 1988.

10.2.8.4 Hand searches

The third type of search is a hand search. This may be made by any member of the public but is usually made by a firm of law searchers who should be bonded to ensure that any loss as a result of an error made by them will be covered. These searches are particularly useful as negative and common searches take time, sometimes two to three weeks, to issue and may be out of date when the result is received. Hand searches ensure that it is possible to carry out searches right up to the date of actual completion of the purchase. It is usual to do a negative search initially and then a hand search to cover the period between the date of the negative search and the date of completion. The negative search may be updated subsequently.

10.2.8.5 Importance of correct instructions for search

In relation to these searches it is important to ensure that a correct and full description of the property is given and also that the correct spelling of the parties' names is given. Regardless of the type of search it is vital that the requisition for the search includes all descriptions by which the land is or was previously known. If in doubt always include alternative descriptions and all alternative spellings. The reason for this is that if searching against Katherine Mullins, any acts of Kate or Katie Mullins will not show. It is for this reason that requisition 13.2 asks if the vendor has ever executed any document in relation to the property in the Irish equivalent or any other variant of his name.

10.2.8.6 Period of search

The general practice is to search back a minimum of twenty years; however, if the vendor has owned the property for thirty years then the search should be against the vendor for that period of thirty years. Each party on title during that twenty-year period must be searched against. Where possible, solicitors should be practical about the length of title shown and accordingly the period in respect of which searches are made.

A Registry of Deeds search must be carried out against all parties on title for the appropriate period. The appropriate period is the *date of the deed* to the person to the *date of the registration of the deed* where the person disposes of their interest in the property ie the subsequent deed.

For example, if B buys from A on 5 May 1952 (registered on 14 May 1952) and then sells to C on 1 July 1963 (registered on 7 August 1963) who, in turn, sells on to D on 8 February 1978 (registered on 3 March 1978) and, on 13 June 1999, D executes a contract selling the property to the present client then, if the 1952 deed is a good root of title, the following searches should be made in the Registry of Deeds:

(a) against B from 5 May 1952 to the date of the registration of his deed to C on 7 August 1963;

(b) against C from 1 July 1963 to the date of the registration of his deed to D on 3 March 1978; and

(c) against D from 8 February 1978 to the date of completion of the purchase.

If the purchaser is obtaining a mortgage it is also necessary to search against him from the date of the contract, ie the date he acquired a beneficial interest in the property, 13 June 1999, to the date of completion.

10.2.8.7 Death on title

The appropriate period is somewhat different if there is a death on title.

If there is a death on title the period to search against the testator is extended. The search must be up to the date of registration of the assent to the beneficiary. If there is no assent the period to search against the testator is up to the date of registration of the subsequent conveyance for value.

If an executor has been appointed the period to search against the executor is from the date of the testator's death to the date of registration of the assent. If the assent has not been registered the search should be up to the date of registration of the subsequent conveyance for value. The beneficiary should be searched against from the date of death of the deceased to the date of registration of the conveyance for sale disposing of his or her interest in the property.

Where there is no will and an administrator is appointed, the period to search against the administrator is from the date of the grant of administration to the date of registration of the assent. If the assent has not been registered the search should be up to the date of registration of the subsequent conveyance for value. The beneficiary should be searched against from the date of death to the date of registration of the conveyance for sale disposing of his or her interest in the property.

In other words, when there is a grant of probate the search against the personal representative must be from the date of death and when there is a grant of administration intestate the search against the personal representative must be from the date of the grant. Any documents that appear on the searches must be explained and, where necessary, discharged or released.

10.2.9 LAND REGISTRY SEARCH

A Land Registry search is carried out when the title being offered is registered in the Land Registry. The search will disclose all details on the folio, ie the current registered owner, the nature of the title (ie whether absolute, good leasehold or possessory), whether or not the land certificate has issued, any dealings pending and any encumbrances appearing (eg whether a land purchase annuity is payable and any cautions or inhibitions registered on the folio). If there is a letter after the number of the folio this must be given as there may be a number of different folios with the same number. For example, Folio 12345, Folio 12345F, Folio 12345L and Folio 12345R are all different folios.

10.2.10 PRIORITY SEARCHES

Section 108 of the Registration of Title Act, 1964 and rules 190 onwards of the Land Registry Rules, 1972 provide for official searches in the Land Registry. The rules in relation to priority searches are particularly important (rules 191 and 192). This search has the added advantage that when the Registrar issues the search he puts an inhibition on the folio. This inhibits all dealings for a period of fourteen days, save the dealing by the party on whose behalf the search was made, ie usually the purchaser or mortgagee. After the fourteen days a further priority search may be applied for; however, this does not continue the previous period. Any applications lodged during the fourteen days will be registered before the new fourteen-day period begins. This search is not commonly done but is recommended where there is a reason to be apprehensive about the financial status of the vendor or where the transaction involves a property of significant value.

10.2.11 ADDITIONAL SEARCHES

Additional searches include searches of the Derelict Sites Register, Housing (Private Rented Dwellings) Register, Register of Dangerous Buildings, Register of Fire Safety Certificates and Register of Multi-Storey Buildings. A further type of search is a bills of sale search which deals with personal chattels, fixtures and crops. This search will be necessary if, for example, the sale includes expensive equipment or shop contents. These additional searches are not dealt with here. For additional information see the lecture by Patrick Sweetman dated 27 February 1998 as part of the CLE Series of Four Seminars on Essential Conveyancing for Practitioners.

10.3   Who Carries Out Searches?

Searches should be prepared by a recognised firm of law searchers with an appropriate level of indemnity insurance. The Law Society and the Joint Committee of Building Societies' Solicitors have confirmed that searches carried out by solicitors are not acceptable (Practice Note, Law Society Gazette, June 1983).

10.4   When are Searches Carried Out?

As stated at **10.1.2.1** the purchaser must make appropriate enquiries in order to be afforded the protection offered by the law to a bona fide purchaser for value. This involves making the appropriate searches prior to completion in order to determine that the title is unencumbered and that other matters such as planning are in order. Generally these searches are carried out prior to completion; however, a prudent conveyancer may also carry out searches prior to contract. For example, due to the principle of caveat emptor a planning search and a search of the Building Control Register should be carried out pre-contract. The vendor may also need to carry out searches pre-contract in order to comply with the Law Society recommendation on negative searches (see Practice Note, Law Society Gazette, July/August 1978) or to properly fulfil his or her duty of disclosure to the purchaser. The vendor has a duty of disclosure in relation to defects on title, rights and liabilities that affect the property and also notices served on the vendor in relation to the property. The vendor may be unable or unwilling to furnish his or her solicitor with certain information about the property or himself or herself and in these circumstances searches may need to be carried out in order to comply with the duty of disclosure. For example, the vendor may have several judgments against him or her but may not know if these have been converted into judgment mortgages.

As a general rule most searches are carried out post-contract and prior to completion.

An exception arises when the purchaser is also mortgaging the property and the completion of the mortgage occurs after completion of the purchase. In that instance the lender will require the searches to be updated to the date of completion of the mortgage. The Law Society Approved Guidelines (1999 edition) in relation to the certificate of title for residential mortgage lending requires that searches must include those against the borrower and, when a purchase is completed in advance of the mortgage, the searches must be updated to the date of the mortgage. The main reason lenders require such searches to be updated is to check the possibility of a judgment mortgage being registered against the property and gaining priority though reference to the case law on this point shows that a lender or purchaser need not be concerned with any judgment registered as a judgment mortgage after completion of the purchase. This is dealt with in more detail at **10.6.1**.

10.5   What to do with the Result of Searches?

The result of the various searches carried out will disclose information in relation to the vendor and/or the property. It may be necessary for the purchaser's solicitor to disclose some of that information to his or her client as it may affect the client's decision to purchase. Alternatively, the purchaser's solicitor may require the vendor's solicitor to confirm that the information or 'acts' appearing on the search do not affect the property being purchased by the client (see Practice Note, Law Society Gazette, December 1997). For example, if the Registry of Deeds search discloses a charge on the property the vendor's solicitor will be required to furnish a discharge on closing, or if the planning search discloses that the property is zoned residential but the client wishes to build a factory then this will obviously impact on his or her decision to purchase.

The purchaser's solicitor makes the searches where necessary in the relevant offices and registers and any act appearing on the results thereof must be explained and/or discharged by the vendor prior to closing. The type of explanation usually offered by the vendor's solicitor is that the act appearing 'does not affect' the property in question. If this is the case the vendor's solicitor should state what the act does affect. The explanation must be noted on the result of the search, signed and dated by the vendor's solicitor.

Any encumbrance affecting the property must be discharged and there must be no other transaction in relation to the property that would adversely affect the title being offered to the purchaser.

10.6   Sets of Searches

10.6.1   GENERALLY

The following sets out the searches that ought reasonably to be required in a general residential conveyancing transaction.

Some of these searches, as listed, are required only if the purchaser is mortgaging the property. The Law Society Approved Guidelines in relation to the certificate of title for residential mortgage lending (1999 edition) require that searches must include those against the borrower from the date of the contract to the date of closing and, when the purchase is completed in advance of the mortgage, the searches must be updated to the date of the mortgage.

The main reason lenders' solicitors ask to have such searches updated is to ensure that a judgment mortgage has not been registered against the property and thus gained priority. However, the case law shows that neither a purchaser for value nor a lender need concern themselves with any judgment registered as a judgment mortgage after completion of the purchase. Once the purchase is completed and the full purchase money paid, a judgment mortgage registered after the date of completion will not affect the property even though the purchase deed and subsequent mortgage have not yet been registered. This is because the vendor no longer has an interest in the property to which the judgment mortgage may attach: see *Tempany v Hynes* [1976] IR 101 and *Re Murphy and McCormack* [1928] IR 479; [1930] IR 322.

10.6.2 SECOND-HAND HOUSES

10.6.2.1 Freehold registered title

When buying a property with a freehold registered title (Land Registry):

The purchaser will require:

(a) Land Registry search against the freehold folio;

(b) judgment search against vendor;

(c) either bankruptcy search (if the vendor is an individual) or Companies Office search (if the vendor is a body corporate) against vendor; and

(d) planning search against the property.

In addition, the mortgagee will require:

(i) up-to-date Land Registry search against the folio (unless the mortgage is contemporaneous with the completion of the purchase), and

(ii) judgment and either bankruptcy search or Companies Office search against borrower and any guarantor of the mortgage.

Note
Sheriff's search and hand search in the Registry of Deeds not required.

10.6.2.2 Leasehold registered title

When buying a property with a leasehold registered title (Land Registry):

The purchaser will require:

(a) Land Registry search against the leasehold folio;

(b) judgment search against vendor;

(c) either bankruptcy search (if the vendor is an individual) or Companies Office search (if the vendor is a body corporate) against the vendor;

(d) sheriff's search against vendor; and

(e) planning search against the property.

In addition, the mortgagee will require:

(i) up-to-date Land Registry search against the folio (unless the mortgage is contemporaneous with the completion of the purchase);

(ii) judgment and either bankruptcy search or Companies Office search against borrower and any guarantor; and

(iii) sheriff's search against borrower.

Note

There is no necessity for a Registry of Deeds search, or a search against the freehold folio.

10.6.2.3 Freehold Registry of Deeds title

When buying a freehold property with unregistered title (registered in the Registry of Deeds):

The purchaser will require:

(a) negative search against all parties on title for the appropriate period;

(b) hand search against vendor from the date to which the negative search is made up to date of closing;

(c) judgment search against vendor;

(d) bankruptcy search (if the vendor is an individual) or Companies Office search (if the vendor is a body corporate) against vendor; and

(e) planning search against the property.

In addition the mortgagee will require:

(i) hand search against borrower from date of contract;

(ii) continuation search in the Registry of Deeds against the vendor to date of completion of mortgage (unless the mortgage is contemporaneous with the completion of the purchase);

(iii) judgment search against borrower; and

(iv) bankruptcy search or Companies Office search against borrower and any guarantors.

Notes

The general practice is to search back a minimum of twenty years. Where possible solicitors should be practical about the length of title shown and accordingly the period in respect of which searches are made. See, however, the comments made at **10.1.2.2** in relation to general condition 19 of the Contract for Sale.

If there is a voluntary conveyance on title a bankruptcy search should be made against the donor.

10.6.2.4 Leasehold Registry of Deeds title

When buying a leasehold property with unregistered title (registered in the Registry of Deeds):

The purchaser will require:

(a) negative search against all parties on title for the appropriate period;

(b) hand search against vendor from the date to which the negative search is made up to date of closing;

(c) judgment search against vendor;

(d) bankruptcy search (if the vendor is an individual) or Companies Office search (if the vendor is a body corporate) against vendor;

(e) sheriff's search against the vendor; and

(f) planning search against the property.

In addition the mortgagee will require:

(i) hand search against borrower from date of contract;

(ii) continuation search in the Registry of Deeds against the vendor to date of completion of mortgage (unless the mortgage is contemporaneous with the completion of the purchase);

(iii) judgment search against borrower;

(iv) bankruptcy search or Companies Office search against borrower and guarantors; and

(v) sheriff's search against borrower.

Notes

The general practice is to search back a minimum of twenty years. Where possible solicitors should be practical about the length of title shown and accordingly the period in respect of which searches are made. See, however, the comments made at **10.1.2.2** in relation to general condition 19 of the Contract for Sale.

If there is a voluntary conveyance on title a bankruptcy search should be made against the donor.

10.6.3   HOUSING ESTATES/NEW HOUSES

10.6.3.1   Freehold or leasehold registered title

When buying a new house where the title is freehold or leasehold and registered in the Land Registry:

The purchaser will require:

(a) Land Registry search against the folio;

(b) bankruptcy search (if the vendor is an individual) or Companies Office search (if the vendor is a body corporate) against registered owner;

(c) judgment search against vendor;

(d) sheriff's search against vendor (leasehold only);

(e) certificate of the developer's solicitor that there are no adverse dealings pending registration, affecting the folio (only required if there are dealings pending); and

(f) planning search against the property.

In addition the mortgagee will require:

(i) judgment search against the borrower;

(ii) bankruptcy search or Companies Office search against borrower and any guarantors; and

(iii) sheriff's search against borrower (leasehold only).

Notes

There is no necessity to obtain a Companies Office search against companies appearing on title other than the vendor, the management company (if any) and any company providing a structural defects indemnity or other guarantee.

If the vendor is different from the builder there is no necessity to do searches against the builder unless some of the purchase money is being released to the builder or his agent (Practice Note, Law Society Gazette, October 1985) or the builder is providing a structural defects indemnity or other guarantee. If the building agreement is with the builder, a Companies Office search should be made pre-contract to ensure that the builder company has not been dissolved.

10.6.3.2 Freehold or leasehold Registry of Deeds title

When buying a new house, where the title is freehold or leasehold and is unregistered (registered in the Registry of Deeds):

The purchaser will require:

(a) Registry of Deeds search against all parties on title for the appropriate period;

(b) judgment search against vendor;

(c) bankruptcy search or Companies Office search against vendor;

(d) sheriff's search against vendor (leasehold only); and

(e) planning search against the property.

The mortgagee will require:

(i) hand search against borrower from date of contract to date of delivery of mortgage;

(ii) judgment search against borrower;

(iii) bankruptcy search or Companies Office search against borrower and any guarantors; and

(iv) sheriff's search against borrower (leasehold only).

Notes

The general practice is to search back a minimum of twenty years. Where possible solicitors should be practical about the length of title shown and accordingly the period in respect of which searches are made. See, however, the comments made at **10.1.2.2** in relation to general condition 19 of the Contract for Sale.

If there is a voluntary conveyance on title a bankruptcy search should be made against the donor.

There is no necessity to obtain a Companies Office search against companies appearing on title other than the vendor, the management company (if any) and any company providing a structural defects indemnity or other guarantee.

If the vendor is different from the builder there is no necessity to do searches against the builder unless some of the purchase money is being released to the builder or his agent (Practice Note, Law Society Gazette, October 1985) or the builder is providing a structural defects indemnity or other guarantee. If the building agreement is with the builder a Companies Office search should be made pre-contract to ensure that the builder company has not been dissolved.

CHAPTER 11

PLANNING

11.1 The Planning Authority

11.1.1 INTRODUCTION

Prior to the coming into force of the first significant Planning Act, the Local Government (Planning and Development) Act, 1963 (the 1963 Act), planning control was exercised in a number of ways.

In rural areas there was little or no need for planning control but in urban situations when grants of land were demised by way of lease, the freehold owner sought to keep some control over the future development of the land by way of covenant that within a specified period the lessee had to erect a building thereon of a certain height and to a certain standard. Much of the development of Georgian Dublin and, later, Victorian Dublin was governed in this way. Prime examples are the development of Mountjoy Square and the surrounding area where Lord Gardiner was a wealthy landowner, Merrion Square, which at the time of its development was regarded as the outskirts of Dublin, and Fitzwilliam Square, where the Earl of Pembroke owned extensive holdings. Further out, Lord Proby owned the lands around Blackrock and the Longford De Vesci Estate were landlords near Dun Laoghaire.

Another influence was the Wide Street Commissioners who laid down certain standards and were responsible for, obviously, widening the main thoroughfares in the centre of the city, principally Westmoreland Street, D'Olier Street, O'Connell Street and the surrounding areas.

The Public Health (Ireland) Acts from 1878 onwards laid down minimum standards governing matters of public health in relation to construction, eg drainage, sewerage, standards for habitable dwellings etc.

Later the Town and Regional Planning Acts, 1934 and 1939 sought to put development on a more formal footing and under these Acts two types of permission, a general permission and a special permission, were available for development purposes.

11.1.2 LOCAL GOVERNMENT (PLANNING AND DEVELOPMENT) ACT, 2000

On 25 August 1999, the Minister for the Environment and Local Government published the Planning and Development Bill, 1999 (the Bill). The stated objective of the Bill was to revise and consolidate in one Act all nine Planning and Development Acts enacted since 1963 and introduce a sustainable development philosophy to the Irish planning system.

PLANNING

The Local Government (Planning and Development) Act, 2000 (the 2000 Act) extensively reformed and consolidated Irish planning law. Among other changes, it included radical new measures in relation to housing supply, in particular the provision of social and affordable houses. It is the first complete review of the planning code since the 1963 Act, and there was major controversy in relation to same.

The Law Society Gazette, April 2000 has comments by the Conveyancing Committee on the Planning and Development Bill, 1999 and the 2000 Act.

On 28 August, 2000, the Local Government (Planning and Development) Act, 2000, was passed. The Act came into force piecemeal as follows:

Part V, Part IX and Part VIII by virtue of SI 349/2000 (1 November, 2000); Part II by SI 379/2000, Part XIV and Part XX by SI 449/2000 (1 January 2001); Part 18 by SI 349/2000, Part 20 by SI 449/2000 and Part XVI by SI 153/2001 (17 April 2001); Part VI chapter 1 by SIs 335 and 336/2001 (28 July 2001); Part V, Part VI chapter 11, s 180 and Part VII by SI 599/2001 (21 January 2001); and finally on 11 March 2002 all other parts of the Planning and Development 2000 Act were commenced by SI 599/2001.

The 2000 Act revised, extended and consolidated the Local Government (Planning and Development) Acts, 1963–1999, so that all the legislation and amendments contained in the Acts of 1963, 1976, 1982, 1983, 1990, 1992, 1993, 1998, and 1999 (in total nine Acts) are now contained in a total of twenty separate parts of the 2000 Act. The purpose of this Act is set out in its title as follows:

*An Act to revise and consolidate the Law relating to Planning and Development, by repealing and re-enacting with amendments, the Local Government (Planning and Development) Acts, 1963–1999; to provide in the interests of the common good, for proper planning and **sustainable development** including the provision of housing; to provide for the licensing of events and control of funfairs; to amend the Environmental Protection Agency Act, 1992, the Roads Act, 1993, the Waste Management Act, 1996, and certain other enactments; and to provide for matters connected therewith.*

The concept of sustainable development appears for the first time in a Planning Act. This phrase is somewhat defined in an address given on 28 September, 1999, by Noel Dempsey T D, Minister for the Environment and Local Government as follows:

'On first glance it can be seen that the proper planning and development of an area has been replaced as the Bill's touchstone by the proper planning and sustainable development. But it goes deeper than a change in terminology. For example, the Development Objectives to be contained in Development Plans reflect the environmental concerns of the modern age. Environmental assessment of regional planning guidelines, development plans and local area plans is provided for. The interface between pollution control, licensing and Planning control has been revised to allow a more holistic approach to be adopted in considering development which requires I P C licences.'

The Act itself does not however set out specific sustainability objectives to put into development plans. Instead the idea seems to be that development plans should be infused with sustainable development concerns. In other words it will be a matter for each regional authority to ensure that the old development plan assesses the sustainability criterion. John Gore-Grimes in his Continuing Legal Education (CLE) lecture, 'Planning and Development Act, 2000', Book One, given on 23 February 2001, gives a good definition of sustainable development as follows:

'Sustainable development can be defined as development which meets the needs of the present without compromising the ability of future generations to meet their own needs. It is achieved by ensuring that environmental concerns are taken into account in all aspects of the planning process so that Development progress is not achieved at the expense of environmental quality.'

11.1.3   DEFINITION

'Planning authority' is defined in the 2000 Act, s 2(1) as:

> (a)   *In the case of a county, exclusive of any borough or urban district therein, the council of the county,*
>
> (b)   *In the case of a county or other borough, the corporation of the borough, and*
>
> (c)   *In the case of an urban district, the council of the urban district, And references to the area of the Planning Authority shall be construed accordingly, and shall include the functional area of the authority* (Dublin Corporation is now Dublin City Council).

In 1993, Dublin County Council was replaced by three new administrative counties which are known as Fingal, Dun Laoghaire/Rathdown and South Dublin. Each of these has a separate council.

11.1.4   FUNCTIONS OF A PLANNING AUTHORITY

The main functions of a planning authority are:

(a)   to prepare and revise development plans: 2000 Act, Part II, ss 9–17;

(b)   to make decisions on individual applications for planning permission: 2000 Act, Part III;

(c)   to use powers of enforcement to ensure compliance with the requirement to obtain planning permission or to comply with the terms and conditions of any permission issued: 2000 Act, Part VIII, ss 151–164;

(d)   to be party to any appeal against a decision made by it whether to grant or refuse permission: 2000 Act, Part VI (1), chapter 111;

(e)   to maintain the public register: 2000 Act, Part I, s 7;

(f)   to examine environmental assessment: 2000 Act, Part X, ss 172–177;

(g)   to make compensation, which arises where planning permission is refused or conditions attached to a planning permission restrict future development of the property: 2000 Act, Part XII, chapters I–III, ss 183–201;

(h)   to develop land itself; the development must not be in material contravention of its own development plan: 2000 Act, Part XI, ss 178–182;

(i)   to acquire land: 2000 Act, Part XIV, ss 210–223;

(j)   to control development on the foreshore: 2000 Act, Part XV, ss 224–228;

(k)   to exercise authority re areas of special amenities: 2000 Act, Part XIII, ss 202–209;

(l)   to exercise powers re housing supply: 2000 Act, Part V, ss 93–101. See also CLE lecture by Patrick Sweetman, 'Planning and Development Act 2000', Book IX, dated 2 March 2001; and

(m)   to exercise powers on architectural heritage: 2000 Act, Part IV, ss 51–92.

11.1.5   EXECUTIVE AND RESERVED FUNCTIONS

The manager of a planning authority exercises the executive function.

A reserved function is one which may only be implemented by resolution of the elected members of the planning authority. Any function of a planning authority which is not specified as being a reserved function is regarded as an executive function. 'Reserved functions' are defined under the 2000 Act, s 2(1). The City and County Management

(Amendment) Act, 1955, s 4 has been much used by individuals over the years and not necessarily in the spirit of its original intention. It allows elected members of the local authority to exercise a degree of control over the officials in the performance of their executive functions.

Section 4(1) of the 1955 Act states:

> *Subject to the provisions of this section, a Local Authority may by resolution require any particular Act matter or thing specifically mentioned in the Resolution and which the Local Authority or the Manager can lawfully do or effect to be done or effected in the performance of the executive function of the Local Authority.*

The decision of the Supreme Court in *P & F Sharpe Ltd v Dublin City and County Manager* [1989] IR 701 held that the elected representatives had a power to give a direction to the manager in regard to a planning permission. This power was not limited to the case of material contraventions only and once the s 4 resolution had been validly exercised the manager was not entitled to exercise any separate or independent discretion as to whether or not he or she would obey it.

The court also went on to state that once the elected representatives decided to operate s 4 then they have to act judicially; this requires them to keep a record of their deliberations. This decision is set out at more detail in O'Sullivan and Shepherd, *Irish Planning Law and Practice*, para 1.650.

In using this provision local representatives tried to control the manner in which the county manager would make his or her decision on behalf of the local authority in relation to a particular planning application. An examination of the use of s 4, as it is known, has shown principally cases where officials of the planning authority have been forced by resolution of the elected representatives to grant permission for particular development proposals, notwithstanding advice to the contrary from the county manager.

The Local Government Act, 1991 had a bearing in relation to general competence of local authorities and reserved functions under that Act. It also provided, in relation to s 4 resolutions, that any notice of a proposal to pass such a resolution relating to the planning application must be signed by not less than three-quarters of the total number of the members elected for the area concerned and not less than three-quarters of the total number of members of the authority must vote in favour.

As the general public became more aware of the influence of planning and the importance to the environment, s 4 resolutions were less frequently encountered to override a decision of the planning authority. *P & F Sharpe Ltd* was applied in *Flanagan v Galway City and County Manager* [1990] 2 IR 66 and in *Griffin v Galway City and County Manager*, 31 October 1990 (unreported). It is clear the court will oblige local representatives to strictly adhere to the rules of procedural justice and the 2000 Act, when giving the county manager a direction under s 4.

11.2   Planning Register

11.2.1   INTRODUCTION

Section 7 of the 2000 Act requires a planning authority to keep a planning register in which all relevant planning information is recorded. It extends considerably, s 8 and s 41 of the 1963 Act, and SI 349/1989 and SI 84/1984, for example: s 7(2)(d), (f), (g), (h), (i), (o), (p), (z)—see below. Not all of the changes are for the better. Note in particular s 7(3), where the planning authority has an obligation to make entries and corrections 'as soon as may be', whereas, under the 1963 Act, it had to do so within seven days. Thus there is no guarantee that a planning register is up to date. Further, there are no sanctions imposed on a local authority which does not keep its register up to date. Section 248 of the 2000 Act allows the information to be provided in electronic form. Further, under s 8, the local authority can require a member of the public to provide it with information within a two-week period (previously fourteen days) after it being so requested.

The register, which incorporates a map (s 7(4)), is available for inspection to members of the public at the offices of the planning authority during office hours (s 7(6)). A certified copy of an entry in the register is regarded as prima facie evidence of the entry without proof of signature or producing the register itself. There is payment of a fee to obtain such a copy (s 7(9)).

Planning authorities are required to publish a weekly list of all planning applications received in a given week, not later than the third working day following that week: Local Government (Planning and Development) Regulations, 1994, SI 86/1994 (the 1994 Regulations), art 30. This list is required to be displayed at the planning office and in each public library for not less than two months beginning on the day on which it is made available.

11.2.2 CONTENTS OF THE PLANNING REGISTER

The planning authority is obliged to enter the following matters:

(a) Any application for permission whether for development, retention of development or for outline permission. Please note (see above) details of such applications are no longer required to be entered within seven days of receipt.

(b) Where an environmental impact statement was submitted in respect of an application. Section 171 provided that the Minister may prescribe information to be contained in the environmental impact statement and this will require regulations.

(c) Where development, to which an application relates, comprises or is for the purposes of an activity in respect of which an integrated pollution control licence, or a waste management licence is required, or a licence under the Local Government (Water Pollution) Act, 1977, is required in respect of discharges from the development. This is a new requirement.

(d) Where the development to which the application relates would materially affect a protected structure, or is situated in an area declared to be an area of special amenity, under s 202. This is a new requirement.

(e) The complete decision of the planning authority in respect of any such application, including any conditions imposed, and the date of the decision.

(f) The complete decision on appeal of the Board in respect of any such application, *including any conditions* imposed (this latter point is a new requirement) and the date of the decision. The italicised words are new.

(g) Where the requirements of s 34(6) in regard to the material contravention of the development plan have been complied with. (This is a new element of the register which helps the collection of evidence for a judicial review.)

(h) Particulars of any declaration made by a planning authority under s 5 (this relates to a declaration and referral on development and exempted development). This is a new requirement.

(i) Particulars of any application made under s 42 to extend the appropriate period of a permission.

(j) Particulars of any decision to revoke or modify a permission in accordance with s 44 (s 44 only applies where the development plan has been amended, and the proposed development no longer applies to it).

(k) Particulars under s 45 of any order, of any decision on appeal, or of any acquisition notice for compulsory acquisition of land for open space.

(l)   Particulars of any notice under s 46 requiring the removal or alteration of any structure, or requiring discontinuance of any use, or the imposition of condition on the continuance thereof, including the fact of its withdrawal, if appropriate. This is a new requirement.

(m) Particulars of any agreement made under s 47 (sterilisation) for the purpose of restricting or regulating the development or use of the land.

(n)   Particulars of any declaration issued by the planning authorities under s 57 (works affecting the character of protected or proposed protected structures) including the details of any review of this declaration.

(o)   Particulars of any declaration issued by the planning authority under s 87 (development and special planning control area) including the details of any review of this declaration. This is a new requirement.

(p)   Particulars of any notice under s 88 in respect of land in an area of special planning control, including, where such notice is withdrawn, the fact of its withdrawal. This is a new requirement.

(q)   Particulars of any certificate granted under s 97 (this is development to which s 96, the provision of social and affordable housing does not apply). This is a new requirement.

(r)   Particulars of any warning letter issued under s 152 including the date of issue of the letter and the fact of its withdrawal if appropriate.

(s)   The complete decision made under s 153 on whether an enforcement notice should issue, including the date of the decision.

(t)   Particulars of any enforcement notice issued under s 154, including the date of the notice and the fact of its withdrawal, or that it has been complied with if appropriate.

(u)   Particulars of any statement prepared under s 188 concerning a claim for compensation under the 2000 Act.

(v)   Particulars of any order under s 205, requiring the preservation of any tree or trees including the fact of any amendment or revocation of the order.

(w) Particulars of any agreement under s 206 for the creation of a public right of way over land.

(x)   Particulars of any public right of way created under s 207.

(y)   Particulars of any information relating to the operation of a quarry provided in accordance with s 261. This is a new requirement.

(z)   Any other matters as may be prescribed by the Minister.

11.2.2.1   The register from a conveyancer's point of view

It is vital to realise that despite the extensive a–z list above, there are several matters which are not included in the register. Therefore, the register alone cannot be relied upon to accurately represent the situation as it actually is. It would be better if all registers were amalgamated into one (eg the Derelict Sites Act Register and any other register or record which the local authority or planning authority is statutorily bound to maintain), so that an examination of the planning register would give solicitors, planners or architects a full picture not just of the permissions applied for and granted, sterilisation orders made, and all other planning related matters, but also all environmental issues, for example, whether or not a commencement notice has been served, whether or not a fire certificate has issued, etc. Therefore, conveyancers when requesting a search from their law searchers should request a search not only on the planning register, but also on the Building Control Act Register, and the Derelict Sites Act Register.

The importance of the necessity given above in every conveyancing transaction to carry out Planning Office searches at pre-contract stage cannot be overemphasised. It has long been accepted that the purchaser's solicitor should make a planning search before the exchange of contract, and this is universally done. However, a solicitor acting for a vendor should also make a planning search before preparing a contract for sale. This has been reiterated many times by the Conveyancing Committee and at various CLE lectures. In his CLE lecture on the Planning and Development Act, 2000, Book Four, John Gore-Grimes explains very succinctly why, as follows. If a vendor's solicitor fails to make such a search, and it transpires that a notice has been served under the Planning and Development Act, the vendor may well be in breach of the obligation provided in the Law Society's General Conditions of Sale, by virtue of general condition 35 which requires a vendor to disclose notices. General condition 35, in requiring the vendor to disclose notices, does offer some comfort to the purchaser. General condition 35 does however, specifically exclude notices, being the contents of a development plan. A notice which the vendor is required to disclose under general condition 35 is one 'in respect of the Subject Property and affecting the same at the Date of Sale'. Apart from the making of pre-contract planning searches when acting both for a vendor and a purchaser, it is now widely accepted within the profession that a vendor's and purchaser's solicitor should raise pre-contract enquiries on planning and indeed other matters to be dealt with by the client. To assist in this, the Law Society has issued pre-contract questionnaires for both vendor and purchaser.

11.3 Development Plan and Development

Part II, ss 9–17, of the 2000 Act (previously s 19(1) of the 1963 Act) deals with development plans, local area plans, regional planning guidelines, and ministerial guidelines and Directives. Section 9 requires every planning authority to make a development plan every six years (previously, this period was five years) which relates to the whole functional area of the authority. Section 9(4) and (5) now requires that regard must be had to the development plans of adjoining planning authorities. This is an attempt at a more integrated planning policy. Section 10(1) defines a development plan as follows:

> a development plan shall set out an overall strategy for the proper planning and sustainable development of the area of the development plan, and shall consist of a written statement and a plan or plans indicating the development objectives for the area in question.

It must contain a written statement with a map indicating the local authority's objectives as well as certain mandatory objectives, see s 10(2)(a)–(m). What it may contain is set out in the first Schedule to the Act. The Minister is given power to add additional objectives which shall, or may be, incorporated in development plans (s 9(4)). Unlike s 19(2) of the 1963 Act, there is no distinction now between urban and rural authorities in relation to objectives.

11.3.1 REVIEW AND VARIATION OF DEVELOPMENT PLAN

Under s 11, a planning authority, not later than four years after the making of a development plan, must give notice of its intention to review its existing development plan, and to prepare a new one for its area.

That notice invites submissions and observations, which may be made in writing to the planning authority within a specified period, which shall not be less than eight weeks (s 11(2)(b)). The planning authority then goes through a consultation procedure which can involve oral hearings, written submissions, and liaison with interested bodies.

Section 11(4)(a) states that within sixteen weeks of this initial notice, the manager of the planning authority is required to prepare a report on the consultations held, and on the submissions and observations received. This report is then submitted to the council members, or a committee of the council members if the council so decides. They may issue directions to the manager regarding the draft plan (s 11(4)(d)), which directions must be issued within ten weeks of the submission of the report to them. The manager then has twelve weeks (s 11(5)(a)) within which to prepare the draft development plan and submit it back to the council members for consideration. They have a further eight weeks within which to make further amendments to the plan. If they make no further amendments, then the draft development plan as submitted to them is deemed to be the draft development plan.

Section 12 is a similar provision to s 21 of the 1963 Act, but there are amendments to time limits for notices etc. There are also new obligations on county managers to prepare reports summarising submissions and observations made, and to make recommendations to the elected members. This draft is then put on public display for a period of not less than ten weeks (s 12(2)(a)) and public notices of its existence issued. Written submissions or observations are invited within the stated period.

Where the new draft development plan proposes the addition or deletion of new protected structures (the old listed buildings) then the planning authority is required to serve notice on the owners or occupiers of such structures (s 12(3)).

Section 12(4) goes on to state that within twenty-two weeks of the notice advising that the draft development plan is on public display, the manager is required to prepare a report on submissions and observations received, and submit it to the council members. This is a new provision which is designed to ensure that development plans are reviewed and adopted within the timescales laid down. The councillors then have twelve weeks to consider the draft plan and the manager's report (s 12(5)(b)) They may accept and adopt the draft development plan as the development plan, or propose alterations. In the case of proposed material alterations, these go on display for a period of not less than four weeks (s 12(7)(b)) and written submissions or observations on the proposed amendments are invited within that period.

Section 12(8)(a) states that the manager of the planning authority within eight weeks from the date of the public notice advising of the proposed amendments is required to make a report of the observations and submissions received on the proposed amendments. The councillors have a further period of six weeks within which to consider the amendments and the manager's report (s 12(9)(b)) and must then make the plan with or without the proposed amendments or subject to any modifications to the amendments as they consider appropriate.

The manager must in his reports take account of the proper planning and sustainable development of the area, the statutory obligations of any local authority in the area and any relevant policy or policies of the government or of any Minister of the government and if appropriate, any observations made by the Minister for Arts, Heritage, Gaeltacht, and the Islands with regard to protected structures.

Section 12(11) restricts the councillors in considering the development plan to considering the proper planning and sustainable development of the area to which that development plan relates, the statutory of any local authority in the area and any relevant policy or policies of the government or of any Minister of the government.

When the plan is made, the planning authority must serve notice on the owner and occupier of any protected structure which has been added to, or deleted from the record of protected structures in the development plan.

If the planning authority fails to make the development plan within two years from the publication of the notice of intention to review the plan, then the manager must make the plan. In doing so, he or she must include so much of the plan as has been agreed by the council members (s 12(14)). This is a new provision.

Interestingly enough, given the detailed timescales listed above, a development plan is not open to challenge by reason only that the timescales of each of the procedures set out in the Act are not complied with (s 12(16)).

Section 12(17) declares that the development plan comes into effect four weeks from the day that it is made.

Section 13 sets out the procedures for variations of the development plan. These provide for the proposed variations to go on public display and public notices to be issued, inviting written submissions and observations. The procedure is similar to that for the adoption of the plan as set out above. However, any variation made to the development plan, unlike the development plan itself, has effect from the day that the variation is made (s 13(11)). Section 15 is a restatement of s 22 of the 1963 Act, but s 15(2) is a new provision which requires the manager of a planning authority not more than two years after the making of the development plan to give a report to the members of the authority on the progress achieved in securing the objectives referred to in sub-s (1).

Section 16 requires the planning authority to make available for inspection and purchase by members of the public copies of the development plan and of variations of same.

Although Patrick Sweetman's Continuing Legal Education (CLE) lecture 'Property Transactions—Liabilities under Planning and Environmental Law' given on 1 December 1992, relates to development plans prior to the 2000 Act coming into force, it is still worth reading, as it sets out general principles and makes observations which are still pertinent under the 2000 Act. He notes that, in urban areas, a development plan will be quite different from one to affect rural areas. Urban areas will have different parts zoned as residential, retail, office, industrial, amenity or a mix of these different users. It will also indicate the density of each mix. The local authority's policy on dealing with the problems of urbanisation such as traffic control, car-parking areas, development of inner city open spaces, road widening etc is set out.

In rural areas zoning would indicate areas zoned purely for industrial use, eg industrial estates, or purely agricultural use in order to preserve the rural amenities.

The development plan also sets out the types of use which would be permitted and those uses which would not be considered. If a proposed use is in an area where a development plan has already indicated it would not permit it, then any application for that use would be turned down. In fact a planning authority may not grant planning permission in material contravention of the development plan unless a prescribed procedure is followed. See also Patrick Sweetman's Continuing Legal Education (CLE) lecture, 'Planning and Development Act, 2000 'Book Two, given on 23 February 2001, especially in relation to material contravention of the development plan.

A planning authority may not grant planning permission which contravenes the development plan unless it adopts a special procedure known as the material contravention procedure (s 34(b)). Previously, the question who decided whether or not a proposed development constituted a material contravention caused not only much debate, but substantial amounts of litigation. A considerable body of case law has built up regarding development in material contravention of the development plan. A number of these have involved halting sites. One of the cases, *O'Leary v Dublin County Council* [1988] IR 150, concerned a proposed halting site on the Dodder Linear Park. The county council argued that any contravention of the zoning from high amenity under the development plan was not 'material' as the development would only involve a small site for five families. As the development plan did not permit residential caravan parks in areas zoned 'high amenity', and if an individual applied for permission for a residential caravan park he or she would be clearly refused, it followed that a development which would, if carried out by an individual, amount to a material contravention of the development plan would likewise be a material contravention if carried out by a local authority.

The case of *Wilkinson v Dublin County Council* [1991] ILRM 605 held that a development may be in material contravention of the development plan if it is inconsistent with the proper planning and development of that area.

In theory, if it is a planning issue, then the local authority should decide, and the courts should not intervene; however, this would result in the effectiveness of the development plan being greatly undermined. See Garrett Simons, 'The Unreasonable Planning Authority: a review of the Application of *O'Keeffe v Bord Pleanala*' 2000 4 IPELJ 164. Where it is suggested that the better view is that it is a question not of planning policy, but rather one which falls to be determined by the courts as a matter of law.

Section 34(b), by introducing a new material contravention procedure, assists somewhat in clarifying the issue.

Before deciding to grant planning permission in material contravention of its development plan, the local authority is required to publish a notice and consider submissions and observations. The councillors must then vote on whether to grant permission and for that vote to be passed, not less than three-quarters of the total number of the councillors must vote in favour (s 34(6)(b)).

Section 4 of the City and County Management (Amendment) Act, 1955 gives the councillors power to direct the county manager to exercise his or her functions in a particular manner. In the past, this section has definitely been used to grant planning permissionin material contravention of a development plan; however, under the 2000 Act where the county manager receives notice of a proposed resolution (s 34(6)(c)) which if passed would require the manager to grant the permission, then the manager will instigate the material contravention procedure outlined above so that s 4 will have no further effect.

If any local county councillors propose an s 4 resolution relating to a proposed grant of planning permission, the notice must be signed by not less than three-quarters of the total number of councillors of the electoral area or areas in which the land, which is the subject of the planning application, is situate (s 34(7)(b)).

As was the situation under the 1963 Act, An Bord Pleanala may decide to grant permission even in material contravention of the development plan. However, the 2000 Act imposes new criteria which must be satisfied, as are set out at s 37(2)(b).

11.3.2   DEVELOPMENT

Development is defined in the 2000 Act, s 3(1) as follows:

> 'Development' in this Act means, save where the context otherwise requires, the carrying out of any works on, in, over, or under land or the making of any material change in the use of any structures or other land.

There are two distinct parts to the definition of development, although they are not always exclusive and sometimes overlap. One refers to the carrying out of 'works' and the other refers to the making of any 'material change of use'.

'Works' are defined in the 2000 Act, s 2 as 'including any act or operation of construction excavation, demolition, extension, alteration, repair or renewal'. 'Alteration', also defined in s 2, includes 'plastering or painting or the removal of plaster or stucco, or the replacement of a door, window or roof which materially alters the external appearance of the structure so as to render such appearance inconsistent with the character of the structure or of neighbouring structures'. Since the 2000 Act, it also applies in relation to protected structure or proposed protected structure where any act of operation involving the application or removal of plaster, paint, wallpaper, tiles, or other material to or from the surface of an interior or exterior of such a structure.

'Unauthorised Structure' means a structure other than a structure which was in existence on 1 October 1964, or a structure, the construction, erection, or making of which was subject to permission for development granted under Part IV of the 1963 Act, or under s 34 of the 2000 Act or which exists as the result of the carrying out of exempted development. Clearly therefore, any structure erected before 1 October 1964 is not an unauthorised structure.

'Unauthorised Development' is for the first time interpreted in s 2 of the 2000 Act as meaning 'in relation to land, the carrying out of any unauthorised works, (including the construction, erection, or making of any unauthorised structure) or the making of any unauthorised use'. This interpretation does not make any reference to unauthorised development prior to 1 October 1964. This is because it does not have to as the essence of the interpretation refers to 'unauthorised works', 'unauthorised structure', and 'unauthorised use', all of which phrases respectively, do make reference to: (a) works commenced on or after 1 October 1964; (b) structures in existence on 1 October 1964; and (c) use commenced on or after 1 October 1964. Therefore, unauthorised development can only have taken place after 1 October 1964.

'Unauthorised Works' are also interpreted by s 2 of the 2000 Act. It means any works carried on, in, over, or under land commenced on or after 1 October 1964, being development other than exempted development or development which is the subject of a permission granted under Part IV of the 1963 Act or under s 34 of the 2000 Act being a permission which has not been revoked, and which was carried out in compliance with that permission or any condition to which that permission is subject.

There is no clear definition of 'use'; rather it is stated negatively. Section 3(2) specifies cases which are to be treated as a material change of use. These include:

(a)   any structure, tree or other object on land used for the exhibition of advertisements;

(b)   placing or keeping vans, tents or other objects for the purpose of caravanning or camping or the sale of goods;

(c)   storage of caravans or tents; and

(d)   the deposit of parts of vehicles, builders' waste, industrial waste, old metal.

Section 3(3) also states that a material change of use arises where a single dwelling is subdivided into two or more dwellings where previously it had been a single dwelling. If the use has remained the same since 1 October 1964, the use is an established use. If the use has changed since 1 October 1964, and permission for a new use was obtained from the local authority, it is a permitted use.

A change of use, by itself, does not constitute development. The change of use must be material. In other words, the degree of the change must be material.

There is a general principle that to constitute a material change of use, the use must be substantially different from the previous use. In practice, whether there has been such a change of use is one of fact and degree. Similarly, there is no definition of 'material change of use' in the 2000 Act and there is a considerable body of case law on what constitutes a material change of use within the meaning of the 1963 and 2000 Acts.

O'Sullivan and Shepherd, *Irish Planning Law and Practice*, point out that the following tests have been suggested:

(a)   Is the change physical rather than mental? (ie a change in the character of the land: eg from residential to commercial; from agricultural to quarry).

(b)   Is the change substantial? Can its effect be measured?

(c)   Is the change one to be taken into account because of its impact on the environment or its increased traffic or demand for services?

There should be a comparison between the present use and the previous use of the land. If the present use is for a quite different purpose then there is a material change. An example would be if a dwellinghouse is changed entirely into barristers' chambers. That would be a material change of use. However, if an engineer decided to work from home and used one room of his house as an office, did not invite clients there, or employ staff, or have a business plate outside, then there would not be a material change of use. Another example often given is of a farm shop for the sale of surplus produce from the farm. Such a use would be ancillary. If the shop included items not produced on the farm then there would be a material change of use.

A material change of use may also happen through intensification of an existing long-established use. The type of questions to be asked to ascertain whether there has been intensification would include:

(a)   Has there been a change from the kind of products previously made?

(b) Is the production method more intense, either by an increase in the workforce or the use of more modern machinery?

(c) Has there has been an increase in traffic, noise or pollution?

(d) Has the area of activity increased or differed? This question is often raised in relation to extracting stone from quarries and there is a substantial body of case law built up in relation to quarrying operations and fully detailed in O'Sullivan and Shepherd.

An added complication is where there is permission for a particular use but it has been underutilised. Its subsequent, more efficient, expanded use might not amount to intensification. Again, a lot of this would depend on the actual facts and the application of the above questions. An example is *Cusack and McKenna v Minister of Local Government*, 1980, High Court (unreported) where the plaintiffs commenced using a portion of a residential house for their solicitors' practice without obtaining planning permission. Prior to this the premises had first been used for a dentist's practice and then for residential flats. Planning permission was not required for the dental practice as that was prior to October 1964. The plaintiffs claimed that there was not a material change of use from a dentist's practice to a solicitors' practice, or if it was development, it was exempted as it was a material change of use within the same class (both uses for the office) and therefore exempt under the then 1977 Regulations. However, at the time the plaintiffs purchased the premises they were used entirely for residential purposes. McWilliam J found on the facts that there was an intervening residential use and therefore any subsequent change was unauthorised. Also such a change would be material as a dental practice and a solicitors' practice had nothing in common.

In assessing whether there has been a material change of use an examination will be made not only as to the use itself but also to its effects. *Cork Corporation v O'Connell* [1982] ILRM 505 concerned an amusement arcade which had been opened in premises previously used as a retail hardware store. The court took into account the large crowds of young people that would be attracted to the area and found a material change of use had occurred. *Mahon v Irish Rugby Football Union*, August 1997, Supreme Court (unreported) concerned local residents seeking an order under the 1976 Act, s 27, as amended, to obtain an injunction against two proposed concerts by U2 at the rugby grounds in Lansdowne Road, Dublin. The plaintiffs argued that the pop concert constituted a change of use and required planning permission. The court held that when assessing whether a change was a material one the court was to have regard to the effects of the change of use on the proper planning of the area in which the land was situated. The court found that the effects on residential amenity, by noise and disturbance caused by light spillage were all materially different in the case of pop concerts to that associated with rugby matches.

'Unauthorised Use' means, in relation to land, use on or after 1 October 1964, being a use which is a material change of use of any structure or other land, being a development other than an exempted development or development which is subject to a permission granted under Part IV of the 1963 Act, or s 34 of the 2000 Act, being a permission which has not been revoked which was carried out in compliance with that permission or any condition to which that permission is subject. Section 2 of the 2000 Act also defines the word 'Use' in relation to land, as not including the use of the land by the carrying out of works thereon. Therefore, clearly, a use which existed prior to 1 October 1964 is not an unauthorised use if it is still in existence now.

11.3.3 ESTABLISHED USE, ABANDONED USE, RESUMPTION OF ABANDONED USE

Where a use was established prior to 1 October 1964 and no enforcement action was taken by the planning authority in the following five years, it was authorised under the

1963 Act, s 2 so long as it continued uninterrupted. There is a similar provision in the 2000 Act, except that the period is seven years (s 157(4)).

There are cases where an established use may be deemed to be discontinued or abandoned. Its subsequent resumption at a later date could constitute development for which permission would be required. There is no clear test as to when a resumption of an abandoned use is regarded as a material change of use. In *Dublin County Council v Tallaght Block Company Ltd* [1982] ILRM 534 the principle was stated that where a previous use of land had ceased for a considerable period of time with no clear intention of resumption then one was entitled to assume that the previous use had been abandoned so that when it was resumed its resumption constituted a material change of use.

A test to apply as to whether a use had been discontinued is to ask:

(a)   Has there been an actual cessation of activity?

(b)   Is there clearly an intention not to resume that activity?

Hence there has to be the intention to abandon the use, and this may be determined from circumstantial evidence, and there has to be the actual cessation as well.

11.4   Exempted Development

11.4.1   INTRODUCTION

The relevant legislation is:

Local Government (Planning and Development) Act, 1963 as amended;
Local Government (Planning and Development) Regulations, 1977 (SI 65/1977);
Local Government (Planning and Development) Regulations, 1994 (SI 86/1994);
Local Government (Planning and Development) Regulations, 1995 (SI 69/1995);
Local Government (Planning and Development) Regulations, 1996 (SI 100/1996);
Local Government (Planning and Development) Regulations, 2000 (SI 181/2000);
Local Government (Planning and Development) Act, 2000; and
Local Government (Planning and Development) Regulations, 2001 (SI 600/2001).

Exempted development is development where an applicant is exempt from the obligation to obtain planning permission. This occurs in the following circumstances:

(a)   where development took place before the commencement of the 1963 Act, ie 1 October 1964;

(b)   where the 2000 Act, s 4 provides that certain types of development are exempt;

(c)   where the Minister exercised his power pursuant to the 1963 Act, s (4)(2) in making regulations providing classes of development to be exempted development. The Minister made exempted development regulations in 1977, which were then replaced by the 1994 Regulations; and

(d)   where the Minister exercises his power pursuant to the 2000 Act, s 4(2)(a) in making regulations providing classes of development to be exempted development. The Minister made exempted development regulations in 2000 which were then replaced by the 2001 Regulations.

The courts have interpreted the exemptions quite strictly in the past. In the Supreme Court decision of *Pillion v Irish Cement Ltd*, 20 November 1986, Supreme Court (unreported) the Chief Justice took the view that developers who avail of the exempted development status are in a special or, in a sense, privileged category as they are not subject to the views or opposition of other persons. It was held that the exempted development regulations 'should by a court be strictly construed in the sense that for a developer to put himself within them he must be clearly and unambiguously within them in regard with what he proposes to do'. Further, the onus lies with the applicant to show that he or she may avail of an exemption as held in the decision of *Lennon v Kingdom Plant Hire*,13 December 1991 (unreported).

11.4.2 DEVELOPMENT PRIOR TO 1 OCTOBER 1964

Development, except for that listed in the 1963 and 2000 Acts, that commenced before 1 October 1964 does not require planning permission as it was in existence prior to the commencement of the 1963 Act.

11.4.3 EXEMPT DEVELOPMENT UNDER THE 2000 ACT, s 4

Section 4(1)(a)–(l) of the 2000 Act provides a number of categories of development where an applicant is exempt from the obligation to obtain planning permission. Certain restrictions apply to these exemptions and it is important to know if any of the exemptions provided in legislation have been restricted in any way. Section 4 of the 2000 Act made significant changes to s 4 of the 1963 Act, which changes are summarised below:

(a) Agricultural exemption, turbury, and initial planting of forestry, are removed from the agricultural exemption because of the significant impact which they have on land and on the surrounding land. Note, the definition of agriculture now includes the training of horses and rearing of bloodstock (s 4(1)(a)). 'Agriculture' is defined in s 2.

(b) The replacement of broad leaf high forest by conifer species is no longer exempted. Conifer species are environmentally unfriendly to wildlife and vegetation excepting foxes and badger (s 4(1)(i)).

(c) Development by a council or county in its own functional area, is exempt. If a planning authority acts outside its own functional area, it is subject to the full rigours of the planning process, unless it is acting for, or on behalf of, or as an employee of the other planning authority where the work is being carried out. Development carried out on behalf of, or jointly, or in partnership with, a local authority is exempt. Obviously, therefore, this means not only development carried out by a local authority itself but by its contractors. Local authority development in the construction of a new road, or maintenance or improvement of an existing road development carried out by a local authority or statutory undertaker re inspecting, repairing, renewing, altering or removing sewers, mains, pipes, cables, overhead wires, including the excavation of a street or other land for that purpose is exempt (s 4(1)(b)–(g)). Note however, Part XIII of the 2000 Act contains a number of restrictions on local authorities carrying out development.

11.4.3.1 Internal and external works: s 4(1)(h)

This is one of the most important exemptions provided for in the 2000 Act. The exemption is divided into two parts, internal and external works:

(a) where development consists of the carrying out of works for the maintenance, improvement or other alterations of any structure being works which affect only the interior of the structure; or

(b) which do not materially affect the external appearance of the structure so as to render such appearance inconsistent with the character of the structure or the neighboring structures.

Internal works

Works which affect only the interior of the structure, such as a partition wall or alterations to an internal layout, do not require permission.

If the interior of the building is listed for preservation in the development plan then the exemption in relation to internal works will not apply: Local Government (Planning and Development) Act, 1976, s 43(1).

External works

Works which do not materially affect the external appearance of the structure so as to render it inconsistent with the character of the structure or the neighbouring structures are exempt. The question of whether development is consistent with the structure or the neighbouring structures can be a vexed one. In *Cairnduff v O'Connell* [1986] IR 73 the issue arose whether an external balcony and staircase to the rear of a Victorian house were exempt under s 4(1)(g). The Supreme Court held that, despite a long interval in replacing the balcony and structure, the works were exempt. The court held that the appearance of the structure was not inconsistent with its own character or that of the neighbouring houses.

In *Dublin Corporation v Bentham*, 22 July 1992, High Court (unreported) an issue arose whether replacing timber sash windows with aluminium windows in a listed building was exempt. The court held that the new windows materially affected the external appearance of the building and rendered the appearance inconsistent with the character of the house itself and were therefore not exempt. However, a number of neighbouring houses had replaced their windows so the development was not inconsistent with the neighbouring structures.

11.4.3.2 Uses incidental to the enjoyment of a dwellinghouse: s 4(1)(j)

This exemption applies only to the use of any structure or other land within the curtilage of a dwellinghouse. There is no Irish definition of curtilage, but the Scottish case of *Sinclair Lockhart's Trustees v Central Land Board* 1951 SC 258 described curtilage as the ground which is used for the comfortable enjoyment of a house or other building. This exemption was examined in the Supreme Court decision of *Dublin Corporation v Moore* [1984] ILRM 339. In this case the parking of ice-cream vans was not incidental to the enjoyment of the dwellinghouse. The parking of a private car is incidental to the enjoyment of a dwellinghouse.

11.4.4 EXEMPT DEVELOPMENT UNDER THE 2001 REGULATIONS

11.4.4.1 Introduction

The Minister has the power pursuant to the 2000 Act, s 4(2)(a) to make regulations providing any class of development to be exempted development.

The 1977 Regulations, which were replaced by the 1994 Regulations as amended by the 2000 Regulations, provided that certain classes of development were exempt from obtaining planning permission. These in turn were consolidated by the Local Government (Planning and Development) Regulations, 2001 (SI 600/2001).

While the previous regulations have been replaced, they are still relevant to development which occurred during their lifespan. For example, particular exempted classes such as swimming pools and golf courses were exempt under the 1977 Regulations, Third Schedule, classes 26 and 27 respectively but were not exempt under the 1994 or subsequent Regulations. However, art 12 of the 1994 Regulations (art 11 of the 2001 Regulations, see also arts 207 and 208) provided that any development that was exempt under the previous regulations continued to be exempted development, provided the development commenced prior to the coming into operation of the 1994 Regulations, ie 16 May 1994.

11.4.4.2 Second Schedule: Generally

The Second Schedule to the 2001 Regulations is divided into four parts, all dealing with classes of exemptions and restrictions relating to same. While a large number of different types of exemptions are provided, it is important to know and to remember that the regulations have provided, in arts 9 and 10, a list of restrictions to the provided exemptions (dealt with at **11.4.6** below). When examining an exemption one must always refer back to the restrictions both in the second column (see below) and in arts 9 and 10 to make sure that the exemption is in fact applicable in the circumstances. For example, class 1 under column 1 provides that 'the extension of a house, by the construction or erection of an extension (including a conservatory) to the rear of the house, or by the conversion for use as part of the house of any garage, store, shed or other similar structure attached to the rear or to the side of the house' is exempt. However, under column 2, there are extensive conditions and limitations listed to this exemption at 1 to 7.

11.4.4.3 Second Schedule, Part I: General

The Second Schedule, Part I deals with exemptions under the heading 'General'. Part I contains a column on the left containing the exemption and a column on the right specifying conditions and limitations to the exemption. Part I is the largest part of the Second Schedule, containing fifty-five classes of exemption. Part I: General is further divided into the following sections:

(a) development within the curtilage of a dwellinghouse (classes 1–13);

(b) development consisting of change of use (class 14);

(c) temporary structures and uses (classes 15–20);

(d) development for industrial purposes (classes 21–22);

(e) development by statutory undertakers (classes 23–32);

(f) development for amenity or recreational purposes (classes 33–37); and

(g) miscellaneous development (classes 38–55).

When examining these exemptions it is also important to check through the restrictions listed in arts 9 and 10 to make sure that the exemption is not removed by virtue of some subsection of that article. An example of this would be if the proposed extension were to be added to a building which is located within an architectural conservation area as listed in the development plan (see art (9)(xii)).

By examining Part I, class 1: General, of the Second Schedule, it is apparent that this exemption relates to extensions to the rear of a dwellinghouse and to the conversion of a garage, store, shed or similar structure attached to the rear or the side of a dwellinghouse.

Prima facie, this type of development does not require planning permission as long as conditions and limitations in column 2 are complied with. An examination of column 2 provides that such extensions are limited in size to less than 40 square metres where the house has not been extended previously. Therefore, if a 20 square metre extension was erected in 1980 there is only provision for a 20 square metre extension now (s 1(a)). Further, in column 2(1)(b) the height of the extension is restricted and the extension may not reduce the private open space to less than 25 square metres (column 2(5)). If there is less than a 25 square metre private open space in the first instance, as often is the case in the inner city, mews developments and new townhouses, then this exemption will not apply at all.

Class 14 of Part I of the Second Schedule provides six circumstances where development consisting of a change of use from one specified use to another specified use would be exempt. These changes of use exemptions largely encourage uses that the planning authorities are in favour of, such as the change of use of two or more dwellings to be used as a single dwelling of any structure previously used as a single dwelling. This exemption encourages the conversion from flats to single dwellings.

Class 50 (a) and (b) deal with the demolition of habitable houses.

11.4.4.4 Second Schedule, Part II: Advertisements

The Second Schedule, Part II deals with exemptions under the heading 'advertisements'. The definition of advertisements may be found in the 2000 Act, s 2. Article 6(2)(b) of the 2001 Regulations provides that development consisting of the use of a structure or other land for the exhibition of advertisements of a class specified in column 1 of Part II of the Second Schedule is exempted development provided that the limitations and conditions in column 2 are complied with. Again, the restrictions provided in art 9 must be examined against these exemptions.

By examining Part II, class 1: Advertisements, of the Second Schedule, it is apparent that this exemption related to advertisements exhibited on business premises relating to the business, or other activity carried on, or the goods or services provided on those premises. There are nine conditions/limitations provided in column 2 that must be complied with. These relate to size, illumination, height, position, location. Further, the restrictions in art 9 must be examined against this exemption. The definition of 'business premises' may be found in the 2001 Regulations, art 5(1) and also should be examined in light of this exemption as hotels and state authority buildings are included within the definition. There are eighteen classes of exemption in Part II: Advertisements.

11.4.4.5 Second Schedule, Part III: Rural

Article 6(3) of the 2001 Regulations provides for the rural development exemptions. These are provided for in Part III of the Second Schedule. These exemptions apply to areas outside the county boroughs, urban districts, specified towns and the excluded areas under s 9 of the Local Government (Reorganisation) Act, 1985. These exemptions are subject to the restrictions listed in art 9 and to the conditions and limitations provided in column 2.

Part III, class 1 of the Second Schedule provides an exemption for the temporary use of any land for the placing of any tent or caravan or for the mooring of any boat, barge or other vessel used for the purpose of camping. There are four limitations/conditions attached to this exemption in column 2. Only one tent/caravan may be placed within 100 metres of another tent/caravan, the length of stay is restricted to ten days, no commercial use or advertisement is permitted and no tent/caravan shall be placed within 50 metres of a public road unless the land is enclosed by a wall, bank or hedge or combination thereof having an average height of 1.5 metres.

11.4.4.6 Second Schedule, Part IV: Use Classes

Article 10 of the 2001 Regulations provides that development which consists of a change of use within any one of the classes specified in Part IV of the Second Schedule and does not involve carrying out any works except works which are exempted, shall be exempted development. This exemption is subject to the proviso that the development will not contravene a condition attached to a planning permission or be inconsistent with a use specified in a permission. The planning conditions attached to a permission should be examined in order to make sure that no restrictions on the use have been imposed. Article 10 does not include the provision that these exemptions are subject to the restrictions in art 9.

Part IV of the Second Schedule, headed 'Classes of Use' contains eleven classes. Clause 1 of Part IV only contains one use, ie use as a shop. The use of a shop, which is defined under the 1977 Regulations very widely, but was revised and restricted in art 8 of the 1994 Regulations, included retail sale of goods, post office, sale of tickets for travel agency, hairdresser, display of goods for sale, hiring of domestic goods or articles, launderette/dry cleaners and reception of goods to be washed, cleaned or repaired. The definition of 'shop' further defined by art 5(1)(a)–(i) of the 2001 Regulations, specifically excludes funeral homes, hotels, restaurants, pubs, sale of hot food off the premises or any use to which class 2 or 3 of Part IV of the Second Schedule applies. Within this class one can change the use from post office to travel agency without obtaining planning permission but cannot change from a post office to a funeral home.

Pursuant to art 10(2)(b) nothing in any class in Part IV shall include any use as an amusement arcade, motor service station, sale, leasing or display for sale/leasing of motor vehicles, taxi business or hire of motor vehicles, scrapyard or breaking of vehicles or for the storage of minerals. Any one of these uses requires planning permission.

11.4.5   FURTHER EXEMPTIONS FOR USES: ART 10

Article 10 actually provides for three specific exemptions for change of use. These exemptions are not subject to the restrictions in art 6 and include the use of not more than four bedrooms in a dwellinghouse as overnight accommodation, provided that same would not contravene a condition attached to a planning permission or be inconsistent with a use specified in a permission. A shop or restaurant provided in a building occupied by or under the control of the State for visiting members of the public is also exempt under art 10.

It should be noted that exemptions relating to change of use may be found in three places in the 2001 Regulations:

(a)   Part I of the Second Schedule: General, class 14;

(b)   art 10; and

(c)   Part IV of the Second Schedule: Use Classes.

11.4.6   RESTRICTIONS TO THE EXEMPTED DEVELOPMENT CLASSES IN PARTS I, II, AND III OF THE SECOND SCHEDULE

Article 9 of the 2001 Regulations provides that development to which art 9 relates (ie Parts I, II and III of the Second Schedule), shall not be exempted for the purposes of the Acts in a number of circumstances. The restrictions should be examined in detail against each exemption claimed, but the main restrictions are found in art 9(1)(a).

If the development would:

(i)   Contravene a condition attached to a planning permission. Often, planning authorities attach a condition that the exempted development provisions in the 2001 Regulations do not apply, particularly in mews/townhouse developments, as they consider that the development potential of a site has reached its maximum. The legality of such conditions has not been tested.

(ii)   Consist of the formation, laying out or material widening of a means of access to a public road, the surfaced carriageway of which exceeds 4 metres in width.

(iii)   Endanger public safety by reason of a traffic hazard or obstruction of road users. Note some signs or illuminated advertising could cause a traffic hazard.

(iv)   With the exception of the exemption relating to porches (Part I, class 7 of the Second Schedule), development which brings the building line forward of the front wall of the building on either side, or beyond a building line specified in the development plan or the draft plan for the area.

(v)   Consist of works under a public road other than connection to wired relay broadcast service, sewer, water/gas main, electricity supply line or cable or works to which classes 25, 26 or 31(a) specified in column 1 in Part I of the Second Schedule relate.

(vi)   Cause interference with a view or prospect of special amenity or special interest which is listed in the development plan or the draft variation or draft new plan.

(vii)   Consist of the excavation/alteration/demolition (other than peat extraction) of places/caves/sites/features or other objects of archaeological/geological/ historical interest, which are listed for preservation in the development plan, draft variation or draft new plan.

(viii) Consist of the extensions, alterations etc of an unauthorised structure or an unauthorised use in a structure. If there is anything unauthorised about a building in terms of planning then all the exemptions in relation to Parts I, II and III are lost.

(ix)   Consist of the alteration/extension/demolition of a building or other structure listed for preservation in the development plan, draft variation or draft new plan. If a building is listed for preservation in the development plan the exemptions relating to extensions etc do not apply.

(x)   Consist of the fencing or enclosure of any land habitually open to, or used by, the public, during the ten years preceding such fencing or enclosure for recreational purposes or as a means of access to any seashore, mountain, lakeshore, river bank, or other place of natural beauty or utility.

(xi)   Obstruct any public right of way.

(xii)   Further to the provisions of s 82 of the Act, consist of, or comprise the carrying out of works to the exterior of a structure, where the structure concerned is located within an architectural conservation area in a development plan for the area, or pending the variation of the development plan, or the making of a new development plan, in the draft variation of the development plan, or the draft development plan, and the development would materially affect the character of the area.

(b)   In an area to which a special amenity order relates, if such development would be development:

    (i)   of classes 1, 3, 11, 16, 21, 22, 27, 28, 29, 31 (other than paragraph (a) thereof), 33(c) (including the laying out and use of land for golf or pitch and putt, or sports involving the use of motor vehicles, aircraft or firearms), 39, 44 or 50(a) specified in column 1, of Part I of the Second Schedule; or

    (ii)   consist of the use of a structure or other land for for exhibition of advertisements of classes 1, 4, 6, 11, 16 or 17 specified in column 1 of Part II of the Second Schedule or the erection of an advertisement structure for the exhibition of any advertisement of any of the said classes; or

    (iii)   of classes 3, 5, 6, 7, 8, 9, 10, 11, 12 or 13 specified in column 1 of Part III of the said Schedule; or

    (iv)   of any class of Parts I, II or III of the Second Schedule, not referred to in subparas (i), (ii) and (iii) where it is stated in the order made under s 202 of the Act that such development shall be prevented or limited;

(c)   if it is development to which Part 10 applies, unless the development is required by, or under, any statutory provision (other than the Act, or these regulations) to comply with procedures for the purpose of giving effect to the Council Directive.

(d)   If it consists of the provision of, or modifications to, an establishment, and could have significant repercussions on major accident hazards.

(2) Subarticle (1)(a)(vi) shall not apply where the development consists of the construction by any electricity undertaking of an overhead line or cable not exceeding 100 metres in length for the purpose of conducting electricity from a distribution or transmission line to any premises.

11.4.7 REFERENCE TO AN BORD PLEANALA UNDER THE 2000 ACT, S 5

Where a question arises as to what in any particular case is or is not exempted development, the question shall be referred to and decided by An Bord Pleanala. An appeal lies against the decision of the Board within four weeks of the date of decision or longer period if the court allows. Sometimes, where enforcement proceedings are initiated by the local authority in relation to unauthorised development they will be adjourned pending a reference to the Board as to the status of the development. The court has absolute discretion whether to adjourn the proceedings or not.

11.4.8 APPLICATION OF EXEMPT DEVELOPMENT REGULATIONS TO CONVEYANCING SOLICITORS

While it is vital that conveyancing solicitors understand what is and is not exempted development, and can find their way through the legislation in relation to same, it is never their responsibility to decide what is, or what is not, exempted development. In other words, where there is the slightest doubt whether or not a development complies with, or does not comply with, the exempted development regulations or s 4 of the 2000 Act, the services of an architect or other suitably qualified person, must be employed and he or she should furnish either a declaration or certificate clearly setting out the grounds which bring the development under the exempt development categories (see **11.11** below). It is very important when are acting for the vendor that the client is asked whether or not he or she is aware of any exempted developments on any part of the premises. Similarly, when acting for a purchaser, the solicitor should specifically request the purchaser (either personally, or request his or her architect) to check the premises being purchased to see if there are any additions or extensions which might conceivably come within the exempted development provisions, or which may indeed require planning permission and then to deal with same appropriately in a special condition (see **11.10.8** below).

11.5 Application for Planning Permission

11.5.1 WHY APPLY FOR PLANNING PERMISSION?

Section 32 of the 2000 Act imposes the general obligation to obtain permission and is basically a restatement of the provisions of s 24 of the 1963 Act as amended. It states that, subject to the other provisions of this Act, permission shall be required under this Part:

> *in respect of any development of land not being exempted development, and; in the case of development which is unauthorised, for the retention of that unauthorised development.*

Section 32 of the 2000 Act does make some changes to s 24 of the 1963 Act, for example: in contrast to the provisions of s 24 (a) of the 1963 Act, there is no statement in s 32 stating that there is no obligation to obtain permission in respect to a development commenced before 1 October 1964. However, in the absence of a reference to development commenced before 1 October 1964, s 32 does not mean that it is necessary to apply for retention permission in respect of developments commenced or completed before 1 October 1964 (see lecture by John Gore-Grimes, 'Planning and Development Act, 2000', CLE, given on 23 February 2001, interpretation section).

Planning permission is required for all development of land which has been carried out since 1 October 1964 and which is not exempted development, or for the retention of unauthorised structures. Further, any person who carries out such a development without obtaining the required planning permission or in contravention of a permission granted is guilty of a criminal offence (see the 1963 Act, s 24 as amended by the 1976 Act, s 3(1); by the 1992 Act, s 20(4) and by the 2000 Act, Part VIII, s 151).

The definition of development in the 2000 Act, s 3(1) is vital therefore in that before proceeding to apply for permission, any good solicitor should satisfy himself or herself as to whether or not permission is required at all. Because, if the development contemplated is not one which requires permission, development should be commenced, as an unnecessary application may permit the planning authority to impose unwelcome conditions or to curtail the operation or activities of the development in some way and it may not be possible to argue at a later date that the application was not necessary. Further, the application should be restricted to those aspects of the development which require permission, ie if it is intended to change the use of only part of a building the entire should not be brought into question or, in the case of retention or continuance, only the unauthorised development should be made the subject of the application.

11.5.2   WHO MAY APPLY?

There is nothing in any of the Planning Acts or regulations which actually specifies who may apply for planning permission. However there is some case law on the point which suggests that the legislature intended to restrict the class to the owner or occupier of the land or somebody acting with their authority. See *Frascati Estates Ltd v Marie Walker* [1975] IR 177 where Henchy J laid down the following rule:

> 'an application . . . to be valid must be made either by or with the approval of a person who is able to assert sufficient legal estate to enable him to carry out the proposed development or so much of the proposed development as relates to the property'.

11.5.3   PROCEDURE TO APPLY FOR PLANNING PERMISSION

Part III of the 2000 Act deals with the making of applications for planning permissions, decisions on those applications, and related matters. Same should be read and followed with great care as the decision of the planning authority may be set aside as having been made without jurisdiction where the applicant has failed to comply with the requirements of the legislation. Compliance with this Part of the Act (ss 32–47 inclusive, and s 50) is a precondition of the exercise of a planning authority's discretion to grant or refuse permission. However, a minor error would not make it invalid as it would be unduly harsh on a developer if a grant for planning permission could be invalidated for some minor infraction of the regulations, especially as the planning authority is empowered, and virtually always does, request further information to remedy any further default in the content of an application. The necessary steps are as follows.

11.5.4   NOTICES

Article 17 of the 2001 Regulations states on the date that the applicant shall:

> *within the period of two weeks before the making of a Planning Application give notice of the intention to make the Application in a Newspaper in accordance with Article 18 and give notice*

of the intention to make the Application by the erection and fixing of a site notice in accordance with Article 18.

The point of this notification is to allow any interested member of the public to make representations or objections in writing and to enable the planning authorities themselves to be made aware of the opinion of the local area towards the proposed development.

The notice in the newspaper must be quite detailed and the requirements for same are found at art 18.

Note that should the planning authority request the applicant to submit an environmental impact statement (EIS) after the application has been lodged, a further newspaper notice may be required.

This is most likely to occur in two cases:

(a) where the application should initially have been accompanied by an EIS (see art 16); or

(b) where the planning authority considers that the proposed development will be likely to have significant effects on the environment.

Article 19 goes on to state that before the lodging of a planning application, the applicant must erect or fix a site notice on the land or structure concerned. While it does not state when this should be done, it cannot be later than the making of the application and it must be maintained in position for a period of at least five weeks from the date of receipt of the planning application and must be renewed or replaced if it is removed or becomes defaced or illegible within that period (see art 20).

Like the notice to the newspaper, the site notice itself must be quite detailed and what exactly it must contain is set out at Form No 1 of the Third Schedule, or as art 19(1)(a) states 'or a form substantially to like effect'. Once again these requirements are strict and the planning authority may request an applicant to give further notice on site where the requirements are not complied with.

Article 24 deals with applications for outline permission and is rather vague in that it states 'in addition to the requirements of art 22(2), be accompanied only by such plans and particulars as are necessary'.

Article 26 deals with the procedure of the planning authority on receipt of a planning application. The planning authority is required to notify certain bodies of planning applications received by it depending on the nature of the application. The bodies which must be served with a notice are listed in art 26(8) essentially 'any person or body who has made a submission or observation in accordance with art 29(1) . . . . or anybody to whom notice was sent in accordance with art 28(2)'. Note that in art 33 the local authority may make a request for further information by notice in writing.

It is more common than not for the local authority to seek further information. While this is frequently done in order to clarify matters, it is also frequently done because local authorities have such a large volume of applications that they are not able to respond within the time period and therefore, by seeking further information, they get to extend that time period. It is also quite common for a local authority to ring the developer and request that he or she seek a time extension which any wise developer will agree to, thus once again giving them additional time in which to review the application.

11.5.5 OBLIGATION OF LOCAL AUTHORITY RE PLANNING FILE

Article 27(1) authorises the planning authority to make available all documents relating to planning applications 'not later than the third working day following a particular week, make available in accordance with subarticle (2) a list of all the planning applications received by the authority during that week'. Any person can inspect the planning file of a particular application at the offices of the local authority during office hours. Each application has an individual file which is cross-referenced according to the planning register reference number to location maps which are also available for inspection. A number of different reference numbers may exist for the same site depending on the number of applications which have been made and this may be quite confusing, as often the planning authority will also maintain separate maps for different periods of years. However, the planning authority is generally very helpful to planning applicants in sorting out same.

These documents remain available for inspection for a period of one month from the date the planning authority gives its decision or, where there are one or more appeals, until each of the appeals is withdrawn or determined or dismissed or, in the case of an appeal against the condition or conditions, only until a direction is given to the planning authority by the Board.

11.5.6   WHO MAY COMMENT ON THE APPLICATION?

Any person or body may make submissions or observations in writing to a planning authority on a particular application. In recent times local communities, often through the vehicle of a residents' association, have become more active in this regard. Section 34(3) gives for the first time in Irish planning law, statutory recognition to submissions and observations made to a planning authority on planning applications. In effect, the planning authority must take into account written submissions or observations made by third parties on the planning application. So, in addition to the application itself, the planning authority shall have regard to any information relating to the application furnished to it by the applicant in accordance with the planning regulations. Note, art 29(1) limits the time in which such a submission or observation must be made to within the period of five weeks beginning on the date of receipt by the authority of the application. The mandatory contents of the submission or observation are set out at art 29(b).

11.5.7   TIME PERIODS

Article 30 sets out the minimum period for determination of a planning application as not until 'after a period of five weeks beginning on the date of receipt of an Application has lapsed'.

While the planning authority must make the decision on the application not earlier than five weeks from its receipt it must not make it later than eight weeks beginning on the date of receipt by the planning authority of the application, ie fifty-six days (see s 34(8) of the 2000 Act). Section 34(8) is so designed to increase the efficiency of the planning control system. The previous nine Planning Acts used days, weeks, and months. Therefore, there was a variation in time periods from anywhere from sixty-nine to fifty-two days; however, under the new Act, it is a clear fifty-six days beginning on the date of the receipt of the application. Further, where additional information is sought, the planning authorities will have an additional four weeks, not two months as previously, to decide on an application other than for applications where an environmental impact assessment is required, or in a material contravention case, or in a case involving risk of major accident or where the application is of such a nature where a major accident may occur which would result in serious consequences, and the planning authority is bound to seek technical advice. If a decision does not issue within the eight-week period, permission is deemed to have been granted by default (see s 34(8)(f)) on the last day of that period. The eight-week period may be extended (and generally is) by the planning authority requesting further information regarding aspects of the application or by consenting (at the request of the applicant, generally prompted by the local authority) to an extension of time for the consideration of the application up to a stated date (see s 34(9)). There is no statutory time limit to the number of time extensions which may be conceded but some authorities restrict it to one only.

The 2000 Act inserts a new provision in relation to planning applications at s 35, in that for the first time a local authority may refuse planning permission for past failures to comply with previous permissions.

Article 37 allows for the withdrawal of planning applications by notice in writing at any time before the giving of the decision of the planning authority.

Section 34(1) provides:

(a) *that where an application is made to a planning authority in accordance with permission regulation for permission for the development of land, and*

(b) *all requirements of the regulations are complied with [. . .]*

the authority may decide to grant the permission subject to, or without conditions, or to refuse it and when dealing with any such application the planning authority is restricted to considering the proper planning and sustainable development of the area, regard being had to the provisions of the development plan, the provisions of any special amenity area order relating to the said area, any European site or other area prescribed for the purposes of s 10(2)(c), and, where relevant, the policy of the government, the Minister, or any other Minister of the government, and the matters referred at s 34(4), and any other relevant provision or requirement of this Act, and any regulations made thereunder. At the time of writing, the relevant regulations are the Local Government (Planning and Development) Regulations, 2001 (SI 600/2001).

Section 34 goes on to provide that the above subsection, together with the following subsections which deal with conditions, applies mutatis mutandis to determinations by An Bord Pleanala. In other words, the planning authority is restricted to considering the proper planning and the development of the area of its authority. Therefore the consideration of any irrelevant factor renders a decision invalid.

Section 34(6), which is rarely invoked, allows the planning authority to grant planning permission for development which would materially contravene the provisions of the development plan but lays down a strict procedure for same and, if a planning authority grants permission in material contravention of the plan without following this procedure, its decision may be quashed in proceedings for judicial review.

An Bord Pleanala, on the other hand, may, at its discretion, grant planning permission for development which would materially contravene the provisions of the development plan. Although An Bord Pleanala is obliged to have regard to the provisions of the development plan, it is not under any statutory duty to give effect to its objectives.

11.5.8 POWER TO IMPOSE CONDITIONS

Section 34(4) of the 2000 Act gives the planning authorities both a general power to attach conditions, and, without prejudice to the general power, express authorisation for certain enumerated conditions. There is an excellent commentary on conditions by John Gore-Grimes in his CLE lecture, 'Planning and Development Act, 2000' Book Two, pp 96–109 given on 23 February 2001. The general power to impose conditions is not without limits, and is subject to a number of limitations laid down by case law. See *Killiney and Ballybrack Development Association Ltd v Minister for Local Government and Templefinn Estates* [1978] ILRM 78, and *The State (Abenglen) v Dublin Corporation* [1982] ILRM 590. The conditions enumerated in s 34(4) are as follows:

(a) The conditions imposed must be for a planning purpose and not for any ulterior one: see *Dunne Ltd v Dublin County Council* [1974] IR 45, where Pringle J expressed the opinion that a condition attached to a planning permission requiring that houses be constructed so as to provide sound insulation against aircraft noise was ultra vires, because the matter could have been more appropriately dealt with by building regulations which the Minister has power to make under the 1963 Act, s 86.

(b) The condition must be fairly and reasonably related to the development permitted. This question very often arises in the case of a condition imposed under s 26(2)(a). The cases of *The State (FHP Properties SA) v An Bord Pleanala* [1989] IRLM 98; [1987] IR 698 and *British Airports Authority v Secretary of State* 1979 SC 200 are dealt with under that heading below.

(c) Conditions must not be unreasonable. A condition attached to a grant of permission may be held by the courts to be void for 'unreasonableness' where it is one which 'no reasonable authority acting within the four corners of their jurisdiction could have decided to impose': *Westminster Bank Ltd v Minister of Housing and Local Government* [1971] AC 508. The question is whether the decision 'flies in the face of fundamental reason and common sense': *The State (Keegan) v Stardust Compensation Tribunal* [1987] ILRM 202; [1992] ILRM 237.

There are many types of conditions which may be imposed. Conditions for requiring roads, open spaces, car parks, sewers, watermains or drains in excess of the immediate needs of the proposed development, conditions restricting the occupation of buildings, conditions requiring matters to be agreed etc.

11.5.9 CONDITIONS RE SIGHT LINES

The Conveyancing Committee of the Law Society in the Law Society Gazette, November 2001 published a guideline in relation to conditions in planning permission re sight lines.

A number of local authorities are imposing conditions in planning permissions requiring the applicant to secure sight lines at the entrance of a house site from the public road. In some cases, the applicants, anticipating the requirement, have offered to provide the necessary sight lines in the application itself; therefore there was nothing on the face of the planning permission to alert anyone of the requirement. The committee pointed out that in at least one case, the applicant offered to reduce the height of the hedge (with the permission of a neighbour who owned the land in question) but no thought was given to what was to happen when the hedge grew again. In another case, the applicant (again with the permission of a neighbour) confirmed that an arrangement had been made with a neighbour to provide an appropriate sight line. In that case the neighbour did not really understand what was required of him and the planning authority in question did not clarify the position. It is not satisfactory that planning authorities in some cases do not deal with the long-term implications.

It seems clear that conditions like this are going to cause problems for architects and engineers who may be asked to certify compliance. It will obviously also cause problems for conveyancing solicitors. Solicitors who are advising clients in relation to the purchase of a property subject to such a condition will have to advise the client very carefully, particularly if the condition is not going to be properly dealt with. In such circumstances, solicitors should point out that they are likely to have a problem certifying title and that there is a clear risk that there will be problems on reselling. The committee advised that such advice should be confirmed in writing. In addition, when acting for a client purchasing a site with the benefit of a planning permission, it is yet another reason to advise clients to have the position regarding the planning permission checked out by a competent person. The committee clearly doubted the wisdom of solicitors briefing an architect or engineer on behalf of their clients in such situations but did recognise that, from time to time, solicitors will find that they will have to do this. The committee feels that such a briefing should be in general terms rather than trying to anticipate all the issues that could arise. However, the issue of sight lines and other easements could be addressed by asking the surveyor to review whether the house, its access and any facilities, such as a septic tank or percolation area or water supply, can be provided without passing over or acquiring rights over land in the ownership of any third party.

Of course, the practical problem here is that an applicant who already owns a site and has received a grant of planning permission subject to such a condition might not realise the full implications of such a condition and might have the house built before realising that there may be a problem. Compliance with the condition may be impossible because it would require the applicant to acquire land perhaps from both adjoining owners to provide the necessary lines of sight. Arguably, the planning authority should not grant permission until the applicant satisfies it that the applicant has such legal rights or perhaps ownership necessary to enable it to comply with any such condition. Planning authorities are ready do this routinely in relation to easements for drainage if a site cannot be drained without a grant of easements over property in the ownership of third parties.

The solicitors faced with such a situation should give the following advice. The best solution is for the client to buy the necessary land so as to put himself or herself in a position of being able to comply with a planning condition and to provide a sight line in a permanent way. If this is not possible or practical (which it will not be in the majority of cases), the client should acquire a grant of easements which will enable him or her to comply properly with the condition. Any grant of easements should be registered on the title of the grantor. If none of this is possible, solicitors should advise clients they will have to qualify title in a manner which may not be acceptable to a lender and that the property may not be resaleable without the problem being regularised. The law agent of one of the main lenders for housing has indicated that a qualification of a certificate of title would not be acceptable if it indicated that the condition about the provision of sight lines in the planning permission had not been complied with. The committee went on to say that it suspected other lenders would take a similar position. Further, it added that an informal arrangement or letters from friendly neighbours are simply not sufficient. It ended its note by saying that it intended to make representation to all relevant parties to try to have a more consistent and reasonable practice applied. Meanwhile this is a very dangerous situation for conveyancing solicitors which needs to be approached very carefully.

11.5.10 SEVERANCE OF CONDITIONS

In *Bord na Mona v An Bord Pleanala and Galway County Council* [1985] IR 205 Keane J said:

'On principle, it seems wrong that a planning permission should be treated as of no effect simply because a condition attached to it, which is nothing to do with planning considerations, is found to be ultra vires. Again, if a condition of a peripheral or insignificant nature attached to a permission is found to be ultra vires, it seems wrong that the entire permission should have to fall as a consequence. But where the condition relates to planning considerations and it is an essential feature of the permission granted, it would seem equally wrong that the permission should be treated as still effective although shorn of an essential planning condition.'

11.5.11 PLANNING PERMISSION BY DEFAULT

Planning permission or approval may be obtained by default where the planning authority fails to give notice to an applicant of its decision on an application which complies with the regulations, within a specified time period, referred to as 'the appropriate period' (see s 34(8)(f)). The decision by the planning authority to grant the permission or approval is regarded as having been given on the last day of that period.

In most cases, the planning authority has a period of eight weeks in which to make its decision, unless a request for further information is made, or the applicant is required to publish a fresh notice of the application, both of which have the effect of extending the period by a further two months from the date of compliance or notice.

The default procedure results in a decision to grant planning permission or approval only where the planning authority does not give notice to the applicant of its decision within the 'appropriate period'.

The default procedure results in a 'decision to grant' planning permission or approval so that an order of mandamus compelling the planning authority to issue a grant of planning permission has to be obtained before development may commence.

'A default permission' may be appealed to An Bord Pleanala (provided that it has made submission or observations on the planning application in question: see s 37(1)(a)) in the same manner as a decision to grant planning permission or approval made within the appropriate period. The default procedure cannot operate to produce a decision which is a material contravention of the development plan, as an order of mandamus 'cannot issue to compel the planning authority . . . to consider an application to do something which would be illegal if done' per Walsh J in *The State (Pine Valley Developments) v Dublin County Council* [1982] ILRM 169.

Similarly, a default permission cannot issue where the planning authority does not have sufficient information to determine whether a proposal is in material contravention of the development plan or not.

11.5.12 REASONS FOR DECISION

The planning authority is obliged to state its reasons for refusing planning permission or approval or for the imposition of conditions attaching to a grant of permission or approval (see 2000 Act, s 34(10)). There is no statutory requirement to provide reasons for the granting of planning permission by the planning authority. It is not clear whether the planning authority has a duty to give all reasons for the refusal of permission. It appears it may extend the reasons for refusal on a second similar application: see *The State (Dino Aprile) v Naas UDC* [1985] ILRM 510. Section 34(10)(b) is a new provision.

11.5.13 GRANT OF PERMISSION

Where the planning authority decides to grant a permission, it is obliged to make the grant 'as soon as may be' after the decision (see s 34(11)(b)).

In the case of a permission by default, it is obliged to make the grant as soon as may be after the period available for a third party appeal has expired; the applicant may be expected not to want to appeal against a default permission. Where an appeal is taken but withdrawn or dismissed by the Board for having been abandoned or as being vexatious, the planning authority is required to make the grant as soon as may be after the appeal has been withdrawn or dismissed. If the Board, having considered an appeal, issues a direction to the planning authority for the attachment, amendment or removal of any condition or conditions, the planning authority is required to make the grant as soon as may be after the giving by the Board of the direction (see s 34(11)).

Note, the grant of planning permission or approval does not entitle a person to carry out any development which requires other licences or permits or is otherwise unlawful.

11.5.14 PERMISSIONS FOR RETENTION OF STRUCTURES OR CONTINUANCE OF USE

The provisions of Part III of the 2000 Act apply in the same way as to the other permissions discussed and consequently the application procedure and the power of the planning authority and An Bord Pleanala to determine applications are identical. It follows, therefore, that the planning authority is not entitled to take into account the prior existence of the unauthorised structure or use in deciding whether to grant or refuse permission, as this is 'a matter which the statute has excluded from the range of its consideration'.

11.6 Planning Appeals

11.6.1 INTRODUCTION

The rules and procedures for making an appeal are set out in Part VI, chapter III, of the 2000 Act, ss 125–146 inclusive and chapter 2 of the 2001 Regulations.

In his introduction to the 2000 Act, the Minister for the Environment stated his intention in relation to appeals procedures of streamlining the system and providing greater efficiency in the output of appeal decisions. While there have been some changes made to the system by the 2000 Act, how the system is to be streamlined is not clear. Appeals to An Bord Pleanala are part of control of development. In other words, decisions of a planning authority involve a two-tier process: the first is a grant of permission under s 34 (see above); the second is the potential for any applicant or any person who has made submissions or observations in writing to the planning application to the planning authority before the decision is made, to appeal to An Bord Pleanala against the decision of the planning authority under s 34 (see s 37(1)(a)). This is one of the most important new provisions under the 2000 Act.

The right to appeal the decision of the planning authority to grant or refuse permission, or to appeal conditions of the planning permission, is *now* restricted to the applicant and to any person(s) who made submissions or observations in writing in relation to the planning application to the planning authority in accordance with permission regulations and on payment of the appropriate fees. Under legislation existing prior to the 2000 Act, there were no standing requirements for the making of an appeal. Any person could appeal before the expiration of the appropriate period. The right of appeal is now much more limited, and persons who wish to appeal, other than the applicant, must be persons who have made submissions or observations on the planning application in question. While it true to say that the right of appeal is now much more limited, there are two exceptions to the general rule set out at s 37(4) and s 37(6). The former states that if a prescribed body should have been notified of a planning application under the planning regulations and the planning authority failed to notify it, that authority or body would be entitled to appeal the decision of the Board, but the Board has power to dismiss any appeal if it considers that the body concerned was not entitled to be sent notice of the planning application in accordance with the planning regulations. The latter exception arises where a person with an interest in land adjoining land in respect of which permission has been granted by the planning authority may within four weeks, and on payment of the appropriate fee, apply to the Board for leave to appeal against the decision of the planning authority under s 34. The application must state the name and address of the person making the application, the grounds upon which the application is made, and a description of the person's interest in the land. Provision is also made for the forwarding by the planning authority of relevant documentation on the planning file to the Board under s 37(6)(c). If the applicant, in making an application to the Board for leave to appeal under this subsection, shows that the development for which permission is being granted will differ materially from the development as set out in the application for permission, by reason of conditions imposed by the planning authority and that the imposition of such conditions will materially affect the applicant's enjoyment of the land, or reduce the value of the land, the Board shall grant the applicant leave to appeal within four weeks from the date of receipt of the application. Within three days of making its decision either to grant or refuse an application for leave to appeal, the Board will notify the planning authority and the applicant, and if leave to appeal is granted, the applicant will have two weeks from the date of notification to bring his or her appeal. Once an application is made under this subsection, the planning authority shall not make any grant of permission unless the application is refused.

11.6.2 TIME LIMITS FOR MAKING AN APPEAL

Section 37(1)(d) states these appeals must be taken within four weeks (it used to be one month), and the time runs from the date of the decision by the planning authority. The time limits provided are very strict and in no circumstances will the time period be extended. Any appeal received by the Board after the expiration of that time limit shall be invalid, as provided for in s 37(3). The Board has no discretion to accept late appeals and a large number of appeals are not processed as they are outside the time period.

11.6.3 APPEALS AND REFERRALS

Part V of the Local Government (Planning and Development) Regulations, 1994 previously set out the procedures for appeals and referrals. These are now contained in Part VI, chapter III, of the 2000 Act (ss 125–146), and chapter 6, arts 151–155 of the Planning and Development Regulations, 2001. There are amendments and changes made in almost all sections of chapter III. Section 125 of the 2000 Act states that chapter III applies to appeals and referrals to the Board. It will not apply to appeals under s 182(4)(b), (the power of a local authority to construct or lay cables etc). Section 126(2), (3), (4) deals broadly with the duties and objectives of the Board in relation to appeals and referrals which were previously dealt with by s 2 of the 1992 Act.

11.6.4 REQUIREMENTS FOR MAKING AN APPEAL

The requirements for making a valid appeal or reference is essentially the same as under the repealed legislation (s 4 of the 1992 Act). An additional mandatory requirement is that the third party appeal should be accompanied by the acknowledgement by the planning authority of the receipt of submissions or observations by it from that third party. Section 127 now also requires that an appeal or referral must state the name and address of any person acting on behalf of the applicant or any person making the referral. In addition to the name and address of the applicant, or person making the referral. In short, s 127 sets out the provisions which an appeal or referral must:

(a) be in writing;

(b) state the name and address of the applicant or person making the appeal or referral;

(c) state the subject matter of the appeal or referral;

(d) state the grounds of the appeal or referral, and the reasons, considerations and arguments upon which they are based;

(e) if the appeal is by a third party under s 37, the appeal must be accompanied by an acknowledgement by the planning authority of receipt of the submissions or observations made;

(f) be accompanied by the relevant fee; and

(g) be made within the period of four weeks, or such extended time as may be allowed under s 37(6) (see above).

An appeal which does not comply with any of the above requirements will be invalid and the requirements apply to persons making an appeal or referral whether or not the request is for an oral hearing. The Board, however, has absolute discretion whether to hold an oral hearing or not.

An appellant will not generally be entitled to elaborate in writing or make any further submissions in writing in relation to the grounds of appeal, or to submit further grounds of appeal and the applicant is given one chance, and one chance only, to comply with the provisions of s 127(1), and to submit documents, particulars or other information relating to the appeal or referral, as the applicant may consider necessary. Any documents or particulars so submitted must be submitted within the time limit or they will not be considered (see s 127(3,4)). As in s 4 of the 1992 Act, the appeal or referral must be sent to the Board by pre-paid post or left with an employee of the Board at the offices of the Board during office hours or by such other means as may be prescribed. If appeal or referral documents are sent by post, they must reach the offices of the Board before the expiration of the four-week time limit, and if delivered, it is necessary that they be left with an employee of the Board personally (see s 127(5)). It is not sufficient that an employee may subsequently come into possession of the appeal documents (see *Graves v An Bord Pleanala* [1997] 2 IR 205, where Kelly J held that an employee of the Board must have the appeal left with him or her personally.

11.6.5 PARTIES AND TIME LIMITS TO AN APPEAL

Section 37(1)(a) deals with parties to an appeal—see above. The planning authority is always a party to an appeal. Section 126 of the 2000 Act which deals with time limits restates with modifications, s 2 of the 1992 Act. It is the object of the Board to ensure that every appeal or referral is determined within a period of eighteen weeks beginning on the date of receipt by the Board of the appeal or referral. In relation to applications for leave to appeal under s 37(6) (see above), the reference to eighteen weeks in s 126 is construed as a reference to fourteen weeks. Section 126(2), while acknowledging the eighteen-week time limit, clearly expects it not to be met on all occasions as it allows the Minister, where it is not met, to make a time-limit within any such period as he or she shall prescribe. Section 126(4) allows the Minister to vary it, either generally or in respect of a particular class or classes of appeals or referrals where it appears necessary for him or her to do so, or by virtue of exceptional circumstances. Section 126(5), further gives the Minister power to give direction to the Board where he or she considers it necessary or expedient to give priority to appeals or referrals which are of strategic, economic, or social importance. Section 141 deals with the time for decisions and appeals (previously s 17 of the 1992 Act). It clarifies the dates from which time limits are to run. With the present building boom the Board is having difficulty in processing appeals within the required period. The main reasons given for delays in processing appeals are:

(a) environmental impact statements have been submitted in conjunction with the appeals;

(b) an oral hearing is held;

(c) new public notices are required;

(d) large cases/complex issues;

(e) in the interest of natural justice the Board requires additional information; and

(f) where the Board raises new matters not raised by the parties an opportunity to make submissions on those new matters must be given.

11.6.6   SUBMISSIONS

Section 128 deals with submission of documents to the Board by planning authorities, (see **chapter 2**, and arts 66 and 168 of the 2001 Regulations). With some changes, it restates s 6 of the 1992 Act, and the provisions affect both appeals and referrals. Section 128 provides that the planning authority must within two weeks (replaces fourteen days) of the date of receipt of a copy of an appeal or referral provide all documentation in relation to an appeal held on its files. Section 129 deals with transmission of submissions or observations to the Board, and by the Board to each other party to the appeal. It essentially restates s 7 of the 1992 Act providing that each other party must receive a copy of the appeal or referral as soon as may be, after the receipt thereof by the Board. Section 130 deals with submissions or observations by persons other than parties to the appeal or referral, and once again, it restates with slight changes s 8 of the 1992 Act (at sub-ss (1)(c), (2) and (3)(b)), and again it deals with both appeals and referrals. It allows submissions and observations to be made by persons other than parties to the appeal and again it sets out regulations about what precisely must be submitted which are very similar to the documents and submissions made under s 127 above. However, while the period is still four weeks, the four weeks run from the day of the receipt of the last appeal, or on the day of the receipt by the Board of the referral or, where the Board requires the applicant to publish a further notice in relation to the appeal or referral from the date of publication of that notice (see s 130(3)).

Section 131 (previously s 9 of the 1992 Act), empowers the Board to request further submissions or observations from a party to an appeal or referral, or to any other person or body in relation to any matter which has arisen.

Section 132 deals with the power of the Board to require submission of documents (previously s 10 of the 1992 Act), in brief it can request any information as it deems necessary for the purpose of enabling it to determine an appeal or referral.

Section 133 provides the Board with the powers in cases where notice is served under s 131 or s 132 above (previously s 11 of the 1992 Act). Section 136 is a new provision which allows the Board to bring the parties to a meeting before the Board in order to discuss the issues arising out of a referral. The convening of such a meeting is at the absolute discretion of the Board, but the Board is bound to keep a written record of the meeting if same is convened.

11.6.7   APPEALS AGAINST CONDITIONS ATTACHED TO DECISIONS

Section 139 deals with appeals against conditions (previously s 15 of the 1992 Act). When an appeal is made against a decision to grant or refuse permission, the appeal will be treated as if the application for permission was made in the first instance to the Board. The entire application will be reconsidered and the appellant may not restrict the Board to considering certain parts of the application. Therefore, if a planning authority granted a very restrictive permission in terms of opening hours and users of a restaurant, it is possible that the Board could grant an even more restrictive permission. It is important to consider the possibility of a less favourable result in terms of the development before appealing a decision. In some cases the appropriate course of action is to consult with the planning authority and to lodge a new revised planning application.

11.6.8   ORAL HEARINGS

Section 134 deals with oral hearings of appeals and referrals (previously s 12 of the 1992 Act), and art 76 of the 2001 Regulations. Sub-sections (2)(c)(ii) and (4) are new. Section 134 provides that a party to an appeal or referral (this does not include an observer) may request an oral hearing on payment of a fee; the Board has absolute discretion on whether or not to hold such an oral hearing. Because of the wording of the section it would be extremely difficult to challenge a decision of the Board not to hold an oral hearing (see *Hynes v An Bord Pleanala* (10 December, 1997 High Court unreported)). There is no requirement on the Board to give reasons why it may have decided not to hold an oral hearing. The section sets out regulations and time limits, and if the regulations are not complied with, or the time limits are not met, the appeal shall not be considered by the Board. The general time limit is a four-week period, and respective starting dates are set out at s 134(1, 2).

Section 135 deals with supplemental provisions relating to oral hearings (previously s 82(4)–(7) of the 1963 Act as amended by the 1976 Act).

The conduct of an oral hearing is left to the discretion of the person conducting it, but there are guidelines given to the inspector at s 135(2) (previously s 82 of the 1963 Act as amended by the 1976 Act). The provisions in relation to requests for oral hearings and the holding of such hearings remain broadly similar to those under the repealed legislation. The ability of an inspector, appointed to conduct an oral hearing in an efficient and orderly manner, is increased by the creation of certain new offences laid out at s 135(7). See *Keane v An Bord Pleanala* (20 June 1995, High Court unreported), which gives the inspector discretion to abbreviate excessive arguments or submissions in the interests of justice. See also the Supreme Court decision in *Lancefort v An Bord Pleanala* [1998] 2 ILRM 401, which requires an objector to raise all legal issues at an oral hearing, in order not to prejudice any subsequent judicial review proceedings. However, in practice, inspectors are frequently unwilling to listen to legal arguments, and have frequently expressed the view that they are concerned only with the planning issues in the appeal. But, as can be seen from above, this is not correct. The legal points should properly be made by the objector irrespective of the inspector's viewpoint. Under the regulations, the inspector is required to prepare a written report of the oral hearing for presentation to the Board. The report contains the inspector's recommendations, and must be available for public inspection. See *O'Keefe v An Bord Pleanala* [1993] 1 IR 39, where it was put beyond dispute that the recommendations of an inspector may not be taken into account by, or followed by, the Board in making its decision.

Section 137 deals with matters other than those raised by parties to the appeal (previously s 13 of the 1992 Act).

11.6.9 DISMISSAL/WITHDRAWAL OF APPEALS

Section 138 (previously s 14 of the 1992 Act) permits the Board to dismiss appeals or referrals if vexatious etc. It adds a new entitlement which allows the Board to reject an appeal if it was made with the intention of delaying the development or to extract money or other inducements from the developer, or any other person (see s 138(1)(a)(ii)).

Section 139 deals with appeals against conditions as opposed to appeals against decisions (previously s 15 of the Local Government (Planning and Development) Act 1992 (see **11.6.7** above)).

Section 140 deals with the withdrawal of appeals, applications and referrals (previously s 16 of the 1992 Act). It allows parties to withdraw appeals or referrals which is new.

11.6.10 REGULATIONS/FEES/EXPENSES RE APPEALS

Section 142 deals with the regulations regarding appeals and referrals (previously s 18 of the 1992 Act). At the time of writing, one such set of regulations has issued, the Local Government (Planning and Development) Regulations, 2001 (SI 600/2001) (see chapter 2, art 66, et al).

Section 143 (previously s 5 of the 1976 Act) requires the Board to have regard to certain policies and objectives. It is stronger than the 1976 Act, in that the Board shall, in

Stages in Appeals under the 1992 Act[1]

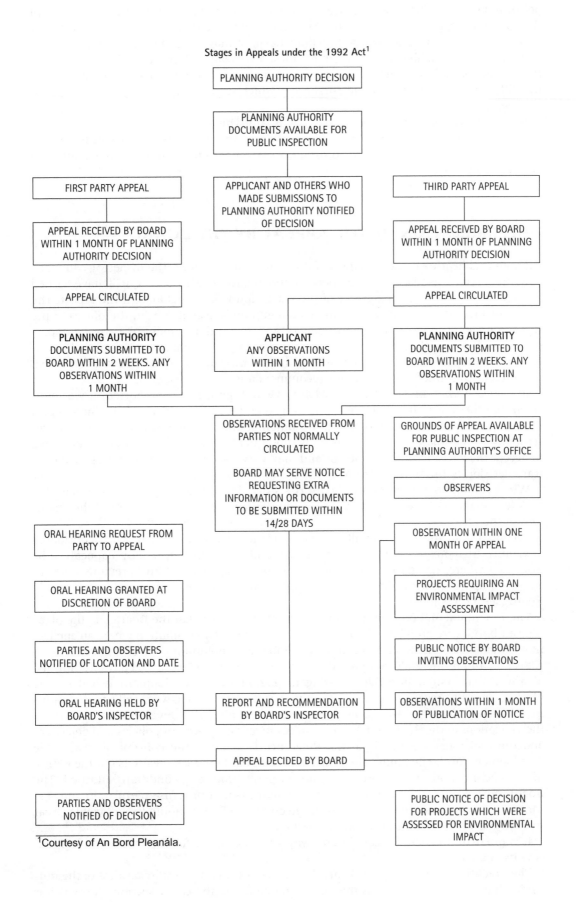

performing its functions, have regard to the policies and objectives for the time being of the government, a State authority, the Minister, planning authorities, and any other body which is a public authority whose functions have, or may have, a bearing on the proper planning and sustainable development of cities, towns, and other areas whether urban or rural. Note that this section makes an attempt in planning terms to lessen, if not remove, the difference between urban and rural areas which were always distinguished in previous legislation.

Section 144 deals with fees payable to the Board. This section is new.

Section 145 (previously s 19 of the 1976 Act) deals with expenses of appeal or referral.

Section 146 enables the Board to assign a person to report on any other matter on behalf of the Board.

11.6.11 DETERMINATION OF THE APPEAL BY THE BOARD

After an oral hearing or examination of the written submissions, the inspector will make a written report available to members of the Board. The inspector will have visited the site in question and an account of the inspection will be included in the report. The inspector's report is usually a very full document and is available from the offices of the Board for a fee. The inspector's report may be a very useful document to assist the understanding of an appeal decision, and is of particular importance if a new scheme of development is proposed on a site. It is also of importance to see if the Board overturned, modified or confirmed the inspector's recommendation.

In *Simmonovich v An Bord Pleanala*, 24 July 1988, High Court (unreported) it was indicated that the Board should appoint one of its members to consider the planning appeal including the inspector's report and all documentation. That member then makes a presentation to the Board where a decision is subsequently made. The Board does not have to accept the decision of the inspector and may vary the recommendation or give a contrary decision (s 146 of the 2000 Act).

When coming to a decision, the Board is restricted to considering the proper planning and development of the area, including the preservation and improvement of the amenities of the area.

Section 138 of the 2000 Act allows the Board to dismiss an appeal if it is considered vexatious, frivolous or without substance or foundation. Further, it allows appeals to be dismissed where, having regard to the nature of the appeal and any previous relevant appeal or approval, it considers that the appeal should not be further considered by the Board (see **11.6.9** above).

The Environmental Protection Agency Act, 1992 provides that the Board and the planning authorities are prohibited from considering environmental pollution where an application is made for permission that requires an integrated pollution control licence.

Section 143 of the 2000 Act provides that the Board is obliged to keep itself informed of any general policy directives relating to planning and development issued by the Minister and has regard to certain objectives. This section effectively reflects more positively than under s 5 of the Local Government (Planning and Development) Act, 1976, the obligations of the Board to take account of current government policies and objectives and those of other identified parties. Reference is made to the concept of sustainable development for the first time. The decision of the Board on the appeal sets out the nature of the decision and, in the case of a grant of permission, any conditions attached. The Board must also state the reasons for the decision to grant or refuse permission and reasons for any conditions imposed. Reasons given by the Board should be sufficiently clear so as to enable the court to review its decision.

It is unlawful to communicate in any way with the Board for the purpose of influencing its decision.

The practice is that every party bears their own costs in an appeal regardless of the outcome. The Board, however, has the power to determine the costs. Section 144 which is new, deals with the Board providing for fees to be made payable to it and s 145 deals with the expenses of the appeal or referral (which effectively restates s 19 of the 1976 Act). Section 146 goes on to outline which documents shall be made available for a period of at least five years commencing on the third working day following the decision of the Board in relation to the matter.

11.6.12 COMPOSITION OF AN BORD PLEANALA

Part VI of the 2000 Act deals with the composition of the Board. It was established in 1977 pursuant to the 1976 Act, s 2. Section 104 of the 2000 Act states that the Board consists of a chairperson, and seven other members. The Minister may by order increase the number of ordinary members. Any such order shall have effect for such period not exceeding five years as shall be specified therein. Section 105 deals with the appointment of a chairperson (previously s 5 of the 1983 Act). The chairperson is selected by the government from a panel of three or fewer candidates recommended by an independent committee. The Minister (s 106 of the 2000 Act) appoints the ordinary members of the Board from various prescribed organisations listed at s 106(1)(a)–(g), this section is a restatement of s 7 of the Local Government (Planning and Development) Act, 1983 with a number of amendments; in particular the panels from which persons for appointment can be nominated have been modified. Section 107 deals with the appointment of a deputy chairperson, and s 108 declares that the quorum for a meeting of the Board shall be three (previously s 12 of the 1983 Act).

11.6.13 JUDICIAL REVIEW OF PLANNING DECISIONS

A judicial review of a planning decision is not a review of the decision itself, but rather of the way that the decision was made. This is the appropriate avenue where the legality of a decision is at issue rather than the merits of the planning matters. Judicial review of planning decisions is governed by s 50 of the 2000 Act (previously the 1963 Act, s 82(3A) and (3B), as substituted by the 1992 Act, s 19(3)).

The time limit for judicial review of planning decisions is different from other judicial review proceedings. An application for leave to apply for judicial review must be made within eight weeks, commencing on the date that the decision was given (s 50(4)(a)(i)).

A challenge to a decision of the planning authority or the Board may only be taken under Order 84 of the Rules of the Superior Courts, 1986 (SI 15/1986). Previously, the period within which an appeal must be brought could not be extended however, the High Court now has the power to extend it in limited circumstances as set out in sub-s (4)(a)(iii) (see also sub-s (4)(d)). Section 50(3) provides that the High Court may stay proceedings pending the making of a decision by the Board, and this is a new provision.

The application must be made by way of notice of motion. The applicant serves the notice of motion, grounding affidavit and statement of grounds (which cannot be amended) within the eight-week period on all the specified parties. A failure to serve the correct party within the eight-week period makes the application for leave invalid. Discovery should be made prior to the application for leave to apply.

Judicial review is a two-stage process. First, leave to apply for judicial review is sought and, if successful, the application is then heard. The first stage is very important as leave to apply for judicial review will not be granted unless the court as per sub-s (4) is satisfied that there are 'substantial grounds', that the applicant has sufficient interest, and that the applicant has made submissions and observations in relation to the proposed development, and that the decision is invalid or ought to be quashed. These new principles as set out above apply only to those decisions of the planning authority and the Board as described in sub-s (4)(a). Substantial interest is not limited to an interest in land or other financial interest, it is a mixed question of law and fact, and depends upon the circumstances of each particular case. Important factors include the impact of the decision upon the applicant's interest, and the degree to which he or she has participated in the planning process, particularly in any appeals to the Board. There is considerable case law on what constitutes substantial grounds. It has been described as a 'high hurdle' by Keane J in the Lugalla case (*Byrne v Wicklow County Council*, 3 November 1994, High Court (unreported)). An appeal to the Supreme Court lies only if the High Court certifies that its decision involves a point of law of exceptional public importance. No appeal lies against the refusal of the High Court to certify a point of exceptional public importance (*Irish Asphalt v An Bord Pleanala* [1996] 1 ILRM 81).

Order 84, rule 20(4) of the Rules of the Superior Courts also requires the applicant for leave to apply for judicial review to have sufficient interest in the matter to which the application relates. The issue of locus standi was recently reviewed by the Supreme Court in *Lancefort Ltd v An Bord Pleanala and the Attorney-General* [1998] 2 ILRM 401. Thus, it is clear that an applicant must satisfy what are effectively three criteria before leave to appeal for judicial review may be granted. First, the applicant must demonstrate that there are 'substantial grounds' for contending that the decision is invalid or ought to quashed. Secondly, the applicant must establish that he or she has a 'substantial interest' in the matter which is the subject matter of the application. Thirdly, the applicant must either have participated in the planning process, or have shown to the satisfaction of the High Court, that there were good and sufficient reasons for not making objections, submissions or observations. There is an exception to the third requirement in the case of prescribed bodies, a member state of the European Community, or a State which is a party to the Trans-Boundary Convention.

11.6.14 GROUNDS FOR JUDICIAL REVIEW

The most common grounds for judicial review are set out below.

11.6.14.1 Unreasonableness/Irrationality

The High Court may grant relief by way of judicial review where a planning authority or the Board acts outside its jurisdiction. The role of the court is not an appeal against the decision but a review of the way the decision was made. The courts will not interfere with the planning decision unless it is so unreasonable that a reasonable local authority would not make it. The Supreme Court decision in *O'Keefe v An Bord Pleanala* [1993] ILRM 237 provided that the planning authority is allowed to accept the weaker of two cases before it and that the court will not intervene in that decision unless there was no evidence before it to reach that decision.

The Supreme Court held that the legislation has unequivocally and firmly placed questions of planning, of the balance between development and the environment, and the proper convenience and amenities of an area within the jurisdiction of the planning authorities and the Board which are expected to have the skill, competence and experience in planning questions. The court is not vested with that jurisdiction, nor is it expected to, nor can it, exercise discretion in relation to planning matters.

The court will not intervene even if it would have reached a different conclusion on the facts presented. Essentially, to claim unreasonableness, the decision must be fundamentally at variance with common sense and be indefensible against plain reason.

Relying on this ground the applicant must establish in evidence all the material that was before the Board when it was making its decision.

11.6.14.2 Breach of natural justice

If the principles of natural justice have been disregarded, then the courts may interfere with the decision. In *Killiney and Ballybrack Development Association v Minister of Local*

Government (1974) 112 ILTR 9, an inspector based his report in part on matters observed at an inspection carried out after the oral hearing which the parties did not have an opportunity to comment on. This decision was set aside.

11.6.14.3 Error on the face of the record

Error on the face of the record may be a ground for judicial review but only if the error disregards the principles of natural justice. An error on the face of the record such as an incorrect site notice may be grounds for judicial review. In *Cunningham v An Bord Pleanala*, 3 May 1990 (unreported), Lavin J held that the newspaper notice was defective in a way that could not be considered trivial or insubstantial.

11.6.14.4 Non-compliance with the planning regulations

Planning permission must be sought in accordance with legislation and in particular the 2001 Regulations. A failure to comply with the regulations may be a ground for judicial review.

11.6.14.5 Time limits

The High Court in determining an application shall act as expeditiously as possible consistent with the administration of justice. The Supreme Court shall act as expeditiously as possible consistent with the administration of justice in determining any appeal in respect of a determination by the High Court of any application referred to above. Section 55(a) provides that the Rules of Court may make provision for the expeditious hearing of an application to the High Court for judicial review.

11.6.14.6 Judicial review from a conveyancing perspective

While it is true that it would be very unusual for a requisition to be raised in relation to judicial review, it could happen. Thus, where a contract is subject to planning, a careful conveyancer should perhaps consider inserting a special condition to the effect that the closing should be postponed until the final decision of the court has been granted by order of the court. Of course, such a condition would make a vendor very unhappy, but from a purchaser's point of view, it could in certain circumstances be vital.

11.7   Enforcement

The remedies available to the local authority (and in some instances to third parties) under the Planning Code are set out below.

It should be noted that the time limits set out below run not only from grants of permission but also from grants of retention permission.

11.7.1   ENFORCEMENT PROCEDURE UNDER THE 2000 ACT

Part VIII of the Planning and Development Act, 2000, comprising ss 151–164 inclusive, has completely changed the enforcement procedures under the 1963 Act (ss 31, 32, 33, 35 and 36). The enforcement of planning control in the 1963 Act was virtually ineffective. Sections 26 and 27 of the 1976 Act and ss 19 and 20 of the 1992 Act were introduced to make planning control more effective, and to a certain degree, this did occur. As conveyancers will not only be dealing with enforcement procedures under the new Act,

'Time Limits for Enforcement Procedures' under the old system as well as the new are given below at **11.7.6**. The structure of the planning enforcement system remains the same in that it is still substantially based on the enforcement notice and the planning injunction.

However, the 2000 Act has introduced a much more streamlined enforcement regime. There are three enforcement mechanisms:

(a) criminal prosecution;

(b) the enforcement notice procedure; and

(c) the planning injunction.

11.7.2 CRIMINAL PROSECUTION

Section 151 (previously s 24 of the 1963 Act as amended) states 'a person who has carried out, or is carrying out, unauthorised development is guilty of an offence'. Sections 156–159 deal with penalties, provisions for prosecution of offences, and the fact that fines imposed are payable to the planning authority. A person convicted of an offence may be ordered to pay the costs of the planning authority in the investigation of the offence, and in the case of the planning injunction, provision is made that the costs may be awarded to either the planning authority or to the person making the application (see s 156).

11.7.3 THE ENFORCEMENT NOTICE PROCEDURE

11.7.3.1 Section 152—warning letter

The warning letter is generally the first part of the enforcement procedure; however, this is not so in all cases. Where representation is made in writing to a planning authority by a person that unauthorised development may have been, is being, or may be carried out, and it appears to the planning authority that the representation is not vexatious or without substance or foundation or it otherwise appears to the authority that unauthorised development, may have been, or is being carried out, then the planning authority shall issue a warning letter to the owner, occupier, or other person carrying out the development, and may give a copy at that time or thereafter to any other person, who in its opinion may be concerned with the matters to which the letter relates. Note, once the local authority reaches a decision that a letter written by a member of the public is well founded, it does not have any discretion, but must issue a warning letter, unless it considers it a matter of a trivial nature. Under sub-s (3) the planning authority shall do so as soon as may be but not later than six weeks after receipt of the representation. However, failure to issue a warning letter will not prejudice the issue of an enforcement notice, or any other decision to take an enforcement action. The warning letter shall contain the information as set out at s 152(4). This is a new procedure not previously provided for in the planning legislation.

11.7.3.2 Section 153—decision on enforcement

This provides for one type of enforcement notice for all types of unauthorised development, not the five notices and warning notices set out under previous legislation. This is a new section, which provides that the planning authority shall investigate subsequent to the issue of a warning letter, and shall make a decision as to whether or not to serve an enforcement notice, and shall include the reasons for the decision in the planning register entry (unfortunately, the time period for this is defined as 'as soon as may be'). Because there is not a time limit put in place between the issue of a warning letter and the completion of the investigations which the planning authority considers necessary, it effectively gives absolute discretion to the planning authority as to whether or not to issue an enforcement notice.

11.7.3.3 Section 154—the enforcement notice

Subsection (3)(a) no longer makes it compulsory to serve the notice on the owner and occupier of the relevant lands as was previously the case (see also sub-s (13)). It may now be served on any other person who in the opinion of the planning authority may be concerned with the matters to which the notice relates.

Subsection (4) is a new provision which states that the enforcement notice takes effect as and from the date of service thereof.

Subsection (5) deals with the contents of an enforcement notice.

Subsection (12) states that an enforcement notice shall have effect for ten years from the date of its service.

Subsection (13) states that the validity of an enforcement notice cannot be questioned by reason only that the person or other persons not being the person served with the enforcement notice was not notified of the service of the enforcement notice.

11.7.3.4 Section 155—issue of enforcement notice in cases of emergency

The procedures for issuing an enforcement notice in normal circumstances, as can be seen from above, are detailed and elaborate, presumably in the hope that if a problem exists it can be dealt with at an early stage and that the complainant is kept fully aware of all decisions being made. Here however, if the local authority is of the opinion that the situation is urgent it can serve an enforcement notice without the need for a warning letter.

11.7.3.5 Section 156—penalties for offences/onus of proof and defences

Rather unusually, given the frequency with which the amounts and the terms of the years to be served are changed, these are dealt with here and not in the regulations. The maximum penalty for conviction on indictment for offences under ss 58(4), 63, 151, 154, 205, 230(3), 239, and 274 is ten million pounds, and/or two years' imprisonment.

Subsection (2) provides increased penalties for continuing offences.

Subsection (6) reverses the onus of proof of prosecutions for an offence under ss 151 and 154. The presumption that the subject matter of prosecution was development and was not exempted development can only be rebutted where the contrary is shown by the defendant. It is not a defence that a person has applied for, or has been granted permission for retention of an unauthorised development since the initiation of the enforcement proceedings, the date of sending of a warning letter, or the date of service of an enforcement notice in a case of emergency. Under s 156(7) it is a defence to a prosecution under s 151 or 152 where the defendant can show that he took all reasonable steps to secure compliance with an enforcement notice under s 154 above.

11.7.3.6 Section 157—prosecution of offences/time limits

This section provides that a planning authority may take summary proceedings for offences created under the Act whether or not the offence was committed in its area. Offences under ss 147 and 148 (declaration by members of the Board of certain interests and requirements affecting members of the Board who have certain beneficial interests) cannot be instituted except with the consent of the Director of Public Prosecutions.

In particular note sub-s (4)(a)(1) which increases the five-year time limit previously introduced by s 19 of the 1992 Act with a seven-year limit. For a discussion on the problems with the five/seven-year limit, see Planning Requisitions below at **11.8.2**.

11.7.4   SECTION 160—PLANNING INJUNCTIONS

Section 160 restates with some amendments s 27 of the 1976 Act. There are some differences. Most importantly, s 160 allows an application to be made for an injunction where 'an unauthorised development has been, is being, or *is likely to be* carried out or continued'. This therefore, allows the court to grant an injunction not just to past and present unauthorised development, but also to potential unauthorised development. Thus, it allows the court to grant quia timet relief in circumstances which the Supreme Court decided were not permissible in *Mahon v Butler* [1997] 3 IR 369. An application for a planning injunction may be made by a planning authority or any other person, whether or not that person has an interest in land. The granting of a planning injunction is entirely at the discretion of the court. Subsection (2) is new in that it allows the court to make positive orders for the carrying out of works. Subsection (5) (a)–(d) now allows relief to be sought from the High Court or the Circuit Court where the rateable valuation of the land, the subject of the application, does not exceed two hundred pounds, or is so determined by the Circuit Court. Subsection (6)(a)(1) and (2) states that the relevant period is now seven years instead of five as prescribed by s 27 of the 1976 Act as inserted by s 19 of the 1992 Act. However, this does not apply where the development concerns the ongoing use of land, and this provision is new. Section 161 deals with costs of applications for injunctions and prosecutions. It allows for fines to be paid to the planning authority, and provides for costs and expenses as incurred by the planning authority in investigating and prosecuting the matter to be paid to it also. This is consistent with the 'polluter pays' principle, and is mirrored in s 159 above.

Section 162 is new. It provides that in any proceedings for an offence under this Act, the onus for proving the existence of any permission granted under Part III shall be on the defendant.

Finally, in relation to enforcement it should be noted that any development required to be carried out on foot of an enforcement notice, or an order under s 60 (see above) does not require planning permission. This provision was omitted in relation to development carried out pursuant to an order under s 27 of the 1976 Act.

11.7.5   ENFORCEMENT FROM A CONVEYANCING PERSPECTIVE

One of the most important questions which the above raises for conveyancers is whether a purchaser's solicitor can be happy with the fact that an unauthorised development was completed either in the case where no planning permission existed more than seven years since the works first commenced, or where the planning permission was granted seven years after the expiration of the life of the planning permission (see **11.12.3** below), being five years or such extended time as allowed by the planning authority, or under s 42 of the 2000 Act. The problems with doing so are listed below at **11.8.2.15**. Unlike the bye-law amnesty discussed at **11.9.1.** below, there is no full planning amnesty although unauthorised developments are immune from general enforcement proceedings under planning legislation after seven years or seven years from the expiration of the planning permission. Subject to some exceptions (previously five years) those unauthorised developments remain unauthorised developments, and from that fact stem serious disadvantages (see below).

11.7.6 TIME LIMITS FOR ENFORCEMENT PROCEDURES PRE-2000 ACT

Nature of Breach of Planning Code	Enforcement Procedure	Legislation	Time Limits
No permission obtained	enforcement notice	1963 Act, s 31	5 years from date the development is carried out
No permission obtained	planning injunction	1976 Act, s 27 (replaced by 1992 Act, s 19(4)(g))	5 years from day the development is substantially completed
Development being or likely to be carried out without permission or in breach of permission	warning notice	1976 Act, s 26	Does not apply once the development is completed
Fear of removal of a tree, feature or other thing the preservation of which is required by a condition in a permission	warning notice	1976 Act, s 26	no time limit
Development not carried out in conformity	enforcement notice	1963 Act, s 35; 1992 Act, s 19(2)	5 years from expiration of life of permission (usually 5 years)
Non-compliance with a permission or a condition therein	planning injunction	1976 Act, s 27 (replaced by 1963 Act, s 31)	5 years from the expiration of the life of the permission (usually 5 years)
Non-compliance with a condition in a permission within time limit specified therein	enforcement notice	1963 Act, s 31	5 years from the date specified in the permission
Non-compliance with a condition in a retention permission within time limit specified therein	enforcement notice	1963 Act, s 32	5 years from the date specified in the permission
Non-compliance with a condition in a permission which does not specify a date for compliance	enforcement notice	1963 Act s 31; 1992 Act, s 19(1)(a)	5 years from date for completion specified in a 'latest date' notice which must be served within life of permission (usually 5 years)
Non-compliance with a condition in a retention permission which does not specify a date for compliance	enforcement notice	1963 Act, s 31; 1992 Act, s 19(i1)(a)	5 years from date for completion specified in a 'latest date' notice which must be served within 5 years from date of retention permission

(continued)

Nature of Breach of Planning Code	Enforcement Procedure	Legislation	Time Limits
Non-compliance with a condition in a retention permission which does not specify a date for compliance	enforcement notice	1963 Act, s 32; 1992 Act, s 19(a)	5 years from date specified in a 'latest date' notice which must be served within 5 years from date of retention permission
Unauthorised use	warning notice	1976 Act, s 26; 1992 Act, s 19(4)	5 years from day on which unauthorised use first commenced
Unauthorised use	planning injunction	1976 Act, s 27 (replaced by 1992 Act, s 19(4))	5 years from day the unauthorised use first commenced. Ten years from the date of service

11.8   Planning Requisitions

11.8.1   INTRODUCTION

Planning requisitions on title have traditionally been raised post-contract. However, there was always a practice among solicitors, when dealing with commercial property, to raise planning requisitions on title pre-contract. This practice is increasingly followed in all conveyancing transactions, particularly in townhouse and apartment developments, and was recommended by John Gore-Grimes in a CLE lecture on the 1996 edition (revised) of the Law Society's Requisitions on Title. When acting for a purchaser he recommends that pre-contract planning requisitions be sent to the vendor's solicitors to include the standard form of Requisitions on Title dealing with planning, Building Control Acts, Fire Services Act, environmental matters and multi-storey buildings. Where a solicitor is acting for a vendor it is important to ensure that these requisitions on title are answered before the contract is prepared, preferably by sending them in duplicate to the vendor client and having him or her respond to same in writing and returned. It is always best to anticipate planning problems and try to solve them before entering into a contract.

Requisition 27 relates to planning and there is a provision at the beginning of the Requisitions on Title whereby any reference to any Act shall include any extension, amendment, modification or re-enactment thereof and any regulation, order, instrument made thereunder and for the time being in force. Thus, there is no need for the full citation of the Planning Acts.

11.8.2   PLANNING REQUISITIONS

The 2001 Law Society Objections and Requisitions on title were issued subsequent to the coming into force of the 2000 Act (see **Appendix 15.1**). However, the requisitions in relation to planning were not updated, hence the questions (sometimes appropriately, sometimes not) refer to the 1963 Act and subsequent legislation under same. Therefore, the comments below in relation to the requisitions must of necessity refer to the older legislation. However, references will also be made to the 2000 Act and the 2001 Regulations where appropriate.

11.8.2.1 Development requisition 27.1

Requisition 27.1 states:

> 'Has there been in relation to the property any development (including change of use or exempted development) within the meaning of the Planning Act on or after the 1st October 1964.'

The purpose of this requisition is to establish whether the premises were developed pursuant to planning permission since 1 October 1964 or whether the premises were built prior to that date. Given the length of time and wide meaning of the word 'development' in the Planning Acts, in the majority of cases, there has been substantial development. It is, of course possible, and it will be clear from the title documents when a building was constructed prior to 1 October 1964. In such a case it is likely that the building was erected on foot of the Town and Regional Planning Acts, which precede the current Planning Code. Generally, the planning documentation in such a case would be retained with the title deeds, but it is not required to have evidence of compliance by way of an architect's certificate (see general condition 36 of the Law Society's General Conditions of Sale). Even where it is clear from the title that the premises were built many years prior to 1 October 1964, this requisition must still be raised. It is possible that further development has taken place by way of addition, alteration, change of use or demolition since 1 October 1964.

It is important that a purchaser's solicitor checks the permissions against the planning search obtained prior to contract to ensure that nothing shows up on the search which has not been furnished. It is also important to check the reference numbers on the permission or the grant of permission or on the building bye-law approval to ensure that these numbers are the same as the numbers referred to in the architect's certificate/opinion. Care should be taken in checking conditions precedent in a planning permission to ensure that they have been complied with before the development commences.

In many situations, such as sales by liquidators or personal representatives who have no knowledge of the property, this requisition will be precluded by contract.

Alternatively the planning warranty will apply.

11.8.2.2 Grant of planning permission: requisition 27.2.a

Requisition 27.2 provides:

> 'In respect of all such developments furnish now (where applicable):
> (a)   Grant of Planning Permission'.

Requisition 27.2.a requires a vendor to furnish copies of all relevant planning permission obtained since 1 October 1964, unless the contract special conditions provide to the contrary. The purchaser must ensure that he or she receives a copy of the grant of permission and not a decision to a grant which may subsequently have been appealed.

11.8.2.3 Outline planning permission and grant of approval: requisition 27.2.b

Where a grant of approval has issued on foot of an outline planning permission it is necessary to obtain both the outline permission and the grant of approval. The outline permission may contain conditions which were not carried through in the grant of approval, but which nevertheless apply and must be complied with. Further, the life of the planning permission is calculated from the date of grant of the outline permission not from the date of grant of approval. Since the 2000 Act, grants of approval no longer issue, the appropriate grant issuing subsequent to an outline permission is now termed a grant of permission.

11.8.2.4 Building bye-law approval: requisition 27.2.c

Building bye-laws are no longer relevant in respect of works completed before 13 December 1989, provided the local authority did not serve a notice in relation to any such works before 1 December 1992. If no copy of the building bye-law approval is available, a purchaser should be prepared to accept a statutory declaration confirming that the works were carried out before 13 December 1989 and as such are deemed to comply with building bye-laws by virtue of the Building Control Act 1990, s 22(7). The declaration must also state that no notice was served before 1 December 1992. Note, however, that special condition 36(b) of the General Conditions of Sale does require the vendor to furnish a copy of such bye-law approval so that, if it is not available, the position should have been covered by the vendor in the special conditions of the contract. Building bye-laws still apply to works carried out after 13 December 1989 and before 1 June 1992.

11.8.2.5 Evidence of compliance with the financial conditions: requisition 27.2.d

The usual means of establishing compliance with financial conditions is by the production of a letter from the local authority confirming that the sum required has been paid or that the appropriate bond is in place. However, under the 2001 edition of the Law Society General Conditions of Sale a vendor may instead produce formal confirmation from the local authority that the roads and services have been taken in charge. This is acceptable as evidence in lieu of receipts for financial contributions and/or the lodgement of bonds.

Where financial conditions fall due for payment on a phased basis, a purchaser is only concerned to ensure that the payment has been paid up to the date when the house was first sold by the developer (see Practice Note, Law Society Gazette, April 1987).

11.8.2.6 Certificate or opinion from an architect or engineer: requisition 27.2.e

It is necessary to furnish a certificate/opinion from an architect or engineer stating that the permission/approval relates to the property and that development has been carried out in conformity with the permission/approval and with the building bye-law approval (if applicable) and that all conditions other than financial conditions have been complied with.

The vendor will have contracted to give this certificate unless the general conditions of the contract have been varied by special condition. The Law Society has approved the format of certificates of compliance (see Law Society Gazette, March 1995). These certificates also contain provisions for exemptions and exceptions and these must be carefully checked and, if found, must be notified to the client. If the exemptions and exceptions are fundamental it is necessary, where a solicitor is also acting for a lending institution and certifying title, to qualify the certificate of title by drawing the lender's attention to the specific exemptions or exceptions referred to in the architect's certificate.

The General Conditions of Sale do not define 'architect' or 'engineer'. The purchaser should establish, in an appropriate case by pre-contract enquiry, the qualifications of the architect or engineer who will give the certificate or should seek a condition in the contract for sale that the certificate to be given will be made by a person whose qualifications are recognised in accordance with Law Society recommendations and that the architect's certificate will be in a format approved by the Law Society (see Law Society Gazette, November 1994). Note, however, that the Law Society recommends that it is unreasonable for solicitors to insist on being furnished with documentation which it was not the practice to furnish at that time. It appears that the practice of furnishing architect's/engineer's certificates/opinions or declarations of compliance became general conveyancing practice in or about the year 1970. The Law Society now recommends that solicitors should only insist on such certificates or declarations on dwellinghouses built since 1 January 1975. Certificates are not required in relation to the original construction of a dwellinghouse built before 1 January 1975. The exemption does not apply to any extensions to dwellinghouses or commercial properties. In other words in any other circumstances, a certificate is required as usual. However, in such a case a special condition must appear in the contract, varying general condition 36.

11.8.2.7 Exempted developments: requisition 27.2.f

'In respect of exempted developments in each case state the grounds upon which it is claimed that the development is an exempted development and furnish a certificate/opinion from an Architect/Engineer in support of such claim.'

It has long been the practice to produce a certificate to confirm that a development was exempt. However, this requisition was only introduced in the 1996 edition of the Law Society Requisitions on Title. Even if it appears at first sight that works are exempt, a careful purchaser should seek such a certificate. This is because virtually every exemption has limitations placed on it; for example, it may be immediately obvious that an extension to a dwelling is less than 40 square metres, but it is not so obvious that the height restriction set out in the 2001 Regulations (class 1, limitation (4)(c)) is complied with or, indeed, that the area of open space in the rear garden has not been reduced below 25 square metres (class 1, limitation (5)). Even where all of the conditions placed on the exemptions have been met, it is necessary to consider the general restrictions on exemptions in the 2001 Regulations, art 9.

The Second Schedule, Part I, of the 2001 Regulations as amended, lists the classes of exemptions with limitations attached and it is very important to look at the definitions contained in art 6, and the restrictions in art 10 when dealing with changes of use. This is really an area beyond the solicitor's field of expertise and it is why it is essential to obtain an architect's certificate of compliance in relation to same.

This is a requisition which must be raised because a planning search will not disclose any information in relation to exempted developments. Further, replies to this requisition should be very carefully made. It is eminently possible, given that the planning history of the premises may go back to 1 October 1964, that the client will not know the planning history of the premises. The solicitor is further handicapped in the giving of his or her replies due to the present inadequacies of the Planning Register, ie searches will not in many cases reveal everything that has occurred. The best method of protection is to adopt the procedures as laid out by John Gore-Grimes in his CLE lecture 'Essential Conveyancing for Practitioners' Lecture 5, p 18, dated July 2001. These procedures are as follows:

(a) make a planning search before allowing a purchaser to sign a purchase contract or before preparing a sale contract for a vendor;

(b) show that search to the client and ask for explanations for any acts appearing thereon;

(c) send out to the client a pre-contract questionnaire along the lines of that attached to the 2001 Contract for Sale issued by the Law Society, expanding where necessary on the planning queries;

(d) carefully check the contract to see if there are any planning exclusions, or whether the planning warranty at condition 36 has been excluded altogether. In such case it will invariably be essential to employ an architect/engineer to examine the house and to examine the planning file in order to report fully;

(e) on all occasions when acting for a purchaser send out before exchange of contract pre-contract requisitions relating to planning and environmental matters;

(f) where there is even the smallest planning defect, and the solicitor is acting for a lending institution as well as for the purchaser, list the defect in the certificate of title.

11.8.2.8   Developments completed after 1 November 1976: requisition 27.3

Requisition 27.3 provides:

> 'In respect of developments completed after the 1st November 1976 furnish now evidence by way of Statutory Declaration of a competent person that each development was completed prior to expiration of the Permission/Approval.'

The provisions of the Local Government (Planning and Development) Act, 1982, s 2(2)(v) set down time limits within which the development must be substantially completed (under the 2000 Act, s 40 is the relevant section). This requisition on title seeks confirmation that the development was completed within the life of the planning permission. Frequently this may be established from the title documents; for example, if there was a lease or conveyance with a building covenant and a certificate of compliance endorsed thereon. In addition, the architect's certificate of compliance should be dated and would have been given upon completion of the property.

Where the planning permission has expired (and no extension has been obtained under the 1982 Act, s 4, see also arts 40/41 of the 2001 Regulations, and s 42 of the 2000 Act) and it is not clear from the title documents when a development was substantially completed, then a purchaser will seek a statutory declaration to confirm that the development was completed within the life of the permission.

If the development is not completed within the time limit it is an unauthorised structure and, consequently, the requisition is of importance. Note that this requisition is, as indicated, only relevant as and from 1 November 1976.

11.8.2.9   Special amenity areas: requisition 27.4.a

Under requisition 27.4 if the property is subject to:

> 'a.   Any Special Amenity Area Preservation Conservation or any other order under the Planning Acts which affects the property or any part thereof',

it is a matter for the purchaser to satisfy himself or herself on these matters by inspection of the Planning Register. This requisition is a very good reason why a planning search should be made by a vendor's solicitor pre-contract. A vendor might very well forget that years ago the façade of the dwelling in sale was the subject of a preservation order. Under the Planning Acts, where such orders are made, the local authority is required to register them in the Planning Register established under the 1963 Act, s 8 (s 7 of the 2000 Act) save for the special amenity areas order. A search in the Planning Register will not reveal if a special amenity order has been made under the 1963 Act, s 42(1) as amended by the 1976 Act, s 40(a), and Part XIII of the 2000 Act. A special enquiry therefore will have to be made of the vendor and, if acting for a purchaser, a special enquiry will have to be made to the local authority by letter to ascertain if a special amenity order is in existence. Under condition 35(b) of the Contract for Sale a vendor is not required to furnish details of the contents of the development plan other than actual or proposed designation for compulsory acquisition and the onus is on the purchaser to carry out a Planning Office search before entering into the contract. Accordingly, frequently the answer to this requisition is 'this is a matter for the purchaser'.

However, where a notice has been served on the vendor or is otherwise known to the vendor, not being a notice in relation to the contents of the development plan, the vendor is obliged to furnish details (see general condition 35).

11.8.2.10 Compulsory purchase or acquisition: requisition 27.4.b

Under requisition 27.4.b it is necessary to ascertain whether the property is subject to:

> 'Any actual or proposed designation of all or any of the property whereby it would become liable to compulsory purchase or acquisition for any purpose under the Planning Acts.'

Under general condition 35(b) of the 2001 edition of the Contract for Sale, if a compulsory purchase order has been made, then the vendor is obliged to put the purchaser on notice. Not to do so would be a fundamental breach. Thus, to fully reply to this requisition it is necessary for the vendor or the vendor's solicitor to consult the development plan and to see if any designation exists. The purpose of the enquiry is not limited to actual or proposed designations for compulsory purchase under the development plan, but presumably also extends to such things as acquisition of public or open space in circumstances envisaged in the 1976 Act, s 25, compulsory dedication of public rights of way as envisaged under the 1963 Act, s 48, and any other sections under the Planning Acts which lead to compulsory purchase or acquisition (or indeed under the 2000 Act). If the local authority has decided to act either under the 1976 Act, s 25 or the 1963 Act, s 48, it is bound to enter such decisions in the planning authority's register and these matters should be discoverable by search. Thus, a prudent purchaser will make his or her own searches prior to contract to confirm whether any such compulsory purchase order has been made or is being considered.

11.8.2.11 Unauthorised development: requisition 27.5

Under requisition it is necessary to ascertain whether there is any unauthorised development as defined in the Planning Acts.

Section 2 of the 2000 Act defines 'unauthorised structure'. That definition is difficult and refers back to permissions granted under the Town and Regional Planning Act, 1934. For conveyancing purposes an unauthorised structure may be taken as being any structure erected after 1 October 1964, which was not built on foot of and in accordance with a planning permission obtained under the current Planning Code and which is not an exempt development.

11.8.2.12 Retention permission: requisition 27.6.a

If there is any such unauthorised development it is necessary to furnish prior to closing:

'A retention permission for such development'.
If there is an unauthorised structure and there is no qualification of general condition 36 of the Contract for Sale, then the vendor is in breach of that warranty and is open to an action for breach of contract by the purchaser. It is likely to prove extremely difficult to complete the sale of the property until such time as that matter is resolved. The purchaser may be prepared to agree that the vendor make an application for retention permission but if that retention permission issues subject to conditions which adversely affect the value of the property then the purchaser would be entitled to compensation (or to rescind). The purchaser is under no obligation to wait until such time as retention permission issues (which usually takes a minimum period of three months, but realistically is more like six) and could serve an appropriate notice under general condition 40 of the Contract for Sale thereby rescinding the contract or, in the alternative, might pursue an action against the vendor for breach of contractual warranty.

11.8.2.13 Evidence of compliance with retention permission: requisition 27.6.b

In the event of unauthorised development it is also necessary to furnish satisfactory evidence of compliance from an architect/engineer with the conditions in the said retention permission.

Where a retention permission is sought and granted it is still essential to have a confirmation from an architect/engineer that the drawings submitted on the application for a retention permission correctly show the development as built and that the conditions of the retention permission have been complied with. This, of course, would not be required where the retention relates only to a change of use and there were no conditions attached (see **11.11.7** below).

11.8.2.14 Evidence that development complies with bye-laws: requisition 27.6.c

If applicable, satisfactory evidence from an architect/engineer that the development substantially complies with the bye-laws or with the regulations made under the Building Control Act, 1990 should also be provided.

Building bye-laws would only be relevant in the areas where building bye-laws apply. See the comments under requisition 27.2(c) above at **11.8.2.4**. The opinion of compliance with the building regulations should be in the Law Society approved format.

Section 19 of the 1992 Act gives some comfort in that the planning authority has a five-year period to use certain enforcement procedures against an unauthorised development. Section 19 of the 1992 Act also provides that a warning notice in relation to any unauthorised use of the land shall not be served after the expiration of a period of five years beginning on the date from which such unauthorised use first commenced (now Part VIII of the 2000 Act, s 157(4)(a)(i) has increased this period to seven years).

However, there is a time limit for s 24 prosecutions under the 2000 Act. While s 19 (s 157(2)(a) of the 2000 Act) gives certain comfort to conveyancers it does not make the unauthorised development authorised and there are certain disadvantages.

11.8.2.15 Disadvantages/problems of relying on the 'five-/seven-year rule'

The disadvantages/problems may be summarised as follows:

(a) In the event of subsequent compulsory acquisition unauthorised developments thereof may not attract compensation.

(b) There is an almost automatic entitlement to compensation under the planning legislation in circumstances where premises have been destroyed by fire and for some reason planning permission to rebuild is refused. However, this is only the case where the premises were, in the first instance, authorised by grant of planning permission.

(c) In certain instances water connections may be refused where the development requiring same is unauthorised (see s 259 of the 2000 Act).

(d) In a situation where an original development was an unauthorised development it may be difficult to obtain a permission for further development or redevelopment of that property.

(e) A development which would otherwise be an exempted development will not be such if same would consist of or comprise the extension, alteration, repair or renewal of an unauthorised structure or a structure, the use of which is an unauthorised use (see 1994 Regulations, art 10(1)(a)(viii)) (see art 9(1)(a)(viii) of the 2001 Regulations).

(f) Most important is the problem experienced by banks and building societies when they are told that the property (or perhaps a part of it which represents a significant part of the purchase price) is a non-conforming development. Many such institutions do not permit any qualification to their certificate of title unless first agreed with them and such agreement may in fact be difficult to obtain and, if agreed, must be in writing. Thus, if a purchaser signs a contract which includes a clause disclosing an unauthorised development more than five years old and relies on the 1992 Act, s 19 (s 157(4)(a)(i) of the 2000 Act) a purchaser's solicitor should, prior to the execution of contract, confirm that the lending institution will accept a qualification on the certificate of title.

(g) Under s 246, the Minister has the power to make regulations for additional fees to be paid to the planning authority. These include fees for the making of submissions or observations in respect of planning permissions, fees for requests and declarations under s 5, fees for the granting of licences or certificates under ss 231, 239, and 254, but most importantly in this instance, the Minister may prescribe that a fee payable to the authority for an application for retention permission shall be in an amount which shall be related to the estimated cost of the unauthorised development, or the unauthorised part thereof as the case may be. This means that the regulations may provide for fees for retention permission to be set at a percentage of the estimated cost of the development, and the memorandum accompanying the Bill of 1999 gives as an example '10% of the cost' of constructing a building. This is a particularly self-defeating provision, because it is after all in the interests of the planning system as a whole that a retention permission should be encouraged rather than discouraged, unless of course, the authority is dealing with a developer who has deliberately created an unauthorised development hoping that the planning authority as a matter of expediency will issue a retention permission rather than order the removal of the unauthorised development and its reinstatement.

Given the length of time since planning legislation, and the increasing number of properties with 'irregularities' in their planning history, and the above problems with the 1992 Act, s 19 (s 157 of the 2000 Act) it is clear that it is more than time for an introduction of a full amnesty on planning matters similar to the building bye-laws amnesty introduced by the Building Control Act 1990, s 22(7).

11.8.2.16 Present use of property: requisition 27.7

The purpose of requisition 27.7 is to establish whether the current use or uses are authorised. Obviously, this is a matter of fact in each case. A vendor's solicitor should ensure that he or she gets full instructions in relation to current uses, particularly where there is more than one. In a private dwellinghouse it may be that part of the property was used as a dentist's surgery or in a commercial building there may be a number of uses and the purchaser will require to know what is the prime use and what ancillary uses apply.

11.8.2.17 Use since 1 October 1964: requisition 27.8

Requisition 27.8 asks whether the property has been used for each of the uses in requisition 27.7 without material change continuously since 1 October 1964.

If the answer to this requisition is 'no' then there has been a development within the meaning of the Planning Acts and the purchaser will be required to produce the appropriate planning permission. Obviously, if no planning permission has been obtained then see requisition 27.5 (at **11.8.2.11** above), and the only means of rectifying the position would be to discontinue the unauthorised use or obtain permission for continuance of such use. It is wise in such circumstances to consider the principles of intensification of user and the abandonment of use. Consider also that the change of use may comprise an exempt development under the 1994 Regulations (now the 2001 Regulations) in which case it is not 'unauthorised use' within the meaning of the 1963 Act, s 2 (now s 2 of the 2000 Act) and accordingly might be said not to be 'a material change'.

11.8.2.18 Applications under Planning Acts and building bye-laws: requisition 27.9

'Give particulars of any application for permission and/or approval under the Planning Acts and the Building Bye-Laws and state the result thereof.'

While requisition 27.9 could cover the permissions as referred to at **11.8.2.2** to **11.8.2.3** above, its real purpose is to obtain details of any applications for planning permission where no decision to grant permission has issued or has been refunded or a permission granted has not been acted upon. The purchaser seeks information in relation to any such application or permission. These may have some use to the purchaser if they are still within their time limit, but if in the ordinary case the permissions have not been acted upon and are more than five years old they may be ignored. The requisition also requests the vendor to produce notification of refusal. This could be of importance to a purchaser who, for example, wished to have a residential property changed into a play school, and in those circumstances where the planning file already discloses a refusal for such change of use.

As building bye-laws have been replaced by the Building Control Act, 1990 and the regulations thereunder, they are only relevant in this context if building bye-law approval was obtained, issued on foot of an application lodged with the local authority prior to 1 June 1992. There is no time limit within which works must be completed on foot of a building bye-law approval.

11.8.2.19 Agreements with planning authority: requisition 27.10

Requisition 27.10 states:

'a.   Has any agreement been entered into with the Planning Authority pursuant to Section 38 of the 1963 Act [now s 47 of the 2000 Act] restricting or regulating the development or use of the property.

b.   If so furnish now copy of same.'

Section 38 of the 1963 Act is one of those matters which will be disclosed in the local authority Planning Register. Sterilisation agreements may be made under the provisions of the 1963 Act, s 38, as extended by the 1976 Act, s 39 restricting or regulating the development or use of property. The point about s 38 is that it is drafted in such a way that it is intended that these sterilisation agreements may be enforced against successors in title. In this way, they are akin to restrictive covenants. They normally arise in a situation where the planning authority is prepared to grant permission for the development of one part of the landowner's holding on condition that another portion of his or her holding is sterilised so that there will be no further development of that other portion in the future (exempted or otherwise) without a further planning permission. Clearly, it is vital that a purchaser knows whether the plot of ground he or she is buying has been sterilised in such a manner. Details of any such s 38 agreement must be registered on the Planning Register so that a purchaser who has carried out his planning search should be aware of the situation.

11.8.2.20 Application for compensation: requisition 27.11.a,b

Requisition 27.11 states:

'a.   Has there been any application for or award of compensation under the Planning Acts.

b.   If so furnish now copy of same.'

A purchaser is also concerned to know whether any compensation has been paid by the planning authority by reason of refusal to grant permission. The Local Government (Planning and Development) Act, 1990 provides that where any such compensation is paid, no development may be carried out on the land in question until such time as the compensation is refunded to the local authority (compensation is dealt with under the 2000 Act at Part XII, in relation to the above requisition, s 190).

11.8.2.21 Registration of statement of compensation: requisition 27.11.c

Requisition 27.11.c asks:

> 'Has a statement of compensation been registered on the Planning Register under Section 9 of the 1990 Planning Act prohibiting development of the property under Section 10 of the said Act' (see s 7(2)(u) of the 2000 Act).

Where compensation is paid, the local authority is required to enter the details on the Planning Register, so that a purchaser who has made his or her enquiries in this regard will be aware of the position before contracts are exchanged. If his or her solicitor knows the purpose for which the client requires the land and that purpose is frustrated by a refusal or by permission which contains onerous conditions, the client must be advised as to what compensation may be claimed and this, of course, will have a very considerable bearing on the purchase price offered, that is if the matter is to proceed at all. A solicitor should never become involved in quantifying the amount of compensation since clearly this is a matter for valuers. Of course, should it have issued prior to contract, general condition 35 of the Contract for Sale applies.

11.8.2.22 Development prior to 13 December 1989: requisition 27.12.a

Requisition 27.12.a provides:

> 'If any development was carried out prior to the 13th of December 1989 and Building Bye-law Approval was either not obtained or not complied with furnish now Declaration that the development was completed prior to the 13th of December 1989 and that no Notice under Section 22 of the Building Control Act 1990 was served by the Building Control Authority between the 1st June 1992 and the 1st of December 1992.'

Requisition 27.12.a is drafted widely enough to capture all works requiring building bye-law approval whether or not they are exempted development. See the comments under requisition 27.2.c at **11.8.2.4** above.

The building control authority could only serve a notice under the Building Control Act, 1990, s 22 where it considers the works constitute a danger to public health or safety. Unfortunately, there is no public register which may be inspected to see whether any such notice was served.

11.8.2.23 Development after 13 December 1989: requisition 27.12.b

Requisition 27.12.b asks:

> 'Has there been any development carried out since the 13th of December 1989 with the benefit of Building Bye-Law Approval. If so furnish now copy of same and draft Engineer's/Architect's Opinion of Compliance.'

A purchaser will require production of a building bye-law approval where the works have been carried out in a building bye-law area between 13 December 1989 and 1 June 1992 or on foot of a bye-law approval applied for prior to 1 June 1992 and will require an architect's certificate of compliance with such building bye-law approval.

When no building bye-law approval has been obtained, a purchaser will require a certificate from an architect to the effect that the works have been carried out in substantial compliance with building bye-laws in force at the date of construction and that had building bye-law approval been applied for, in the view of the architect, it would have been granted. Under the Law Society General Conditions of Sale a purchaser is not required to accept such certificate unless the special conditions so provide, although the fact of accepting such certificate is well established.

11.8.2.24 User of property from 1 October 1964: requisition 27.13

Requisition 27.13 states:

> 'Furnish now Statutory Declaration by a competent person evidencing user of the property from the 1st October 1964 to date.'

In this requisition, the purchaser is asking for a statutory declaration by a competent person evidencing user of property from 1 October 1964 to date. Inevitably the answer is 'vendor declines'. There are immense practical difficulties, particularly as more and more time passes, of obtaining somebody competent to give a declaration which dates back to 1964. However, a purchaser seeking to rely on an established use dating pre-1964, for example, where a house has been divided into a number of residential units, will insist upon appropriate evidence confirming such established use.

11.8.3 BUILDING CONTROL REQUISITIONS

Requisition 28 refers to the Building Control Act, 1990 and any regulations or instrument thereunder (referred to collectively as 'the regulations').

The Building Regulations are a code of practice to ensure that structures/buildings are built according to the best code of practice and that the layout takes best advantage of fire escapes, sound control, ventilation, hygiene, drainage and waste disposals, stairways, ramps and guards, fuel and energy conservation in the interest of health, safety and welfare of the users of these buildings. Whether or not there has been compliance with same is a job for the engineer/architect, not the solicitor.

11.8.3.1 Requisition 28.1

> 'Is the property or any part thereof affected by any of the provisions of the Regulations.'

If any works have been carried out since 1 June 1992, other than on foot of a building bye-law approval application which was made prior to that date, then the answer here is 'yes' unless one of the exemptions applies.

11.8.3.2 Requisition 28.2

> 'If it is claimed that the property is not affected by the Regulations state why. Evidence by way of a Statutory Declaration of a competent person may be required to verify the reply.'

In most cases the answer would be that 'no works have been carried out since 1 June 1992 so that the Building Regulations do not apply'.

Where there is doubt as to when the works were completed, a statutory declaration confirming that the works were completed prior to that date may be sought. Where it is claimed that the works are exempt from any requirement to comply with the regulations, the position may need to be confirmed by declaration or certificate of an appropriate person.

11.8.3.3 Requisition 28.3

> 'If the property is affected by the Regulations furnish now a Certificate/Opinion of Compliance by a competent person confirming that all necessary requirements of the Regulations have been met.'

This certificate should be in a form acceptable to the Law Society, ie the Law Society format or the (RIAI) March 1993 edition (see Law Society Gazette, March 1995).

The building regulations certificate must be signed by a competent person and it should be checked to ensure that there are no reservations or exceptions in it. If there are they will have to be specifically referred to in the certificate of title furnished by the purchaser's solicitor by way of a qualification on title.

11.8.3.4   Requisition 28.4

'a.   Has a Commencement Notice been given to the Building Control Authority in respect of the property.

b.   If so furnish now a copy of the same.'

Where no copy of the commencement notice is available, a purchaser need not be unduly concerned. Failure to obtain a commencement notice is an offence under the 1990 Act. However, a subsequent owner of the property has not committed that offence and the local authority has no power to take action against the property (as opposed to an individual) arising out of the failure to obtain such a commencement notice. However, it is considered good practice to obtain a copy of the commencement notice where it is available.

11.8.3.5   Requisition 28.5.a

'If the property is such that a Fire Safety Certificate is one of the requirements of the Regulations:

a.   A copy of the Fire Safety Certificate must be attached to and referred to in the Certificate of Compliance which should confirm that the works to the property have been carried out in accordance with the drawings and other particulars on foot of which the Fire Safety Certificate was obtained and with any conditions of the Fire Safety Certificate.'

None of the Law Society recommended certificates specifically refers to the conditions attached to a fire safety certificate, but rather certifies that the works have been carried out in general compliance with the Building Regulations. As compliance with the fire safety certificate conditions forms part of the Building Regulations, the Law Society and the RIAI Certificates of Compliance incorporate compliance with any requirements of the fire safety certificate. Where a purchaser is furnished with either the standard Law Society format of certificate or the RIAI version, then same is acceptable.

11.8.3.6   Requisition 28.5.b

'Confirm that no appeal was made by the Applicant for such Certificate against any of the conditions imposed by the Building Control Authority in such Fire Safety Certificate.'

Only the applicant may appeal a decision to issue a fire safety certificate or any conditions attached. If any appeal was lodged it would appear on the register of fire safety certificates maintained by the local authority pursuant to the Building Control Regulations, 1991, art 19.

11.8.3.7   Requisition 28.6

'a.   Has any Enforcement Notice under Section 8 of the Building Control Act 1990 been served.

b.   If so, furnish now a copy of the Notice and a Certificate of Compliance made by a competent person.'

Where works have not been designed or have not been constructed in conformity with the Building Regulations, the building control authority may serve such an enforcement notice. This notice must be served within a period of five years commencing on the date of completion of the works or of material change in the purpose for which the building is used. Obviously, where no works have been carried out and there has been no change of use since 1 June 1992, no such notice can have been served.

11.8.3.8 Requisition 28.7

'If any application has been made to the District Court under Section 9 of the Building Control Act 1990 furnish details of the result of such application.'

Under requisition 28.7, a person on whom an enforcement notice has been served may make an application to annul, modify or alter such interest. No such application may be made unless works have been carried out since 1 June 1992.

11.8.3.9 Requisition 28.8

'a.   Has any application been made to the High Court under Section 12 of Building Control Act 1990.

b.   If so furnish a copy of any Order by the Court and evidence of any necessary compliance with such order by a Certificate of a competent person.'

This is a procedure similar to the 'planning injunction' procedure under the 1976 Act, s 27 (as amended) (see s 160 of the 2000 Act). It allows a building control authority to apply to the High Court for an order requiring the removal, alteration or making safe of any structure, service, fitting or equipment or the discontinuance of any works, or restricting or prohibiting use of a building until the removal, alteration or making safe of any structure, service, fitting or equipment, or the discontinuance of any works as the case may be have been effected. There is no time limit within which such action must be made.

11.8.3.10 Fire Services Act, 1981: requisition 29

Requisition 29 is a pre-contract requisition and any purchaser who buys a premises which is open to the public, or a flat, is liable to have a notice served on him or her by the fire officer and it is often a costly business to comply with the fire officer's requirements. Before purchasing any such property the client should be advised to check with the fire officer to ensure no notices have been served and that no notices are contemplated. However, while this letter should be sent, it is conveyancers' experience that no response is received.
Requisition 29(1) asks:

'a.   Have any Notices been served under the Act.

b.   If so furnish now copies of same.

c.   Are there any proceedings pending under the Act.'

This requisition makes enquiries as to whether any notice has been served or whether any proceedings are pending under the Fire Services Act, 1981, but in reality the information can only be obtained from the vendor client.

11.8.3.11 Requisition 29(2)

'a.   Has the property ever been inspected by the Fire Authority for the functional area within which the property is situate.

b.   If so what were its requirements.'

Requisition 29(2) enquires as to whether the property has been inspected by the fire officer and whether the requirements of the fire officer have been complied with. The requisitions on title also enquire as to whether there are any outstanding requirements of the fire officer which have not been complied with and request the certificate from the fire office authority confirming compliance with any work which the fire officer requires to be done. Obtaining these certificates from the fire officer is a very difficult matter. It is important to serve at least one month's notice on the fire authority, both in respect of the applications for a new licence and for applications for renewals.

There is a misconception that the Fire Services Act, 1981 applies to residential dwellinghouses. The Act does not apply to residential dwellinghouses other than flats and the reply in cases of residential dwellinghouses is always 'not applicable'. Nevertheless, in cases where the Fire Services Act does apply the non-compliance with the fire services notices incurs heavy penalties and possible court proceedings. Under the requisition, apart from asking whether any notices have been served, the vendor is asked to furnish copies of same and to state whether or not proceedings are pending.

11.8.3.12 Environmental: requisition 31

Under the Law Society's Contract for Sale, the purchaser is, pursuant to general condition 16, 'deemed to buy with full notice of the actual state and condition of the subject property'. It should, however, be noted that under general condition 35 a purchaser may seek to rescind the sale if the purchaser is sure that the vendor, prior to the sale, failed to notify the purchaser of a relevant notice or information.

Requisition 31 provides, inter alia:

'1.   Has any notice certificate order requirement or recommendation been served upon or received by the Vendor or has the Vendor notice of any intention to serve any notice relating to the property or any part of it under or by virtue of or pursuant to the European Community Act 1972 by way of the implementation of directives for the control or prevention of pollution or preservation or improvement of the environment or any law relating to the Environment whether Irish Law European Community Law any common or customary law or legislation any order rule regulation directive statutory instrument bye-law or any legislative measure thereunder; ("the Environmental Controls").

2.   Furnish now any notice certificate order requirement or recommendation so received.

3.   Has the same been complied with?'

The vendor is required to confirm that no notice, certificate, order, requirement or recommendation has been served upon him or her or that the vendor has not been notified of any intention to serve such notice etc under the various environmental statutes and regulations listed. If the vendor has been served with copies, these should be furnished to the purchaser, and if notices etc require work to be carried out, this question also must be answered, if necessary with a certificate from a competent person.

Requisition 31.4 asks whether the vendor is aware of any breach of the environmental controls in respect of the property.

Few vendors will be aware in dwellinghouse situations of breach of any environmental controls in respect of their property. If a vendor is aware of such breach he is asked to give full particulars. It should be stressed, however, that this chapter deals with requisitions on title only for residential sale and very different criteria attach to a sale of farmlands, factory lands or industrial premises.

11.8.4 LOCAL GOVERNMENT (MULTI-STOREY BUILDINGS) ACT, 1988: REQUISITION 35

11.8.4.1 Introduction

The Local Government (Multi-Storey Buildings) Act, 1988 (the 1988 Act) came into effect on 14 November 1988 and affects all multi-storey buildings which were not completed on or before 1 January 1950. As defined in the Act, a multi-storey building is a building comprising five or more storeys (and a basement is regarded as a storey). The Act applies to such buildings whether residential, apartments, office blocks, hotels or any other buildings.

From 1 June 1992 the provisions of the 1988 Act ceased to have effect except in cases coming within the transitional provisions of the Building Control Act 1990, s 2(2). Multi-storey buildings started at 1 June 1992 with the benefit of building bye-law approval or, in the event of building bye-law approval not having issued, but the plans for building bye-law approval having been lodged, will require the usual certificates and must comply with the 1988 Act. In the event of planning permission having issued for multi-storey buildings where no building bye-law approval or plans have been lodged, the provisions of the 1988 Act will not apply and the buildings must be erected in accordance with the Building Regulations. If work is commenced on a multi-storey building after 1 June 1992 and before 1 August 1992, no fire safety certificate was required under the Building Regulations.

11.8.4.2 What is a multi-storey building: requisition 35.1

Requisition 35.1 asks:

> 'Is the property or any part of the property a multi storey building within the meaning of the 1988 Act or does it form part of a development in which there is a multi storey building with which it shares a common Management Company.'

Requisition 35.1, which asks whether the property in sale is a multi-storey building (ie a five-storey building, including basement, with which it shares a common management company built since 1 June 1950) appears quite simple. However, what is a factual question has caused problems in that difficulties have arisen on the definition of what is and what is not a storey. Where any dispute arises counsel's opinion should be sought.

11.8.4.3 Regulation of multi-storey building: requisition 35.2

If the building is a multi-storey building, is it governed by: (a) the regulations as defined in requisition 28, or (b) the 1988 Act?

The point of requisition 35.2 is to establish whether the building is covered by the 1988 Act or whether it is governed by the Building Control Act, 1990. The provisions of the 1988 Act ceased to have any effect from 1 June 1992 except for cases coming within the transitional provisions of the Building Control Act 1990, s 2(2). Effectively, the provisions of the 1988 Act have been fully replaced by the Building Control Act 1990, together with the regulations made thereunder.

Each local authority is required by the 1988 Act to prepare and maintain a register of multi-storey buildings located in its area. This refers to five-storey buildings, including basement, completed after 1 January 1950. The local authorities are compelled to serve notice on the owners of multi-storey buildings requiring them to furnish a certificate in accordance with the 1988 Act, s 3, and there is an obligation on the local authority to take follow-up action to ensure that the relevant certificate is submitted. This obligation on the local authorities' part to seek certificates only relates to multi-storey buildings which were completed between 1 January 1950 and 14 November 1988 when the Act came into force. Once an owner is served with a notice by the local authority, the owner is obliged to furnish a certificate to the local authority in one of the forms referred to in s 3 of the Act. Once an owner has been served with a notice all arrangements associated with submitting the certificate, including engaging a competent person to carry out works to be certified and submission of certificate, are the responsibility of the owner. The certificate must cover the entire building and a certificate relating to a part of a building only is meaningless. Where a multi-storey building is completed after commencement of the 1988 Act (14 November 1988) and before the coming into force of the Building Control Act, 1990, there is an automatic duty on the owner to apply for a certificate and this must be done before the building or any part of it is occupied. Local authorities who own multi-storey buildings are not excluded from the provisions of the Act. If no notice was served there is no obligation under the Act.

Section 3 of the Act sets out the various kinds of certificates which the owner of a building may furnish to the local authority. There are several different certificates depending on the building's characteristics:

(a) The first certificate specifies that the building is not a specified building as defined in the Act.

(b) If the building is a specified building, the certificate can certify either:

(i) that the building is built in accordance with the appropriate codes of practice and standards;

(ii) that the occupiers of the building and the persons in its vicinity will not be exposed to risks related to robustness of the building unduly in excess of those which would be present in the building which is covered at (i) above;

(iii) all reasonable actions have been taken to minimise, as is practical, the risks of accidental damage to the building.

(c) The Act requires one appraisal and one certificate in respect of each building and there is no continuing requirement to submit further certificates on a regular basis, save under the provisions of s 5, which require that no action be carried out which would nullify a certificate under s 3 without the prior submission of a further certificate.

(d) A competent person to sign the said certificate has been defined by s 1 of the Act. In practice, nearly all buildings completed before the coming into force of the 1988 Act have been served with a notice by the relevant authority, and in almost all cases the relevant certificates have been deposited with the local authority and are available for inspection. This obligation since the passing of the Act, is on the owner of the buildings to file a multi-storey Building Act Certificate with the local authority and experience has shown that in almost all cases this has been done. Since the passing of the Building Control Act, 1990, and as and from 1 June 1992, save and except for the transitional provisions already referred to, there is no need to file any certificate with the local authority and the architect's certificate of compliance dealing with the Building Regulations is sufficient.

(e) The onus is placed on a competent person, usually a chartered engineer with structural engineering experience, to make an appraisal of an existing building, for a response to accidental overload is a complex task involving detailed examination and the exercise of a large degree of engineering judgment. The Act provides for severe penalties for certificates which are inaccurate, or in any way misleading. In some cases engineers carrying out the appraisal have formed the opinion that the building could have insufficient robustness or resistance for accidental damage. In some cases they have also concluded the amount of disturbance to the building by opening up joints etc to meet the necessary inspections to ascertain the position would be excessive. For example, Harcourt House and Canada House on the corner of St Stephen's Green and Earlsfort Terrace were cases where a certificate could not be signed without very considerable expenditure being incurred in rendering the building sufficiently robust to resist accidental damage. The purpose of the Act is to ensure that reasonable action is taken to make a building safe, if this is required.

11.8.4.4   Requisition 35.3

'a.   If the answer to [requisition 35.1] above is in the negative because the entire building was constructed prior to the 1st day of January 1950 furnish now a statutory declaration by a person who can prove satisfactorily that the building was so constructed.

b.   If the answer to 2. b above is in the affirmative reply to Requisitions 4–9 below.'

The first part of requisition 35.3 requires a statutory declaration to be produced in a case where a multi-storey building was constructed prior to 1 January 1950. In obvious cases, this declaration is rarely furnished, but in cases where the completion of the building was in or about 1 January 1950 a declaration should be insisted upon.

The second part of this requisition states that if the building is a multi-storey building built from 1 January 1950, answers must be furnished to requisitions 35.4–35.9 (inclusive).

11.8.4.5   Requisition 35.4

Requisition 35.4 provides:

'a.   Has a notice been served by the local authority under section 2(2) of the 1988 Act.

b.   If so furnish now a copy of same.

c.   Whether or not such a notice has been served and the construction of the building was completed prior to the 14th November 1988 furnish now a certificate from a competent person in accordance with Section 3(a) or a declaration in accordance with Section 3(b) of the 1988 Act.'

It would be extremely rare that a local authority would not by now have served a notice on the owner of the multi-storey building requesting the submission of a certificate in respect of any building completed prior to 14 November 1988. Therefore part (b) of this requisition merely asks for a copy of the local authority's notice. Such notice may not always be available but the most important document is the certificate signed by a competent person in accordance with s 3(a), or a declaration in accordance with s 3(b), of the 1988 Act. Requisition 35.4.c requests either an s 3(a) certificate or an s 3(b) declaration as to whether or not the local authority has served a notice on the owner of any building completed before 14 November 1988. The fact that the local authority omitted to request a certificate in an appropriate case does not relieve the owner of the building from obtaining such a certificate.

11.8.4.6   Requisition 35.5

'Where a Certificate has been submitted to the Local Authority pursuant to Section 3 of the 1988 Act:

a.   State whether or not the same is in accordance with the appropriate form provided for in the Regulations made and in force under the 1988 Act.

b.   Furnish now a copy of the said Certificate.'

These regulations came into force in 1990 under the 1988 Act setting out the prescribed form of certificate. Requisition 35.5.a asks if the certificate is in the prescribed form and 5(b) asks for a copy of the certificate.

11.8.4.7 Subsequent work on a building: requisition 35.6

Requisition 35.6 asks

'a. Has any work been carried out to the building which might nullify the effect of a Certificate furnished in accordance with Section 3 and require a further certificate in accordance with Section 5 of the 1988 Act.

b. If so furnish now a certified copy of such certificate.'

One certificate issues only in respect of each building. However, there is an exception provided for in the 1988 Act, s 5. If work has been carried out which effectively nullifies the certificate which has already been furnished in accordance with s 3, a further certificate is required under s 5 and the requisition calls for the production of this additional certificate.

11.8.4.8 Requisition 35.7

Requisition 35.7 provides:

'If the building is a multi-storey building the construction of which was not completed prior to the 14th of November 1988 furnish now a certified copy of the certificate in the prescribed form submitted to the Local Authority pursuant to Section 4 of the 1988 Act.'

As stated above, any building completed after 14 November 1988 does not require the local authority for the area to serve a notice requesting a certificate. These certificates must be submitted by the owner/developer to the local authority before any part of the building is occupied.

11.8.4.9 Requisition 35.8

Requisition 35.8 asks:

'Have any notices been served under the 1988 Act which have not yet been complied with.'

The local authority is entitled to serve notices under the 1988 Act requiring certain works to be carried out to ensure that the building is robust. This requisition requires the vendor to produce such notices (if any) which have been served.

11.8.4.10 Requisition 35.9

Requisition 35.9 provides:

'Where any Certificate has been submitted to the Local Authority under the 1988 Act furnish a letter from the Local Authority confirming that the Certificate has been placed on the Register.'

This was a new requisition, put in for the first time in the 1996 edition of the Law Society's Requisitions on Title and the purpose of it is to establish evidence of compliance with the 1988 Act. The register is a public register and any person is entitled to inspect it and to certify that the certificate has been submitted to the local authority and that the certificate, if such be the case, has been placed on the register.

11.9   The Building Regulations

11.9.1   INTRODUCTION

The Building Control Act, 1990 and the regulations made under it are referred to collectively as 'the Building Regulations'. The relevant legislation is:

Building Control Act, 1990;
Building Control Regulations, 1991 (SI 305/1991);
Building Control Act 1990 (Commencement Order 1991) (SI 304/1994);
Building Regulations 1991 (SI 306/1991);
Building Control Regulations 1991, Technical Guidance Documents;
Building Control (Amendment) Regulations, 1994 (SI 153/1994);
Building Regulations (Amendment) Regulations, 1994 (SI 154/1994);
Building Control Regulations, 1997 (SI 496/1997);
Building Regulations, 1997 (SI 497/1997);
Building Regulations Advisory Body Order (SI 348/1998);
Building Control (Amendment) Regulations, 2000 (SI 10/2000);
Building Regulations (Amendment) (3) Regulations, and 2000 (SI 179/2000);
Building Regulations (Amendment) (2) Regulations 2000 (SI 249/2000); and
Building Regulations (Amendment) (3) Regulations 2000 (SI 441/2000).

Prior to the Building Control Act, 1990, such controls as existed arose by virtue of building bye-laws made under the Public Health (Ireland) Act, 1878, s 41, the Public Health (Amendment) Act, 1890, s 23 and the Dublin Corporation Act, 1890, s 33. Unlike the Building Control Act, which replaced building bye-laws, building bye-laws did not apply throughout the country; nor indeed were they obligatory; they were made in the following areas only: Bray UDC, Dublin Corporation, Dublin County Council, Dun Laoghaire Corporation, Cork Corporation, Galway Corporation, Limerick Corporation, Naas UDC.

In areas where local authorities had made building bye-laws it was necessary to obtain a building bye-law approval before carrying out structural works or other works involving draining, sewerage, disposal, etc. Such an approval could not be obtained retrospectively. Therefore, technically, the absence of a building bye-law approval was a defect which could not be cured other than by demolishing the structure. Accordingly, in such a situation it became established practice to accept the certificate of an architect confirming that the works complied with the building bye-laws as of the date the works were carried out, that in the opinion of the architect bye-law approval would have been granted if it had been applied for, and it is not uncommon to come across such architects' opinions on title: see Law Society Gazette, March 1986.

Section 22(7) of the Building Control Act, 1990 abolished the necessity to obtain bye-law approval from 1 June 1992. The effect of this is that there is no longer any need to obtain bye-law approval for development in areas where bye-law approval was required. The Building Control Authority had six months from 1 June 1992 to object to developments which were carried out prior to 13 December 1989. If no notice was served before

Time Period	Building Bye-laws	Amnesty re Building Bye-laws	Building Regulations
From 1890 to 1 June 1992	Building bye-laws apply. Possibility of amnesty if conditions met.	Amnesty applies if conditions met ie work carried out prior to 13 Dec 1989 *and* no notice served by local authority by 1 Dec 1992.	Building Regulations do not apply.

(continued)

Time Period	Building Bye-laws	Amnesty re Building Bye-laws	Building Regulations
Prior to 13 Dec 1989	Building bye-laws apply. Possibility of amnesty if conditions met.	Amnesty re bye-laws if conditions met ie work carried out prior to 13 Dec 1989 *and* no notice served by local authority by 1 Dec 1992.	Building Regulations do not apply.
13 Dec 1998 to 1 June 1992	Building bye-laws apply. No possibility of amnesty.	Amnesty re bye-laws does not apply. Architect's cert or BBL approval necessary.	Building Regulations do not apply.
Post 6 June 1992	Building bye-laws apply if works carried out pursuant to bye-law approvals applied for prior to 1 June 1992.	Amnesty re bye-laws does not apply.	Building Regulations apply unless works carried out pursuant to bye-law approvals applied for prior to 1 June 1992.

1 December 1992 in respect of works carried out prior to 13 December 1989 the works are deemed to have been built in accordance with the bye-law. However, building bye-laws are relevant in relation to works carried out between 13 December 1989 and 1 June 1992 and works carried out pursuant to bye-law approvals applied for prior to 1 June 1992.

11.9.2   INTRODUCTION TO THE BUILDING CONTROL ACT, 1990

The Building Control Act, 1990 has three main purposes:

(a)   to replace the existing system of building bye-laws (applicable in particular areas) with a national building control system;

(b)   to improve the regulation of building standards by providing for additional matters including energy conservation, the needs of the disabled, the efficient use of resources and the encouragement of good building practice. In particular, the Act enabled the Minister to make fire safety a central feature of Building Regulations; and

(c)   the designation of a range of local authorities and building control authorities provides for the alignment of existing fire authorities (under the Fire Services Act, 1981) with building control authorities.

Thus, the Building Control Act, 1990 and the regulations made under it (as listed at **11.9.1**) provide a statutory basis for the making and administration of regulations for control of building. It constitutes a system for regulating building works and lays down minimum standards for design, construction, workmanship, materials etc. Different standards apply depending on the use of the building.

   The Building Control Act, 1990 sets out a new system to regulate building practice. The new framework provides the Minister for the Environment with the power to make Building Regulations. To date there have been seven statutory instruments and one statute (see above) which set out in great detail the new requirements. The Act imposes a duty on everybody to comply with these regulations. The regulations are a code of practice to ensure that structures are built to that code.

The regulations are divided into twelve sections as follows:

(1) structure;

(2) fire;

(3) site preparation resistance to moisture;

(4) materials and workmanship;

(5) sound;

(6) ventilation;

(7) hygiene;

(8) drainage and waste disposal;

(9) heat-producing appliances;

(10) stairways, ramps and guardrails;

(11) conservation of fuel and energy; and

(12) access for disabled people (extended considerably by the 2000 Regulations).

The Department of the Environment has issued technical guidance documents in relation to each section. It is not obligatory to follow the technical guidance documents but doing so certainly constitutes prima facie compliance with the regulations.

The 2000 Regulations came into force on 1 January 2001, and they amend Part M of the Building Regulations, 1997 by requiring that all new dwellings should be visitable by people with disabilities. They make a number of technical amendments to the existing Part M.

11.9.3   APPLICATION AND COMMENCEMENT

The main provisions of the Building Control Act, 1990 came into force on 1 June 1992. From that date all works for the erection of buildings or the material alteration or extension or change of use of existing buildings must comply with the regulations unless the works are covered by any of the exemptions specified below.

The Building Regulations, 1997 and the Building Control Regulations, 1997 consolidate the earlier regulations made in 1991 and amended in 1994. The 1997 Regulations came into operation on 1 July 1998 and they apply in relation to works commenced, or a material change of use taking place, on or after 1 July 1998. However, where a fire safety certificate has been issued under the Building Control Regulations, 1991 and 1994 then the earlier Building Regulations apply in respect of works or material change of use covered by that fire safety certificate, provided that the works commence, or the change of use takes place, before 31 December 2002. The old Building Regulations will continue to apply in relation to works or change of use occurring prior to 1 July 1998.

11.9.4   EXEMPTIONS FROM THE BUILDING CONTROL ACT, 1990

The Building Control Act, 1990 is similar to the Planning Acts in that certain classes of development are exempt. The principal exemptions from the requirements to comply with the regulations are listed below.

(a) Works commenced before 1 June 1992 or works carried out on foot of a building bye-law approval application which was made prior to 1 June 1992: see Building Regulations, 1991, art 7.

(b) Alterations to buildings which do not affect the structural or fire safety aspects of the building: see Building Regulations, 1997, art 11(1).

(c) Detached domestic garages with a floor area not exceeding 25 square metres (originally 23 square metres as per Building Regulations, 1991, art 6(1)(h) and, by virtue of the Building Regulations (Amendment) Regulations, 1994, art 6(1)(i) increased to 25 square metres) and height of not more than 3 metres or, in the case of a pitched roof, 4 metres: see Building Regulations, 1997, Third Schedule, class 1.

(d) Single-storey detached buildings in the grounds of a dwellinghouse with a floor area not exceeding as above, initially 23 square metres and, since 1994, 25 square metres, a height of not more than 3 metres or, in the case of a pitched roof, 4 metres, and used exclusively for recreational or storage purposes as opposed to use for trade or business or human habitation: see Building Regulations, 1997, Third Schedule, class 2.

(e) Single-storey extensions to existing dwellings ancillary to a dwelling and consisting of a conservatory, porch, car port or covered area with a floor area not exceeding 25 square metres (or 2 square metres in the case of a porch) and a height less than 3 metres or, if a pitched roof, 4 metres: see Building Regulations (Amendment) Regulations, 1994, art 6 and Building Regulations, 1997, Third Schedule, class 3.

(f) Certain temporary structures: see Building Regulations (Amendment) Regulations, 1994, art 6(1)(e)–(h), Building Regulations, 1997, Third Schedule, classes 11, 12, 13.

(g) A single-storey glasshouse where not less than three-quarters of its total external area is comprised of glass and it is used solely for agriculture and it is detached from any other building: see Building (Amendment) Regulations, 1994, art 6(1)(l), Third Schedule, class 4.

(h) A single-storey building which is detached from any other building and which is a building used solely for agriculture and is used exclusively for the storage of materials or products, for the accommodation of plant or machinery, or in connection with the housing, care or management of livestock and is a building where the only persons habitually employed are engaged solely in the care, supervision, regulation, maintenance, storage or removal of the materials, products, plant, machinery or livestock in the building and which does not exceed 300 square metres in floor area: see Building Regulations (Amendment) Regulations, 1994, art 6(1)(m), Third Schedule, class 5.

(i) The design or construction of a building which is carried out by or on behalf of a building control authority or material change of use of a building in the possession of a building control authority where the building or works will be situated within the functional area of the building control authority concerned: see Building Control Act, 1990, s 4.

(j) The regulations do not apply to a building for mining or quarrying, other than a house or building used as offices, laboratories or showrooms, a building the construction of which is subject to the Explosives Act, 1875, a building subject to the National Monuments Acts, 1930–1994, a building constructed for and used by the Electricity Supply Board as its generating transmission or distribution station, a temporary dwelling as defined by the Local Government (Sanitary Services) Act, 1948: see Building Control Regulations, 1994, art 6(1)(a)–(d), Third Schedule, classes 6–10.

(k) Lighthouses: Building Regulations, 1997, Third Schedule, class 14.

(l) Article 8 of the Building Regulations, 1997, which operates from 1 July 1998, creates a new emphasis in relation to certain buildings themselves as opposed to works to buildings. These buildings are exempt from the regulations if they come within one of the classes set out in the Third Schedule, provided that they comply with the conditions attaching to the relevant class.

11.9.5 COMMENCEMENT NOTICES

When a development is subject to the Building Regulations, the nature of the development determines the level of control under the scheme. For all works and uses to which the Building Regulations apply a commencement notice must be submitted to the building control authority when a proposed development is likely to be commenced, thus enabling it to consider whether it will inspect such a development and determine whether or not it complies with the regulations. These commencement notices, since the 1997 Regulations, must be submitted not less than fourteen days and not more than twenty-eight days before the commencement of works (previously it was seven and twenty-one days). The requirement to serve a commencement notice and what information it must contain is laid down in the Building Control Regulations, 1997, art 8 (previously the Building Control Regulations, 1991 arts 6 and 7)

(a) the address of the building and its use or proposed use;

(b) a description of the proposed works or change of use;

(c) the name of:

(i) the owner;

(ii) any other person who is carrying out the works (eg the builder);

(iii) the person from whom the plans of the works can be obtained (eg the architect); and

(iv) the person from whom notification of the pouring of foundations and the covering up of any drainage system can be obtained (eg the builder).

Oddly enough there is no need to name the designer or to supply plans.

11.9.6 EXEMPTIONS FROM THE NEED TO SERVE COMMENCEMENT NOTICES

The following developments are exempt from the need to serve commencement notices:

(a) works exempt from the requirement to comply with the Building Regulations as set out at **11.9.4** above;

(b) works carried out by a building control authority in its own area;

(c) Garda stations, military barracks, courthouses and certain other buildings for officers of the State, and certain works carried out for national security reasons (Building Control Regulations, 1997, art 6);

(d) provisions of services, fittings and equipment to a building not involving a material alteration; and

(e) exempt development under the Planning Acts except:

(i) where a fire safety certificate is required; or

(ii) for material alterations (other than minor works) in a shop or office or industrial building.

In short, in determining whether a Commencement Notice is required in any particular case to which the Building Regulations apply, it is simply necessary to ask:

1. whether planning permission is required; or

2. whether a fire safety certificate is required.

If the answer to either question is yes, then one must obtain and serve a commencement notice.

11.9.7 DEFINITIONS

'**Material alteration**' is an alteration where the works, or any part of the work carried out by itself, would be subject to the requirement of the regulations concerning structure of fire safety (Building Regulations, 1991, art 10(2)).

'**Minor works**' mean works consisting of the installation, alteration, or removal of fixture or fittings or works of a decorative nature (Building Regulations (Amendment) Regulations, 1994, art 4).

'**Shop**' is defined in the Building Control (Amendment) Regulations, 1994, art 4 as including a building used for retail or wholesale trade or business (including retail sales by auction, self-selection and over-the-counter wholesale trading, the business of lending books or periodicals for gain and the business of a barber or hairdresser) and premises to which the public is invited to deliver or collect goods in connection with their hire, repair or other treatment, where they themselves may carry out such repairs or treatments. It is also defined in the 1997 Regulations, art 5.

'**Office**' is defined as including premises used for the purpose of administrative or clerical work, including writing, book-keeping, sorting papers, filing, typing, duplicating, machine calculating and drawing and the editorial preparation of matter for publication, handling money (including banking and building society works) or telephone system operation: see Building Regulations (Amendment) Regulations, 1994, art 4 and Building Regulations, 1997, art 5(4).

'**Industrial building**' is defined as including a factory or other premises used for manufacturing, altering or preparing, cleaning, washing, breaking-up, adopting or processing any article generating power or slaughtering livestock: see Building Regulations (Amendment) Regulations, 1994, art 4 and Building Control Regulations, 1997, art 5(4).

'**Guest building**' means a building (other than a hostel or hotel) providing overnight guest accommodation for reward and includes a guesthouse: see Building Control Regulations, 1997, art 5(4).

'**Day centre**' means a building used for the provision of treatment or care to persons where such persons do not stay overnight and includes a day-care centre, a pre-school, a creche and a day nursery: see Building Control Regulations, 1997, art 5(4).

'**Repair/Renewal**' means works of maintenance or restoration of a routine nature relating to (a) the keeping of a building in good condition or working order, or (b) the return of the fabric of a building to its original condition (see Building Control Regulations, 1997, art 5(4)). Note here the omission of the works 'or former state' in the new definition, which could well prove to be significant.

'**Works**'. The Building Control Regulations, 1997, art 5(4) defines works as any act or operation in connection with the construction, extension, alteration, repair or renewal of a building.

'**Domestic garage**'. Under the Building Control Regulations, 1997, art 5(4), a domestic garage means a building ancillary to a dwelling which is suitable for use for the storage of a motor vehicle or vehicles and is not used for the purpose of any trade or business.

Note that the definitions differ from those in the Local Government (Planning and Development) Regulations, 2001.

11.9.8 FIRE SAFETY CERTIFICATES

The Regulations under the Building Control Act, 1990 re Fire came into effect on 1 August 1992. By virtue of arts 11 and 12 of the Building Control Regulations, 1997, it is mandatory to obtain a fire safety certificate before work commences on a development in relation to:

    (a)   the erection of a building;

    (b)   the material alteration in:

        (i)   a day-centre;

        (ii)   a building containing a flat;

      (iii) a hotel, hostel or guest premises;

      (iv) an institutional building;

      (v) a place of assembly;

      (vi) a shopping centre

other than a material alteration consisting solely of minor works;

(c) a material alteration in a shop, office or industrial building where:

      (i)   additional floor space has been provided within the existing building; or

      (ii) the building has been subdivided into a number of units for separate occupancy;

(d) the extension of a building by more than 25 square metres. This is not to be confused with the exemption under the Planning Regulations, ie 40 square metres; and

(e) a material change of use of a building to which Part B of the First Schedule to the 1991 Regulations (being the Fire Regulations) applies.

Please note that the Fire Services Act, 1981 remains unaffected by the Building Control Act, 1990 and all of the enforcement powers of a fire officer under the Fire Services Act remain.

Definitions of an institutional building, an industrial building, a flat, a shopping centre, etc may be found in the Building Regulations, 1997, art 5(4). In particular note the definition of flat which was amended in the 1994 Regulations and in the 1997 Regulations and is now defined as a separate and self-contained premises constructed or adapted for residential use and forms part of a building from some other part of which it is divided horizontally, ie duplex apartments are clearly flats under this definition.

11.9.9 APPLICATION FOR FIRE SAFETY CERTIFICATE

The application for a fire safety certificate must be in the prescribed form and be accompanied by a detailed plan showing compliance with the Fire Regulations and particulars of the proposed use. Any application which does not contain the necessary information is invalid. The Fire Regulations are comprehensive and must be complied with. The application is almost as demanding as an application for planning permission and requires a lodgement of plans, floor plans, elevations, and calculations to show that the proposal does comply with the Fire Regulations. It should be lodged at the same time as the application is made for a planning permission to try to save time. The building control authority keeps a register of applications for fire safety certificates. If the application is accepted by the building control authority it sends out a receipt to the applicant and the building control authority has a two-month period in which to make its decision, either to grant permission with or without conditions or to refuse permission. A refusal, or grant of permission imposing conditions, must provide reasons. If the authority fails to reach a decision within that time a default procedure, akin to that applicable to a planning application, applies, whereby the certificate must automatically issue to the applicant. Again, as with a planning application, there is a procedure whereby an applicant may appeal to An Bord Pleanala against the decision of an authority either in part or in its entirety.

Again, the building control authority may or may not inspect the development but it has wide powers if the developer proves uncooperative. It is an offence to carry out works or make a material change of use without first obtaining a fire safety certificate.

11.9.10 EXEMPTIONS TO THE REQUIREMENT TO OBTAIN A FIRE SAFETY CERTIFICATE

The following developments are exempt from the requirements to obtain a fire safety certificate:

(a)   works exempt from the requirement to comply with the Building Regulations;

(b)   works commenced, or material change of use, made before 1 August 1992;

(c)   a building (other than a flat) the proposed use for which is as a domestic dwelling;

(d)   works carried out by the building control authority in its own area;

(e)   provision of services, fittings and equipment to a building not involving a material alteration;

(f)   a material alteration consisting only of minor works in a building containing a flat, hotel, hostel or guesthouse, an institutional building, a place of assembly or shopping centre;

(g)   a material alteration in a shop, office or industrial building unless additional floor space has been provided within an existing building or the building has been subdivided into a number of units for separate occupancy;

(h)   works carried out to a building in compliance with the notice served under the Fire Services Act, 1981, s 20; and

(i)   certain single-storey buildings used solely for agriculture (the definition of 'agriculture' is identical to that contained in the Local Government (Planning and Development) Act, 1963), but differs from the definition of 'agriculture' contained in the Planning Development Act, 2000. See art 11(2)(a)–(d) of the Building Control Regulations, 1997, for a list of these exemptions.

11.9.11 DISPENSATIONS/RELAXATIONS

An application to the authority for dispensations or relaxations of Building Regulations may be made. If no decision is made by the authority within two months, the dispensation or relaxation is deemed to have been granted (see Building Regulations, 1997, art 14). There is an appeal procedure if an applicant is dissatisfied with the authority's decision, the appeal again lying to An Bord Pleanala. The Minister for the Environment also has power to dispense with or relax any regulations in respect of any particular class of building operation, works or material alteration, subject to such conditions as he deems appropriate.

11.9.12 ALTERATION OR EXTENSION OF EXISTING BUILDINGS

The Building Regulations apply to all material alterations (not being repair or renewal) or extensions of existing buildings, in that all works done must comply with the regulations. In addition, the alteration or extension cannot result in a new or greater contravention of the regulations.

11.9.13 LIABILITY, PENALTIES AND ENFORCEMENT

Failure to comply with any requirements of the Building Control Act, 1990 or the regulations is an offence. Fines of up to €10,000 and/or a term of imprisonment not exceeding two years, may be imposed for failure to comply with the regulations or failure to comply with an enforcement notice. If the offence is committed by a company with the consent or contrivance of, or is attributable to any neglect on the part of, any director, manager, or secretary of that company, that person shall also be guilty of that offence.

Enforcement notices may be served by the authority on the owner of the building or any other person involved in the works. It may set out the works required to ensure compliance with the regulations or may prohibit the use of a building or part of it until these works are done. The authority has power to enter a building and carry out the remedial works if the enforcement notice is not complied with and may recover the costs from the owner or the person who carried out works in breach of the regulations as a simple contract debt. The authority also has power to enter buildings to inspect them and any plans or documents relating to the works and to take samples of materials being used (see Building Control Act, 1990, ss 7–8).

There is a limitation period of five years from completion of the works or change of use after which no enforcement notice may be served. The Act also provides for a procedure similar to the planning injunction under the Planning Act, 1976, s 27 (as amended by the 1992 Act), and the 2000 Act, s 160 whereby the authority may seek a High Court order requiring alterations, the making safe of any structure, the discontinuance of works, or prohibiting the use of a building where the authority considers that there is substantial risk to health or safety. There is no time limit on this action being taken.

The Building Control Act, 1990 (see s 21) specifically prohibits the taking of any civil proceedings for contraventions of the Act or the regulations. However, the Act does impose strict liabilities on designers and builders for which they may be held liable in contract or tort to their client or third parties without proof of negligence against them.

11.9.14 MULTI-STOREY BUILDINGS

The Local Government (Multi-Storey Buildings) Act, 1988 does not apply to buildings commenced after 1 June 1992, save where built on foot of a building bye-law approval applied for on or before that date. The 1988 Act does still apply to multi-storey buildings constructed between 1 January 1950 and 1 June 1992. 'Single storey buildings' is defined in the Building Regulations, 1997, art 5 as a building consisting of a ground storey or a basement storey only. Further, the same article goes on to define a basement storey as a storey which is below the ground storey or, where there is no ground storey, a storey the top surface of the floor of which is situate at such a level or levels that some point in its parameters is more than 1.2 metres below the level of the finished surface of the ground adjoining the building in the vicinity of that point.

11.10 Planning Warranty

11.10.1 INTRODUCTION

General condition 36 of the Law Society General Conditions of Sale (2001) is entitled 'Development' and deals with the question of planning matters generally. This condition has been changed slightly in the 2001 edition of the Law Society General Conditions of Sale as compared with the 1995 edition. General condition 36, which is the only warranty contained in the Contract for Sale, provides a purchaser with a warranty by the vendor that all developments on or to the property since 1 October 1964 comply with all the requirements of the Planning Acts and, where applicable, building bye-laws and building control regulations. The warranty does not cover/extend to building bye-law approvals in respect of development or works carried out prior to 13 December 1989.

The warranty goes further in that if a planning permission has been implemented then the vendor warrants that the conditions expressly notified with any permission by any competent authority in relation to and specifically addressed to any development or works were substantially complied with. See CLE lecture by John Gore-Grimes, 'The 2001 Edition of the Law Society Contract for Sale', given on 6 February 2002.

General condition 36 is divided into four sections: (a), (b), (c) and (d).

11.10.2 GENERAL CONDITION 36(a)

11.10.2.1 Generally

Where general condition 36(a) is left intact, ie not varied or deleted in the Special Conditions, it puts the vendor in the position of furnishing a warranty that the planning permission in relation to the property is fully in order and that there has either been no development whatsoever since 1 October 1964 that requires planning permission, building bye-law approval, or building control approval or that all necessary planning permissions and building bye-law approvals/building control approval have been obtained and the conditions contained therein have been complied with. The warranty at condition 36(a)(1)(ii) warrants that if a planning permission had been implemented, the conditions expressly notified with any such permission by any competent authority in relation to and specifically addressed to any development or works were complied with substantially; for example, when an engineering department of a local authority issues requirements which are notified with a planning permission, the vendor is warranting compliance with same even where they are not specifically incorporated in the permission. A vendor must be satisfied that no competent authority issued conditions with any planning permission which were not incorporated in the condition. If the vendor is in any way unsure of the position the appropriate special condition should be inserted in the contract to vary the warranty.

The full significance of condition 36(a) must be appreciated by all vendors, who must disclose any planning irregularity in the special conditions of the contract. Failure to do so will leave the vendor open to an action for breach of warranty, apart from the fact that it may be extremely difficult to compel the purchaser to complete the sale. It is a very significant warranty as it basically calls on the vendor to stand over all planning matters in relation to a property for a period of time in excess of thirty-five years. Where the vendor is simply unaware of the planning history of the property, the warranty in general condition 36 should be restricted to cover only the period in respect of which the vendor has the appropriate knowledge. The importance of this condition is highlighted by a marginal note in the printed General Conditions of Sale which reads:

'In cases where property is affected by an unauthorised development or a breach of Condition/Conditions in a Permission/Approval amounting to a non-conforming development or where the Bye-Law Amnesty covered by Section 22(7), Building Control Act, 1990 is relevant, it is recommended that same be dealt with expressly by Special Condition.'

If it later transpires that matters are not as warranted in condition 36(a), the purchaser could have a right of action against the vendor for breach of warranty, which in turn could have serious financial implications for a vendor long after the transaction may have been completed (see general condition 48).

Refer to practice note in Law Society Gazette, May 2000, pertaining to blanket exclusion of general condition 36.

11.10.2.2 Breach of warranty

If the extent of the warranty has not been limited by the vendor prior to the execution of contracts and the vendor is subsequently found to be in breach of it, a purchaser is in a strong position. Patrick Sweetman, in a CLE lecture entitled 'Property Transactions/ Liabilities under Planning and Environmental Law', given on 1 December 1992 (on 'Property Development/Planning & Environmental Issues of the 1990s') succinctly puts it as follows:

'The consequences of a breach of this warranty could be:

1. That the purchaser would have right of action in damages for breach of warranty.

2. The purchaser may be able to walk away from the contract.

3. Even if the purchaser wishes to complete the sale, substantial delays will be incurred, so that the vendor will remain responsible for the property and will not receive the balance of proceeds until either the planning breach is resolved (normally by retaining a retention planning permission) or the parties agree to terms of settlement.'

General condition 51(d) of the Contract for Sale provides for submission to arbitration of disputes as to the materiality of any matter for the purpose of general condition 36(a) (ie breach of the planning warranty). Arbitration may take considerable time and it may suit the parties to agree to set aside an agreed sum, being a portion of the consideration, and to close the sale, leaving the planning issue to be decided subsequently. The purchaser accepting such a situation would need to satisfy himself as to the worst possible scenario arising from the planning breach and ensure that sufficient sums are retained to cover it.

Often no monetary payment would be sufficient to safeguard a purchaser's position, for example, if there was a dispute as to whether a particular use was an established use since 1 October 1964. A purchaser would be unlikely to take the risk that continuance of use of permission might be granted, as he or she could be left with a property utterly useless to his requirements.

Hence the importance of a vendor's solicitor fully advising the vendor of the extent and importance of this warranty and that all developments, bearing in mind that development as defined in the Planning Acts includes material change of use, are disclosed to the solicitor to enable the context of the warranty to be limited to when drafting the contract.

11.10.2.3 Building bye-law approval and general condition 36

Section 22(7) of the Building Control Act, 1990 provides that no enforcement action will be taken, and building bye-law approval will be deemed to have been granted, in respect of all works carried out prior to 13 December 1989 unless the local authority served a notice before 1 December 1992, stating the works constituted a danger to public health or safety. Therefore, it is not necessary for a purchaser to concern himself or herself with building bye-laws in respect of works carried out prior to 13 December 1989 unless such a notice was served. However, appropriate evidence must be produced to show that the works were carried out prior to 13 December 1989 and that no notice was served. This is usually given by way of a statutory declaration by the vendor. However, despite this amnesty it is required that general condition 36 of the Conditions of Sale be varied in the Special Conditions in reference to same. The Law Society Conveyancing Committee advises that the full vigour of the rest of condition 36 will continue to operate under the general condition as so varied (see Law Society Gazette, September 1993).

11.10.2.4 Extensions

Many house extensions and garage conversions are exempt developments. Previously, if the property was in an area where building bye-laws apply, the works lost their exempt status by reason of the Local Government (Planning and Development) Regulations, 1977 (SI 65/1977), art 11(1)(a)(iv) if no building bye-law approval was obtained or the works did not comply with the bye-law approval. However, those regulations have been revoked and replaced with the Local Government (Planning and Development) Regulations, 2001

(SI 600/2001) so that, provided the works are exempt under the 2001 Regulations, such previously unauthorised development now enjoys exempt status.

11.10.3 PRODUCTION OF DOCUMENTATION

General condition 36(d) requires production of all permissions and approvals, fire safety certificates and, if available, commencement notices under the Building Regulations. The words 'if available' are inserted in the light of the Law Society recommendation that a solicitor should not insist on production of a commencement notice if it is not readily available (see Practice Note, Law Society Gazette, November 1994).

11.10.4 FINANCIAL CONDITIONS

General condition 36(e)(i) requires that a vendor shall on or prior to completion furnish to the purchaser evidence of compliance with all financial conditions. Alternatively, the vendor may provide formal confirmation from the local authority that the roads and services abutting the said property have been taken in charge by it without requirement for payment of money in respect of same. This is, in effect, an extension of the Law Society's recommendation (issued with the Gazette, May 1987) in relation to second-hand houses in housing estates. The recommendation states that where solicitors are dealing with a second or later purchase of residential houses where the roads and services are in charge of the local authority, then they should not be concerned with enquiries as to compliance with financial conditions in a planning permission, unless the purchaser's solicitor is on notice of some problem. If a solicitor is acting for the first purchaser buying a newly constructed house in a housing estate, he or she is only entitled to obtain copies of receipts for financial payments required to be paid up to the date of completion of the purchase. As a matter of practice, if the local authority issues a letter confirming that the roads and services have been taken in charge, then such a letter will be accepted as satisfactory evidence of compliance with financial conditions.

Further, in relation to letters of compliance with financial contributions, it is commonplace for a local authority to agree to accept payment of financial contributions from a builder/developer by way of stage payments. Thus, if the property is purchased in the early stages of a large development, often the only evidence of compliance with the financial conditions will be a letter from the local authority confirming that the stage payments have been discharged to date because the next payments do not become due until a later date. There is a Law Society recommendation of April 1987 (Law Society Gazette) where it is recommended that it is only necessary to produce letters confirming compliance with financial conditions up to the date of the first purchase of the dwellinghouse, and frequently a vendor's solicitor will refer a purchaser's solicitor to said recommendation. However, it cannot be repeated often enough, that a vendor relying on this recommendation, or indeed any other, in relation to general condition 36, must insert the appropriate special condition in the contract. Note this recommendation applies only to housing estates and not to once-off houses on individual sites or, indeed, to commercial property. Note, however, that if the roads and services have been taken in charge since the dwellinghouse was completed, a letter of charge from the local authority should be obtained. In that instance evidence of compliance with the financial conditions becomes unnecessary.

See also the Conveyancing Committee recommendation (Law Society Gazette, February 1989) which provides that a solicitor may certify either from his or her own personal knowledge or from an inspection of the local authority records that the roads and services are in charge of the local authority.

Section 180 of the 2000 Act is a new provision, and deals with taking charge of building estates. It requires planning authorities to take housing estates in charge where requested by a majority of the residents or the developer, once the estate is complete. It applies to development which includes the construction of two or more houses etc. It must have been completed to the satisfaction of the planning authority. This section applies to a development in respect of which a permission was granted under s 34 of the 2000 Act, or under Part IV of the 1963 Act, which means that estates already in existence qualify to be taken in charge provided that they comply with the conditions of s 180. If however, the estate is unfinished, the obligation to take it in charge does not arise during the seven-year period when enforcement action may be taken by a planning authority to ensure completion of the estate. If however, enforcement proceedings have not been taken within the seven-year period, the planning authority shall take the estate in charge where requested to do so by a majority of qualified persons who own or occupy the houses in question. The procedure is initiated under s 11 of the Roads Act of 1993. See CLE lecture by Patrick Sweetman, 'Planning and Development Act, 2000', Book IV.

11.10.5 CERTIFICATES/OPINIONS

General condition 36(e)(ii) requires the production of a certificate or an opinion on compliance with planning and bye-law requirements from an architect or an engineer or other person professionally qualified to so certify or opine. The Conveyancing Committee of the Law Society has set out recommended criteria in relation to the qualifications of the persons offering certificates or opinions on compliance and these are contained in the Law Society's Newsletter issued with the October 1994 Gazette. However, the General Conditions of Sale do not define 'architect' or specify who is competent to certify or opine and, accordingly, the identity and qualifications of a person who will approve compliance with planning and building control requirements should be established by the purchaser before contracts are exchanged.

General condition 36(e)(ii) also provides that the certificate or opinion to be furnished must confirm that all conditions expressly notified with the permission by a competent authority, and especially directed to and materially affecting the property or any part of it, have been substantially complied with. The standard Royal Institute of the Architects of Ireland (RIAI)/Law Society Forms of Opinion cover these conditions, unless specifically excluded, and in such a case it is necessary to get an additional certificate from a third party to show compliance. If a vendor is agreeing to give a certificate covering such conditions issued by a competent authority, he or she must first check that his or her architect/engineer will be in a position to do so. It is not unusual in major commercial developments for planning conditions to specifically require the agreement or compliance with the requirements of the competent authority and the architect in overall charge will generally refer in the opinion of compliance to a certificate of sub-contractors confirming compliance, for example, with a fire officer.

Never in any of these certificates/opinions will there be a reference to compliance with financial conditions in any permission. Neither the RIAI Forms of Opinion nor the Law Society Specimen Certificates of Compliance cover such conditions so that conveyancers dealing with second-hand property must delete this condition by an appropriate special condition unless they may obtain a supplemental certificate from an architect or engineer covering the point. If a vendor is agreeing to give a certificate containing this provision, he or she should first check that an architect or engineer is in a position to do so.

In relation to second-hand houses bought before 31 December 1975, the Law Society has recommended that, as it was not the practice at that time to furnish an architect's certificate of compliance, a purchaser's solicitor should not insist on one now (see Practice Note, Law Society Gazette, January/February 1993). However, three points should be noted. If a vendor seeks to rely on this recommendation there must be a restriction placed on the warranty contained in general condition 36(a) by inserting an appropriate special condition. Further, the recommendation relates to second-hand houses built prior to 31 December 1975 only. It does not relate to any other type of property. The planning permission should, of course, always be obtained.

General condition 36(f)(i),(ii), which is new to the 2001 contract, provides that where the vendor has furnished certificates or opinions on compliance, *the vendor shall have no liability* on foot of the warranties expressed in general condition 36(a) or (b) in respect of any matter with regard to which the architect's certificate/opinion is erroneous or inaccurate unless the vendor was aware at the date of sale that same contained any material error or inaccuracy. If, subsequent to the date of sale and prior to completion thereof, it is established that any such certificate or opinion is erroneous or inaccurate, then, if the vendor fails to show that before the date of sale the purchaser was aware of the error or inaccuracy, or that same is no longer relevant or material, or that same does not prejudicially affect the value of the subject property, the purchaser may by notice given to the vendor rescind the sale.

11.10.6 BUILDING CONTROL ACT, 1990

General condition 36(b) warrants that the provisions of the Building Control Act, 1990 and the regulations thereunder have been complied with. The warranty is to the effect that where the provisions of the Building Control Act or the regulations thereunder apply to the design or development of the property or any activity in connection therewith, that there has been substantial compliance with the Act and regulations. The vendor is required to produce a certificate or opinion by an architect or a professionally qualified person competent to certify compliance confirming such substantial compliance 36(e)(ii) (see general condition).

If such warranty is excluded in the General Conditions of Sale, a purchaser should satisfy himself or herself as to compliance with the regulations prior to exchange of contracts by way of pre-contract enquiries. The Law Society has issued a standard set of Requisitions on Title in relation to same (see Planning Requisitions at **11.8**).

11.10.7 CONTINUANCE OF WARRANTY

General condition 36 should be read in conjunction with general condition 48, which provides that all obligations and provisions under the contract which are not implemented by a deed of assurance and which are capable of continuing or taking effect after completion shall enure and remain in full force and effect. Thus, a purchaser would have a remedy against the vendor even where the planning difficulty only came to light after the sale had been completed. Patrick Sweetman, in a CLE lecture on Planning Law, on 20 April 1999, gives a series of examples of the appropriate wording in drafting a special condition which will protect the vendor from the full rigours of the warranty in general condition 36 and yet not be so complex or all excluding so as to put off a purchaser or seriously affect the purchase price.

11.10.8 SAMPLE SPECIAL CONDITIONS

The following are some sample special conditions which might be inserted into a contract in order to protect the vendor from the full rigours of the warranty in general condition 36.

11.10.8.1 Example 1

Problem

Vendor in Dublin built an extension to his house of less than 23 square metres in 1982. No application for bye-law approval was sought or obtained.

Answer

This fact should be stated in simple terms in the special conditions. If the vendor is able to furnish an architect's certificate in the form recommended by the Conveyancing Committee of the Law Society confirming compliance with bye-laws as at the date of construction, then the special condition should indicate such a certificate will be forthcoming.

Specimen draft clause

> The Vendor constructed an extension less than 23 square metres to the premises in sale in or about 1982. No application for Bye-Law Approval was made or obtained at the time. The Vendor shall furnish on closing Architect's Certificate in the form recommended by the Law Society confirming that from his inspection the works substantially comply with Bye-Laws as at the time of construction. No requisition, objection or enquiry shall be raised by the Purchaser in relation to said extension. General Condition 36 is amended in this respect.

If the vendor is not able to furnish such an architect's certificate then, as the extension was built prior to 13 December 1989, the amnesty under the Building Control Act, 1990, s 22(7) applies and the extension is 'deemed to comply unless notice was served prior to 1 December 1992 that the works constituted a danger to public health or safety'. In such circumstances the vendor should offer a statutory declaration stating when the works were carried out and that no notice was served. An example is set out below:

Specimen draft clause

> The Vendor constructed in or around 1982 an extension to the premises in sale which said extension is less than 23 square metres. No application for Bye-Law Approval was sought or obtained. The Vendor relies on the benefit afforded by Section 22(7) of the Building Control Act 1990 and shall furnish on closing Statutory Declaration of Vendor stating when the works were carried out and that no notice was served on the Vendor by the Local authority in relation to said premises as at 1 December 1992. The Purchaser shall accept said Statutory Declaration and no further requisition, objection or enquiry shall be raised in relation to same. General Condition 36 is amended in this respect.

11.10.8.2 Example 2

Problem

A downstairs wc/cloakroom was installed under the stairs of an existing house in March 1990 in the Dublin area. No bye-law approval was sought.

Answer

Special conditions in the contract should state this fact. As the work was done between 13 December 1989 and 1 June 1992, it is necessary for the vendor to furnish an architect's certificate to say that no bye-law approval was sought but there was substantial compliance. This is another example similar to above and the Law Society recommended form should be used. It would also be advisable to have a statutory declaration from the vendor confirming when the work was carried out.

The difference between this example and example 1 is that the vendor cannot avail of the amnesty under the Building Control Act, 1990, s 22(7). Hence as bye-law approval was required and not obtained, technically a retention permission is required. However, as it is now 2002 and the work was carried out in March 1990, it should be noted that the work was carried out in March 1990 which was before the coming into force of the Building Control Act, 1990 on 1 June 1992. Previously the vendor could have relied on the protection offered by the Local Government (Planning) and Development Act, 1992, s 19, but this Act was repealed by the Planning and Development Act, 2000. The position is now covered by s 157(4) of the 2000 Act whereby no warning letter or enforcement notice can be issued after seven years from the date of commencement of the development. The vendor should give a statutory declaration to this effect (see draft clause below).

Specimen draft clause

> A downstairs wc/cloakroom was installed in the premises in sale in or around March 1990. No Bye-Law Approval was sought. The vendor shall furnish an architect's certificate stating that no Bye-Law Approval was sought at the time the work was carried out but as far as he/she is able to ascertain from an inspection now of the work there was substantial compliance with the Bye-Laws in force at the time. The vendor shall also furnish a Statutory Declaration stating when the work was carried out and that the Vendor has received no warning letter or enforcement notice from the Local Authority or Planning Authority and the vendor relies on section 157(4) of the Planning and Development Act, 2000 in this regard.

11.10.8.3 Example 3

Problem

Three-storey residential house with basement portion used continuously as an office since 1988. No planning permission obtained for change of user of this portion of the house.

Answer

State fact in special conditions. As the user has been for more than seven years, the planning authority cannot issue a warning letter or enforcement notice nor make an application to the High Court or Circuit Court for a planning injunction (now— s 157(4) and s 160 of the Planning and Development Act, 2000).

The difference between Examples 1 and 2 and Example 3 is that the 'Development' consists of a change of use for which no permission was obtained. Example 1 and Example 2 relate to 'Developments' consisting of works carried out.

A suitable special condition in the contract would be as follows :

Specimen draft clause

> The basement portion of the premises in sale has been used continuously as offices since 1988. No application was made for planning permission for change of use. The vendor will furnish a Statutory Declaration stating when said uses are commenced and confirming that he has received no notice from the Local Authority or planning authority in relation to same nor has any planning injunction been obtained. The vendor relies on the benefit afforded by Section 157(4) of the Planning and Development Act, 2000. The purchaser purchases the said premises with full knowledge of the position and no objection, requisition or enquiry shall be raised in relation thereto. General Condition 36 is amended in this respect.

11.10.8.4 Example 4

Problem

House constructed in 1973. No architect's certificate available.

Answer

State fact in special conditions. Furnish planning permission and bye-law approval and refer to Practice Note, Law Society Gazette, January/February 1993. Special condition should state the facts and refer to Law Society recommendation and that general condition 36 is varied accordingly.

11.10.8.5 Example 5

Problem

Warehouse built in 1967. Planning permission but no architect's certificate available.

Answer

The vendor should be advised to engage the services of an architect who should attend at the planning office and inspect the plans on foot of which the planning permission issued (and bye-law approval if the warehouse was situate in an area to which bye-laws applied). This is unlikely to be possible in the major urban areas. The architect should then make a visual inspection of the building as constructed and furnish a certificate of compliance. If no architect's certificate is forthcoming, the purchaser must be put on notice in the special conditions of the contract. The recommendation of the Conveyancing Committee set out in January/February 1993 Practice Notes of the Law Society Gazette relates only to private residential property. As the warehouse was constructed post-1 October 1964 planning permission was required (as well as bye-law approval if in a bye-law area) and an architect's certificate must be furnished as it is a non-residential building.

11.10.8.6 Example 6

Problem

Retention permission obtained.

Answer

A special condition should draw attention to the retention permission. It is important to check that the vendor is in possession of the grant of permission for the retention of the unauthorised development and not the notification of decision to grant permission. This is because there could have been an appeal before the grant issued or the possibility of a change in the conditions in the grant (this is unlikely but still a possibility). A retention permission should be treated in the same way as an ordinary planning permission in that an architect's opinion should be furnished confirming compliance with the conditions in the retention permission. The opinion of the architect should state that he or she prepared the plans which were lodged with the application for retention permission and he or she confirms the plans lodged on foot of which the retention permission issued reflect the present building. If the retention is for use only with no condition attached then a vendor's declaration is appropriate.

There may also be conditions attached to that retention permission and if that is the case the architect's opinion must state those conditions have been met. It is not usual but should there be a condition in the planning permission which requires financial contribution/payment then the vendor must furnish a receipt in discharge of that condition.

11.10.8.7 Example 7

Problem

Vendor constructed an extension of 20 square metres to rear of dwellinghouse in 1996 and in 2000 added a conservatory to the rear of the house measuring 16 square metres.

Answer:

At the time the extension was constructed in 1996 the limit for exempted development was 23 square metres and hence there was no problem in relation to that extension. Now the total floor area of the extension and the conservatory total 36 square metres. However SI 181/2000 (which came into force on 22 June 2000) amended Part 1, Sch 2, Class 1 of the 1994 Regulations which relates to dwellinghouses. In this case the extension of 2000 taken together with the previous extension in 1996 does not exceed 40 square metres in total and the vendor has confirmed that the area of private open space at the rear is not less than 25 square metres. It should be noted that an extension includes a conservatory.

Specimen draft clause

> A ground floor extension to the rear of the dwellinghouse was constructed in 1996 which said extension had a floor area of 20 square metres. In 2000, the vendor constructed a conservatory to the rear of the dwellinghouse which has a floor area of 16 square metres. The vendor shall furnish an Architect's Opinion that the works carried out in 1996 and 2000 were exempt from Planning Permission and further thereof an Architect's Opinion on compliance with building regulations in relation to said extensions shall be forthcoming.

11.10.9 CONSEQUENCES OF NON-DISCLOSURE

As previously stated at **11.10.2**, in view of the warranty in general condition 36, non-disclosure of any problem prior to the signing of contracts may have serious consequences. The most serious is the rescission of the contract by the purchaser and proceedings issued for the return of the deposit and any damages. It is very likely, by that stage that the vendor client will have already entered into a binding contract for the purchase of another house based on the proceeds of the sale of the problem property being available by a certain date. In turn, the vendor is caught in not having the funds to complete his or her own purchase and, at the very least, is exposed to a claim on the interest of the balance due as per the provisions of his or her contract to purchase. Another consequence of a breach of warranty is an action for damages by the purchaser based on the diminution of market value of the property, as a result of the planning situation not being in order. Again, this may have consequences for the vendor who would be relying on receiving a certain sum of money for the property to enable him or her to purchase an alternative property. In the worst case scenario he or she may sue his or her solicitor for negligence in such a case.

A further consequence is that the purchaser may insist on retention permission being obtained before completing the purchase. Retention permission has the same time intervals as an application de novo and the same time period for appeals. It could add at least another three months to the completion date as well as the expense involved in the application, the architect's certificate and the vendor's exposure in the meantime under his or her contract for the purchase of the alternative house.

If acting for the purchaser, a pre-contract planning search would have revealed information regarding any planning application. In particular a survey report on the structure of the house will also have commented on the existence of any extension or user. This has the benefit of drawing the purchaser's attention to it and will allow the raising of further enquiries pre-contract. If the special conditions have not been amended the purchaser, in addition, has the benefit of the warranty.

Even where a vendor has revealed planning problems and they have been dealt with in the special conditions by his or her solicitor, there might still be a problem and it is then up to the purchaser and his or her advisers to assess the situation and ascertain whether it may be rectified and at what cost and whether a renegotiation of the purchase price is required.

However, a further problem then arises in that the purchaser's solicitor is often required to furnish a certificate of title to the purchaser's lending institution and any problem in relation to planning must be brought to the attention of the lending institution's advisers prior to contract and their written requirements obtained. The borrower/purchaser may not be in a position to comply with them before proceeding. While naturally a certificate of title is better not qualified, there are occasions, particularly in relation to planning, where it is necessary to do so. There is an excellent article on same by Patrick Sweetman at a CLE lecture on Planning Law dated 28 April 1999.

11.11 Architect's Certificates of Compliance

11.11.1 INTRODUCTION

It is now a standard requirement for conveyancers acting for a purchaser of a property that the development conforms to the Planning Acts, building bye-laws and all Building Regulations.

The practice of seeking certificates of compliance with planning permission has been gradual and became everyday practice in the early 1970s: see Law Society Gazettes December 1979, June 1980, August 1989, May 1990 and January/February 1993.

11.11.2 WHY IS AN ARCHITECT'S CERTIFICATE OF COMPLIANCE REQUIRED?

The need for architects' certificates of compliance was also partly brought about by the spread of lending by building societies to the country where previously house lending had been largely dealt with by local authorities under the Small Dwellings Acts. The tighter enforcement of the Planning Acts and the Fire Services Act were further reasons why people became more careful and, indeed, such documentation became an element of title.

11.11.3 WHO SHOULD CERTIFY COMPLIANCE?

The Conveyancing Committee of the Law Society recommends that it is reasonable for solicitors to accept certificates or opinions on compliance from:

(a) persons with a degree or diploma of degree standard in architecture, eg a Bachelor of Architecture;

(b) persons who have been in practice as architects on their own account for ten years;

(c) chartered engineers;

(d) persons with a degree in civil engineering;

(e) persons who have been in practice on their own account as engineers in the construction industry for ten years;

(f) qualified building surveyors;

(g) persons from another jurisdiction in the EU whose qualification is entitled to recognition in Ireland under the Architect's Directive. See Patrick Sweetman and Eammon Galligan, 'Planning—recent developments in conveyancing practice' (1994) IPELJ vol 1, no 4, 38.

In general, therefore, such certificates or opinions on compliance issued by engineers, building surveyors, architects or persons in sole or partnership practice providing architectural services on their own account for a period of at least ten years are acceptable to conveyancers. However, occasionally certifiers may be asked to provide confirmation or verification of the adequacy of their professional indemnity insurance. Most architects tend to resist giving details of their insurance unless this is sought by their own client or is part of their conditions of engagement. There is an EEC Directive No 85/384/ EEC: 'The Architect's Directive', where a proposal has been submitted to the European Commission to amend the directive to include persons whom the Minister for the Environment certifies have, over a period of at least five years immediately prior to the coming into force of the directive, pursued architectural activities, the nature and importance of which, in the opinion of the Minister, give that person an established right to pursue his or her activities. A list of those persons with the requisite experience has been prepared by the Department of the Environment. Any person on that list to whom a certificate has been issued under the proposed amendment will also come within the definition of an architect. It is the duty of solicitors to exercise caution in relation to the qualifications of a person from whom they will recommend acceptance of certificates of compliance. The reason for this is obvious—if a solicitor advises the client to accept a certificate of compliance in relation to a development, eg a house or house extension, from a person who is not adequately qualified and a problem arises, the solicitor will almost certainly be sued for negligence on the basis that he or she should not have accepted the certificate from a person who is not adequately qualified.

Thus when advising a client on a house purchase transaction regarding any material point such as whether a certificate of compliance relative to a house or an extension is in an acceptable form or is given by a person with an acceptable qualification, solicitors should apply a threefold test:

(a) In the solicitor's own opinion, is the particular package in order and in accordance with good conveyancing practice?

(b) Will it be acceptable under the rules or guidelines for the bank or building society from whom the client is borrowing?

(c) Will it be acceptable to most other solicitors if the property were to be put up for sale again in the near future?

If the answer to any of these questions is in the negative, a solicitor normally advises his or her client not to accept the situation and advises the client not to proceed with the transaction unless the difficulty is resolved.

If a query arises over the qualification of a person giving a certificate, the solicitor should take care to make it clear that he or she is not making the decision but is advising the purchaser, and that the final decision as to whether or not to proceed with the purchase is the client's responsibility. Most purchasers, particularly those borrowing, tend to be cautious and accept their solicitor's advice, but some will take a commercial judgment and proceed despite what the solicitor perceives as a problem. Obviously, if a client decides to proceed despite the solicitor's concern, it is imperative for the solicitor to confirm the advice in writing. A solicitor should also bear in mind that, while the Law Society will assist and advise its members in regard to such practice, none of this can absolve the individual solicitor from his or her responsibility to the client. In other words, each solicitor must look at each individual case on its own merits.

11.11.4 STANDARD FORMS OF COMPLIANCE

Following the introduction of the Building Regulations, 1991 (SI 306/1991) and the Building Control Regulations, 1991 (SI 305/1991) the Royal Institute of the Architects of Ireland (RIAI) issued a set of five Standard Forms of Opinion on Compliance for use by its own members. The Incorporated Law Society has recommended that the March 1993 edition of these forms is acceptable. Forms 1, 2 and 3 concern compliance with building regulations. Form 4 concerns compliance with planning permission and/or exemption from planning control and Form 5 concerns compliance with planning permission and/or building bye-law approval. See also the Law Society Gazette August/September 1997. An additional Form 1A was issued in March 1997. Form 1A concerns compliance of an apartment dwelling with Building Regulations. Further the Conveyancing Committee subsequently agreed with the Institution of Engineers of Ireland (IEI) and with the Association of Consulting Engineers in Ireland (ACEI) on the format of a certificate of compliance with Building Regulations for completion by a structural/civil chartered engineer in cases only where a lead architect is appointed to the project. This certificate was published in the Conveyancing Handbook in Appendix 8 at pp A8.1 to A8.5 (BR SE 9101). The most recent architect's certificate to be agreed by the RIAI and the Law Society is a Form 1B, issued in June 2001, which relates to an architect's opinion on compliance of an apartment dwelling with Building Regulations for use where a professional architectural service has been provided at the design and construction stage of a relevant building or works. (See **Appendix 11.1.**)

The Law Society has produced its own forms of certificates of compliance dated 7 May 1993 (see Law Society News, published November 1993). There are two forms dealing with compliance with planning requirements and building bye-laws, one for full service and the other for part only service, and two which concern compliance with planning and Building Regulations (full service and part service only). (See **Appendix 11.2.**)

The RIAI recommends to its members that they use its standard forms. Other certified professions generally follow the Law Society version.

The RIAI suggests that persons accepting forms from its members should check that the persons completing the forms are in fact members of the Institute and that the form carries the RIAI membership stamp. It also recommends that the original printed form be used rather than photocopies as this makes it very much easier to check that no amendments or alterations have been made to standard wording.

Frequently certificates of compliance are offered which are neither in the RIAI format nor the Law Society format. The RIAI form is often adopted without incorporating the definitions contained in the original version. This, of course, renders the document unintelligible. Care should be exercised when one is offered a form which is not in the RIAI or Law Society format to ensure that it covers the essential information.

In the Law Society Gazette, November 2001, the Conveyancing Committee issued a warning in relation to IEI/ACEI certificates of compliance. The Conveyancing Committee had previously agreed with the IE Ireland and with the ACE Ireland on the format of a certificate of compliance with Building Regulations for completion by a structural/civil chartered engineer in cases were a lead architect is appointed to the project. This certificate was published in the Conveyancing Handbook in Appendix 8 at pp A8.1 to A8.5 (BR SE 9101). A prominent warning was published in the Handbook on the front page of the specimen certificate of compliance to the effect that this form was intended for use only by a consulting engineer in the situation where a lead architect had also been appointed to the project. Despite this warning, this form is being offered by some vendors, in relation to projects where no architect has been involved, as the sole evidence of compliance with both planning and Building Regulations. The form has not been designed to meet this type of situation and under normal circumstances should not be used or accepted in connection therewith. The committee proceeded to confirm that the form relates only to compliance with Building Regulations and a further certificate of compliance with planning should always be obtained from the lead architect appointed to the project. It is suggested therefore that in projects where the consulting engineer leads the project, one or other of the specimen forms of compliance at pp 7.41 to 7.52 of the Conveyancing Handbook be utilised with appropriate adaptations.

11.11.5 WHAT IS THE ESSENTIAL INFORMATION?

The following is a checklist of the requirements for a certificate of compliance. At the very least it should:

(a) specify the qualifications of the persons who will give the certificate;

(b) specify the means of knowledge of the person giving the certificate (ie details of the inspection and knowledge of the plans, drawings and all the particulars on foot of which the planning permission and fire safety certificate are issued);

(c) confirm that the planning permission and fire safety certificate relate to the development being conveyed;

(d) confirm that the design of the development is in substantial conformity with the Building Regulations;

(e) confirm that the development is in substantial compliance with the planning permission;

(f) that a Commencement Notice has been served in applicable cases;

(g) that the conditions of the Fire Safety Certificate have been complied with;

(h) where the planning permission covers a large development of which works being certified form part and that larger development has not yet been completed, confirm that the general conditions of the planning permission have been substantially complied with in so far as it is reasonably possible up to the date of the issue of the certificate;

(i) not contain any qualifications or exceptions which are not generally acceptable in practice such as those that are in the RIAI forms. When necessary independent evidence of compliance with matters excluded from forms of certificate should be obtained;

(j) be dated and signed; and

(k) be an original.

It is fundamental in certifying compliance with the Building Regulations that the issue of the design of the works be dealt with. Where the certifier did not design the building a further certificate should be obtained from an appropriate person certifying compliance with the design elements. Also, copies of certificates upon which the certificate relies should be appended (see Practice Note, Law Society Gazette, August/September 1997).

Building bye-laws do still apply to some larger developments and, in particular, to housing estates where application for building bye-law approval was made prior to 1 June 1992. The form of architect's certificate which certifies compliance with planning requirements and building bye-laws for a house in a new housing estate is set out in the Law Society Gazette of November 1979, as amended by the Gazette of June 1982, and is still offered in some cases and, indeed, is perfectly acceptable.

Where a home extension which would be an exempted development was built without building bye-law approval, because building bye-law approval could not be issued retrospectively, the Law Society has issued a recommendation in the Gazette of March 1986 re the certificate to be accepted.

Where a property has been purchased with the assistance of a bank or building society loan, the purchaser's solicitors are frequently required to give a certificate of title. That certificate will generally have to show 'a good marketable title' has been obtained by the purchaser and that all current conveyancing recommendations of the Law Society have been followed.

Where an architect's certificate or opinion is not in the RIAI standard format or in the form prescribed by the Law Society, a solicitor may not be in a position to give the certificate of title sought.

A purchaser's solicitor should agree the format of the architect's certificate to be produced on completion and the qualification of the person who will give that certificate before signing a contract, otherwise a dispute may arise as to the form of certificate to be produced and a purchaser may find himself or herself unable to satisfy his lending institution as to the existence of a good marketable title or, at least, could be compelled to accept a certificate which is less than it should be.

329

11.11.6 INTEGRATED POLLUTION CONTROL (IPC) LICENSING

The recent introduction of Integrated Pollution Control Licensing under the Environmental Protection Agency Act, 1992 will necessitate a whole new set of enquiries in the conveyancing process where activities licensable by the Agency are concerned. The Law Society has not yet adopted a standard form of requisitions on title or conditions to accommodate the new Integrated Pollution Control (IPC) regime. Some of the significant features from the conveyancing perspective have been outlined by Patrick Sweetman, 'Recent Developments in Conveyancing Practice' IPELJ (1994) vol 1, no 3.

11.11.7 CERTIFICATES OF COMPLIANCE WITH RETENTION PERMISSION

Where a retention permission has been applied for and obtained it is still necessary for a purchaser to seek for confirmation by way of a letter of opinion by a suitably qualified person that the drawings submitted for the retention application correctly showed the actual structure for which permission to retain was applied for. If there are conditions to the grant of permission to retain, the certifier should go on to deal with these in the usual way. No certificate of compliance should be required where the permission related only to the retention of a change to use, where no conditions were attached. However is it reasonable to accept a title in a case where permission to retain an extension to a dwelling-house was obtained more than ten years ago and no certification of compliance is available? The Conveyancing Committee in the Law Society Gazette of May 2000 (see also November Gazette 1997) takes the view that in the light of the provisions of the 1992 Act, it is reasonable for the solicitor not to require certified compliance in such a case unless there is an evident problem. When acting for a vendor in such a case, a solicitor preparing a contract should put in a special condition putting the purchaser on notice of the position and providing that no requisition or objection shall be made due to lack of certification. In that way before signing a contract a purchaser has an opportunity of getting advice on the matter and, if necessary, of getting advice from an experienced architect or engineer.

11.12 Analysis of Planning Documentation

11.12.1 INTRODUCTION

The first thing to establish when examining planning documentation is what type of planning document is being looked at. This simple instruction is not always so simply complied with as there are several types of planning permissions which unfortunately all look very similar as, indeed, their names are equally similar. Therefore, it is important to look very carefully at the document being held. Some of the various types of planning documentation are set out below.

11.12.1.1 Outline planning permission

The grant of an outline planning permission does not authorise development. It is an agreement in principle and requires a grant of approval (post the 2000 Act, grant of permission) on foot of the outline permission before development may commence. The nature and character of outline planning permission has been changed substantially by s 36 of the 2000 Act (see below). However, given that conveyancers will, of course, be looking at planning permissions which issued before the new Act it is necessary to go into some detail on what those provisions in relation to outline permission were before addressing the changes wrought by the Act.

Article 3 of the Local Government (Planning and Development) Regulations, 1994 defined it as permission for development subject to the subsequent approval of the details. It established the *principle* of the acceptability of the development and could not subsequently be reassessed by the planning authority. The grant of outline permission in effect bound the planning authority to grant the development subject to conditions regulating the details of the proposal when an application consequent on such outline permission was made.

This arose from the statement of Barrington J in *The State (Pine Valley Development Ltd) v An Bord Pleanala* [1982] ILRM 169, who summarised the law as follows:

(a) a full permission in respect of which detailed plans must be lodged and on foot of which, if granted the development may immediately commence;

(b) an outline planning permission in which the applicant seeks approval in principle for the proposed development, which, if granted, does not authorise the commencement of development until the applicant has obtained an approval; and

(c) an approval which is a detailed approval by the planning authority of the development permitted in principle under the outline permission and which authorises the developer to commence the development.

It followed from this that the outline permission set the parameters within which the planning authority had to consider the application for an approval and that it was not open to the planning authority, at the approval stage, to reopen matters which have already been granted under the general terms of the outline permission.

It therefore appeared that outline permission, followed by an approval, was equivalent to a full permission. Thus, a developer having obtained his outline permission had gone a certain length of the road and when he applied subsequently for an approval, the planning authority was only concerned with the detail whereby the developer proposed to complete the development already approved in principle by the planning authority. However, in recent times in particular (see *Irish Asphalt v An Bord Pleanala* [1997] 1 ILRM 81) it had been decided that if there was a significant change in planning circumstances the planning authority could reconsider its decision. The court had more or less determined that outline permission could be effectively overturned at approval stage or substantially. So the situation on what exactly a developer was entitled to expect from such permission was unclear.

The main value of outline planning permission (prior to and post the 2000 Act) is that, at a relatively low cost (in terms of the designer's fees at least), it allows the principle of the development to be established and sets the parameters within which the planning authority must consider an application for subsequent approval. This type of planning permission is particularly valuable in the case of large sites where development may take place over a long period of time and whose precise architectural details could not be formulated at an early stage. In such cases it establishes the acceptability of the overall concept and allows for a series of approval applications to be lodged for individual sections as the proposal is further clarified.

Full planning permission was (prior to the 2000 Act) obtained in two different ways:

1. notification of *decision* to grant outline permission ⎫ outline
2. notification of *grant* of outline permission ⎬
3. notification of *decision* to grant approval ⎭ permission
4. notification of *grant* of **approval**

OR

1. notification of *decision* to grant permission
2. notification of *grant* of **permission**

Therefore, when given a grant of permission/approval one knows whether outline has issued by looking at the wording. If it says 'approval' then a grant of outline permission has issued and must be obtained. Post the 2000 Act, grants of 'approval' will cease to issue.

Section 36 of the Planning Act 2000 cures the uncertain status of an outline permission created by previous planning legislation and case law as outlined above. It provides the basis in primary legislation for outline permission where previously this was dealt with only in regulations. An outline permission does not authorise the carrying out of the development to which the permission relates until the subsequent *permission* has been granted under the 2000 Act. As a result of these new provisions the word *approval* will disappear from the planning vocabulary (see above).

In particular the provisions at sub-s (3)(a) and (b) should be noted:

(a) *Where outline permission has been granted by a planning authority, any subsequent application for permission must be made not later than three years beginning on the date of the grant of outline permission, or such period, not exceeding five years, as may be specified by the planning authority.*

(b) *The outline permission shall cease to have effect at the end of the period referred to in paragraph (a) unless the subsequent application for permission is made within that period.*

The section continues, however, to give the planning authority discretion to extend the life of the outline permission from three to five years. Outline permissions are in a special category in relation to the time limit of duration of the permission (see **11.12.3** below). In general under s 40, the duration of a planning permission is limited to five years. Section 41 of the Act provides that the planning authority or the Board may, having regard to the nature and extent of the development, and any other material considerations, specify the period in excess of five years during which the permission will be effective. Section 42 provides that a planning authority may, in relation to an application as regards a particular permission, extend the normal five-year period by such additional period as the authority considers requisite to enable the development to which the permission relates to be completed, subject to certain requirements. However, the provisions of ss 40, 41 and 42 do not apply to outline permissions.

Section 36(4) provides an important amendment which greatly strengthens the value of an outline permission by providing that the planning authority will not be able to refuse permission at the subsequent application on the basis of a matter agreed by the planning authority when the outline permission was granted, provided that the authority are satisfied that the proposed development is within the terms of an outline permission. Subsection (5) provides that no appeal can be brought to the Board under s 37 against the decision of a planning authority to grant permission consequent on the grant of outline permission in respect of any aspect of the proposed development which was decided in the grant of outline permission. The time for the third party objector to make an objection was by making a submission or observation on the outline permission after the date of lodgement and before the date of the decision and appealing the outline permission after the decision within the four-week period.

The provisions at s (36)(4) and (5) will be particularly welcome for developers in circumstances were they have obtained outline planning permission as it significantly limits the opportunity of the planning authority to revisit matters decided in the course of the grant of outline permission when considering an application for full planning permission. Likewise, having outline planning permission will limit the ability for appeals to be brought against decisions on an application based on the previous outline planning permission. This is a significant change to the pre-existing position.

The Planning and Development Regulations, 2001, art 21 place restrictions on outline applications in that they may not be made for permissions for retention of the development or for development which would consist of or comprise the carrying out of works to protected structures or a proposed protected structure, or development which comprises or is for the purposes of an activity requiring an IPC licence or waste licence. Article 22 goes on to list the contents of planning applications generally.

11.12.1.2 Notification of a decision to grant permission/approval

A notification of a decision to grant permission/approval is *not* a full permission. Essentially, it is a notice of intention to grant permission/approval (post the 2000 Act, permission only). During a period of four weeks (prior to the 2000 Act, one month) beginning on the date of the making of this decision, the applicant may appeal it or some conditions in it, to An Bord Pleanala. Where there is no appeal, the planning authority will formally give the grant of permission at the end of the appeal period. The applicant must not commence work until the final grant of planning permission issues.

11.12.1.3 Notification of grant of permission/approval

This is the actual planning permission. Since the 2000 Act, Grants of Approval no longer issue. The word 'approval' is no longer used in connection with outline permission.

11.12.1.4 Notification of grant of permission on appeal

After the notification of decision to grant permission issues, if it is appealed to An Bord Pleanala, the applicant will receive from An Bord Pleanala either the grant of permission with or without whatever conditions the Board considers appropriate or, if the Board so decides, a refusal of permission.

11.12.1.5 Notification of permission for retention

This application would be made where an unauthorised development has taken place and permission is sought to retain it. These circumstances would occur, for example, where no planning permission had ever been granted, or it had been granted but the building had not been erected in compliance with it, or there was an unauthorised use. One of the merits of this type of planning, unlike a proposed development, where its effect can only be gauged from drawings, is that its actual impact is evident and calculable. This approach should not be relied upon in order to avoid seeking planning permission before starting work as there is no guarantee permission for retention will be granted, or indeed the applicant may be required to carry out costly modifications. Note permission for retention does not automatically absolve the solicitor from prosecution if enforcement action has already been taken against him or her (see **11.7** above).

11.12.1.6 Notification of permission for continuance of use

11.12.2 PLANNING DOCUMENTATION CHECKLIST

Once it is decided what type of planning permission exists the following checklist should be applied:

(a) Is it a final grant?

(b) Does it relate to the property in question? If there are any doubts about this check with the architect's certificate of identity which should tie in the planning permission with the property.

(c) What is the expiry date of the planning permission? ie is the planning permission still alive? (see below)

(d) Was the property substantially completed within the lifespan of the planning permission? (see below)

(e) Check the conditions attached to the planning permission. The Local Government (Planning and Development) Act, 2000, s 34(4) sets out various types of conditions which a local authority may include in a planning permission, that is not to say that the local authority is in any way restricted to those conditions. However, the general power to impose conditions is not without limits and is subject to a number of limitations laid down by case law. It may impose any conditions it considers appropriate in the context of the proper planning and development of the area, provided, of course, that they are reasonably related to the application made. Although this section is similar to s 26(2) of the 1963 Act, there are some new conditions. Note that the conditions which dealt with the provision to collect financial contributions are no longer in the start of this section but are dealt with under ss 48 and 49 of the 2000 Act. The types of conditions may be divided into roughly five categories. These sections deal with development contributions and supplementary development contribution schemes.

11.12.2.1 Conditions regulating development works

For example, in the context of housing estates, it is quite common to find a condition which provides that certain houses not be built. This should be watched carefully, as the planning site number and the subsequent house number are not always the same and it is unfortunately not unheard of for a developer to erect houses which the planning permission required to be omitted. Therefore, an architect's certificate certifying same should be obtained.

Another example of a condition which may be imposed is that which would require that part of the larger development be ceded to the local authority and conveyancers, on notice of this requirement from reading the conditions, should ensure that it has been complied with.

11.12.2.2 Conditions precedent

Conditions precedent are obviously conditions which must be complied with before a development may proceed. A typical example is conditions requiring that steps be taken to protect trees or preserve open spaces. Another example would be the building of spine roads. Check whether an architect's certificate may cover these conditions or whether a third party, for example, the local authority, has to confirm it in writing. In other words, when on notice that a condition precedent has not been complied with, it is *not* sufficient to rely on the production of an architect's opinion on compliance. Each situation has to be examined on its own merits.

11.12.2.3 Financial conditions

There are two main types of financial conditions. The local authority often requires a developer to make a contribution towards the provision of services for the development—in large-scale developments the financial condition may be expressed as a certain sum per house/industrial unit. The second type of condition relates to a bond for the satisfactory completion of the common areas within the development prior to the local authority taking them in charge.

This condition may be made in the form of an indemnity bond or cash lodgement or guarantee from a body approved by the local authority.

Bonds are often arranged in stages so that a bond may be obtained covering only a portion of the development. However, provided that the developer furnishes evidence that the financial conditions have been complied with for the particular property, he or she may safely proceed (see Law Society Gazette Practice Note, April 1987).

With regard to bonds in relation to roads and services the architect's certificate will not show whether same has been complied with and a receipt from the local authority must be obtained or a letter from the local authority confirming that same has been complied with.

Sections 48 and 49 of the 2000 Act set out a new regime in respect of financial contributions. It is designed to ensure that there is some transparency in connection between the amounts collected from developers from infrastructural works and infrastructural works carried out by the local authority with these monies. These sections deal with the inclusion of contributions as conditions attached to planning permissions.

11.12.2.4 Conditions restricting future development

Conditions restricting future developments are increasingly common especially in urban areas where the size of gardens being sold with dwellinghouses, for example townhouses, is limited.

Frequently there is a prohibition against what would normally be exempt development on such a property provided it fell within the criteria, eg conservatories. Another example would be in relation to commercial property where there is a prohibition on advertising signs or a direction in relation to shop fronts. It is absolutely vital to alert the client to the existence of such a condition as the Local Government (Planning and Development) Regulations, 1994, art 10(1)(a)(i) (under the 2001 Regulations, art 9) which provides that any development referred to in the Second Schedule will not be exempt if it contravenes a condition attaching to a permission under the Acts, or is inconsistent with the use specified in a permission. Another typical condition, particularly on the east coast, restricts the use of a property to members of the family of the applicant. This occurs in cases where a farmer wishes to develop a site on part of his farm and the local authority does not wish to encourage linear development. In the past, by reason of the absolute wording of the condition, problems arose because no lending institution would lend on the security of the property. This clearly gave rise to problems in financing the construction of the dwelling. In addition, of course, it made it impossible to sell the house.

Where such a condition is encountered, an application for a new planning permission to free the property of this condition may be made. Local authorities noting all of the above problems nowadays tend to provide that the house when first constructed on a site be occupied by an applicant or member of his or her family.

11.12.2.5 Conditions incorporating previous permissions

When an alteration to or a revision of an existing permission has been obtained, the revised planning permission often incorporates the terms of the earlier permission. Clearly in such a case it is necessary to obtain a copy of the earlier permission and the terms of same should be read very carefully.

11.12.3 HOW LONG DOES A PLANNING PERMISSION LAST?

The Local Government (Planning and Development) Act, 1982, s 2 provided for a limit on the life of a planning permission (s 40 under the 2000 Act). The standard duration of a planning permission is five years from the date of the grant of the permission by the planning authority or An Bord Pleanala. A longer period may be allowed if the development is complex (see s 41). Note that the time runs from the granting of the permission. The decision of the planning authority on an application for approval/permission may be appealed to An Bord Pleanala, and this is a fact which should be taken into account.

If planning permission expires and an application for a new permission of the same development is made, the planning authority may refuse permission or attach significantly different conditions. This may happen if planning policies required for the proper planning and development of the area have changed in the interim. Prior to 1982, the situation in relation to the life of a planning permission was somewhat complex.

The current position is:

(a) from 1 November 1982, the average life of a planning permission is five years (see (d) below);

(b) for planning permission granted between 1 November 1976 and 31 October 1982 it was seven years from the grant or until 31 October 1987, whichever was the earlier date;

(c) for planning permission granted before 1 November 1976, the property had to be completed by 31 October 1983; if not it was an unauthorised development and in need of a retention order;

(d) withering permissions: s 96(15) of the 2000 Act. Any planning permission issued on foot of an application made after 25 August 1999 and before the local authority housing strategy is incorporated in this development plan will lapse as of 31 December 2002, or two years from the date planning permission was granted whichever is the later in respect of so much of the development, the external walls of which have not been completed.

This provision is clearly designed to allow planning authorities to impose social/affordable housing conditions in developments which are being constructed on foot of planning permissions issued before the housing strategy is in place. There is great uncertainty as to how the provisions will operate in practice and they could result in major delays in completing residential schemes, while the developer goes back to the planning authority for a new planning permission. See the article by Patrick Sweetman, 'Recent Developments in Conveyancing Practice', Irish Planning and Environmental Law Journal, vol 7, no 4.

The above time limits are subject to two exceptions:

(i) under the Local Government (Planning and Development) Act, 1982, s 3 (s 41 of the 2000 Act) the planning authority has the power to grant permission for a period of more than five years; and

(ii) if the five-year period established with the Local Government (Planning and Development) Act, 1976, s 29 had been extended to a date later than that provided for, the later date applies.

In certain circumstances the planning authority may extend the period of validity over a planning permission, but only where substantial work has been carried out during the lifetime of the permission and the planning authority is satisfied that the development will be completed in a reasonable time.

Under the Local Government (Planning and Development) Act, 1987, s 4 (s 42 of the 2000 Act) provision is made for the extension of these time limits where substantial works were carried out during the relevant period and a further extension where failure to carry out the works during the extended period was due to circumstances outside the control of the developer; 'substantial' is unfortunately not defined: it is suggested that substantial works comprise either works which show an intention of completing the scheme or alternatively works which would be an eyesore or otherwise contrary to good planning or development if left unfinished. See *Frenchurch Properties Ltd v Wexford County Council* [1991] ILRM 769 where it was held that a planning authority is entitled to have basic views and policies regarding what is in a general sense 'substantial works'. It may amount perhaps to as much as 40 to 50 per cent of the development, but the planning authority must decide each case on its merits and much would depend on the size and scale of the development, ie a small proportion of works being required have been carried out in a larger development. In this particular case Lynch J decided that the manufacture of a floor slab and steelworks off the site was works within the definition because these items were especially made and could not be used otherwise.

Outline permission is in a special category in relation to time limits for a permission. See **11.12.1.1**.

11.12.4 A GENERAL APPROACH TO A PLANNING QUESTION

Every practitioner approaches the checking of any planning issue in his or her own way. Below is one possible approach to a planning question.

In relation to the original building/use and each extension/change of use (in date order of occurrence), see **1(2)** below and **11.8.2.14** above re loss of exemption. Is there:

1. planning permission?

2. building bye-law approval/compliance with Building Regulations?

3. an architect's certificate of compliance with 1 and 2?

1.   *Planning permission*

In relation to planning, any development must have planning permission or be exempt from same.

Sources of exemptions are as follows:

1. pre-1963 (1/10/1964);

2. s 4 of the 1963 Act and 2001 Act;

3. under the 1977 Regulations;

4. under the 1994 Regulations;

5. under the 2000 Regulations; and

6. under the 2001 Regulations.

See **11.4** above.

If it is not exempt and there is no planning permission there are three possibilities:

(1) Apply for retention permission:
     There are some problems with this; it takes a long time to process the application, and retention permission may be refused. Further if retention permission is granted it might be granted with conditions which do not suit. Above all an application for retention permission invalidates the 'five-year rule/seven-year rule' (see **11.8.2.14** above).

(2) Rely on the 'five-year rule/seven-year rule':
     Section 19 of the Local Government (Planning and Development) Act, 1992 (replaced by s 157(4)(a)(i) of the 2000 Act) introduced what has become commonly known as the 'five-year rule/seven-year rule'. It does not say that an unauthorised development after five years/seven years becomes authorised. It merely says that the local authority after a period of five years/seven years may not serve an enforcement notice or take proceedings. However, this has certain consequences, which must be explained to your client (see **11.8.2.14**).

(3) Knock it down/cease the unauthorised use.

2.   *Bye-law approval/compliance with Building Regulations*

If there is no bye-law approval

(1) Check that the property is situate in an area where building bye-laws applied (see **11.9.1** above) because, if it is not, then obviously same did not have to be obtained.

(2) If it is in such an area, and same was not obtained, then see if it is now possible that an architect will certify that while bye-law approval was not obtained the development would have complied with same if it had been applied for (see Law Society Gazette, March 1986 and see **11.9.1** above).

(3) See if the bye-law amnesty applies. Section 22(7) of the Building Control Act, 1990 abolished the necessity to obtain bye law approval from 1 June 1992. The

building control authority had six months from 1 June 1992 to object to developments which were carried out prior to 13 December 1989 and provided no notice was served before 1 December 1992, the works will be deemed to have been built in compliance with the bye-laws (see **11.9.1** above).

Note: it is the usual practice to accept a vendor's declaration in relation to same. The precedent declaration below also incorporates a paragraph re the five-/seven-year rule:

STATUTORY DECLARATION

I,   of   aged eighteen years and upwards **DO SOLEMNLY AND SINCERELY DECLARE** as follows:

1. The property to which this Declaration relates is (hereinafter called 'the Property').

2. I say that I purchased the Property on the   day of   200   .

3. During the course of my ownership of the Property I have not received any Enforcement or other Notices under the Local Government (Planning and Development) Acts, 1963 to 1992 from the Planning Authority or any other person.

4. I say that Section 22 of the Building Control Act, 1990 has been explained to me and I say that the works carried out by me to the Property were carried out prior to the 13th of December 1989.

5. I say that no Notice has been served on me from the Building Control Authority in connection with works carried out to the Property within six months of the 1st of June 1992 stating that the works constituted a danger to public health or safety.

6. I say that Section 19 of the Local Government (Planning and Development) Act, 1992/ Section 157(4)(a) of the Local Government (Planning and Development) Act, 2000. has been explained to me and I say that as the 'works' to the Property had been completed for more than five years/seven years, it is my opinion that the Planning Authority are precluded from serving Enforcement Notices under the aforesaid Planning Act. It is also my opinion that the Local Authority is also precluded, in the circumstances from serving Warning Notices under Section 26 or Enforcement Notice under Section 37 of the 1976 Planning Act/Section 152 of the Local Government (Planning and Development) Act, 2000.

7. I make this solemn Declaration conscientiously believing the same to be true from facts within my own knowledge and belief and for the benefit of

DECLARED by the said

who is personally known to me at

in the City of Dublin, this   day of   , 2002

_____

COMMISSIONER FOR OATHS/
PRACTISING SOLICITOR

However building bye-laws are relevant in relation to works carried out between 13 December 1989 and 1 June 1992 and works carried out pursuant to bye-law approval applied for prior to 1 June 1992.

In relation to compliance with Building Regulations if they have not been complied with there is no 'solution', 'amnesty', 'five-year rule' etc.

3. *Architect's certificate of compliance*

In relation to all developments (including those that are exempt and in relation to those that have retention permission, see **11.11.7** above) an architect's certificate of compliance with planning/bye-laws/Building Regulations is required. However, note in relation to residential properties, there is a Law Society recommendation (Law Society Gazette of

January/February 1993) which states that prior to 1st December 1975 as it was not the practice to obtain architect's certificates of compliance it is recommended the same are not sought now in relation to residential properties only.

It is vital that in relation to all of the above, any 'solution', 'amnesty', 'five-/seven-year rule', 'Law Society recommendation' etc which may apply does not mean that you are in compliance with general condition 36. Therefore, if your planning is not absolutely perfect, general condition 36 of the Contract for Sale will have to be amended or deleted. Some examples of the appropriate Special Conditions are included in the Conveyancing Manual.

APPENDIX 11.1

RIAI Architect's Opinions on Compliance

ARCHITECT'S OPINION ON COMPLIANCE WITH BUILDING REGULATIONS

(FORM FOR USE WHERE A PROFESSIONAL ARCHITECTURAL SERVICE HAS BEEN PROVIDED AT THE DESIGN AND CONSTRUCTION STAGE OF THE RELEVANT BUILDING OR WORKS)

FORM 1

MARCH 1993 ISSUE

Reprinted May 2002

Published by Royal Institute of the Architects of Ireland in agreement with the Law Society for use in appropriate circumstances.

ADVICE NOTES

This Opinion should only be completed when the architect is satisfied that the Relevant Building or Works is in compliance with the requirements of the Building Control Act.

a   Insert the full name of your employer [not his agent].

b   Insert the full address of your employer.

c   Insert a precise description of the building, part of a building, or works to which this Opinion relates. Your description should be sufficiently precise as to ensure exclusion of other works attached to, associated with or otherwise connected to the Relevant Building or Works.

d   Insert a precise description of the services you provided as described in your terms of appointment, as, for example, *'Schedule A services of the 11 December 1992 RIAI Conditions of Appointment'*. Make particular reference to any variation from standard services, especially where this may involve services provided during the course of construction.

e   Confirm by insertion of one of the following phrases, that the Design of the Relevant Building or Works is in substantial compliance with the Building Regulations.

   [a]   I am of the opinion that the Design of the Relevant Building or Works is in Substantial Compliance with the Building Regulations.

   OR

   [b]   I am of the opinion that the Design of the Relevant Building or Works is in Substantial Compliance with the Building Regulations. I have received Confirmations from those detailed at Schedule A hereto, stating that elements of the Relevant Building or Works which they designed have been designed in Substantial Compliance with the Building Regulations. This Opinion relies solely on those Confirmations in respect of such elements.

f   Confirm by insertion of one of the following phrases, either that a Fire Safety Certificate to be detailed at Schedule B relates to the Relevant Building or Works, or that the Relevant Building or Works qualifies for exemption from the requirements to obtain a Fire Safety Certificate.

   [a]   I am of the Opinion that the fire Safety Certificate detailed at Schedule B hereto relates to the Relevant Building or Works and was obtained in accordance with the provisions of the Building Control Act and the Building Regulations.

   OR

   [b]   I am of the opinion that the Relevant Building or Works is exempt from any requirement for the making of an application for a Fire Safety Certificate by virtue of its being a building which is proposed to be used as a dwelling (other than a flat).

   OR

   [c]   I am of the opinion that the Relevant Building or Works is exempt from any requirement for the making of an application for a Fire Safety Certificate by virtue of being works commenced or a material change of use made before 1 August 1992.

g   Confirm by insertion of one of the following, either that a Commencement Notice to be detailed at Schedule C was served and insert the date of service, or that the Relevant Building or Works is exempt from the requirement for such notice.

[a]   The Commencement Notice, detailed at Schedule 'C' hereto relates to the Relevant Buildings or Works and was served as required under the terms of the Building Control Act on . . . . (date).

OR

[b]   I am advised by the Employer that the Commencement Notice detailed at Schedule C hereto and relating to the Relevant Building or Works was served as required under the terms of the Building Control Act on . . . . (date)

OR

[c]   The Relevant Building or Works is exempt from any requirement requiring the service of a Commencement Notice by virtue of its being exempted development for the purposes of the Local Government (Planning and Development) Acts, 1963 to 1992, and being a class of building or works to which Part III of S.1 305 of 1991 does not apply.

h   Insert the date of your inspection on site. The date should not be earlier than the date of practical completion but as soon as practicable thereafter.

i   Confirm by insertion of one of the following phrases, that the Construction of the Relevant Building or Works is in Substantial Compliance with the Building Regulations.

[a]   . . . the Construction of the Relevant Building or Works is in Substantial Compliance with the Building Regulations.

OR

[b]   . . . the Construction of The Relevant Building or Works is in Substantial Compliance with the Building Regulations. I have received Confirmations from those detailed at Schedule A hereto, that the Relevant Building or Works has been constructed in Substantial Compliance with the Building Regulations. This Opinion relies on Visual Inspection and on those Confirmations.

j   Insert at [a] one of the following, describing the inspections carried out during Construction.

[i]   Inspections carried out by the architect resident on site during the construction stage, being part of the services described at 2 above.

OR

[ii]   Periodic inspections carried out by the architect during the construction stage, being part of the services described at 2 above.
[note: frequent or constant inspection is not part of Standard Services]

k   Enter the Contractor/specialist/consultants' details and also the element(s) to which the Confirmation relates.

l   Enter the relevant details.

m   enter date of issue which should be as close as is practically possible to the inspection date.

n   Sign your name in full, state your RIAI membership number, and use your membership stamp in the space provided.

RIAI ARCHITECT'S OPINIONS ON COMPLIANCE

ARCHITECT'S OPINION
ON COMPLIANCE WITH BUILDING REGULATIONS
January 2001 Print

[FORM FOR USE WHERE A PROFESSIONAL ARCHITECTURAL SERVICE HAS BEEN PROVIDED AT THE DESIGN AND CONSTRUCTION STAGES OF THE RELEVANT BUILDING OR WORKS]

1. I am a Registered Member of The Royal Institute of the Architects of Ireland, this being a qualification listed in Directive 384/85/EEC of the European Community, retained by[a]

    . . . .

    . . . . (hereinafter called 'the Employer')

    of[b] . . . .

    to furnish an Opinion on the compliance with *Building Regulations* of[c]

    . . . .

    . . . .

    . . . .

    [hereinafter called *'the Relevant Building or Works'*].

    This opinion is issued solely for the purpose of providing evidence for title purposes of the compliance of the *Relevant Building or Works* with the requirements of the *Building Control Act*. Except insofar as it relates to such compliance it is not a report on the condition or structure of the *Relevant Building or Works*.

2. I have provided the following architectural services in connection with the *Relevant Building or Works*[d]

    . . . .

    . . . .

    . . . .

    . . . .

3. DESIGN[e]

    . . . .

    . . . .

    . . . .

    . . . .

4. FIRE SAFETY[f]

    . . . .

    . . . .

    . . . .

    . . . .

5.   COMMENCEMENT[g]

. . . .

. . . .

. . . .

. . . .

6.   INSPECTION[h]

On[h] . . . . ('the Inspection Date') I carried out an *Inspection* of the *Relevant Building or Works* for the purposes of (a) comparing such with its *Design* and (b) establishing its substantial compliance with the *Building Regulations*.

7.   CONSTRUCTION

It is the responsibility of those concerned with the construction of *the Relevant Building or Works* to ensure the compliance of such with the *Building Regulations*.

I am of the opinion that[i]

. . . .

. . . .

. . . .

. . . .

. . . .

DEFINITIONS

'Building Control Act'
means the Building Control Act, 1990 and any statutory modification or re-enactment thereof current at the date of the Commencement Notice referred to at Schedule C hereto.

'Building', 'Works', 'Construction' and 'Design' have the meanings respectively assigned by the *Building Control Act*.

'Building Regulations'
means regulations made under the *Building Control Act*.

'Confirmations'
means statements received from the persons detailed at Schedule A hereto, confirming substantial compliance of elements of *the Relevant Building or Works* with *Building Regulations*.

'Substantial Compliance' when applied to Design
means that the Design of the Relevant Building or Works, is in accordance with *the Building Regulations*, saving and excepting such deviations as would not in my opinion warrant the issue of enforcement proceedings as provided for in the *Building Control Act*.

'Substantial Compliance' when applied to Construction
means that such Construction of the Relevant Building or Works, as is evident by Visual Inspection, is in accordance with the Building Regulations, saving and excepting such deviations as would not in my opinion warrant the issue of enforcement proceedings as provided for in the *Building Control Act*.

RIAI ARCHITECT'S OPINIONS ON COMPLIANCE

'Visual Inspection' means

[a][j] . . . .

. . . .

. . . .

and

[b]   the Inspection of the *Relevant Building or Works* as existed on the Inspection Date. For the purposes of the Inspection no opening up was carried out. The inspection was therefore superficial only and took no account of works covered up, inaccessible or otherwise obscured from view.

SCHEDULE A: CONFIRMATIONS[k]

Contractor: . . . .

Of: . . . .

Element: . . . .

. . . .

Consultant/Specialist: . . . .

Of: . . . .

Qualification/profession: . . . .

Element: . . . .

Consultant/Specialist: . . . .

Of: . . . .

Qualification/profession: . . . .

Element: . . . .

Consultant/Specialist: . . . .

Of: . . . .

Qualification/profession: . . . .

Element: . . . .

Consultant/Specialist: ....

Of: ....

Qualification/profession: ....

Element: ....

___

Consultant/Specialist: ....

Of: ....

Qualification/profession: ....

Element: ....

___

SCHEDULE B: FIRE SAFETY CERTIFICATES[L]

Building Control

Authority: ....

Reference number: ....

Date of issue: ....

Decision Order number: ....

Date: ....

___

SCHEDULE C: COMMENCEMENT NOTICES[L]

Building Control

Authority: ....

Date of lodgement: ....

Reference number, if available: ....

THIS OPINION DOES NOT IN ANY WAY WARRANT REPRESENT OR TAKE INTO ACCOUNT:

Construction carried out or changes made to the *Relevant Building or Works* after the Inspection Date.

RIAI ARCHITECT'S OPINIONS ON COMPLIANCE

Date of Issue[m] . . . .

Signed[n]   . . . .
Registered Member of The Royal Institute of the Architects of Ireland

The RIAI is aware that persons are using the affix 'MRIAI' who are not members and who are not eligible to be members. Verification of membership can be obtained from the RIAI or by means of a current RIAI Membership stamp.

ARCHITECT'S OPINION ON COMPLIANCE OF AN APARTMENT DWELLING WITH BUILDING REGULATIONS

**FORM FOR USE FOR APARTMENTS WHERE A PROFESSIONAL
ARCHITECTURAL SERVICE HAS BEEN PROVIDED IN THE DESIGN
AND
A SITE INSPECTION SERVICE HAS NOT BEEN PROVIDED IN THE
CONSTRUCTION OF THE RELEVANT BUILDING OR WORKS
AND
WHERE THE ARCHITECT HAS NOT ADMINISTERED
THE BUILDING CONTRACT**

FORM 1A
(APARTMENTS)

This opinion is based on a visual inspection of the completed apartment and is issued in the matter of licences and consents only. It is not a report on the condition of the apartment nor does it relate to elements of the construction which are covered up, inaccessible or otherwise obscured from view. The RIAI advises that matters not evident by visual inspection may be material to the matter of substantial compliance.

FEBRUARY 2000 ISSUE

Reprinted January 2001

*Published by Royal Institute of the Architects of Ireland in agreement with the Law Society
for use in appropriate circumstances.*

ADVICE NOTES

This Opinion should be completed only by the Architect involved in the project at Design Stage and when the Architect is satisfied that the Relevant Building or Works is in compliance with the requirements of the Building Control Act. Members are advised that this opinion should be issued only where HomeBond confirmation of registration is available. Where such confirmation is not available Members should exercise the greatest care and caution if considering issuing an Opinion.

a   Insert the full name of your employer [not his agent].

b   Insert the full address of your employer.

c   Insert a precise description of the apartment to which this Opinion relates and of the development of which the apartment forms part.

d   Confirm by insertion of one of the following phrases, either that a Commencement Notice to be detailed at Schedule C was served and insert the date of service, or that the Relevant Building or Works is exempt from the requirements of such notice.

> *[a]   The commencement Notice, detailed at Schedule 'C' hereto relates to the Relevant Building or Works and was served as required under the terms of the Building Control Act on . . . . (date).*

> OR

> *[b]   I am advised by the Employer that the Commencement Notice detailed at Schedule C hereto and relating to the Relevant Building or Works was served as required under the terms of the Building Control Act on . . . . (date).*

e   Insert the date of your inspection on site. The date should not be earlier than the date of practical completion but as soon as possible thereafter.

f   Enter the Contractor/Specialist/Consultants details and also the element(s) to which the Confirmation relates.

g   Enter relevant details.

h   Enter date of issue which should be as proximate as possible to the inspection date.

i   Sign your name in full, state your RIAI membership number and use your membership stamp in the space proviced.

j   Members are advised that an Opinion On Compliance can be issued using this form only where confirmations are received from:

- The structural engineer responsible for the design of the structure.

- The contractor

- HomeBond (confirming registration)

- Specialist sub-contractors and suppliers including those responsible for the following:

  — Smoke Alarms

  — Fire Alarms

  — Fire Detection Systems

— Emergency Lighting

— Fire Doors

— Lifts

— Fire Stopping and Fire Barriers

— Mechanical Ventilation

ARCHITECT'S OPINION
ON COMPLIANCE WITH BUILDING REGULATIONS
March 1997

(FORM FOR USE FOR APARTMENTS WHERE A PROFESSIONAL ARCHITECTURAL SERVICE HAS BEEN PROVIDED AT THE DESIGN STAGE AND A SITE INSPECTION SERVICE HAS *NOT* BEEN PROVIDED AND THE ARCHITECT HAS *NOT* ADMINISTERED A BUILDING CONTRACT)

1   I am a Registered Member of the RIAI, this being a qualification listed in Directive 384/85/EEC of the European Community, retained by[a]

. . . .

. . . . (hereinafter called 'the Employer')

of[b] . . . .

to furnish an Opinion on the compliance with *Building Regulations* of[c]

Apartment . . . .

including such parts of the common and amenity areas, supporting, serving or leading to that Apartment to which the Building Regulations apply and those elements of the development of which it forms part, which materially affect the substantial compliance of such Apartment with the Building Regulations (the said Apartment, areas and elements being hereunder together referred to as 'the Relevant Building or Works').

Forming part of the development . . . . ('the Development')

This opinion issued solely for the purpose of providing evidence, for title purposes, of the compliance of the *Relevant Building or Works* with the requirements of the *Building Control Act*. Except insofar as it relates to such compliance, it does not include any opinion on the condition or structure of the *Relevant Building or Works*. It should be noted that a site inspection service was not provided.

2   I have provided the following architectural services in connection with the Development.

    (i)   Preparation and lodgement of drawings and documents on foot of which planning permission for the Development was granted.

    (ii)   Preparation and lodgement of drawings and documents on foot of which the Fire Safety Certificate for the Development detailed at Schedule B was granted.

    (iii)   Interpretation of information for the contractor.

    (iv)   Visual Inspection of the Relevant Building or Works.

PERIODIC INSPECTION OF THE WORK UNDER CONSTRUCTION DID NOT FORM PART OF THIS SERVICE NOR HAVE I ADMINISTERED THE BUILDING CONTRACT.

3   DESIGN

I am of the opinion that the Design of the Relevant Building or Works is in substantial compliance with the Building Regulations. I have received confirmations from those detailed at Schedule A hereto stating that elements of the Relevant Building or Works which they have designed are in Substantial Compliance with the Building

Regulations. This opinion relies solely on those confirmations in respect of such elements.

4   FIRE SAFETY

I am of the opinion that the Fire Safety Certificate detailed at Schedule 'B' hereto relates to the Relevant Buildings or Works and was obtained in accordance with the provisions of the Building Control Act and the Building Regulations.

5   COMMENCEMENT[d]

. . . .

. . . .

. . . .

. . . .

6   INSPECTION[e]

On . . . . ('the Inspection Date') I carried out a Visual Inspection of the completed *Relevant Building or Works* for the purposes of (a) completing such with its *Design* and (b) establishing its substantial compliance with the *Building Regulations*.

This opinion does not in any way warrant, represent or take into account construction carried out or charges made to the Relevant Building or Works and/or the Development after the Inspection Date.

7   CONSTRUCTION

It is the responsibility of those concerned with the construction of the *Relevant Building or Works* to ensure the compliance of such with the *Building Regulations*.

I have not provided a full architectural service in the course of the construction of the Relevant Building or Works and a site inspection service was not provided nor have I administered a Building Contract. I am therefore unable to comment on, methods of construction, materials used, and elements of the *Relevant Building or Works* not evident by Visual Inspection. *I am of the opinion*, based solely on the service described at 2 above, that such construction of the Relevant Building or Works as is evident by Visual Inspection is in substantial compliance with the Building Regulations and in preparing this Opinion on Compliance I have relied on such Visual Inspection and confirmations from the contractor, the structural engineer, specialist sub-contractors and suppliers as detailed in Schedule A.

RIAI ARCHITECT'S OPINIONS ON COMPLIANCE

SCHEDULE A: CONFIRMATIONS[f]

BUILDING CONTRACTOR

Contractor: . . . .

Of: . . . .

Element   Construction of the Relevant Building or Works

STRUCTURAL ENGINEER[f]

Contractor: . . . .

Of: . . . .

Qualification/profession: . . . .

Element   Design of Structural Elements

MECHANICAL VENTILATION[f]

Consultant/Specialist: . . . .

Of: . . . .

Qualification/profession: . . . .

Element   Design and Installation of Mechanical Ventilation

LIFT[f]

Consultant/Specialist: . . . .

Of: . . . .

Qualification/profession: . . . .

Element   Design and installation of lift

FIRE ALARM[f]

Consultant/Specialist: . . . .

Of: . . . .

Qualification/profession: . . . .

Element   Design and Installation of Fire Alarm

SMOKE ALARM[f]

Consultant/Specialist: . . . .

Of: . . . .

Qualification/profession: . . . .

Element   Design and Installation of Smoke Alarm

FIRE DETECTION SYSTEM[f]

Consultant/Specialist: . . . .

Of: . . . .

Qualification/profession: . . . .

Element   Design and Installation of Fire Detection System

EMERGENCY LIGHTING[f]

Consultant/Specialist: . . . .

Of: . . . .

Qualification/profession: . . . .

Element   Design and Installation of Emergency Lighting

FIRE DOORS[f]

Consultant/Specialist: . . . .

Of: . . . .

Qualification/profession: . . . .

Element   Design and Installation of Fire Doors

FIRE STOPPING/FIRE BARRIERS[f]

Consultant/Specialist: . . . .

Of: . . . .

Qualification/profession: . . . .

Element   Design and Installation of Fire Stopping

SCHEDULE B: FIRE SAFETY CERTIFICATES[f]

Building Control Authority: . . . .

Reference Number: . . . .

Date of Issue: . . . .

Decision Order Number: . . . .

Date: . . . .

SCHEDULE C: COMMENCEMENT NOTICES[g]

Building Control Authority: . . . .

Date of Lodgement: . . . .

Reference Number, if available: . . . .

DEFINITIONS

'Building Control Act'
means the Building Control Act, 1990 and any statutory modification or re-enactment thereof current at the date of the Commencement Notice referred to at Schedule C hereto, or (if the Relevant Building or Works is exempt from the requirements for such Notice) at the date of the commencement thereof.

'Building', 'Works', 'Construction'
have the meanings respectively assigned by the *Building Control Act 1990*.

'Design'
has the meaning assigned by the Building Control Act 1990.

'Building Regulations'
means regulations made under the *Building Control Act*.

'Confirmations'
means statements, *copies of which are annexed hereto* received from the persons detailed at Schedule A hereto, confirming substantial compliance of elements of *the Relevant Building or Works* which they have designed or constructed/installed with *Building Regulations*.

'Substantial Compliance' when applied to Design
means that the Design of the Relevant Building or Works, is in accordance with *the Building Regulations*, saving and excepting such deviations as would not in my opinion warrant the issue of enforcement proceedings as provided for in the *Building Control Act*.

'Substantial Compliance' when applied to Construction
means that such Construction of the Relevant Building or Works, as is evident by Visual Inspection, is in accordance with the Building Regulations, saving and excepting such deviations as would not in my opinion warrant the issue of enforcement proceedings as provided for in the *Building Control Act*.

'Visual Inspection'
means the Inspection of the completed *Relevant Building or Works* as existed on the Inspection Date, which inspection was limited to:

— Visual Inspection of Apartment
— Visual Inspection from the exterior of the common and amenity areas supporting, serving or leading to the Apartment.
— Visual Inspection of the service ducts servicing the Apartment where accessible.
— Visual Inspection of external areas.
— For the purposes of the Inspection no opening up was carried out. The inspection was therefore superficial only and took no account of works covered up, inaccessible or otherwise obscured from view.

RIAI
MEMBERSHIP STAMP

Date of Issue[h] . . . .

Signed[i and j]   . . . .

Registered Member of The Royal Institute of the Architects of Ireland

The RIAI advises that matters not evident by Visual Inspection may be material to the matter of substantial compliance.

The RIAI is aware that persons are using the affix 'MRIAI' who are not members and who are not eligible to be members. Verification of membership can be obtained from the RIAI or by means of a current RIAI Membership stamp.

THE ROYAL INSTITUTE OF THE ARCHITECTS OF IRELAND

• FOUNDED 1839 •

ARCHITECT'S OPINION ON COMPLIANCE OF AN APARTMENT DWELLING WITH BUILDING REGULATIONS

(FORM FOR USE WHERE A PROFESSIONAL ARCHITECTURAL SERVICE HAS BEEN PROVIDED AT THE DESIGN AND CONSTRUCTION STAGE OF THE RELEVANT BUILDING OR WORKS)

FORM 1B
(APARTMENTS)

JUNE 2001 ISSUE

Published by Royal Institute of the Architects of Ireland in agreement with the Law Society for use in appropriate circumstances.

ADVICE NOTES

This Opinion should only be completed when the architect is satisfied that the Relevant Building or Works is in compliance with the requirements of the Building Control Act. Members are advised that this opinion should be issued only where Home Bond confirmation of registration is available. Where such confirmation is not available Members should exercise the greatest care and caution if considering issuing an opinion.

a   Insert the full name of your employer [not his agent].

b   Insert the full address of your employer.

c   Insert a precise description of the apartment to which this opinion relates and of the development of which the apartment forms part.

d   Insert a precise description of the services you provided as described in your terms of appointment, as, for example, *'Schedule A services of the 11 December 1992 RIAI Conditions of Appointment'*. Make particular reference to any variation from standard services, especially where this may involve services provided during the course of construction.

e   Confirm by insertion of one of the following phrases, that the Design of the Relevant Building or Works is in substantial compliance with the Building Regulations.

    [a]   *I am of the opinion that the Design of the Relevant Building or Works is in Substantial Compliance with the Building Regulations.*

    OR

    [b]   *I am of the opinion that the Design of the Relevant Building or Works is in Substantial Compliance with the Building Regulations. I have received Confirmations from those detailed at Schedule A hereto, stating that elements of the Relevant Building or Works which they designed have been designed in Substantial Compliance with the Building Regulations. This Opinion relies solely on those Confirmations in respect of such elements.*

f   Confirm by insertion of one of the following phrases, either that a Fire Safety Certificate to be detailed at Schedule B relates to the Relevant Building or Works, or that the Relevant Building or Works qualifies for exemption from the requirements to obtain a Fire Safety Certificate.

    [a]   *I am of the Opinion that the fire Safety Certificate detailed at Schedule B hereto relates to the Relevant Building or Works and was obtained in accordance with the provisions of the Building Control Act and the Building Regulations.*

    OR

    [c]   *I am of the opinion that the Relevant Building or Works is exempt from any requirement for the making of an application for a Fire Safety Certificate by virtue of being works commenced or a material change of use made before 1 August 1992.*

g   Confirm by insertion of one of the following, either that a Commencement Notice to be detailed at Schedule C was served and insert the date of service, or that the Relevant Building or Works is exempt from the requirement for such notice.

    [a]   *The Commencement Notice, detailed at Schedule 'C' hereto relates to the Relevant Buildings or Works and was served as required under the terms of the Building Control Act on . . . . (date)*

OR

[b]   *I am advised by the Employer that the Commencement Notice detailed at Schedule C hereto and relating to the Relevant Building or Works was served as required under the terms of the Building Control Act on . . . . (date)*

OR

[c]   *The Relevant Building or Works is exempt from any requirement for the service of a Commencement Notice by virtue of its being exempted development for the purposes of the Planning and Development Act, 2000 (or, as the case may be, any other Acts which it superseded) and being a class of building or works not necessitating the procurement of a Fire Safety Certificate.*

h   Insert the date of your inspection on site. The date should not be earlier than the date of practical completion but as soon as practicable thereafter.

i   Confirm by insertion of one of the following phrases, that the Construction of the Relevant Building or Works is in Substantial Compliance with the Building Regulations.

[a]   *. . . the Construction of the Relevant Building or Works is in Substantial Compliance with the Building Regulations.*

OR

[b]   *. . . the Construction of The Relevant Building or Works is in Substantial Compliance with the Building Regulations. I have received Confirmations from those detailed at Schedule A hereto, that the Relevant Building or Works has been constructed in Substantial Compliance with the Building Regulations. This Opinion relies on Visual Inspection and on those Confirmations.*

j   Insert at [a] one of the following, describing the inspections carried out during Construction.

[i]   *Inspections carried out by the architect resident on site during the construction stage, being part of the services described at 2 above.*

OR

[ii]   *Periodic inspections carried out by the architect during the construction stage, being part of the services described at 2 above.*
[note: frequent or constant inspection is not part of Standard Services]

k   Enter the Contractor/specialist/consultants' details and also the element(s) to which the Confirmation relates.

l   Enter the relevant details.

m   enter date of issue which should be as close as is practically possible to the inspection date.

n   Sign your name in full, state your RIAI membership number, and use your membership stamp in the space provided.

ARCHITECT'S OPINION
ON COMPLIANCE WITH BUILDING REGULATIONS
June 2001 Print

[FORM FOR USE WHERE A PROFESSIONAL ARCHITECTURAL SERVICE HAS BEEN PROVIDED AT THE DESIGN AND CONSTRUCTION STAGES OF THE RELEVANT BUILDING OR WORKS]

1. I am a Registered Member of The Royal Institute of the Architects of Ireland, this being a qualification listed in Directive 384/85/EEC of the European Community, retained by[a]

    . . . .

    . . . . (hereinafter called 'the Employer')

    of[b] . . . .

    to furnish an Opinion on the compliance with *Building Regulations* of[c] Apartment .

    . . . .

    including such parts of the common and amenity areas, supporting, serving or leading to that Apartment to which the Building Regulations apply and those elements of the development of which it forms part, which materially affect the substantial compliance of such Apartment with the Building Regulations (the said Apartment, areas and elements being hereunder together referred to as 'the Relevant Building or Works') forming part of

    . . . .

    ('the Development').

    This opinion is issued solely for the purpose of providing evidence for title purposes of the compliance of the *Relevant Building or Works* with the requirements of the *Building Control Act*. Except insofar as it relates to such compliance it is not a report on the condition or structure of the *Relevant Building or Works*.

2. I have provided the following architectural services in connection with the *Relevant Building or Works*[d]

    . . . .

    . . . .

    . . . .

3. DESIGN[e]

    . . . .

    . . . .

    . . . .

4. FIRE SAFETY[f]

    . . . .

    . . . .

    . . . .

5.   COMMENCEMENT[g]

. . . .

. . . .

. . . .

6.   INSPECTION[h]

On[h] . . . . ('the Inspection Date') I carried out an *Inspection* of the *Relevant Building or Works* for the purposes of (a) comparing such with its *Design* and (b) establishing its substantial compliance with the *Building Regulations*.

7.   CONSTRUCTION

It is the responsibility of those concerned with the construction of *the Relevant Building or Works* to ensure the compliance of such with the *Building Regulations*.

I am of the opinion that[i]

. . . .

. . . .

. . . .

. . . .

. . . .

DEFINITIONS

'Building Control Act'
means the Building Control Act, 1990 and any statutory modification or re-enactment thereof current at the date of the Commencement Notice referred to at Schedule C hereto.

'Building', 'Works', 'Construction' and 'Design' have the meanings respectively assigned by the *Building Control Act*.

'Building Regulations'
means regulations made under the *Building Control Act*.

'Confirmations'
means statements received from the persons detailed at Schedule A hereto, confirming substantial compliance of elements of *the Relevant Building or Works* with *Building Regulations*.

'Substantial Compliance' when applied to Design
means that the Design of the Relevant Building or Works, is in accordance with *the Building Regulations*, saving and excepting such deviations as would not in my opinion warrant the issue of enforcement proceedings as provided for in the *Building Control Act*.

'Substantial Compliance' when applied to Construction
means that such Construction of the Relevant Building or Works, as is evident by Visual Inspection, is in accordance with the Building Regulations, saving and excepting such deviations as would not in my opinion warrant the issue of enforcement proceedings as provided for in the *Building Control Act*.

'Visual Inspection' means

[a][j] . . . .

. . . .

. . . .

and

[b] the Inspection of the *Relevant Building or Works* as existed on the Inspection Date. For the purposes of the Inspection no opening up was carried out. The inspection was therefore superficial only and took no account of works covered up, inaccessible or otherwise obscured from view.

SCHEDULE A: CONFIRMATIONS[k]

Contractor: ....

Of: ....

Element: ....

....

_____

Consultant/Specialist: ....

Of: ....

Qualification/profession: ....

Element: ....

_____

Consultant/Specialist: ....

Of: ....

Qualification/profession: ....

Element: ....

_____

Consultant/Specialist: ....

Of: ....

Qualification/profession: ....

Element: ....

_____

Consultant/Specialist: ....

Of: ....

Qualification/profession: ....

Element: ....

_____

RIAI ARCHITECT'S OPINIONS ON COMPLIANCE

Consultant/Specialist: . . . .

Of: . . . .

Qualification/profession: . . . .

Element: . . . .

SCHEDULE B: FIRE SAFETY CERTIFICATES[L]

Building Control

Authority: . . . .

Reference number: . . . .

Date of issue: . . . .

Decision Order number: . . . .

Date: . . . .

SCHEDULE C: COMMENCEMENT NOTICES[L]

Building Control

Authority: . . . .

Date of lodgement: . . . .

Reference number, if available: . . . .

THIS OPINION DOES NOT IN ANY WAY WARRANT REPRESENT OR TAKE INTO ACCOUNT:

Construction carried out or changes made to the *Relevant Building or Works* after the Inspection Date.

RIAI
MEMBERSHIP STAMP

Date of Issue[m] . . . .

Signed[n] . . . .
Registered Member of The Royal Institute of the Architects of Ireland

The RIAI is aware that persons are using the affix 'MRIAI' who are not members and who are not eligible to be members. Verification of membership can be obtained from the RIAI or by means of a current RIAI Membership stamp.

ARCHITECT'S OPINION ON COMPLIANCE WITH BUILDING REGULATIONS

(FORM FOR BUILDERS OR WORKS IN CONNECTION WITH WHICH A DESIGN ONLY SERVICE HAS BEEN PROVIDED AND WHERE A FIRE SAFETY CERTIFICATE IS NOT REQUIRED)

FORM 2

MARCH 1993 ISSUE

Reprinted June 2000

Published by Royal Institute of the Architects of Ireland in agreement with the Law Society for use in appropriate circumstances.

ADVICE NOTES

This Opinion should only be completed when the architect is satisfied that the Relevant Building or Works is in compliance with the requirements of the Building Control Act.

a   Insert the full name of your employer [not his agent].

b   Insert the full address of your employer.

c   Insert a precise description of the building, part of a building, or works to which this opinion relates. Your description should be sufficiently precise as to ensure exclusion of other works attached to associated with or otherwise connected to the Relevant Building or Works.

d   Before issuing an Opinion using this Form, satisfy yourself that the Relevant Building or Works qualifies for exemption from the requirement to obtain a Fire Safety Certificate.

> *[i]   . . . the Relevant Building or Works is exempt from any requirement for the making of an application for a Fire Safety Certificate by virtue of its being a building which is proposed to be used as a dwelling (other than a flat).*

OR

> *[ii]   . . . the Relevant Building or Works is exempt from any requirement for the making of an application for a Fire Safety Certificate by virtue of being* works commenced *or* a material change of use *made before 1 August 1992.*

e   Confirm by insertion of one of the following phrases, either that a Commencement Notice was served and insert the date of service, or that the Relevant Building or Works is exempt from the requirement for such notice.

> *[i]   The Relevant Building or Works is exempt from any requirement requiring the service of a Commencement Notice by virtue of being exempted development for the purposes of the Local Government (Planning and Development) Acts, 1963 to 1992 and being a class of Building or Works to which part iii of S.1 305 of 1991 does not apply.*

OR

> *[ii]   I am advised by the Employer that a Commencement Notice relating to the Relevant Building or Works was served as required under the terms of the Building Control Act on . . . . (date)*

f   Insert the date of your inspection on site. The date should not be earlier than the date of practical completion but as soon as practicable thereafter.

g   Enter date of issue which should be as close as is practically possible to the Inspection Date.

h   Sign your name in full, state your RIAI membership number, and use your membership stamp in the space provided.

ARCHITECT'S OPINION
ON COMPLIANCE WITH BUILDING REGULATIONS
March 1993 Issue

[FORM FOR USE FOR BUILDINGS OR WORKS IN CONNECTION WITH WHICH
A DESIGN-ONLY SERVICE HAS BEEN PROVIDED AND WHERE A FIRE SAFETY CERTIFICATE
IS NOT REQUIRED]

1. I am a Registered Member of the Royal Institute of the Architects of Ireland, this being a qualification listed in Directive 384/85/EEC of the European Community retained by[a]

    . . . .

    . . . . (hereinafter called 'the Employer')

    of[b] . . . .

    to furnish an Opinion on the compliance with *Building Regulations* of[c]

    . . . .

    . . . .

    . . . .

    [hereinafter called *'the Relevant Building or Works'*].

    This Opinion is issued solely for the purpose of providing evidence for title purposes of the compliance of the *Relevant Building or Works* with the requirements of the *Building Control Act*. Except insofar as it relates to such compliance it is not a report on the condition or structure of the *Relevant Building or Works*.

2. I have provided architectural services in the matter of the architectural design of the *Relevant Building or Works*.

3. DESIGN
    I am of the opinion that the *Design* of the *Relevant Building or Works* is in Substantial Compliance with *the Building Regulations*.

4. FIRE SAFETY
    I am of the opinion that[d] . . . .

    . . . .

    . . . .

5. COMMENCEMENT[e]

    . . . .

    . . . .

    . . . .

6. INSPECTION

    On[f] . . . . ('the Inspection Date') I carried out a *Visual Inspection* of the *Relevant Building or Works* for the purposes of (a) comparing such with its *Design* and (b) establishing its substantial compliance with *the Building Regulations*.

7.   CONSTRUCTION

It is the responsibility of those concerned with the construction of the *Relevant Building or Works* to ensure the compliance of such with *the Building Regulations*.

I did not provide professional services in connection with the construction of the *Relevant Building or Works*.

In the absence of evidence of independent professional inspection of the Relevant Building or Works in the course of construction, I am unable to comment on methods of construction, materials used, and elements of the Relevant Building or Works, not evident by *Visual Inspection*.

I am of the opinion that such construction of the *Relevant Building or Works* as is evident by *Visual Inspection* is in Substantial Compliance with *the Building Regulations*.

DEFINITIONS

'Building Control Act' means the Building Control Act 1990 and any statutory modification or re-enactment thereof current at the date of the Commencement Notice aforesaid.

'Building', 'Works' and 'Construction' have the meanings respectively assigned by the *Building Control Act*.

'Building Regulations' means regulations made under the Building Control Act.

'Design' has the meaning assigned by the *Building Control Act*, but excepting such design as could, in my opinion, reasonably be outstanding pending the construction stage.

'Substantial Compliance' when applied to Design
means that in my opinion the Design of the Relevant Building or Works, is in accordance with *the Building Regulations*, saving and excepting such deviations as would not in my opinion warrant the issue of enforcement proceeding as provided for in the *Building Control Act*.

'Substantial Compliance' when applied to Construction
means that such Construction of the Relevant Building or Works, as is evident by Visual Inspection, is in accordance with the Building Regulations, saving and excepting such deviations as would not in my opinion warrant the issue of enforcement proceedings as provided for in the Building Control Act.

'Visual Inspection' means the inspection of the Relevant Building or Works as existed on the Inspection Date. No opening up was carried out. The inspection was therefore superficial only and took no account of works covered up, inaccessible or otherwise obscured from view.

THIS OPINION DOES NOT IN ANY WAY WARRANT, REPRESENT OR TAKE INTO ACCOUNT:

Construction carried out or changes made to the *Relevant Building or Works* after the Inspection Date.

RIAI
Membership Stamp

Date of Issue[g] . . . .

Signed[h]   . . . .
Registered Member of The Royal Institute of the Architects of Ireland

The RIAI advises that matters not evident from Visual Inspection may be material to the matter of Substantial Compliance.

The RIAI is aware that persons are using the affix 'MRIAI' who are not members and who are not eligible to be members. Verification of membership can be obtained from the RIAI or by means of a current RIAI Membership stamp.

ARCHITECT'S OPINION ON EXEMPTION FROM BUILDING REGULATIONS

(FOR USE ONLY FOR BUILDING OR WORKS EXEMPT FROM ANY NEED FOR COMPLIANCE WITH BUILDING REGULATIONS)

FORM 3

MARCH 1993 ISSUE

Reprinted June 2000

Published by Royal Institute of the Architects of Ireland in agreement with the Law Society for use in appropriate circumstances.

ADVICE NOTES

This Opinion should only be completed when the architect is satisfied that the Relevant Building or Works is exempt from any need to comply with the Building Regulations.

a   Insert the full name of your employer [not his agent].

b   Insert the full address of your employer.

c   Insert a precise description of the building, part of a building, or works to which this Opinion relates. Your description should be sufficiently precise to ensure exclusion of other works attached to associated with or otherwise connected to the Relevant Building or Works.

d   Confirm by insertion of one of the following phrases, that the Relevant Building or Works is exempt from the requirement to comply with the Building Regulations.

    [i]   I am advised by the Employer that the Relevant Building or Works were commenced prior to 1 June 1992 and based on this information I am of the opinion that the Relevant Building or Works is exempt from any need for compliance with the Building Regulations.

    OR

    [ii]   I am of the opinion that the Relevant Building or Works is exempt from any need for compliance with The Building Regulations, by virtue of its being works to which Building Byelaws apply, and for which approval was given on foot of plans, which, in accordance with such Byelaws, were deposited before 1st June 1992.

    OR

    [iii]   I am of the Opinion that the Relevant Building or Works is exempt from any need for compliance with The Building Regulations, by virtue of being a building subject to the National Monuments Acts, 1930 to 1987 or works in connection therewith.

e   Enter date of issue.

f   Sign your name in full, state your RIAI membership number, and use your membership stamp in the space provided.

ARCHITECT'S OPINION
ON EXEMPTION FROM BUILDING REGULATIONS
March 1993 Issue

[FOR USE ONLY FOR BUILDINGS OR WORKS EXEMPT FROM ANY
NEED FOR COMPLIANCE WITH BUILDING REGULATIONS]

1. I am a Registered Member of the Royal Institute of the Architects of Ireland, this being a qualification listed in Directive 384/85/EEC of the European Community retained by[a]

    . . . .

    . . . .

    . . . . (hereinafter called 'the Employer')

    of[b] . . . .

    to furnish an Opinion on exemption from *the Building Regulations* of[c]

    . . . .

    . . . .

    [hereinafter called *'the Relevant Building or Works'*].

    This Opinion is issued solely for the purpose of providing evidence for title purposes of the exemption from the need for the *Relevant Building or Works* to comply with the requirements of the *Building Control Act*. Except insofar as it relates to such exemption this Opinion is not a report on the condition or structure of the *Relevant Building or Works*.

2. EXEMPTION[d]

    . . . .

    . . . .

    . . . .

DEFINITIONS

'Building Control Act' means the Building Control Act 1990 and any statutory modification or re-enactment thereof current at the date of this opinion.

'Building' and 'Works' have the meanings respectively assigned by the *Building Control Act*.

'Building Regulations' means regulations made under the Building Control Act.

RIAI
MEMBERSHIP STAMP

Date of Issue[e] . . . .

Signed[f] . . . .

Registered Member of The Royal Institute of the Architects of Ireland

The RIAI is aware that persons are using the affix 'MRIAI' who are not members and who are not eligible to be members.

Verification of membership can be obtained from the RIAI or by means of a current RIAI Membership stamp.

THE ROYAL INSTITUTE OF THE ARCHITECTS OF IRELAND

· FOUNDED 1839 ·

ARCHITECT'S OPINION ON COMPLIANCE WITH PLANNING PERMISSION AND/OR EXEMPTION FROM PLANNING CONTROL

FORM 4

MARCH 1993 ISSUE

Reprinted November 2000

*Published by Royal Institute of the Architects of Ireland in agreement with the Law Society
for use in appropriate circumstances.*

ADVICE NOTES

General Note

This Opinion refers only to the Planning Acts as hereinafter defined.

This Opinion on Compliance should not be issued for developments which clearly contravene the Planning Laws. Architects giving an opinion are strongly advised to refrain from qualifying the opinion beyond the limits prescribed in this Advice Note. They are particularly urged to refrain from attaching schedules of work or omissions which attach to such qualifications.

Completing the Form

a   Insert the full name of your employer [not his agent]

b   Insert your employer's full address. This need not be the Relevant Development address.

c   Describe in full the Relevant Development. This description should define specifically the development or the part of the development on which the opinion is issued and may differ from the development described in the Planning Orders. A careful description will help to minimise the risk of misrepresentation.

d   Delete as appropriate either Planning Permission, exemption from control, or such combinations as are appropriate in each use.

e   Insert a precise description of the services you provided as described in your terms of appointment, for example, 'Schedule A services of the 11 December 1992 RIAI Conditions of Appointment'. Make particular reference to any variation from standard services.

f   Enter the date of your inspection of the Relevant Documents.

g   Enter the date of your Visual Inspection of the Relevant Development.

h   Insert the appropriate paragraph from the following using the wording in italics:

[i]   *. . . , based on the services provided as described at 2 above, and on a comparison of the Relevant Development with the Relevant Documents, the Relevant Development is in Substantial Compliance with the Planning Orders.*

This paragraph relates to the Relevant Development which has been granted planning permission and has been carried out in Substantial Compliance with that permisson.

OR

[ii]   *. . . , the Relevant Development is exempted development as defined by the Planning Acts, by virtue of its being a class of development described as such at*

. . . .

This paragraph relates to a Relevant Development which qualifies as exempted development within the meaning of the Planning Acts. Insert the appropriate exemption reference from the Acts or Regulations.

Note that development which clearly contravenes the Building Regulations, but which would otherwise be exempted from the provisions of the Planning Acts, may not be exempted development by reason of such contravention. No Opinion on Compliance should be issued in such circumstances.

Note also that the cumulative effect of subsequent or previous development may affect the Substantial Compliance or exemption of the Relevant Development: for example the floor area of an original dwelling house may only be increased by an aggregate of the exempted floor area whether by conversion(s) and/or extension(s).

i   This clause is applicable to developments such as housing estates, apartment developments, retail and industrial developments where Opinions are issued prior to the completion of the development.

   ... the conditions of the Planning Orders relating to the overall Development(s) of which the Relevant Development forms part, have been substantially complied with insofar as is reasonably possible at this stage of the Development.

j   If the service you are providing is solely the single inspection referred to at 4, strike out the words 'inter alia'.

k   Schedule here conditions of the Planning Permission, compliance with which cannot be established from the Relevant Documents on the public record, or from your own records, where you are the architect for the Relevant Development.

l   Insert the date of issue of the Opinion. It is good practice to ensure that the date of issue and the date of inspection of the files and development are as close as practicable.

m   Sign your name in full, state your RIAI membership number, and use your membership stamp in the space provided.

n   See Advice Note c as to the description of the Relevant Development.

o   Enter the precise description of the development, using the wording on the Planning Order, for each separate Planning Permission.

ARCHITECT'S OPINION
ON COMPLIANCE WITH PLANNING PERMISSION
AND/OR EXEMPTION FROM PLANNING CONTROL
March 1993 Issue

1.   I am a Registered Member of The Royal Institute of the Architects of Ireland, this being a qualification listed in Directive 384/85/EEC of the European Community, retained by[a]

. . . .

. . . . (hereinafter called 'the Employer')

of[b] . . . .

to furnish an Opinion on the Compliance of[c]

. . . .

. . . .

[hereinafter called *'the Relevant Development'*] with Planning Permission and/or exemption from planning control within the meaning of the Planning Acts.

This Opinion is based on the Visual Inspection only of the Relevant Development carried out for the purpose of comparison of such with the *Relevant Documents*. It is issued solely for the purpose of providing evidence for title purposes of the compliance of the *Relevant Development* with Planning Permission and/or exemption from planning control within the meaning of the Planning Acts.[d] Except insofar as it relates to such compliance/exemption[d] it is not a report on the condition or structure of the *Relevant Development*.

2.   I have provided the following architectural services in connection with the *Relevant Development*[e]

. . . .

. . . .

3.   On[f] . . . . I inspected the *Relevant Documents* at the offices of

. . . .

['the relevant Planning Authority'] for the purposes of comparison of the *Relevant Development* with the *Relevant Documents*. I confirm that the Planning Orders in the Schedule hereto (hereinafter called *'the Planning Orders'*) are those registered in respect of and relating to the *Relevant Development*.

4.   On[g] . . . . ('the Inspection Date') I carried out a *Visual Inspection* of the *Relevant Development* for the purposes of comparison of the *Relevant Development* with the *Relevant Documents*.

5.   I am of the opinion that[h] . . . .

. . . .

. . . .

RIAI ARCHITECT'S OPINIONS ON COMPLIANCE

6.   I am also of the opinion that[i] . . . .

. . . .

. . . .

DEFINITIONS

'*Planning Acts*' means the Local Government (Planning and Development) Acts, 1963 to 1992 and any statutory modification or re-enactment thereof current at the Date of Issue of this Opinion and all Regulations, Statutory Instruments and Orders made under or pursuant to the said Acts and for the time being in force.

'*Substantial Compliance with the Planning Orders*' means that:

[a]   the *Relevant Development* is constructed in accordance with the said Planning Orders saving and excepting such minor deviations which in my opinion do not constitute a contravention of the proper planning and development of the area as expressed through the said Planning Orders and the Development Plan, and

[b]   such minor deviations do not warrant the issue of enforcement proceedings by the relevant Planning Authority as provided for in the Planning Acts.

'*Relevant Documents*' means inter alia[j] those drawings and documents, available at the date at 3 above for public inspection on the planning file, which were submitted to, and on foot of which, the Planning Authority issued the Planning Orders.

'*Visual Inspection*' means an inspection of the Relevant Development as existed on the Inspection Date. No opening up was carried out. The inspection was superficial only and therefore took no account of works covered up or inaccessible.

This opinion does not in any way warrant, represent or take into account any of the following matters:

1.   The accuracy of dimensions in general save where incorporated by virtue of the conditions of the Planning Orders.

2.   The following conditions, compliance with which cannot be established[k]

Register Ref.	Condition[s]
Register Ref.	Condition[s]
Register Ref.	Condition[s]

3.   Matters in respect of private rights or obligations.

4.   Matters of financial contribution and bonds.

5.   Development of the property which may occur after the Inspection Date.

6.   Any other development attached to, associated with or otherwise connected to the Relevant Development, save insofar as such other development may affect the Substantial Compliance with the Planning Orders or exemption from Planning Control within the meaning of the Planning Acts of the Relevant Development.

RIAI
MEMBERSHIP STAMP

Date of Issue[l] . . . .

Signed[m]   . . . .

Registered Member of The Royal Institute of the Architects of Ireland

376

SCHEDULE attached to the Opinion on Compliance with Planning Permission for[n]

i   Development[o]   ....

....

Register Reference No: .... Date: ....

Decision Order No: .... Date of Grant of Permission: ....

ii   Development[o]   ....

....

Register Reference No: .... Date: ....

Decision Order No: .... Date of Grant of Permission: ....

iii   Development[o]   ....

....

Register Reference No: .... Date: ....

Decision Order No: .... Date of Grant of Permission: ....

iv   Development[o]   ....

....

Register Reference No: .... Date: ....

Decision Order No: .... Date of Grant of Permission: ....

· FOUNDED 1839 ·

ARCHITECT'S OPINION ON COMPLIANCE WITH PLANNING PERMISSION AND/OR EXEMPTION FROM PLANNING CONTROL AND/OR BYE LAW APPROVAL

FORM 5

MARCH 1993 ISSUE

Reprinted June 2000

Published by Royal Institute of the Architects of Ireland in agreement with the Law Society
for use in appropriate circumstances.

ADVICE NOTES

On Architects Opinion on Compliance

GENERAL NOTE

This Opinion refers only to the Planning Acts and Building Bye Laws as hereinafter defined.

This opinion on Compliance may not be issued for developments which clearly contravene the Planning Laws or Building Bye Laws. Architects giving an opinion are strongly advised to refrain from qualifying the opinion beyond the limits prescribed in this Advice Note. They are particularly urged to refrain from attaching schedules of works or omissions which attach to such qualifications.

COMPLETING THE FORM (letters relate to notation letters):

a.   Insert the full name of your employer (not his agent).

b.   Insert the full address of the employer. This need not necessarily be the Relevant Development Address.

c.   Describe in full the Relevant Development. This description should define specifically the development or the part of the development on which the Opinion is issued and may differ from the development described at paragraph 2 below.

d.   Delete as appropriate either Planning Permission, Bye Law Approval or exemption from control or such combinations as are appropriate in each case.

e.   Insert a precise description of the services you provided as described in your terms of appointment, as, for example, Schedule A Services of the 11 December 1992 RIAI Conditions of Appointment. Make particular reference to any variation from standard services.

f.   Enter the date(s) of your inspection of the planning file (Relevant Documents).

g.   Enter the date(s) of your Visual Inspection of the Relevant Development.

h.   Insert the appropriate paragraph from the following using the wording in italics;

   (a)   *. . . based on the services provided as described at 2 above, and on a comparison of the Relevant Development with the Relevant Documents, the Relevant Development is in Substantial Compliance with the Planning Orders.*
   This paragraph relates to a Relevant Development which has been granted planning permission and has been carried out in Substantial Compliance with that permission.

   (b)   *based on the services provided as described at 2 above, and insofar as a Visual Inspection of the Relevant Development can reasonably disclose, the Relevant Development is in Substantial Compliance with the Building Bye Laws.*
   This paragraph relates to a Relevant Development which has been granted a Building Bye Law approval and has been constructed in Substantial Compliance with the Building Bye Laws.

EXEMPTED DEVELOPMENTS;

   (c₁)   *. . . the Relevant Development is exempted development as defined by the Planning Acts being . . .*

379

This paragraph relates to a Relevant Development which qualifies as exempted development within the meaning of the 1963 Planning Act.

(c₂)   . . . the Relevant Development is exempted development as defined by the Planning Acts by virtue of it being a class of Development described as such at. . .

This paragraph relates to a Relevant Development which qualifies as exempted development within the meaning of the Planning Acts and which has been granted a Building Bye Law approval. Therefore this paragraph must be accompanied by paragraph h(b) above, and will refer to exempted development carried out on foot of the Local Government (Planning & Development) Regulations S.I. 65 of 1977.

(c₃)   . . . that the Relevant Development would have qualified as exempted development as defined by the Planning Acts by virtue of it being a class of development described as such at . . . . save that a Building Bye Law Approval Order was not obtained.

This paragraph relates to a Relevant Development which would have qualified as exempted development under the Planning Acts had Building Bye Law Approval been obtained. Therefore this paragraph must be accompanied by paragraph h(d) above, and will refer to exempted development carried out on foot of the Local Government (Planning & Development) Regulations S.I. 65 of 1977.

DEVELOPMENTS WITHOUT BYE LAWS;

(d)   . . . whereas a Building Bye Law Approval Order was not obtained, and insofar as a Visual Inspection can reasonably disclose, the Relevant Development is in substantial compliance with the Building Bye Laws, saving and excepting those requiring the giving of notice and, submission of documents for receipt of approval, prior to the commencement of development.

This paragraph relates to a Relevant Development constructed without having obtained a Building Bye Law Approval which in your opinion has been constructed in Substantial Compliance with the Building Bye Laws.

Depending on which of the above paragraphs are included in the Opinion, part or all of paragraph 3 may be struck out as appropriate.

Note that the cumulative effect of subsequent, or previous development may affect the substantial Compliance or exemption of the Relevant Development; for example the floor area of an original dwelling house may only be increased by an aggregate of the exempted floor area whether by conversion(s) and/or extension(s).

Note also that development which clearly contravenes the Building Bye Laws, but which would otherwise be exempted from the provisions of the Planning Acts, may not be exempted development by reason of such contravention. No Opinion on Compliance should be issued in such circumstances.

i.   This clause is applicable to developments such as housing estates, apartment developments, retail and industrial developments where Opinions are issued prior to the completion of the development

. . .the conditions of the Planning Orders relating to the overall development(s) of which the Relevant Development forms part, have been substantially complied with insofar as is reasonably possible at this stage of the development(s).

j.   If the service you are providing is solely the single inspection referred to at 4, strike out the words inter alia.

k.   Insert at (a) one of the following, describing the inspections carried out during Construction.

[i]   Inspections carried out by the architect resident on site during the construction stage, being part of the services described at 2 above.

OR

[ii]   Periodic inspections carried out by the architect during the construction stage, being part of the services described at 2 above.

Where no service was provided in the course of construction strike out section (a) or enter 'not applicable'.

l.   Schedule here conditions of the Planning Permission, compliance with which cannot be established from the Relevant Documents on the public record, or from your own records, where you are the architect for the Relevant Development.

m.   Insert the Date of Issue of the Opinion. It is good practice to ensure that the Date of Issue and the dates of inspection of the files and development are as close as practicable.

n.   Sign your name in full, state your RIAI membership number, and use your membership stamp in the space provided.

o.   Enter the wording at 1 (see Advice Note c) used to describe the Relevant Development.

p.   Enter the precise description of the development, using the wording on the Planning Order, for each separate Planning Permission.

q.   Enter the precise description of the development using the wording on the Building Bye Law Order for each separate approval.

ARCHITECT'S OPINION ON COMPLIANCE WITH PLANNING PERMISSION AND/OR EXEMPTION FROM PLANNING CONTROL AND/OR BYE LAW APPROVAL
March 1993 Issue

1. I am a Registered Member of The Royal Institute of the Architects of Ireland, this being a qualification listed in Directive 384/85/EEC of the European Community, retained by[a]

    . . . . (hereinafter called 'the Employer')

    of[b] . . . .

    to furnish an Opinion on the Compliance of[c] . . . .

    . . . . [hereinafter called 'the Relevant Development'] with Planning Permission and/or Bye Law Approval and/or exemption from planning control within the meaning of the Planning Acts[d].

    This Opinion is issued solely for the purpose of providing evidence for title purposes of the compliance of the Relevant Development with Planning Permission and/or (if applicable) Building Bye Law Approval and/or (if applicable) exemption from planning control within the meaning of the Planning Acts. Except insofar as it relates to such compliance it is not a report on the condition or structure of the Relevant Development.

2. I have provided the following architectural services in connection with the Relevant Development[e] . . . .

    . . . .

3. On[f] . . . . I inspected the Relevant Documents at the offices of . . . . ('the relevant Planning Authority') for the purposes of comparison of the Relevant Development with the Relevant Documents. I confirm that the Planning Orders at Schedule A hereto are those registered in respect of and relating to the Relevant Development, and that the Building Bye Law Orders at Schedule B hereto are those registered in respect of and relating to the Relevant Development.

4. On[g] . . . . ('the Inspection Date') I carried out a Visual Inspection of the Relevant Development for the purposes of comparison of the Relevant Development with the Relevant Documents.

5. I am of the opinion that[h] . . . .

    . . . .

    . . . .

6. I am also of the opinion that[i] . . . .

    . . . .

    . . . .

DEFINITIONS

'*Planning Acts*' means the Local Government (Planning and Development) Acts, 1963 to 1992 and any statutory modification or re-enactment thereof current at the Date of Issue of this Opinion, and all Regulations, Statutory Instruments and Orders made under or pursuant to the said Acts and for the time being in force.

'*Substantial Compliance with the Planning Orders*' means that:

(a) the *Relevant Development* is constructed in accordance with the said Planning Orders saving and excepting such minor deviations which in my opinion do not constitute a contravention of the proper planning and development of the area as expressed through such Planning Orders and the Development Plan, and

(b) such minor deviations do not warrant the issue of enforcement proceedings by the relevant Planning Authority as provided for in the Planning Acts.

'*Building Bye Laws*' means Bye Laws referred to in Section 22(1), Building Control Act, 1990 and applicable before the coming into operation of that Act.

'*Substantial Compliance with Building Bye Laws*' means that the *Relevant Development* is constructed in accordance with the said Building Bye Law Orders saving and excepting such minor deviations that in my opinion do not warrant the issue of enforcement proceedings.

'*Relevant Documents*' means inter alia[j] those drawings and documents, available on the date at 3 above for public inspection in the planning file, which were submitted to, and on foot of which, the Planning Authority issued the said Planning Orders and/or the said Building Bye Law Orders.

'*Visual Inspection*' means

(a)[k] . . . .

. . . . and

(b) an inspection of the Relevant Development as existed on the Inspection Date. No opening up was carried out. The inspection was therefore superficial only and took no account of works covered up, inaccessible or otherwise obscured from view, and which may be fundamental to the matters hereby opined.

THIS OPINION DOES NOT IN ANY WAY WARRANT, REPRESENT OR TAKE INTO ACCOUNT:

a. The accuracy of dimensions in general save where incorporated by virtue of the conditions of the Planning Orders.

b. Structural Calculations except where prepared and submitted by the undersigned.

c. The following conditions, compliance with which cannot be established.[l]

d. Matters in respect of private rights or obligations.

e. Matters of financial contribution and bonds.

f. Development of the property which may occur after the Inspection Date.

g. Any other development attached to associated with or otherwise connected to the Relevant Development save insofar as such other development may affect Substantial Compliance with the Planning Orders or Substantial Compliance with the Building Bye Laws.

RIAI ARCHITECT'S OPINIONS ON COMPLIANCE

Date of Issue[m] . . . .

Signed[n] . . . .
Registered Member of The Royal Institute of the Architects of Ireland

SCHEDULE A Attached to the Opinion on Compliance for[o] . . . .

Development[p] . . . .

. . . .

Register Reference No. . . . . Date: . . . .

Decision Order No: . . . . Date of Grant of Permission: . . . .

Development[p] . . . .

. . . .

. . . .

Register Reference No. . . . . Date: . . . .

Decision Order No: . . . . Date of Grant of Permission: . . . .

SCHEDULE B

Development[q] . . . .

. . . .

Register Reference No. . . . . Date: . . . .

B.B.L. Order No. Date: . . . .

Development[q] . . . .

. . . .

Register Reference No. . . . . Date: . . . .

B.B.L. Order No. Date: . . . .

OPINIONS ON COMPLIANCE: FEES

The RIAI recommends that fees for opinions on compliance should be charged on the basis of £1.75 per square metre of building size plus a time charge calculated at the appropriate rate based on one half of the time involved in preparing the opinion, subject to a minimum charge of £150 and a maximum of £10,000.

APPENDIX 11.2

Law Society Forms of Certificates of Compliance

LAW SOCIETY CONVEYANCING HANDBOOK
CHAPTER 7   PLANNING
PLANNING/BUILDING REGULATIONS
FORMS OF CERTIFICATE OF COMPLIANCE

LAW SOCIETY FORMS OF CERTIFICATES OF COMPLIANCE

The Conveyancing Committee has been working for a considerable period on the preparation of new forms of Certificates of Compliance to replace the form of certificate of compliance with Planning and Building Bye-Laws originally published by the Law Society in the Gazette in November 1978.

Four new forms of certificate of compliance and a memorandum explaining their important features are attached.

The RIAI have published a set of five Architects Opinion on Compliance and the RIAI have very kindly agreed to send a full set of these five specimen forms to each firm of solicitors in the Country. With this Newsletter is a memorandum explaining their important features as far as the Law Society are concerned.

The Committee would prefer Solicitors to get certificates of compliance on the Law Society forms and Solicitors should try to negotiate that its forms will be used where possible.

It is suggested that Solicitors should insert the RIAI forms and the attached documentation in their copy of the Conveyancing Handbook. As soon as all the guidelines are issued the Committee will be revising Chapter 7 of the Handbook which deals with planning.

The Committee is aware that Solicitors have tended to exercise caution in relation to the qualifications of persons from whom they will accept certificates of compliance. The reason for this is obvious. If a Solicitor advises a client to accept a Certificate of compliance in relation to a development such as a house or a house extension from a person who is not adequately qualified and a problem arises the Solicitor will almost certainly be liable in negligence on the basis that he should not have accepted or recommended acceptance of the certificate from a person who was not adequately qualified.

When advising a client in a house purchase transaction regarding any material point such as whether a Certificate of Compliance relative to a house or extension is in an acceptable form or given by a person with an acceptable qualification Solicitors usually apply a threefold test:

1.   In the Solicitor's own opinion is the particular matter in order and in accordance with good conveyancing practice?;

2.   Will it be acceptable under the rules or guidelines of the Bank or Building Society from whom the client is borrowing?; and,

3.   Will it be acceptable to most other Solicitors if the property were to be put up for sale again in the near future?

If the answer to any of these questions is in the negative the Solicitor will normally advise his or her client not to accept the situation and to advise the client not to proceed with the transaction unless the particular difficulty is resolved. Solicitors apply somewhat similar tests in relation to commercial property but obviously the requirements are more variable and more stringent in relation to the same.

If a query arises over the qualification of a certifier the Solicitor should take care to make it clear that he or she is not making the decision but is advising the purchaser and that the final decision in the matter of whether to proceed with the purchase or not is the clients. Most purchasers, particularly those borrowing, will tend to be cautious and accept their Solicitor's advice but some will take a commercial judgment and proceed despite what the Solicitor perceives as a problem. Obviously if a client decides to proceed despite the Solicitor's concerns, it is good practice for the Solicitor to confirm the advice in writing. Solicitors should also bear in mind that while the Law Society will assist and advise its members in regard to best practice none of this can absolve the individual solicitor from his responsibility to the client. Each solicitor must look at each individual case on its own merits.

The Committee is carrying out a review of this whole area and will issue further guidelines when the practice in relation to the use of the various certificates has settled down. The Society intends to hold several seminars to explain the certificates and to assist practitioners in dealing with the complicated issues that arise in relation to this increasingly complex area.

The Conveyancing Committee is preparing draft requisitions pending revision of the printed forms and these will be issued as soon as possible.

LAW SOCIETY FORMS OF CERTIFICATE OF COMPLIANCE FOR CONVEYANCING

The Society has prepared four forms of certificate of compliance *which are set out at the end of this newsletter*. These are:-

1. A certificate of compliance with planning permission and building regulations, full service.

2. A certificate of compliance with planning permission and building regulations, part service.

3. A certificate of compliance with planning permission and building bye-laws, full service.

4. A certificate of compliance with planning permission and building bye-laws, part service.

Part Service means that the certifier designs the house, obtains planning permission therefor but does not make periodic inspections in the course of construction and gives a certificate based on one inspection when the house is practically completed.

Full Service means a case where the certifier designs the house, obtains planning permission therefor and makes periodic inspections while the building is being constructed.

Normally a certifier would give a full service in connection with larger developments and part service would only arise in connection with speculative developments.

These forms have been agreed with the following professional bodies and will be used when appropriate by their Architects and Building Surveyors. Enquiries regarding membership can be made to the contact points listed below where a register is kept.

1. The Irish Architects Society. It has its registered offices at 35 Fitzwilliam Place, Dublin 2. Phone Number (01)6688685. The Honorary Secretary is John C. O'Grady, 67 Grosvenor Road, Dublin 6. Phone Number (01)4979990 and (01)4979620. Fax Number (01)4976777.

2. The Incorporated Association of Architects and Surveyors, Irish Branch. It has its office at Hogan House, Hogan Place, Dublin 2. Phone Number (01)6613022, Fax (01)6613130.

3. The Architects and Surveyors Institute. Its Secretary is Arthur Dunne who can be contacted at 7 Woodbine Park, Blackrock, County Dublin—Phone Number (01)2694462. Its memberships officer's name is Des Holmes—Phone number (01)2862369.

4. The Society of Chartered Surveyors, 5, Wilton Place, Dublin 2, Phone Number (01)676 5500, (01)6763276. The General Secretary is Tony Smyth.

The following points should be noted:-

1. There are notes at the end of each form which are intended to assist those filling them in.

2. The forms are not sacrosanct and should be adapted to meet the circumstances of any particular case.

3. Compliance of the design with building regulations is just as important as compliance of the construction and, therefore the form of certificate of compliance based on the original agreed form of certificate of compliance originally published in 1978, which did not separate design and construction, would not be appropriate in relation to certification of compliance with building regulations.

389

4.   The Building Control Act and the Regulations thereunder provide for a notice called a Commencement Notice to be given to the Building Control Authority by relevant parties. While Building Control Authorities keep a register for their own use neither the Act nor any of the Regulations give the public a right of access to it and after a lapse of time, there will be extreme difficulty and indeed it may often prove impossible to establish whether a Commencement Notice was or was not served in relation to any particular development. It is clearly very important for the maintenance of good standards of building that Building Control Authorities monitor building standards. The service of Commencement Notices in every case will be an important ingredient in this process. The maintenance of such standards however and taking a tough line with persons who fail to serve Commencement Notices or breach the Act or Regulations is a matter for the Building Control Authorities. It hardly seems reasonable however that the failure to serve a Commencement Notice should make a particular property unsaleable. The effect of not serving the Commencement Notice in any case is that the person or persons carrying out the development commits an offence but this should not impact on a subsequent owner. In most cases, therefore, it seems reasonable for Solicitors for subsequent owners not to concern themselves unduly about whether a Commencement Notice was served or not. The Committee sees no point in insisting on the production of a copy of the Commencement Notice if such copy is not readily available.

5.   The Building Control Act and the Regulations thereunder also impose an obligation on the relevant parties to apply for a Fire Safety Certificate in relation to all new structures other than single dwellings, (not being flats) and in relation to any material developments by way of extension alteration or change of use. The Building Control Regulations provide for an official register to be kept of all applications for Fire Safety Certificates and the decision in relation thereto and whether an appeal was made against the decision. This Register will be available to the public. It is clear that Fire Safety Certificates and their compliance are going to be of vital importance for Conveyancers. The tenor of the Act and the relevant Regulations obviously intend that a Fire Safety Certificate would be obtained before the development commences. Indeed where a FSC is required in relation to the erection of any building or the material extension or alteration of any building it is an offence to start work without first getting the Fire Safety Certificate. It is already clear that this is not always going to happen, particularly in relation to fitting out buildings where retailers are in a hurry to get a shop open. The Fire Safety Certificate procedure is a paper exercise only. Plans, specification and various particulars are submitted and in due course the Building Control Authority, assuming the submissions are in order, issues the Fire Safety Certificate either subject to conditions or not which in effect says that provided that the development is carried out in accordance with the details submitted, and presumably any conditions thereof, that it complies with the Fire Section of the Building Regulations. Solicitors are already being asked to accept situations where the development is carried out first and the Fire Safety Certificate is obtained later. There does not seem to be any serious problem for a subsequent owner in accepting such a situation because any offence is committed by the party or parties obliged to obtain the Fire Safety Certificate or carrying out the work. Solicitors should take care that the Certificate of Compliance they get deals fully with the situation. It would be particularly important to have clear confirmation in such a case that any conditions of a Fire Safety Certificate had been complied with.

6.   The Committee has been advised that it would be almost impossible for an Architect or Engineer who was not involved in the design to certify compliance of a structure or works with the Building Regulations or with a Fire Safety Certificate. Even in the case of fitting out a building therefore it would be extremely unwise for a person to have such work commenced unless an appropriately qualified person

whose certificate was likely to be accepted by conveyancers was involved in the design of the work and made sufficient inspections to be able to later issue a certificate of compliance.

7. Most commercial and industrial buildings have Architects and Engineers involved in the design and making inspections while the building work is being carried out. Most largescale housebuilding is designed by an Architect or Engineer but is not inspected in the course of construction. The Architect or Engineer in due course gives a certificate of compliance based on a single visual inspection at completion. Most once-off houses do not have an Architect or Engineer involved and this and extensions and conversions to private houses is the sector where most problems are likely. Persons borrowing from a Building Society when building a new house are normally required to have an appropriately qualified person involved who will be able to certify that they designed and carried out inspections of the structure at certain stages of construction. It seems likely that there are going to be problems for some people who have houses built, converted or extended without professional guidance and indeed some houses are likely to be unsaleable as a result.

8. In relation to Building Bye Laws, Solicitors should note the provisions of Section 22 (7) of the Building Control Act, 1990, where an amnesty is granted to work carried out prior to the 13th December 1989, and approval of such works under the Building Bye Laws is deemed to have been granted. Proceedings shall not be taken on the basis of non compliance with Building Bye Laws unless before 1st December 1992 the Local Authority served a notice on the owner stating the works constituted a danger to public health or safety.

9. The Committee has agreed to monitor the operation of the forms of certificate with the Professional bodies mentioned above and to review them in the light of experience. The use of the two certificates referring to Building Bye-Laws will gradually disappear over the next five years.

10. It has been decided not to advise Solicitors to ask for confirmation or verification of the existence and adequacy of certifiers Professional indemnity Insurance. The position in this respect will be kept under review.

RIAI FORM OF ARCHITECTS OPINION ON COMPLIANCE FOR CONVEYANCING PURPOSES[1]

Most Architects in Ireland are members of the Royal Institute of Architects of Ireland. This institute has offices at 8 Merrion Square, Dublin 2, Phone Number (01)6761703. Its General Secretary is John Graby.

The RIAI has recently published five[2] forms of Architects opinion on compliance. These are:

Form 1. ARCHITECT'S OPINION ON COMPLIANCE WITH
BUILDING REGULATIONS
This is a form for use where a professional Architectural service has been provided at the design and construction stage of the relevant building or works.

Form 2. ARCHITECT'S OPINION ON COMPLIANCE WITH
BUILDING REGULATIONS
This is a form for use for Buildings or works in connection with which a design only service has been provided and where a fire safety certificate is not required.

LAW SOCIETY FORMS OF CERTIFICATES OF COMPLIANCE

Form 3.   ARCHITECT'S OPINION ON EXEMPTION FROM
BUILDING REGULATIONS
This form is for use for Buildings or works exempt from any need for compliance with building regulations.

Form 4.   ARCHITECT'S OPINION ON COMPLIANCE WITH
PLANNING PERMISSION AND OR EXEMPTION FROM
PLANNING CONTROL

Form 5.   ARCHITECT'S OPINION ON COMPLIANCE WITH
PLANNING PERMISSION AND/OR BYE-LAW APPROVAL

The following points should be noted regarding these certificates:-

1.   Copies can be obtained at a cost of £3 each from the RIAI.

2.   The RIAI forms refer at the commencement to its member being a registered member of the RIAI this being a Qualification listed in directive 384/85/EEC (The Architects Directive). The Society feels that this is completely unnecessary and should not be included in certificates by Irish Architects in relation to domestic developments.

3.   Form 4 of the RIAI forms deals only with compliance with planning and/or exemption from Planning control. The Society feels that this is a good idea and will probably adopt a similar practice when it revises its own forms.

4.   All five forms have attached advice notes as to their completion. In the Society's opinion both the certificates and the advice notes are quite complicated and not very user friendly. Solicitors should check that any certificate they are asked to accept has been completed prima facia in accordance with the advice note. This is not to say that the advice notes should be followed slavishly merely that they should only be departed from for good reason. The Society would have preferred the certificates to be given on the certifiers notepaper as is envisaged in the Society's own forms. Also details such as the Architects membership number and the membership stamp are not something that the Society feels are necessary but if Solicitors are accepting an RIAI form of certificate it is probably better to get these details completed. The former will facilitate checking an Architects qualifications. The Society has never recommended that Solicitors advise clients to accept certificates of opinion based solely on the membership of any Institute and has not changed its view in this respect.

5.   The original form of Architects certificate of compliance was drafted jointly by the Law Society and the RIAI and was published as an agreed form. The five new forms were prepared by the RIAI. A sub-committee of the Conveyancing Committee agreed on behalf of the Society to recommend that Solicitors accept these forms in appropriate cases. This recommendation relates to the March, 1993 issue of the forms and subsequent forms. Earlier editions contained some printing errors.

6.   Form 3; Architects Opinion on Exemption from Building Regulation deals with different situations where relevant buildings or works are exempted from the Buildings Regulations for one reason or another. One of the alternative suggested wordings reads:

> 'I am advised by the Employer that the Relevant Building or Works were commenced prior to 1st June 1992 and based on this information I am of the opinion that the Relevant Building or Works is exempt from any need for compliance with the Building Regulations.'

The information given to the architect is of course hearsay and any solicitor would seek corroboration of the facts from someone who was actually aware of his own knowledge that the work had in fact so commenced. This would normally be confirmed by statutory declaration.

Full Service

Buildings

Regs

Planning

SPECIMEN CERTIFICATE

CERTIFICATE OF COMPLIANCE

I, ... CERTIFY as follows:-

1. I am an . . . . having qualified as such at . . . . in the year . . . . and I am a Member of The . . . .

2. I have been in independent private practice on my own account since the year . . . . or thereabouts

   OR

   I am a Partner in (or a Member of) the above named Firm of . . . . in independent private practice.

3. I am the . . . . /my said Firm are the . . . . retained by . . . . to design and make periodic inspection during the course of construction of . . . . (insert precise description of buildings or works) . . . known as . . . . . . situate at . . . . in the . . . . of . . . . such building or works being hereinafter referred to as 'the Relevant Works'.

4. The Plans and other particulars on foot of which there were granted or issued the Permission/Approval and the Fire Safety Certificate mentioned respectively in paragraphs 5 and 6 hereunder were prepared by me/by my said Firm.

5. The Grant of Permission/Approval–Decision Order No. . . . . dated . . . . the . . . . day of . . . . , 19 . . . . Planning Reference No. . . . . – relates to the Relevant Works.

6. The Fire Safety Certificate (Reference No. . . . .) dated the . . . . day of . . . . , 19 . . . . also relates to the Relevant Works.

7. The Relevant Works and the services thereof have been designed in substantial conformity with the Building Regulations made pursuant to the Building Control Act, 1990.

8. Commencement Notice of the intention to undertake the Relevant Works was duly given on the . . . . day of . . . . in accordance with the Building Control Regulations, 1991 and such Notice contained or was accompanied by the information and particulars prescribed by the said Regulations.

9. I made periodic inspections of the Relevant Works during the construction thereof AND in my opinion the construction of the same complies substantially with the Grant of Permission/Approval mentioned in Paragraph 5 hereof and substantially with all the said Building Regulations applicable thereto.

10. No Planning Permission other than that referred to at paragraph 5 aforesaid is pertinent to the Relevant Works.

11. I consulted with the Fire Authority and ascertained its requirements in relation to the Relevant Works AND in my opinion the said requirements have been complied with in the erection thereof.

12. The conditions of the Permission/Approval referred to at paragraph 5 relating to the Estate of which the Relevant Works form part have been substantially complied with in so far as is reasonably possible at this stage of the development of such Estate BUT this paragraph is not to be taken as extending to conditions for the payment of financial contributions or the giving of security for satisfactory completion compliance with which is not within my competence to certify.

13. In the event that the Relevant Works and the site works pertaining thereto have not been built and/or laid out exactly in accordance with the said Permission/Approval any disparity is unlikely to affect the planning and development of the area as envisaged by the Planning Authority and expressed through such Permission/Approval.

14. TAKE NOTE that this Certificate is issued solely with a view to providing evidence for title purposes of the compliance of the Relevant Works with the requirements of Planning Legislation and of the Building Control Act, 1990 and the Regulations thereunder. Except insofar as it relates to compliance with the said requirements and Regulations it is not a report or survey on the physical condition or on the structure of the Relevant Works NOR does it warrant, represent or take into account any of the following matters :-

   (a) the accuracy of dimensions in general save where arising out of the conditions of the Permission/Approval or the Building Regulations aforesaid

   (b) the following conditions, compliance with which cannot be established:
   Planning Reference No: . . . . Conditions . . . .
   Planning Reference No: . . . . Conditions . . . .

   (c) matters in respect of private rights or obligations

   (d) matters of financial contribution and bonds

   (e) development of the Relevant Works which may occur after the date of issue of this Certificate.

Dated the . . . . day of . . . . 19 . . . .

Signed . . . .

NOTES: The original of the foregoing Certificate should be furnished on the Certifier's headed notepaper.

The following advices (referenced to the correspondingly numbered paragraphs above) are for the guidance of the Certifier, and should <u>not</u> be incorporated in or added to the Certificate, of which they do not form part.

5. Insert here details of all Grants of Permission which are pertinent to the Relevant Works. (If there is more than one such Permission or if there is an Approval on foot of an Outline Permission, appropriate adjustments should be made throughout the Certificate).

   OR

   If the subject matter is exempted development as defined by the Local Government (Planning and Development) Acts, 1963 to 1992, so indicate and state why.

6. Insert here details of all pertinent Fire Safety Certificates

   OR

   If there was no requirement for the obtaining of a Fire Safety Certificate, so indicate and state why.

7/9. Where elements of design, inspection or construction involve others, it may be appropriate to refer to, and attach, Certificates from such others, and to indicate the measure of reliance placed on same.

8. Insert here details of all Commencement Notices

    OR

    If no Commencement Notice was required to be given, so indicate and state why.

11. This paragraph should be included where there is a requirement in the Grant of Permission/Approval to consult with the Fire Authority or the Fire Officer.

12. Include this paragraph where the Relevant Works form part of an Estate.

13. Ensure that the Relevant Works accord with the planning unit which is the subject of the Permission/Approval.

14. The list of non-warranted items may be expanded to include structural calculations where there is available a separate Certificate/Report covering same from an Independent Structural Engineer.

LAW SOCIETY FORMS OF CERTIFICATES OF COMPLIANCE

SPECIMEN CERTIFICATE

CERTIFICATE OF COMPLIANCE

I, ... certify AS FOLLOWS:

1. I am an . . . . having qualified as such at . . . . in the year . . . . AND I am a member of The . . . .

2. I have been in independent private practice on my own since the year . . . . or thereabouts

    OR

    I am a Partner in (or a Member of) the above named Firm of . . . . in independent private practice.

3. I am the . . . . /my said Firm are the . . . . retained by . . . . to design the . . . . (insert precise description of building or works) . . . . situate at . . . . in the . . . . of . . . . such building or works being hereinafter referred to as 'the Relevant Works'.

4. The Plans and other particulars on foot of which there was granted the Permission/Approval mentioned in paragraph 5 hereunder were prepared by me/by my said Firm.

    OR

    I visited the office of the Planning Authority and there inspected the house plans, estate layout plan, specifications and other drawings and documents which were represented by the Planning Authority as those on foot of which the Permission/Approval mentioned at Paragraph 5 hereunder was granted.

5. The Grant of Permission – Decision Order No. . . . . dated the . . . . day of . . . . , 19 . . . . Planning Reference No. . . . . relates to the Relevant Works.

6. The Relevant Works and the services thereof were designed by me/my said Firm in substantial conformity with the Building Regulations made pursuant to the Building Control Act, 1990.

7. Commencement Notice of the intention to undertake the Relevant Works was duly given on the . . . . day of . . . . in accordance with the Building Control Regulations, 1991 and such Notice contained or was accompanied by the information and particulars prescribed by the said Regulations.

8. I have inspected the Relevant Works AND in my opinion the construction thereof complies substantially with the Permission/Approval mentioned in paragraph 5 hereof.

9. The position of the Relevant Works and of the site thereof is in substantial compliance with the estate layout presented to the Planning Authority in so far as the estate has been completed.

10. No Planning Permission other than that referred to at paragraph 5 aforesaid is pertinent to the Relevant Works.

11. The conditions of the Permission/Approval referred to at paragraph 5 relating to the Estate of which the Relevant Works form part have been substantially complied with in so far as is reasonably possible at this stage of the development of such Estate BUT this paragraph is not to be taken as extending to conditions for the payment of financial contributions or the giving of security for satisfactory completion compliance with which is not within my competence to certify.

12. In the event that the Relevant Works and the site works pertaining thereto have not been built and/or laid out exactly in accordance with the said Permission/Approval any disparity is unlikely to affect the planning and development of the area as envisaged by the Planning Authority and expressed through such Permission/Approval.

13. I did not supervise the construction of the Relevant Works and my inspection thereof, which was made on the . . . . day of . . . . 19 . . . . was visual only. This inspection did not entail the opening up of works, which had been fully/substantially completed on said date. To the extent that such inspection allowed, and not taking into account matters which were inaccessible to me, I am of the opinion that the Relevant Works have been constructed in substantial compliance with the Building Regulations aforesaid.

14. TAKE NOTE that this certificate is issued solely with a view to providing evidence for title purposes of the compliance of the Relevant Works with the requirements of Planning Legislation and of the Building Control Act, 1990 and the Regulations thereunder. Except insofar as it relates to compliance with the said requirements and Regulations it is not a report or survey on the physical condition or on the structure of the Relevant Works NOR does it warrant, represent or take into account any of the following matters:-

   (a) the accuracy of dimensions in general save where arising out of the conditions of the Permission/Approval or the Building Regulations aforesaid

   (b) the following conditions, compliance with which cannot be established:

   Planning Reference No: . . . . Conditions . . . .

   Planning Reference No: . . . . Conditions . . . .

   (c) matters in respect of private rights or obligations

   (d) matters of financial contribution and bonds

   (e) development of the Relevant Works which may occur after the date of the said inspection.

Dated the . . . . day of . . . . 19 . . . .

Signed . . . .

NOTES: The original of the foregoing Certificate should be furnished on the Certifier's headed notepaper.

The following advices (referenced to the correspondingly numbered paragraphs above) are for the guidance of the Certifier, and should *not* be incorporated in or added to the Certificate, of which they do not form part.

4. If the subject matter is exempted development as defined by the Local Government (Planning and Development) Acts, 1963 to 1992, so indicate and state why.
   (Delete Paragraph 5/renumber subsequent Paragraphs).

5. Insert here details of all Grants of Permission which are pertinent to the Relevant Works. (If there is more than one such Permission or if there is an Approval on foot of an Outline Permission, appropriate adjustments should be made, throughout the Certificate).

6/13. Where elements of design, inspection or construction involve others, it may be appropriate to refer to, and attach, Certificates from such others, and to indicate the measure of reliance placed on same.

7. Insert here details of all Commencement Notices.

OR

If no Commencement Notice was required to be given, so indicate and state why.

11. Include this Paragraph where the Relevant Works form part of an Estate.

12. Ensure that the Relevant Works accord with the planning unit, which is the subject of the Permission/Approval.

14. The list of non-warranted items may be expanded to include structural calculations where there is available a separate Certificate/Report covering same from an Independent Structural Engineer.

Full Service/

Building Bye-Laws

Planning

SPECIMEN CERTIFICATE

CERTIFICATE OF COMPLIANCE

I.   . . . CERTIFY as follows:

1. I am an . . . having qualified as such at . . . in the year . . . . AND I am a member of The . . .

2. I have been in independent private practice on my own account since the year . . . or thereabouts

OR

I am a Partner in (or a Member of) the above named Firm of . . . in independent private practice.

3. I am the . . . . /my said Firm are the . . . . retained by . . . . to design and make periodic inspection during the course of construction of . . . . (insert precise description of building or works) . . . . known as . . . . situate at . . . . in the . . . . of . . . . such building or works being hereinafter referred to as 'the Relevant Works'.

4. The Plans and other particulars on foot of which there was granted or issued the Permission/Approval and the Notice of Approval mentioned respectively in paragraphs 5 and 6 hereunder were prepared by me/by my said Firm.

5. The Grant of Permission/Approval – Decision Order No. . . . . dated the . . . . day of . . . . 19 . . . . Planning Reference No. . . . . relates to the Relevant Works.

6. The Notice of Approval under the Building Bye-Laws, which Notice is dated the . . . . day of . . . . 19 . . . . and was issued under Reference Number . . . . also relates to the Relevant Works.

7. The Relevant Works and the services thereof have been designed in substantial conformity with the relevant Building Bye-Laws for the time being in force.

8. I made periodic inspections of the Relevant Works during the construction thereof AND in my opinion the construction of the same complies substantially with the Permission/Approval mentioned in Paragraph 5 hereof and substantially with all the said Building Bye-Laws applicable thereto.

9. No Planning Permission other than that referred to at Paragraph 5 aforesaid is pertinent to the Relevant Works.

10. I consulted with the Fire Authority and ascertained requirements in relation to the Relevant Works AND in my opinion the said requirements have been complied with in the erection thereof.

11. The conditions of the Permission/Approval referred to at Paragraph 5 relating to the Estate of which the Relevant Works form part have been substantially complied with in so far as is reasonably possible at this stage of the development of such Estate BUT this paragraph is not to be taken as extending to conditions for the payment of financial contributions or the giving of security for satisfactory completion compliance with which is not within my competence to certify.

12. In the event that the Relevant Works and the site works pertaining thereto have not been built and/or laid out exactly in accordance with the said Permission/Approval any disparity is unlikely to affect the planning and development of the area as envisaged by the Planning Authority and expressed through such Permission/Approval.

13. TAKE NOTE that this Certificate is issued solely with a view to providing evidence for title purposes of the compliance of the Relevant Works with the requirements of Planning Legislation and of the Building Bye Laws. Except insofar as it relates to compliance with the said requirements it is not a report or survey on the physical condition or on the structure of the Relevant Works NOR does it warrant, represent or take into account any of the following matters:-

    (a) the accuracy of dimensions in general save where arising out of the conditions of the Permission/Approval or the Building Bye-Laws aforesaid

    (b) the following conditions, compliance with which cannot be established:

    Planning Reference No: . . . . Conditions . . . .

    Planning Reference No: . . . . Conditions . . . .

    (c) matters in respect of private rights or obligations

    (d) matters of financial contribution and bonds

    (e) development of the Relevant Works which may occur after the date of issue of this Certificate

Dated the . . . . day of . . . . 19 . . . .

Signed . . . .

NOTES: The original of the foregoing Certificate should be furnished on the Certifier's headed notepaper.

The following advices (referenced to the correspondingly numbered paragraphs above) are for the guidance of the Certifier, and should *not* be incorporated in or added to the Certificate, of which they do not form part.

4/5. If the subject matter is exempted development as defined by the Local Government (Planning and Development) Acts, 1963 to 1992, so indicate and state why. Further, so far as relevant, adjust the word of Paragraph 4 to cover the plans and particular prepared for Bye-Law purposes.

5. Insert here details of all Grants of Permission which are pertinent to the Relevant Works. (If there is more than one such Permission or if there is an Approval on foot of an Outline Permission, appropriate adjustments should be made, throughout the Certificate).

6. Insert here details of all pertinent Notices of Approval. (If there is more than one, appropriate adjustments should be made throughout the certificate)

    OR

    If there was no requirement to obtain Building Bye-Law Approval, so indicate and state why.

7/8. Where elements of design, inspection or construction involve others, it may be appropriate to refer to, and attach, Certificates from such others, and to indicate the measure of reliance placed on same.

10. This Paragraph should be included where there is a requirement in the Grant of Permission/Approval to consult with the Fire Authority or the Fire Officer.

11. Include this Paragraph where the Relevant Works form part of an Estate.

12. Ensure that the Relevant Works accord with the planning unit, which is the subject of the Permission/Approval.

13. The list of non-warranted items may be expanded to include structural calculations where there is available a separate Certificate/Report covering same from an Independent Structural Engineer.

LAW SOCIETY FORMS OF CERTIFICATES OF COMPLIANCE

Part Service/
Building Bye-Laws
Planning

SPECIMEN CERTIFICATE

CERTIFICATE OF COMPLIANCE

I, ... CERTIFY as follows:

1. I am an . . . . having qualified as such at . . . . in the year . . . . AND I am a member of The . . . .

2. I have been in independent private practice on my own account since the year . . . . or thereabouts

   OR

   I am a Partner in (or a Member of) the above named Firm of . . . . in independent private practice.

3. I am the . . . . /my said Firm are the . . . . retained by . . . . to design the . . . . (insert precise description of building or works) . . . . situate at . . . . in the . . . . of . . . . such building or works being hereinafter referred to as 'the Relevant Works'.

4. (a) The Plans and other particulars on foot of which there was granted the Permission/Approval mentioned in Paragraph 5(a) hereunder were prepared by me/by my said Firm.

   (b) The Relevant Works and the services thereof were designed by me/my said Firm in substantial conformity with the relevant Building Bye-Laws for the time being in force

   OR

   I visited the office of the Planning Authority and there inspected the house plans, estate layout plan, specifications and other drawings and documents which were represented by the Planning Authority as those on foot of which:

   (i) was granted the Permission/Approval mentioned at Paragraph 5 (a) hereof

   AND

   (ii) was issued the Notice of Approval referred to at Paragraph 5 (b) hereof.

5. (a) The Grant of Permission – Decision Order No. . . . . dated the . . . . day of . . . . 19 . . . . Planning Reference No . . . . relates to the Relevant Works

   (b) The Notice of Approval under the Building Bye Laws which Notice is dated the . . . . day of . . . . 19 . . . . and was issued under Reference Number . . . . relates to the Relevant works.

6.   I have inspected the Relevant Works and in my opinion the construction thereof complies substantially with the Permission/Approval mentioned in Paragraph 5 (a) hereof.

7.   The position of the Relevant Works and of the site thereof is in substantial compliance with the estate layout presented to the Planning Authority in so far as the estate has been completed.

8.   No Planning Permission other than that referred to at Paragraph 5 (a) aforesaid is pertinent to the Relevant Works.

9.   The conditions of the Permission/Approval referred to at Paragraph 5 (a) relating to the Estate of which the Relevant Works form part have been substantially complied with in so far as is reasonably possible at this stage of the development of such Estate BUT this paragraph is not to be taken as extending to conditions for the payment of financial contributions or the giving of security for satisfactory completion compliance with which is not within my competence to certify.

10. In the event that the Relevant Works and the site works pertaining thereto have not been built and/or laid out exactly in accordance with the said Permission/Approval any disparity is unlikely to affect the planning and development of the area as envisaged by the Planning Authority and expressed through such Permission/Approval.

11. I did not supervise the construction of the Relevant Works and my inspection thereof, which was made on the . . . . day of . . . . 19 . . . . was visual only. This inspection did not entail the opening up of works, which had been fully/substantially completed on said date. To the extent that such inspection allowed, and not taking into account matters which were inaccessible to me, I am of the opinion that the Relevant Works have been constructed in substantial compliance with the relevant Building Bye-Laws as stipulated for in the Notice of Approval mentioned in Paragraph 5 (b) hereof.

12. TAKE NOTE that this Certificate is issued solely with a view to providing evidence for title purposes of the compliance of the Relevant Works with the requirements of Planning Legislation and of the Building Bye-Laws. Except insofar as it relates to compliance with the said requirements it is not a report or survey on the physical condition or on the structure of the Relevant Works NOR does it warrant, represent or take into account any of the following matters:-

(a) the accuracy of dimensions in general save where arising out of the conditions of the Permission/Approval or out of the Building Bye-Laws aforesaid.

(b) the following conditions, compliance with which cannot be established:

Planning Reference No: . . . . Conditions . . . .

Planning Reference No: . . . . Conditions . . . .

(c) matters in respect of private rights or obligations

(d) matters of financial contribution and bonds

(e) development of the Relevant Works which may occur after the date of the said inspection

Dated the . . . . day of . . . . 19 . . . .

Signed . . . .

NOTES: The original of the foregoing Certificate should be furnished on the Certifier's headed notepaper. The following advices (referenced to the correspondingly numbered paragraphs above) are for the guidance of the Certifier, and should <u>not</u> be incorporated in or added to the Certificate, of which they do not form part.

4. If the subject matter is exempted development as defined by the Local Government (Planning and Development) Acts, 1963 to 1992, so indicate and state why, and make consequential adjustment in Paragraphs.

5. (a) Insert here details of all Grants of Permission which are pertinent to the Relevant Works. (If there is more than one such Permission or if there is an Approval on foot of an Outline Permission, appropriate adjustments should be made, throughout the Certificate).

   (b) Insert here details of all pertinent Notices of Approval.

   OR

   If there was no requirement to obtain Building Bye Law Approval, so indicate and state why.

4(b) Where elements of design, inspection or construction involve others, it may be
& 11. appropriate to refer to, and attach, Certificates from such others, and to indicate the measure of reliance placed on same.

9. Include this Paragraph where the Relevant Works form part of an Estate.

10. Ensure that the Relevant Works accord with the planning unit, which is the subject of the Permission/Approval.

12. The list of non-warranted items may be expanded to include structural calculations where there is available a separate Report covering same from an Independent Structural Engineer.